Scottish Rural Society
in the Sixteenth Century

For my Mother
and
In memory of my Father

Scottish Rural Society
in the
Sixteenth Century

MARGARET H.B. SANDERSON

JOHN DONALD PUBLISHERS LTD.
EDINBURGH

© Margaret H.B. Sanderson, 1982

ISBN 0 85976 027 8

Printed in Great Britain by
Bell & Bain Ltd., Glasgow

Preface

THIS book grew out of a study of landholding and tenancy, in particular the spread of feu-ferm tenure, on church lands in the sixteenth century, undertaken for a post-graduate degree at Edinburgh university. The subject has been widened to include secular lands in order to give a fuller picture of Scottish rural society in the period. The emphasis is on social history: in particular the structure of society and the rights of tenants and small proprietors in the land which they possessed and were dependant upon.

With a clearer picture of these central questions in mind it may be possible to go on to investigate the quality of sixteenth-century life for the generality of the people. An attempt has been made, in the final chapter of this book, to break this further ground with the aid of the virtually untapped source material in the Registers of Testaments.

Other writers have dealt fully with national politics, the Reformation, Scottish trade and pre-Improvement agriculture in books that appear in the Bibliography but, as these subjects form an important framework to the present study, they are discussed where appropriate. The paucity of source material for the Highlands has made the study almost entirely that of Lowland society, with the exceptions of parts of Argyll and the highland districts of Perthshire.

I should like to thank Professor Gordon Donaldson for first interesting me in 'the feuing of kirklands', from which this study grew. My thanks are due to the Duke of Hamilton and Brandon for permission to quote from the rental of Arbroath abbey at Lennoxlove, and to the Earl of Eglinton and Winton, the Earl of Leven and Melville and the Earl of Morton for permission to publish the results of extensive research into their archives, deposited in the Scottish Record Office, and to quote from them. Quotations from legal records and from private archives gifted to the Scottish Record Office are published with the approval of the Keeper of the Records of Scotland, Dr John Imrie, and those from Alloway Barony Court Book with the permission of the Provost and Councillors of Kyle and Carrick District Council, as successors to the Royal Burgh of Ayr.

I am grateful to the Editors of the following for allowing me to make use of material previously published by me in their publications and journals: the Ayrshire Archaeological and Natural History Society, *Northern Scotland*, the Company of Scottish History and Editors of the *Scottish Historical Review*, and the Scottish Church History Society. I am indebted to Miss Myrtle M. Baird for her expert assistance while preparing the Index and reading the proofs, and to Moira Robertson for typing the Index.

Margaret H.B. Sanderson

Contents

List of Maps

List of Abbreviations

A.A.N.H.S.	Ayrshire Archaeological and Natural History Society
A.D.C.	Acta dominorum concilii
A.D.C.S.	Acta dominorum concilii et sessionis
A.P.S.	*Acts of the parliaments of Scotland*
Bann. Club	Bannatyne Club
H.M.C.	Historical Manuscripts Commission
H.M.S.O.	Her Majesty's Stationery Office
Mait. Club	Maitland Club
N.L.S.	National Library of Scotland
N.S.A.	*New Statistical Account of Scotland*
O.S.A.	*Old Statistical Account of Scotland*
R.F.C.	Register of abbreviates of feu charters of kirklands
R.M.S.	*Register of the great seal*
Royal Comm.	Royal Commission on Ancient and Historical Monuments (Scotland)
R.P.C.	*Register of the privy council*
R.S.S.	Register of the privy seal (unprinted)
R.S.S.	*Register of the privy seal* (printed)
S.H.R.	*The Scottish Historical Review*
S.H.S.	The Scottish History Society
S.R.O.	The Scottish Record Office
S.R.S.	The Scottish Record Society
T.A.	*Accounts of the Treasurer of Scotland*

Note: Where short titles are used in chapter notes, these are given in brackets after the first use of the full title. Location of manuscripts and the names of publishing societies of printed works are given only with the first reference.

1

The National Setting

'I was at that schooll the space of almost fyve yeirs, in the quhilk tyme, of publict news I remember I hard of the mariage of Hendrie and Marie, King and Quein of Scots, Seignour Davie's slauchter, of the King's mourder at the Kirk of Field, of the Quein's taking at Carbarri, and the Langsyd field . . . Also, I remember weill how we past to the heid of the muir to sie the fyre of joy burning upon the stiple heid of Montrose at the day of the King's birthe . . .'[1]

James Melville, *Autobiography and Diary* (Wodrow Society)

THE history of sixteenth-century Scotland is full of familiar landmarks so that, until memorising dates went out of fashion, every Scottish schoolboy was expected to be able to attach an event, unhesitatingly, to such dates as 1503, 1513, 1560, 1567 and 1603. It is significant that these very landmarks — the marriage of James IV and Margaret Tudor, the defeat of Flodden, the Reformation-rebellion, the deposition of Queen Mary and the succession of her son, James VI, to the throne of England — should be bound up with the revolution in Anglo-Scottish relations. The turning of the Scottish government away from the traditional alliance with France towards alignment with England, the traditional enemy, was gradual, it was not inevitable and it relied for success at a critical moment on the active stage of a religious revolt but, by 1603, it was complete and it made the Scotland of James VI's latter years a very different place from the Scotland of his great-grandfather, James IV.

In the minority of James V, between 1513 and 1528, the division of sympathy between Anglophile and Francophile became clear-cut as the disillusioned Scottish nobles showed reluctance to invade England in the half-hearted campaigns that followed Flodden and the experiment of a French-bred regent, the duke of Albany, failed and gave place to the government of the Anglophile earl of Angus, husband of the queen-mother, Margaret Tudor. Queen Mary's long minority brought the rivalry of France and England in Scotland to a head with the making and unmaking of a marriage alliance with England and the ultimate marriage of the young queen to the heir to the French throne, in 1558. Hard on the heels of this, however, came the Treaty of Berwick of 1560, which brought the Scottish reformers and the Lords of the Congregation English support, and the Treaty of Edinburgh of the same year, which removed the French presence from Scotland. After the failure of Queen Mary's personal government her son, on reaching his majority, waited, with more tact and patience than his mother had done, to be recognised as Queen Elizabeth's heir and in 1603 became king of Great Britain.

Although it was a time of change, there were a number of constant factors in sixteenth-century Scottish life. In internal politics the nobles continued to dominate, their activities thrown into relief against the dark background of three successive royal minorities. Their attachment to the Francophile or Anglophile parties was complicated by the age-old dynastic struggle among Hamiltons, Douglases and Lennox Stewarts, fought out in the persons of the earls of Arran, Angus and Lennox with their allies. Even the opposition to Queen Mary's marriage with Darnley and the brief farce of a rebellion which marked it, as well as support for her in the civil war that followed her deposition in 1567, can partly be attributed to the Hamilton-Lennox rivalry over their claims to stand next in line to the throne.

The influence of the great nobles, whom James V had antagonised, Mary had fallen foul of and James VI had manoeuvred with so successfully in the interests of royal authority and the peace of the realm, was drawn off somewhat after the union of the crowns when a number of them followed the king to London and the Scottish court, as a stimulus to political and cultural life, was removed.

Parallel to these far-reaching changes in diplomacy, which aligned and eventually united Scotland with England, ran a revolution in religious life which passed through several stages, linking Scotland, successively, with Lutheran Germany, Calvinist Geneva, Huguenot France and the cultural centres of the Reformed Netherlands.

Although the Scottish Reformation came late, comparatively speaking, its statement of belief ratified by parliament a generation after Luther's protest of 1517 and almost thirty years after Henry VIII's Act of Supremacy, it was no less radical for that. Support for reform had been growing since the end of the fifteenth century and had affected all classes. Until the Council of Trent, after which the Roman Catholic Church had authoritative answers to the arguments of heretics, ecclesiastical authority in Scotland was on the offensive, in a rigorous campaign to punish heretics, not to argue with them. Protestantism in the 1530s and 1540s ranged from the popular Lutheranism of the common folk to the partly political motives of Anglophile lairds, some of whom were in the pay of Henry VIII after the debacle of Solway Moss and death of James V, in 1542.

Signs of more cogent religious protest came with the preaching of George Wishart, executed for heresy in 1546, who had had firsthand knowledge of Calvinist Geneva and whose mantle was to fall on John Knox in the late 1550s. Gradually, as it began to realise where opposition was coming from — not just disgust at clerical standards but theological propositions — the church, led in the 1550s by Archbishop John Hamilton, took up a defensive attitude, trying to explain the traditional doctrines to the faithful, in documents such as Hamilton's Catechism, in an attempt to lessen the impact of the protestant teaching.

At the same time the lay leadership of the Reform party became more formidable, now including members of the nobility and men of the standing of James Stewart, commendator of St Andrews priory and a natural son of James V. Their leadership culminated in armed resistance to the government of the French Queen-Regent, Mary of Guise, in 1559-60, when with English help the Lords of the Congregation drove the French out of Scotland. Parliament thereafter, although having only doubtful authority in the matter, ratified the Confession of Faith, the official statement of Reformed doctrine drawn up by the ministers.

A 'settled polity', or church order, took longer to emerge than had the statement of faith. When it did it was less of an indigenous creation than those of Lutheran Germany or Anglican England, partly because it came much later, partly because those who worked it out, often tussling over it, were drawing not only on the beliefs and experience of protestants in other countries, notably France and England, but were influenced by political pressures at home. Above all, it was the astute King James VI who was largely responsible for the workable amalgam of episcopal and presbyterian systems which he left behind him when he departed for London in 1603.

For the ordinary Scot at parish level the period of the Reformation was marked by both continuity and change. The violent, iconoclastic phase of the revolt was short-lived and localised, mainly confined to the vicinities of Edinburgh, Dundee and Perth. Very many parishioners found that 'old priest' and 'new presbyter' were one and the same man; it has been estimated that about half of the clergy in charge of parishes soon after the Reformation had been in orders before 1560, many of them in the same or nearby parishes.[2] For tenants on church lands there was virtually no dislocation in the pattern of rural life in the years around 1560 — the landlord, probably a careerist cleric or virtual layman, was very likely an absentee landlord anyway — and the estate officers continued to lift the rents as usual. There was no official 'dissolution of the monasteries' in Scotland — their property had long been slipping into lay hands by commendatorships and feuing of the lands — and the monks continued to live out their lives in many cases in the precincts enjoying their *portions,* or salaries, for their lifetimes.

However, there were some new and unfamiliar aspects of religious life. The church service became centred on the preaching of the Word and exposition of the faith, the internal arrangements of the kirk drawing attention to the pulpit rather than the communion table, the latter being often set up for the purpose, with the communicants seated around it, emphasising the corporate character of the communion service. However, the Lord's Supper, although central to Reformed doctrine, in spite of the Reformers' ideals, became almost as infrequent as attendance at the parish mass had latterly been. When it was celebrated, the parishioners received both bread and wine. During services the congregation participated in the praise, taking enthusiastically to the *Gude and Godly Ballatis,* some of which were thinly disguised songs, and to the tuneful metrical psalms.

The participatory role of the Reformed congregation was also seen in the work of the elders, although many members of kirk sessions were used to being on the jury of the barony court. Public repentance took the place of private confession, although public penance had not been unknown before the Reformation. The reading of the Bible in English diminished the use of Scots in church but gave Scotsmen of all classes a new field for argumentative exchange of ideas.

Positive benefits, although never operated without difficulty and hampered for many years by lack of money, were the Reformers' intentions that each congregation should support its own poor and that there should be some kind of school in every parish, an advance on the well-meaning but piecemeal arrangements for the poor and education in the late middle ages, particularly in rural areas. The biggest achievement at parochial level to result from the Reformation-settlement was a resident parish ministry able to teach their congregations. The fact that the first generation of pastors were often poorly paid and housed tended to bring them nearer to the people, while their educational standards were on the whole higher than those of their predecessors, the parish curates.

Two important conditions of economic progress, external peace and internal stability, were largely lacking for more than half of the sixteenth century, but were gradually achieved in the later personal reign of James VI and almost assured by the time of his succession to the English crown. Peace with England meant an end to the tramping of invading armies across some of the best agricultural land in Scotland. The Border counties ceased to be an international problem and became a domestic one within the united kingdom.[3] Merchants could travel or send their cargoes by sea with greater safety than formerly, although even near the end of the sixteenth century the activities of shipmasters-cum-pirates were a diplomatic problem.

If peace came slowly, the other preconditions of economic progress — capital and enterprise — were for long lacking. In the small towns, the conservative merchant guilds who dominated the councils were more concerned with preserving their privileges, especially vis-a-vis the craft incorporations, than with breaking new ground in commerce and industry. In the countryside, any development of natural resources, such as coal and salt, was in the hands of the landowners, nobles and lairds, who controlled the materials and labour force, and most income still came from the land itself.

If overseas trade was pursued with some vigour, along routes laid down over the centuries, it was because as a small, comparatively poor country on the fringe of Europe Scotland was vitally dependent on her European trading links for industrial raw materials such as iron, wood and dyestuffs, and for supplies of grain in times of dearth. As it happened, her essentially rural character helped her to produce commodities which were welcome in northern European countries: skins, hides, fish, coal and heavy quality linen. The benefits of Scotland's overseas trade, however, were not only material but cultural; both medieval and post-Reformation scholars and students found their way in large numbers to European universities, where many Scots throughout the sixteenth century were to be found not only among the student bodies but on the teaching staffs. As the trade with France declined, due to the realignment of Scotland's diplomatic associations after the Reformation, the centuries-old links with the trading and cultural centres of the Baltic and the Low Countries became stronger than ever and the Scots colonies there increased in size and influence.[4]

In this book we are concerned with rural Scotland in the lifetimes of those generations who lived, roughly speaking, between Flodden and the Union of the Crowns, during which time historic changes took place in political and religious life and more gradual changes in economic development and in cultural and educational opportunities. Life went on at local level, sometimes affected and sometimes untouched by changes of national importance.[5]

Notes

1 Melville's home at that time was at Over Logie, 'bot twa myles' from Montrose.
2 G. Donaldson, *The Scottish Reformation,* 85
3 T. I. Rae, *The Administration of the Scottish Frontier, 1513-1603,* 232
4 S.G.E. Lythe, *The Economy of Scotland in its European setting, 1550-1625,* 247-254
5 A list of important events in Scotland, England and Europe begins on page 244

2

The Barony

'my lord followis . . . the tennandis of Stobwod that thai ar unlauchfull tenentis be the commone eittyne of corne and distruccione of thair nychtboris.'

Court Book of the Barony of Carnwath, 150

A BIRD'S eye view of Scotland in the sixteenth century would have given the impression that the built-up areas, if we can so describe the burghs, had been cut out of the predominantly rural landscape, whereas today the countryside increasingly looks like the gaps between towns, at least in those parts of the country where most people live. Then, most Scots were landward men living in the open country. Yet, in spite of what it might have looked like from the air — a patchwork of scattered settlements — rural society was closely-knit. The local unit of rural life was the barony, in social terms a community living within geographically and legally defined limits, using the same methods of cultivation, living on the fruits of their own labour, served by the same local amenities, paying rent to the same landlord and going about their everyday business under the same rules and customary laws made and enforced in the barony court to which they all owed attendance.

A barony might be as small as one or two modern farms put together but it was, nevertheless, a defined local unit. There was no standard size or average valued rental. An earldom, in social and geographical terms, was a bunch of baronies, however many or scattered or separately administered. The baronies which made up a lordship or *regality,* that is a territorial jurisdiction within which the baron had almost royal powers, might be separated by considerable distances as a result of the way in which lands had been acquired over the years. Newbattle abbey, for instance, held the baronies of Newbattle in Midlothian and Monkland in Lanarkshire, Kinloss abbey those of Kinloss in Moray and Strathisla in Banffshire, Holyrood abbey those of Broughton in Midlothian, now inside modern Edinburgh, and Kerse in Stirlingshire. In the world of lay landlords, the earl of Morton held baronies in Lanarkshire, Midlothian, Fife, Kinross and Perthshire by the end of the sixteenth century.

In a sense the baron was a local government officer, the governable parts of Scotland being divided into baronies so that it could be administered on behalf of the crown. He held his lands by virtue of a charter which defined his holdings as *in liberam baroniam* — in free barony — with the right to hold a court for the administration of public justice in the king's name and to which the tenants brought disputes and matters concerning the internal affairs of the community. The land could be divided up, and even given away, with the king's consent. The jurisdiction could not be divided — in lawyer's language it was *unum quid* — and the right to dispense public justice that went with it could be given away only by the king, who had delegated the power in the first place. Each barony had a head place, *caput,* where the head courts of the year were usually held, in the earlier feudal period often the strong place or castle of the baron. However, with the proliferation of baronies in the later middle ages, many of them had no castle and the *caput* was often a selected territory named in the charter, at which the baron took sasine — formal possession — of the property.[1]

Whatever it meant to the lawyers, to the rural dweller the barony was where he lived and worked. Methods of cultivation and types of farming varied from one district to another, depending on the nature of the soil and the prevailing climate, mainly arable in some parts, pastoral in others, mixed in many. Settlements tended to follow the arable land, sometimes on raised ground where drainage was better, or stood about a kirk or a mill, at a ferry, crossroads or other communication-point, near coal pits, salt pans or lime kilns, or around a castle or monastery or the buildings of an outlying grange. The names of these settlements, kirktoun, milntoun, coaltoun, ferrytoun, castletoun and monktoun, still perpetuate their memory all over the country. Not only that, but the names given to the working parts of a settlement itself often survive too, to be found today within the oldest parts of a bigger urban area; so in Paisley, clinging to the walls of the monastery, were the Seedhill, Bellmeadow, Wellmeadow, Quarrelhill, Grevisland, Oxshawhead and Oxshawside, the Goosecroft and the Gallowhill.[2] In the little settlement of Scone, now entirely gone, were Marnock's croft, the Chapel yards, the Dovecot croft, Goosecroft, Cruikitacre and Sandyhill.[3] Depending on its size, a barony might contain anything from a dozen to twenty such touns, or even more, all roughly conforming to the natural, remarkably workable pattern of a self-supporting settlement.

Not all distinctly named territories in a barony as they appear in rentals, however, can have been actual townships, some being simply intensively cultivated areas held by tenants in nearby settlements who often had holdings in more than one place. The kind of estate records which list people and places, such as rentals and surveys of occupancy, often show tenants with scattered holdings. For example, a list of arrears of money rent drawn up by Melrose abbey's chamberlain of Kylesmure in 1529 shows a number of tenants in this position, including 'John Reid in Sok' who held land in Cowfaldschaw and Nether Meiklewood, two non-adjacent territories.[4] In the second half of the sixteenth century the feu charters which turned many small tenants into proprietors often reveal their scattered or neighbouring holdings, then being consolidated into feus. John Duncan, who lived in the small burgh of Kinloss in 1564, for instance, held a 'tenandry' in the surrounding district consisting of six acres in the Cellarer's Cruik, Milncruik and Sclaterland, a quarter of Alehoustack and Woodland and an acre called Whiteacre.[5] Many individual examples could be cited to show the scattered nature of tenant holdings on the jointly cultivated or shared farms of the baronies. The houses, built by the tenants themselves, were a mixture of stone, turf and wattle, strengthened by beams which were among the householder's most valuable furniture, with a smoke-hole in the rigging of the thatched roof, low doors and unglazed windows. They were quickly assembled, easily dismantled structures. In 1513 a man in the barony of Alloway was asked to compensate a widow, whose holding he had taken over, with six merks of money, several small pieces of land and 'ane biggit hous to duell in for hyr lyftyme'.[6] A year later, in the same barony, when a son was admitted to his late father's holding, it was arranged that if he and his mother were unable to live together 'the said Margaret sall haif the housis that ar biggit and scho sall help the said Gilbert to the bigging of ane hous of ane cuppill'.[7] Dwellings would appear wherever holdings were created, or subdivided, new land taken in or woodland cleared.

Through a sizeable township ran the loan along which cattle were driven to pasture and the oxen or horses to the ploughing. Around the settlement lay the cultivated ground, *infield* land under constant cropping and *outfield* land occasionally allowed to lie fallow. The land was turned over by the jointly owned plough team or by the plough animals of more prosperous tenants, in the run-rig pattern of cultivation strips, varying numbers of which formed the tenants' holdings. Around the cultivated land rose the great outer, or head, dyke made of turf and beyond lay the moss, undrained land that yielded peat for fuel and turf for building, the commonty which provided common grazing for the community's stock and the low-lying meadowland near the river, allowed to flood naturally and coveted for its richer pasture. On the high land were the shielings or summer pastures with their folds and herds' bothies.

Having sketched the classic late-medieval farmtoun, we must admit that the picture is just a little too tidy. Our ideas of what the rural landscape was like before the so-called revolution in agriculture are mostly derived from the writings of the eighteenth-century 'improvers', who were often inclined to magnify their own achievements by setting them alongside the backwardness of their forebears and whose descriptions of the bad old days of Scottish agriculture have been uncritically back-dated into the seventeenth and sixteenth centuries without sufficient examination of the evidence that has survived from those times. This evidence, from the barony court books, rentals and other estate papers, tends to suggest that our picture of 'pre-improvement' rural society is more static than was actually the case.

The fact is that the countrywide pattern, could we have seen it from our bird's eye view, would have appeared extremely varied, a genuinely living, changing pattern. From one tract of arable land to another, from farm to farm, the size of holdings varied. In some places, so it appears from rentals, smallish tenants cultivated the land jointly and were jointly responsible for the whole rent. Other lands were divided into quarters among four tenants, or into a variety of shares, in anything down to thirty-second parts. How these tenants worked out their shares of the farm on the ground is another matter on the mechanics of which we have little information, except in rare recorded cases where the business was difficult or led to a dispute. In 1468 the Grange of Balbrogie was leased by the abbot of

Coupar Angus to twenty-one persons, husbandmen and cottars, 'and thai sall divide the settingis amangis thameselves'.[8] No doubt it was largely left to the tenants to sort out. If, as seems to have been the case, tenant families held holdings for generations, reallocation would take place only occasionally. The way in which the land was thus divided up among the tenants is reflected in the many ways in which it is designated and identified in rentals. Even within one barony it might be described in acreage or merklands, in ploughgates (oxgangs), perhaps at its valued rental such as 13s 4d land or 6s 8d land, or in quarters, thirds or other proportions. Land was often referred to by a place-name derived from its size or situation, such as 'Meikle' or 'Little', 'Over' or 'Nether', 'Easter' or 'Wester', 'sunny half' or 'shady half'. In a list of the tenants and occupiers of the touns of Stobo and Eddleston in 1580 the cultivated lands are variously identified in oxgangs, merklands, in nominal money value (which by that time represented less than the actual rent), and in one or two places by a name associated with a local amenity, such as 'mill lands', 'brewlands' and 'smiddy lands'.[9]

Not only was there variety in the size of holdings and in the way in which farmtouns and arable land were set to tenants but there appears in the sixteenth century to have been a movement towards consolidation of holdings. On the church estates this movement was encouraged by the fairly rapid conversion of many leases into feus, turning many quite small tenants into proprietors — owner occupiers — something which we shall be looking at for its own sake later. We can understand feuars, whose possessions had now become heritable in their families, wishing to consolidate their holdings, and here and there we find evidence of this in the records. At Letham in the barony of Monimail in Fife, in 1596, six men who had feued scattered pieces of that toun agreed to consolidate their holdings by exchange 'sua that everie ane of thaim haif thair awin portioun thairof liand togidder and out of rin-rig'. In the barony of Boarhills, also in Fife, in 1577, the feuars came to a similar arrangement, 'bearing that the said lands then lay in rin-rig and on that account they sustained great loss and inconvenience . . .'[10]

But a certain amount of consolidation may have been under way even before and apart from feuing. In rental books such as those of the abbeys of Coupar Angus and Paisley and the archbishopric of Glasgow we find tenants constantly exchanging holdings with neighbours and relations, in all likelihood in order to gain possession of adjacent land units.[11] In the barony of Glasgow, betweeen 1528 and 1540, John Bargelly and his son Thomas acquired four portions of the lands of Shettleston, including a bit forfeited from a man sentenced to death in the archbishop's court, and by the 1560s the family holding was big enough to be split in two between a brother and sister, the latter receiving her share as her marriage portion.[12] Alexander Jackson, a Coupar Angus tenant, acquired three separate pieces of Carsegrange between 1542 and 1554 and, on the point of taking them in feu in 1559, he acquired a fourth piece on another tenant's resignation.[13]

While it is true that, when a tenant was said to occupy a third or six acres of a toun, we have no way of telling whether this meant a block of land or the sum total of several scattered holdings, and although the latter may often have been the case, as with a tenant of the earl of Morton who was said to possess 'ane husbandland through the toun of Langnewtoun',[14] yet consolidation was probably on the increase. It seems to be suggested by the fact that the medieval practice of periodic reallocation of rigs among the tenants was largely dying out in Lowland Scotland by the sixteenth century and by the fact that many rentals, both lay and ecclesiastical, show tenant families in possession of the same holdings one generation after another. Signs of deliberate enclosure have been detected on the lands of Coupar Angus abbey, where even in the fifteenth century it was assumed that tenants would try to add to their holdings, 'and eftir as tha haf mar in mailyn (holdings) thai sal haif mar in sowmys (grazing)'.[15]

How did the movement towards consolidation of holdings affect the infield/outfield system which we have come to think of as standard practice? It is easy to picture the formation of bigger holdings on infield land, constantly under crops, but what about outfield? Did the possessors agree among themselves about when it should lie fallow and did it suit all of them to allow it to lie fallow at the same time? At Alloway in Ayrshire those who had *ley* land — fallow land — were required to till the outer rig of it to prevent their cattle from straying on to their neighbours' sown land'.[16] A complaint by two tenants in the barony of Keillour in Perthshire against other two 'that wranguslie and agane the law withaldis fra thame ther outfield', suggests that the outfield had been divided among the tenants.[17] The distinction between infield and outfield land may have been clearer-cut in earlier days when joint-holding and communal cultivation were regular practice than in the sixteenth century with its increase in substantial tenant farmers with their *fixed run-rig* holdings, rarely reallocated, and their tendency to consolidate their holdings into adjacent blocks.

The daily life of the rural communities is to be found in the pages of the barony court books, often lively documents in which legal jargon may run alongside the colloquial speech of witnesses. Those in the case of William Anderson, who had attacked Andrew Mitchell in Carnwath, reported how Anderson had

come with ane hand ax and Rolland Cok with ane swerd and buklar and lay in William Graham's yart behind his hous, among the hemp, and baid thair ane lang tyme . . . and Andrew Mitchell was cumand hame ridand fra the mercat of Lanark fer withtin the nycht, throw the toun of Carnwyth, the said William Anderson, met hym and pullit him of his hors and kest hym in ane myr and dang him with his neiffis (fists) and feit and bludit hym, and the said Andrew Mitchell criit murther, the quhilk the nychtburis hard and come furth, baith mene and wiffis, and fand the said William Anderson lyand apone the said Andrew Mitchell and tuk hym up and put thaim sindry (apart) . . . . The quhilk deposiciones of the saidis preiffis and witnes, the inquest beand riply awisit, hafand God before, etc., come in curt agane and delivirit all in ane voce . . . and fand William Anderson in the blud and bludwit . . . .[18]

At Eglinton in 1576 a tenant admitted having seen another one build a house with stone from a ruinous chapel:

John Galston, sworn and admittit, deponis that Alan Rankin biggit ane littill hous wyt the stanis of the chapell and put (removed) nane of the grund, and that umqle (the late) sir Jasper Montgomery gaf to the said Allan saye mekill tymmir as was the dur (door) cheikis, and syn knawis not . . . .[19]

Another Eglinton tenant described how three of his neighbours

wyt forseyth (foresight) felony . . . wait on hym to have slane hym . . . and stickit hym wyt ane quheynar (whinger) behynd the ryt lug . . . and spulzeit (stole) fra hym his quhenzear and his purss wyt fyf pundis mone therin and his bonat . . . .[20]

All tenants had to attend at least the three head courts of the year or send substitutes, and there was pressure to attend the intermediate courts so that there would be a sufficient number of suitors from whom to choose the jury. The tenants *were* the court. From them were chosen the jury, or assise, and the officers of the court — the officer or serjeant who summoned attendance, *fenced* the court formally so that business could begin, confiscated the goods of offenders and installed the baron bailie in office, the other servants of the court who assisted him, the *dempster*, or doomster, who pronounced the judgement, or *doom*, of the court, and the *sworn men* who were called upon to advise the jury from background examination of a case. The sworn men of Glasgow barony once asked for an increase in the daily allowance given to them to compensate for loss of farming time as they had been 'meikle irkit . . . and drawin fra ther labor'.[21] The *birlaymen*, or boorlaw men, appointed to settle disputes or hand back stolen property which had been recovered, sometimes formed a separate little court and may have been less democratically chosen than the jury of tenants. At Urie, at any rate, in 1617, they appear to have been chosen by an ordinance of the court, although this may have followed a popular election not recorded in the court book.[22] The *eveners* were appointed to measure and demarcate holdings where need for this arose and they, of course, were also barony men. The clerk of the court was a professional, perhaps already employed by the baron in his own affairs, and was often a local notary.

The baron himself might preside, especially at the head courts and at Whitsunday when new tenants were received, but he was often represented by the bailie or the latter's deputy. In the 1520s we find even as preoccupied a superior as David Beaton presiding in the regality court of Arbroath abbey.[23] In the court book of Carnwath, between 1523 and 1542, Lord Somerville presided at forty-nine out of seventy-six meetings of the court.[24] In the latter part of the century we find the earl of Eglinton presiding at only three out of fifteen sessions,[25] whereas William Douglas of Lochleven, whose main residence was in Kinross, was present at the barony court of Keillour in Perthshire on six out of ten occasions, sometimes in company with his bailie.[26] Where a barony or regality court belonged to a burgh, certain of the bailies and town council held the court. From the expression 'aldermen, bailies and standing commissioun' in Alloway barony court book it seems that the magistrates of Ayr, to whom that barony belonged, chose some of their number, probably in rotation, to hold the court.[27] The presiding officer, or the baron himself in these circumstances, however, was there simply to see to it that the laws and procedure were honoured. Judgement was given by those who attended and served as the jury.

The courts met at irregular intervals, more or less as need arose. Often, the date of the next meeting would be announced at the end of the previous one, otherwise the officer would ride round the barony warning the tenants to attend. The head courts were usually held at the *caput* but on other occasions wherever the baron thought fit, indoors or out of doors, sometimes at the place where the business on hand had arisen, as when the barony court of Urie met at Cowie mill to sort out the strained relations between tenants and the miller.[28] At Elgin the bishop of

Moray's regality court often met in the cathedral chapter house or treasury, 'jewale hous' as the latter was called,[29] that of Holyrood's barony of Broughton in the Canongate tolbooth,[30] while that of Eglinton met variously at 'the mansioun place', 'the court stane' and in the 'garden', 'lower yard' and 'forth-ludging' of the castle itself.[31] At Arbroath the court was held in the precincts, in what was known as the 'regality court house'.[32] At Glasgow the archbishop's bailie, the laird of Minto, held the meetings in his own lodging in the city.[33] The court of Urie, where the local authority of the laird, Hay of Urie, was gradually undermined by that of his superior, the earl of Errol, met in a variety of places, from the houses of tenants in Woodhead and Cowie to the 'barn of Andrew Allardyce in Woodheid' and the schoolhouse of Urie.[34] Tenants were fined for failure to attend court or to send substitutes, for speaking out of order or for slipping away before the end of the proceedings, a temptation when the court was held out of doors.

Through service as officers and jurymen, or simply by frequent attendance, tenants became as knowledgeable about the law of the court as about the weather that controlled their environment. Yet, in many baronies, those who took an active part in affairs tended to be drawn from a reservoir of repeatedly named individuals who were constantly called upon to sit in judgement on what was, after all, their neighbours' business. Life was essentially public, everybody knew everybody else in the barony, and a tenant felt his wrongs had been righted only after the whole story had been heard and he himself justified in court in a public way that we would now resent. There was much petty bickering and tale-bearing. The barony court existed before the post-Reformation kirk session, and those who spied on and reported the wrongdoings of their neighbours to the courts had nothing to learn from the elders and their 'searchers'. Although in the middle ages the baron had been careful to keep his court free of the interfering arm of Holy Kirk in matters that did not concern her, there were times when, as the local secular power, he did back up church authority. In the Whitsunday court at Alloway in 1529, for example, tenants were warned against defiance of the church's censures for more than forty days and the penalty for adultery included the loss of a holding.[35] In post-Reformation times, when the church authorities, in the form of the ruling elders, were one's equals and neighbours, the two local courts often worked hand in hand, often composed of the same people, sitting on session and assise. The 'black books' of both sometimes contained the names of a nucleus of habitual troublemakers whom they had to deal with over and over again.

Punishment fell for similar reasons in both courts: transgression of the law in the absolute sense, the moral law of God or the common law of the realm, and breach of the social and material rules which safeguarded the integrity of the community. Trouble arose for both authorities from the fact that membership of each community, congregation and barony, was not from choice but for geographical reasons. Perhaps there was a little more flouting of the kirk session than of the baron's court for, after all, the minister and elders had no power to hang you and divine retribution seemed further away than the hardship that might follow the loss of a holding. In the case of the kirk session only the punishment was carried out in public, the preliminary questioning taking place in private before the minister and elders when full confession and repentance might help to mitigate the sentence, whereas in the barony court, although the evidence of witnesses was usually taken by the jury out of court, statements of the facts behind a complaint or the frequently lengthy allegations of a pursuer were often heard *in* court. When the indictment was recited many a culprit had his character read. One man in the barony of Spynie who was accused of stabbing another and had been confronted in court with the knife with which he had forced open a coffer of his victim's, stealing from it a quantity of gold, was told that this money could not possibly be his own:

ye being ane puir man haiffing onlie ane croft of land of fyve schillingis schawing (sowing) and using na uther honest traid to won your living, spendis, waistis and consumes in drinking ryatuslie mair nor ony in the toun of Kinneduart . . . .

Moreover, he was known to have spent three rose nobles in drink in Elgin in three days, 'quhilk ye culd nocht deny'.[36]

The criminal jurisdiction of the barony court was more or less confined to cases of theft and slaughter, provided the thief was caught red-handed and the killer taken in the act. The obvious difficulties in dealing with cases of slaughter meant that this crime slipped more and more into the courts of the king's justiciars whose records are full of it. No cases of slaughter came before the barony court of Carnwath during the nineteen years covered by its surviving court book. It did crop up elsewhere, however; a man was acquitted of the crime at Spynie in 1593 and a neighbour hanged for it three years later.[37] The death penalty was inflicted for other crimes, including house-breaking and theft, the gallows hill being a familiar landmark and the gallows itself an important piece of baronial equipment. Some baronies had more than one; at Yester they cheerfully used a spare one in place of the kitchen brace when the latter had to be sent to the smith to be mended.[38] A criminal might be beheaded instead of hanged; in Breadalbane the 'heiding axe', kept in the guardhouse of Balloch castle, turns up faithfully in the regular inventories of the castle's plenishings.[39]

In the barony of Spynie in Moray both men and women were hanged, beheaded or drowned for the local pastime of sheepstealing, drowning taking place in the River Lossie, on one occasion after the court had conveniently met 'upoun the water syd of Lossie'.[40] One man, who was said to have made his living at sheep-stealing — one wonders how much the Elgin fleshers knew about him — and who was hanged for the crime, gave the officer some trouble in finding proof of his guilt until the sharp-eyed officer spied a cow picking wool out of the top of the house, whereupon a search resulted in the discovery of several salted carcases in the rigging of the roof. The man's wife, who was also hanged, was caught trying to conceal the rest of the telltale mutton: 'thow the said Christiane ran away with sum soddin muttoun in thy bosom, quhilk thy neighbouris saw'.[41] In 1608 a woman in Glasgow barony, accused of having stolen corn from a neighbour's barn, was given another chance but was warned that a second offence would mean drowning 'bot (without) ony assys'. She had disposed of the corn to a third party to avoid being caught with it in her possession.[42] In the barony of Cally

'Charlie McMorane sumtyme in Colvone (Colvend) and now vagabond', was drowned for the theft of a horse and some hanks of yarn.[43]

Many holders of baronies were given wider powers by the crown, their lands being erected into *regalities* in which they enjoyed almost royal powers over criminal cases, including those called the four pleas of the crown, murder, arson, rape and robbery, which were usually reserved for the royal justiciar's court. In a regality, from which the authority of the king's writs and the activities of his officers were excluded, the baron could have his own justiciar's court, keep his own chancery for issuing brieves, running in his own and not in the king's name, so that certain legal business could begin, such as the recognition of heirs, and in a few cases might even have his own mint. Many nobles, bishops and monasteries held their lands in regality, making them like local monarchs, largely independent of royal authority.

It is in the internal, largely non-criminal business of the barony courts, however, that we find the normal pattern of rural life. The land itself was of first importance and so closely were the tenants identified with it that the clerk of Urie barony court could use the expression, 'the laird, with consent of his haill grund ...'[44] To ensure that the lord received his due from the land, every effort was made to see that it was continually cultivated and to avoid breaks in occupancy. The general policy of tenant-continuity was due less to benevolence than to common sense. Vacant holdings and those to which nobody could lay a clear claim reverted to the landlord to be re-set by him. Tenants were penalised just as severely for neglecting to cultivate their holdings as for failure to pay their rent in time, since the first fault would lead to the second. At Alloway they were warned that if they could not labour their own ground it would be set to their neighbours, and one man was prosecuted for 'postponing to occupy his mailing, depriving the toun (i.e. the burgh of Ayr, the superior) of the profit thereof'.[45] A tenant accused of *wrongful occupation* was allowed to sow and harvest that year's crop before being removed; David Farquhar in Alloway, wrongly occupying the holding of Adam Wilson, was allowed not only to sow and harvest the ground but also to claim some compensation from Wilson, the rightful holder.[46] Holdings were re-set although the rent or other dues might be in arrears, if security was given for payment. Tenants with doubtful rights of possession were left in occupation until their cases could be properly heard in court; in 1533 a Dunfermline abbey tenant who was found to be in possession four or five years after the expiry of his lease was allowed to remain 'quhill he be ordourly callit (i.e. to appear in court) and justly put thayr fray'.[47]

Although in a sense land mattered more than people, the lord did not have it all his own way, for he was not above the law of his own barony. His complaints against tenants came before the barony court, where the accused had opportunity to defend themselves. At other times the tenants might raise actions against him. In 1595 the barony court of Alloway found in favour of a tenant who had disputed the action of the burgh in leasing a holding during his minority, to which he claimed the right of possession.[48] Careful regulation of the occupancy and cultivation of the ground helped to defend the respective rights of landlord and tenant and protected the interests of both. Although in practice many tenant families often held their holdings from one generation to another, in many places there was a formal re-setting of the ground at Whitsunday and an allocation of vacant holdings whose number was increased by the judicial removals which took place at that term. Those due for renewal were re-let, in most cases to the same people on the same conditions as before, and those tenants who held by life leases were required to produce their titles in court for examination, to make sure that they were keeping the terms of their leases. 'The Whitsonday court and assedatioun (setting) of the barony' is the heading on the first page of the Alloway court book, when the magistrates of Ayr met 'in plane Witsonda' for the purpose. Here, according to the court book, holdings were re-let systematically — 'set to him as before' is the phrase used over and over again — and rentallers, that is those who held life leases, who failed to produce their rentals for inspection, 'so that the judges may know how every tenant uses his mailing and keeps the acts and statutes', were fined 22s.[49]

Not only were holdings re-set but they were often physically redefined, or *delt*, in order to discourage tenants from encroaching on their neighbours' lands over the years. Violation of the limits of delt land or of an 'act of daill' led to many. disputes in the barony court, much deliberation by the sworn men, and subsequent measuring and 'stobbing' by the eveners. In 1510 Andrew Johnson in Alloway was accused of having laboured and sown a rig of land which had been assigned to the pursuer 'in his daill'.[50] In the last analysis dealing the holdings was a matter for the baron to decide, yet, if it was done without his knowledge, he could not simply overrule what had been done but had to bring the matter into the barony court as a complaint against tenants. The earl of Eglinton appeared as a pursuer in his own court in a case of this kind in 1576:

> The quhilk daye, tuching the evyning and als gud for als gud (i.e. equally) of the merkland in Mylntoun, occupiit be Andrew Gardner, younger, and Walter Young, the said Walter allegeis that the tua was delt for othyr. My Lord repellit the samyn, allegeis in respect the samyis was not delt wyt his Lordship's consent therto, and at na tenentis had nor sall have power to daill ony landis outin his Lordship (i.e. without his knowledge), nethyr nor for thrie yeris wyout his consent therto, of the quhilkis the said Andrew requirit actis (i.e. an extract from the court book for himself) . . .[51]

Good, newly cultivated land might be delt in acres, the name *acredales* occurring in different parts of the country. In fact, there is a sense in which *dales* denoted pieces of land, usually larger than the rigs on the run-rig, given to tenants in addition to their holdings in the run-rig area. In the barony of Carnwath a widow who held 15s worth of land asked to have part of 'the intak of the Caldlaw' and was granted 'her daill efferand to (appropriate to) her 15s.'[52] Meadowland, pasture and moss were delt, as well as arable; in 1515 an Alloway tenant complained that another had 'tilled part of his delt meadow'.[53] Husbandmen with large holdings were sometimes prosecuted for creating acredales on their own land, bringing in subtenants to do the cultivating.

Surreptitious attempts to increase the size of a holding were pounced on, usually as the result of a neighbour's complaint; tilling another's daill, ploughing up parts of the well-fertilised loan, or a right-of-way or meadow land, sowing on

the other side of a broken march dyke. Encroachment sometimes led to such confusion that a general redefinition of holdings became necessary, as when the
tenants of the barony of Stane agreed to abide by the earl of Eglinton's 'act of
daill'.[54] Good neighbourhood in the literal sense meant honouring the boundaries
of one's neighbour's land, a problem which gave rise to countless acts of the
barony court; dykes must be kept in repair, weeds kept under control, corn eaten
by straying animals compensated for, neighbours' agreements made publicly in
court and not by private arrangement. Many cases of assault and blood-drawing
which are sometimes construed as mere lawlessness must have been the result of
disputes over cultivation, the business which occupied the time and energy of most
people, including the young. It was surely the reason behind the argument in the
barony of Glasgow during which one tenant laid about another with 'ane fute
spaid'.[55] The barony court handled many matters which also came before the
burgh courts of urban communities; enforcement of the payment of debts, of
servants' fees, of money promised under contract, failure to return property which
had been pledged or loaned. One man at Alloway, with predictable lack of
success, sued a neighbour for a white hat which the latter admitted to having
borrowed but had lost at the battle of Flodden.[56] Disputes arose out of the continual buying and selling of victual and animals among the members of the rural
community, such as the sale by one Dunfermline tenant to another of what was
described as 'ane falty horse'.[57]

The maintenance of internal law and order in the barony, as distinct from
public justice, occupied a lot of the court's time, from the brawls which were apt
to accompany the annual fair to those which ended in blood-drawing, which could
mean a fine in court, a *wite* as it was called, hence the term *blood-wite*. Culprits
would try to wriggle out of paying the fine by admitting that blood had been
drawn but denying responsibility for it — denying the wite. It was sometimes
difficult to sort out what had actually happened in a disturbance. Two characters
at Carnwath took refuge in the explanation that 'it was in play and nocht in
ernyst.'[58] Barony officers were often *deforced* — forcibly prevented from carrying
out an order of the court, usually to confiscate stock or other goods; an offender's
neighbours would sometimes join him in waylaying the officer and retrieve the
animals that were being driven off. Deforcement was regarded seriously by the
court and might result in the loss of holdings or in imprisonment. Similar penalties
were inflicted for attempts to cultivate land or use stock or crops which the baron
had *fenced* or placed under *arrestment* by an act of the court, legally setting them
aside as it were until a case was examined or a debt paid. All these offences were
taken as being violations of an act of the court made in the baron's name, and
were therefore looked upon as offences against the lord of the ground himself;
'fylin of his grund with violent blud', 'forssin of his offesar', breking of his fens'.[59]
A law-abiding community, cultivating the ground and regularly paying rent to the
baron, meant that he was better able to fulfil his duties to the crown. The tenants
were the lord's men, although not in any sense of personal bondage. What was
theirs was his and what was his was the king's. At least, that was the theory, for

there would always be those who acted the heavy landlord on the one hand and the overmighty subject on the other.

Microcosm of rural society and public order that it was, the barony was a conservative community. This was inevitable, for it had a legal framework, its function depended on the maintenance of the status quo in its institutions and way of life, and the conservatism of the people was reinforced by their dependence on the land and the rhythm of agriculture. An important positive element in this way of life was the smooth-running of those institutions to be found in all baronies that brought profit to the landlord and amenity to the inhabitants and were often operated on a monopoly basis. Of these the most important was undoubtedly the grain mill, or mills, at which all grain grown in the barony must be ground. The land was said to be *thirled* to the barony mill, those who cultivated the land being known as the *sucken,* another instance of the tenants' identification with the land itself. The superior received the *multure,* tax on the grain ground, which might be paid in cash or in actual grain, and the miller got his perquisite, the *knaifship.* The miller was responsible for keeping the mill in good working order and only he was supposed to supervise the milling process, since he alone was accountable and could not complain of injustice if he allowed others to interfere with the work. Millers in the barony of Glasgow were warned not to allow their wives or women servants to put the tenants' 'stuff' into the mill, and were instructed to scour the mill thoroughly after grinding malt so that the incoming meal could be ground properly; one of them had a new knaifship measure made for him by a cooper on the baron-bailie's orders.[60] Nobody trusted the miller, but the tenants were not to be trusted either; those at Urie were forbidden to interfere with the millstones during grinding, and those in Glasgow barony were warned that there must be no selling of grain directly from the ground to the mealmakers.[61] At Urie the millers were given remarkably wide powers in being made 'officers to themselves' with power to confiscate the moveables of those who failed to present grain to be ground.[62] Where a mill, grain or fulling mill, was leased to a tacksman trouble might follow for, since he was usually responsible for the upkeep of the buildings and machinery and for the collection of the multures which he often received with his lease, he was sometimes unscrupulous in his demands. The tenants of Alloway successfully complained against the tacksman who tried to make them 'bring hame' new millstones while they were in the middle of the harvest, a matter he ought to have attended to before they began to cut the grain.[63]

Other amenities such as the smithy and the brewhouse — lands being thirled to the latter as to the mill — might be leased to tenants whose services in smith work and brewing would count as part of the rent. Besides, barony smiths and brewers might be entitled to certain payments from other tenants. Steven Smith, smith in the barony of Urie, complained that the tenants refused to pay his 'smeddie boll', explaining that 'the smeddie collis was risseyn to hiecher prycis and mair scant to be had', as a result of which rise in the cost of materials 'he was unable to susteyn the wark of the grund' without loss to himself.[64] In the same barony James Duncan, brewer, paid two stones of 'brew chres' (brewing tallow) as rent in kind for his alehouse and croft, and James Millin was prosecuted for failure to pay his 'brew lauche', tax due for his liberty of brewing ale.[65] A herd was paid by the tenants whose stock was pastured on the commonty, and since he was a barony servant attacks upon him were regarded as a serious offence, almost as if they had been made upon a barony officer. There were attempts by the courts to ensure that where new pasture was acquired a herd was employed to control the grazing stock; at Eglinton those with pasture on the moss were ordered to pay a herd among them, and at Monimail repair of the folds and the payment of a herd were enjoined.[66] At Glasgow tenants were caught trying to graze their animals during the night, possibly to avoid the herd's fee or simply to steal extra use of the pasture.[67]

There were many negative rules which made the barony a closed community to outsiders, the 'outtintoun men'. Subtenants must not be brought in from outside, widows must not re-marry outsiders, must not re-marry at all, in fact, without the baron's consent and his knowledge of who was going to take over their holdings, and tenants must not take leases of land outwith the barony and thus serve two masters. At Alloway in 1517 a man lost his tack for not remaining in the barony 'in the heid of thyn awin mailing'.[68] In regalities which possessed a burgh, care was taken to refer cases correctly either to the lord's burgh or landward court. Barony men cited to appear before another court could be *repledged* to that of their own baron, while no tenant was allowed to pursue another before judges other than an assize of their own barony, only barony men being permitted to serve on the assize or to appear as witnesses.

In spite of the procedure of repledgation of tenants to their lord's own court, relations between the barony courts and those of other authorities were not always easy. Ordinary folk resented the lengthy and costly procedures of the medieval church courts and tried to avoid them, as they tried to avoid payment of the hated kirk dues, but if the baron happened to be an ecclesiastic it would be easier to bring pressure to bear on the tenants when summoning them to appear before the church courts. By the time the authority of medieval canon law had declined, much of the effectiveness of the barony courts themselves was already eroded. Criminal jurisdiction was first to go — passing to the justiciar and sheriff — until by the seventeenth century the barony court was very largely concerned with administrative business and petty squabbles. It should be emphasised, however, that the criminal powers of the barony court remained in theory; it was only in practice that they faded. Even in civil actions the power of the local courts lessened as time went on. From mid-sixteenth century onwards more and more inhabitants of baronies brought appeals before the Lords of Council and Session in the supreme civil court in Edinburgh, including many customary tenants, as we shall see later. One such tenant from the barony of Inchaffray in Perthshire found himself beaten up in the High Street of Edinburgh by the landlord's servants for daring to raise an action against him in the Court of Session.[69] We find the professional advocates who defended these people in court defining and upholding the 'use' and 'lovable custom' of the baronies and influencing the judges into over-turning the decisions of barons against their tenants. On the other hand, the Lords sometimes upheld the local authority of barons against that of the central government's representatives, as when they upheld the complaint of John Lennox, baron of Cally, against Lord Maxwell, the king's steward of Kirkcudbright, who had interfered with Lennox's right to search a house in his barony for a suspect thief.[70]

Not only the tenants but the barons themselves looked to royal authority to give strength to their arm, eroding the power of their own local courts in the process. This could easily happen where the baron was a royal official or enjoyed a good measure of royal favour. The earl of Cassillis, as the king's bailie of Carrick, had a second chance to bring the tenants of his own barony to trial.[71] Sir Robert Barton, the Comptroller, holding the royal gift of the *ward* of young Lord Drummond, presided over the latter's barony court of Auchterarder from 1514 to 1520.[72] Sir Robert Melville of Murdocairney, Treasurer of the realm, was baron of Monimail at the end of the sixteenth century.[73] In 1532 the abbot of Dunfermline, George Durie, and the administrator of the abbey, his uncle, Archbishop James Beaton, referred a case from the regality court to the Lords of Council and Session with the result that royal letters arrived calling on the regality bailies and their deputies to stop proceedings in the case, which the bailies and their deputies 'with honor and reverence obeit'.[74] However localised rural life might be, there were always ways and means by which the king's authority could penetrate into it.

Notes

1 W. C. Dickinson, *Court Book of the Barony of Carnwath* (S.H.S.), Introduction, *passim (Carnwath)*

2 Register of feu charters of Paisley abbey (Paisley public library), *passim* (Paisley charters)

3 Rental of Scone (S.R.O.), RH 9/3/163

4 M.H.B. Sanderson, *The Mauchline Account Books of Melrose Abbey* (A.A.N.H.S.) *(Mauchline Account Books)*

5 Register of feu charters (S.R.O.), ii, fo. 185r (R.F.C.)

6 Alloway barony court book (S.R.O.), B6/28/1, fo. 89r (Alloway)

7 *Ibid.,* fo. 99r

8 C. Rogers, *Register of Cupar Abbey* (Grampian Club), I, 177 *(Cupar)*

9 Newbattle muniments (S.R.O.), GD40/1/741

10 Leven and Melville muniments (S.R.O.), GD26/4/688

11 See Appendix A

12 J. Bain, *Diocesan registers of Glasgow* (Grampian Club) I, 186, 189 *(Glasgow registers)*

13 *Cupar,* II, 19, 51, 117; *R.M.S.,* IV, 1788

14 Morton muniments (S.R.O.), GD 150/1429

15 *Cupar,* I, 228

16 Alloway, B6/28/2, fo. 3r

17 Keillour barony court book (S.R.O.), RH 11/41/1, fo. 4r (Keillour)

18 *Carnwath,* 199

19 Eglinton muniments (S.R.O.), GD 3, Barony court book, fo. 18r

20 *Ibid.,* fo. 31r

21 Regality court book of Glasgow (S.R.O.), RH 11/32/3/1, 1605 (Glasgow regality)

22 D. G. Barron, *Court book of the barony of Urie* (S.H.S.), 24 *(Urie)*

23 G. Hay, *History of Arbroath,* 112-127

24 *Carnwath, passim*

25 Eglinton muniments, GD 3, Barony court book, *passim*

26 Keillour, *passim*
27 Alloway, B6/28/1, fo. 66r
28 *Urie*, 14
29 *Extracts from the register of the regality of Spynie* (Spalding Miscellany II), 122, 127, 129 *(Spynie)*
30 *Records of the Canongate, 1561-88* (Maitland Club Misc., II), pp. 283-359
31 Eglinton muniments, GD 3, Barony court book, *passim*
32 R. L. Mackie and S. Cruden, *The Abbey of Arbroath: Official Guide* (H.M.S.O.), 41
33 Glasgow regality, *passim*
34 *Urie*, 12, 24, 25, 29
35 Alloway, B6/28/1, fo. 165r
36 *Spynie*, 125
37 *Ibid.*, 120, 132
38 Yester writs (S.R.O.), GD28/1838
39 Breadalbane muniments (S.R.O.), GD 112/22/2
40 *Spynie*, 132, 134
41 *Ibid.*, 129
42 Glasgow regality, 30 April 1608
43 Broughton and Cally muniments (S.R.O.), GD 10/450
44 *Urie*, 6
45 Alloway, B6/28/1, 22 January 1510
46 *Ibid.*, B6/28/1, fo. 14v
47 J. Webster and A. A. M. Duncan, *Regality court book of Dunfermline*, 93 *(Dunfermline regality)*
48 Alloway, B6/28/1, fo. 23r
49 *Ibid.*, B6/28/1, fo. 22v
50 *Ibid.*, B6/28/1, 2 May 1510
51 Eglinton muniments, GD 3, Barony court book, fo. 51r
52 *Carnwath*, 9
53 Alloway, B6/28/1, 24 January 1515
54 Eglinton muniments, GD3, Barony court book, fo. 9r
55 Glasgow regality, 15 April 1607
56 Alloway, B6/28/1, 18 November 1516
57 *Dunfermline regality*, 103
58 *Carnwath*, 108
59 *Ibid.*, civ
60 Glasgow regality, 1611
61 *Ibid.*, 1611
62 *Urie*, 29
63 Alloway, B6/28/1, fo. 15r
64 *Urie*, 8
65 *Ibid.*, 26
66 Eglinton muniments, GD3, Barony court book, fo. 46r; Leven and Melville muniments, GD 26/2/1, fo. 3r
67 Glasgow regality, 30 April 1608
68 Alloway, B6/28/1, 4 February 1517
69 Register of acts and decreets (S.R.O.), xii, fo. 472r (Acts and decreets)
70 Broughton and Cally muniments, GD 10/447
71 Bailie court book of Carrick (S.R.O.), RH 11/14/1, fo. 3v (Carrick)
72 Drummond charters (S.R.O.), GD 160/118/11
73 Leven and Melville muniments, GD 26/2/1
74 *Dunfermline regality*, 78

3

Running the Estates

'To ane pyper to play to the scheraris in harvest, £4'.

Douglas of Lochleven accounts, 1574: RH 9/1/3

ESTATE management is perhaps too formal a description to apply to the running of his affairs by a small farmer who kept his account book in his pocket, yet both he and the lord of a regality, whose officers managed his widespread lands for him, had the same basic business to attend to, collecting their income and keeping account of how it was spent. Apart from salaries attached to government appointments and income derived from trade or the practice of a profession, nearly all income came from the land or, more correctly, from the rents of those who cultivated it. The extent to which the landlord controlled the land from which he expected his rents to come might vary throughout his estate, depending on how the land was *set* and how it was *occupied*. Therefore, the landlord and those who handled his rents had to know who the occupants were and what dues they ought to pay annually.

Land was either *in the hands* of the baron or it was *set* to others on a variety of conditions. The *Mains* of the barony, a name which survives in hundreds of places on the modern map and is sometimes referred to locally as 'the home farm', which often lay near the baron's dwelling and produced food for his household, was not usually leased out to tenants but remained in his hands, cultivated by his servants and tenants or, in the sixteenth century — by which time the tenants' labour services had often been commuted to cash payments — by hired agricultural workers, some of whom no doubt came from tenant families. We find, however, that here and there the Mains itself was coming to be leased, especially in baronies belonging to churchmen, who tended to be absentee landlords. At Torpichen, for example, leasing of the Mains was underway in the first half of the century; although it was then said that the major part of it was 'in my lord's hands and holds a plough of eight oxen with the *bonage* (commuted harvest work) of the barony', it was also stated that 'ther is set out of the Mains certain acres to the cottars of the toun (of Torpichen) extending to twenty acres, of which each acre should pay yearly of maill 5s, and a hen'.[1]

Other parts of the barony besides the Mains might be in the lord's hands, for a variety of reasons. He might take over land to which the right was in dispute or which had been *violently occupied*, that is, by someone who had no right to it and who had been legally dispossessed of it by the barony court. The land might be in *ward*, that is, in the lord's hands during the minority of an heir, if it was held heritably, or it might be a holding which had been forfeited by a tenant who had in some way broken the customary law, 'the lovable custom', of the barony.

Next to the land actually in his hand the baron had fairly firm control over the use of land set to tenants in what was known as *steelbow*, where the stock and seed were given to the tenant with the ground, a contractual arrangement found not only in the Lowlands but also in the Highlands of Scotland, whereby the tenant was obliged to deliver to the landlord at the expiry of the contract — possibly made from year to year — certain profits of the land and stock, such as grain, butter, cheese and the young of the animals. Some steelbow holdings were of long standing, others may have been a way of dealing with newly cultivated land. While there had been some commutation of steelbow dues by the sixteenth century, it is clear from testaments that actual steelbow victual and animals were paid by some tenants still.

Lands held in steelbow may seem a sort of half-way arrangement between the Mains, which was entirely in the lord's hands, and land which was completely leased out. But, in effect, steelbow land was rather like Mains land because the cultivation was done by the tenants, who were formerly bound to cultivate the Mains, and there was a guarantee of returns for the lord's kitchen.

A third way in which the landlord could closely control the use of the ground, particularly with regard to stockrearing and dairy produce, was to lease pasture land and dairy farms to tenants who reared the stock and, once a year, rendered an account of the animals in their possession. The reckoning often took place at Beltane or at midsummer.

In the 1540s the earl of Eglinton, holding his courts of the baronies of Eglinton and Ardrossan, 'made Beltane' with some of his *bowmen*, as these tenants were called:

> At Irvin the 11 day of maii 1545, quhilk day my lord of Eglinton maid beltan with Rob Torrence in Hairschaw. Remanis with him the said day, fyfe tyde ky, ane ferrow kow and twa yield ky, ane ox beist of thrie yeir auld . . . the haill nowmer 14 beistis . . .
>
> 20 September 1545, deliverit till Arthure Dunlop to put in the Hairschaw, with thir gudis abone wryttin, fyfe . . . beistis of twa yeir auld, four . . . stirkis, thre ox beistis of twa yeir auld and ane ox stirk, quhilkis gudis wes of the ferm stirkis (i.e. rents in kind) of Ardrossan . . . .[2]

Here, stock from the rents in kind of one barony, Ardrossan, is transferred to another, Eglinton. At Corriehoill in the barony of Ardrossan thirteen animals were counted, with the memorandum, 'and restis (remains) to cum to the ketchin, 2 wedderis and ane yeild ewe'.

These *bowgangs*, or *bowtouns*, as they were called, set to bowmen, were to be found in all parts of the country; sheep from the Bowtoun set to John Steidman by the laird of Lochleven, 'yearly to deliver to the said John 280 lambs and John to deliver agane to the laird at Beltane 240 rochth hoggis';[3] fifty stones of cheese from Glenbrue belonging to the laird of Glenorchy and 'held in bowing';[4] cheese from thre 'bow ky' held by tenants of the lordship of Hamilton, 'each cow paying two stones cheese to my lord's house';[5] 352 stones of cheese from Glendaruel in Argyll, 'set in bowhous under my lord's ky'.[6] The bowings, like steelbow holdings and the Mains, meant produce for the lord's kitchen and were probably thought of together by the chamberlain of the barony. An interesting memorandum, drawn up about 1567, of 'My Lord of Menteith's bowgangs and manis, usit be erlle Jone his guidschir', suggests the link between them:

Item, Bosresly, where Lucas Fisher was Bowman
Item, Insere where Murdoch and Janet Wood paid ferm and kane cheese
Item, Blairinros bowgank to me lord . . . .
Item, a merkland in John McEwine hand and another merkland bowgank to me lord
Item, Glassyll ane bowgank to me lord
Item, Gartdreny ane gret bowgank
Item, Awchmoyr ane mens
Item, Inche moy ane manis
Item, the £5 of Cracksuttie manis and bowgank
Item, the 8 merkland of Inche made in ane park be me lordis fader, planesit (plenished) with meris
And as to the 40s land of Downante it paid nevir but maill silver, sik as the rental buk specifeis and malowris (maillers, who paid only money rent) evir duelland thair this hunder yeir bygain quhilk weill knawin be me lordis rentall buk.[7]

In this one memorandum land is said to be in bowing, leased, in Mains, in parkland for the grazing of brood mares and held for money rent only: a good example of the variety of land-use. In the barony of Torpichen one farm, 'the Hochcottis', formerly 'ane bow place', was said to be set for silver maill and rent in grain, with 'sown oats, bere, eight oxen, six ky and forty ewes in teilbow',[8] and at Fauldhouse in the same barony it was laid down that the land should normally be set for money and victual, 'induring my will', but that at any time it might become a bowgang, at least in part: another reminder of changing land-use to suit the landlord's purpose. The laird of Wamphray, Gilbert Johnston, however, had to bring an action into his own barony court in order to establish his claim to a *bowstead* which he had had built on the lands of Hessilbank, witnesses being called to name the bowmen and one of them stating that his father had given the laird the wood 'to big ane bow' there.[9]

The point in all this is that by keeping land in his own hands, as Mains land or for other reasons, or by setting it in steelbow or to a bowman as a dairy or sheep farm, the baron was able to control the land-use and make sure that he got returns for the use of his household.

He had less direct control over land which was leased out to the tenants in the more normal way, which accounted for the bulk of the estate. Admittedly, where land was leased for a number of years, the baron had the right of review when the lease fell due for renewal but, as we shall see in a later chapter, renewal was in many cases automatic and the conditions were rarely changed.[10] Any deliberate attempt to raise the rent was met with protest from the tenants, who regarded this as a violation of the custom of the barony. Where land was leased to a tenant for his lifetime, this could also come under review, at the death of the tenant, but, as we shall also see later, renewal of life-leases was even more automatic. Although in some barony court books there is evidence that tenants who held for life were required to present their titles regularly for inspection, this was only to ensure that they were keeping their part of the agreement.[11] Therefore, having once leased the ground on this contract-like basis, that is, continued possession in return for prompt payment of rent and performance of 'due service', the baron's returns from the land and the extent of his control over it remained more or less fixed. Some variations in the returns might be realised if rents in grain were sold at market prices from year to year.

The landlord benefited even less from land which was held from him heritably, by charter. This happened where nobles and ecclesiastical landlords, who themselves held their land by charter from the king as his tenants-in-chief, had vassals under them who similarly held from them in the feudal pyramid. Many cadet branches of noble families and relatives of substantial lairds as well as many small proprietors held land heritably, side by side with those who held by lease. These vassals, *heritors* or *freeholders*, as they were called, passed the land automatically to their heirs according to the law of succession, with virtually no right of review by the superior. What is more, their annual dues consisted of fixed money payments which represented the old feudal *ward* duty, supplemented by certain periodic *casualties* payable to the lord when the heir succeeded while under age, when he married and when he subsequently entered into his inheritance. The use of the land — the *property* right — was defined in the charter once and for all and was largely out of the lord's hands. Heritable holdings were most common on lay estates but they did occur on church land here and there; the Ochterlonies of Kellie, for example, held their lands heritably from the abbot of Arbroath. On the church lands *feu-ferm* holding gradually replaced leases, and the feuars of kirklands, like the heritors and freeholders of lay estates, paid their lords an annual, fixed, money feu-duty and certain casualties at intervals. Feu charters also gave the feuar an increased use of the land itself and took it a step further away from the superior's control. A roll of landholders in the regality of Stow, part of the estates of the archbishops of St Andrews, lists twelve freeholders, nine feuars and ninety-seven tenants who held by lease.[12]

There would always be some land on an estate which for one reason or another brought the landlord in nothing at all in a given year, a fact which had to be noted in the chamberlain's accounts. Memoranda by Lord Oliphant's chamberlain in 1595 reflect the rigours of rural life: 'the sixth rig of Aberdargie occupied by Andrew Drone, who departed in poverty fra the samyn . . . The wobstar's rowme (the weaver's holding), lying waste, who left in poverty'.[13] Land might be completely out of the baron's hands because he had *wadset* it, that is, alienated it in return for a loan of money, during the non-payment of which the creditor, known as the wadsetter, collected the rents and was for all practical purposes the proprietor. Occasionally the legal memoranda and surveys of estates compiled for the information of guardians, trustees and creditors reveal the considerable extent to which land might be wadset; in the 1570s, for instance, Lord Forbes's debts on wadset land amounted to 14,000 merks.[14]

Several officers, of whom the most important were the bailie and the chamberlain, were responsible for the management of the property, monitoring the occupancy of the land, dealing with transgressions of the customary law by tenants, and accounting for all incoming revenue and outgoing expenses. Quite often these officers, the bailie and chamberlain would operate through or with the assistance of deputies, and would reply on serjeants and other subordinate officers to actually carry out their commands, and on clerks to help them record the business, in barony court books, account books and rentals. These personnel were usually local people, tenants themselves or at least relatives of the landlord, and would be known to the inhabitants of the baronies; they did not have the impersonal character of modern administrators.

We have already seen the baron bailie at work. He took charge of the public side of affairs. Through him the landlord's will was seen to be done as he presided in the court and maintained law and order through his officers and serjeants. Good relations between a baron and his bailie were essential and, since the lord might spend a considerable time away from home, the bailie had to be trusted to act in his interests in his absence. One way to ensure this was to appoint a relative or substantial tenant as bailie, and so we find Montgomeries acting for the earl of Eglinton, Ogilvys for Lord Ogilvy and Gordons for the earl of Huntly and, on the other hand, on church estates, Huntly himself as bailie of the Gordon bishop of Aberdeen, a Chisholm bailie at Dunblane and a Colville at Culross abbey.

The bailiary of many monastic estates had become hereditary by the sixteenth century, which caused difficulties because, whereas the bailiary might get stuck in one family, usually one of local influence, the lord of regality or baron, in the person of abbot or commendator, changed from time to time. Resentment of the continuous authority of a hereditary bailie increased as monastic lands came to be regarded as pieces of private property by the families of lay commendators and ambitious ecclesiastics. The days when the head of a religious house looked gratefully to the support of an influential local magnate were passing. For a bailie who might himself be a tenant on the church estate in question, as in the case of Learmonth of Dairsie, bailie of the archbishopric of St Andrews, or whose lands adjoined it, the office strengthened his hand over his own tenants and those of his neighbours. People sometimes complained that bailies and their deputies pursued private quarrels under cover of officialdom. When the feud between Alexander Cunningham, the post-Reformation commendator of Kilwinning abbey, and the hereditary bailie, the earl of Eglinton, was at its height in 1579 it was stated before the privy council that the commendator 'for sindrie reasonabill causis baith of dedlie feid and utheris, hes obtenit his haill tenentis and servandis exemit fra the said Erllis jurisdictioun in all civile and criminale caussis'.[15] We can imagine the predicament of tenants faced with the rival demands of two local authorities. Earlier in the century the Hamilton abbot of Kilwinning, had refused for almost two years to recognise the earl's father as hereditary bailie.[16]

Grants of bailiary sometimes reserved certain executive powers to the superior. Although Learmonth of Dairsie, bailie of St Andrews, was also coroner of the archbishop's regality court, he was not allowed to actually hold a justice-ayre without the latter's licence, and the Learmonths took an oath of fidelity to the archbishop on appointment.[17] The earl of Arran, as bailie and justiciar for the archbishop of Glasgow in the 1540s, was not permitted to appoint or remove officers without the archbishop's consent.[18] The earl of Morton, who became bailie of Dunfermline abbey in 1574, was banned from creating *ad hoc* bailies, as they were called, to give sasine of land in the regality.[19]

Arrangements for payment of the bailie's fee varied. If he were paid an outright sum, this would most likely be given to him by the chamberlain when the accounts were made up; in the 1580s the earl of Morton's chamberlain gave £10 to Lord Maxwell, bailie of the barony of Preston,[20] and in 1593 the chamberlain of Arbroath paid £9 to Lord Ogilvy, the hereditary bailie, in name of the superior, Lord John Hamilton.[21] On church land the bailie was sometimes paid from the teinds, which were, strictly speaking, not rents but dues from the inhabitants as parishioners of parishes annexed to the religious house in question. Wallace of Craigie, as bailie of Paisley abbey's barony of Monkton in Kyle, received as his salary a quantity of meal from the teinds of some of the abbey's Ayrshire parish kirks.[22] Very often a bailie was paid from the rents in grain, which he could then sell at market prices, so that his fee varied from year to year. Sometimes, if he held land himself on the estate concerned he was simply given a rebate of his own rent; the earl of Argyll was paid from the feu-duty of the lands of Farnell which he held from the landlord, the bishop of Brechin,[23] and Kerr of Cessford from lands which he held from the commendator of Kelso.[24] Lord Boyd was paid partly from his own rents and partly from fines imposed in the court of the archbishop of Glasgow, over which he presided as bailie.[25]

Some sixteenth-century grants of bailiary were in the form of feu charters, making the office hereditary in the grantee's family. Sometimes a separate obligation was drawn up at the time of the appointment defining the bailie's powers and responsibilities. Hugh Campbell of Loudoun, the king's sheriff of Ayr, who was made bailie of Melrose abbey's Ayrshire barony of Kylesmure in 1521 by Abbot Robert Beaton, signed an agreement at the time which was meant to remind him that he must not regard the barony of Kylesmure a part of his own — as it happened — neighbouring lands. He undertook not to tax the tenants, demand carriage service from them for himself, lift fines in the barony court or nominate a deputy to preside there without the abbot's licence, and not to take his friends hunting and hawking over the farmland. On the positive side he agreed to take the part of the abbey in all controversies, oversee the 'inputting and outputting' of tenants and, when asked to do so, 'red and devoid ony stedyng' in spite of any 'freindschip' or 'manrent' between himself and the tenant concerned. Campbell's agreement pinpoints well the likely areas of friction between the baron and his bailie, who in this case was required to pledge his rents, lands and moveables for the honouring of his obligation.[26]

The chamberlain of the barony dealt with the finance, assisted by officers and serjeants who uplifted and gathered in the rents, and by clerks who kept the books. There were areas in which his responsibility overlapped that of the bailie. He might be asked, for example, to furnish evidence of a tenant's right to a holding or the amount of rent due by a tenant whose case was before the barony court. The chamberlain of Kilwinning abbey once personally confronted at his dwelling a tenant who was being prosecuted for arrears of rent.[27] To be able to trust the man who handled the income was just as essential as trusting the bailie who represented the baron's authority. Again, a relative was often chosen for this job, or a tenant or trusted friend. In earlier times the office of chamberlain of a church estate would have been held by an ecclesiastic, often a member of the convent of a monastery, but by the early sixteenth century it was passing more and more frequently into the hands of a layman, although those who handled the internal finance of a monastic community, such as the almoner or 'master of the petty commons', were often members of the convent, and as late as 1571 a canon of Inchaffray, William Ruthven, was chamberlain there.[28] Bishop George Brown of Dunkeld, in the early years of the sixteenth century, made James Fenton, the precentor of the cathedral, chamberlain 'owing to his business ability'.[29] By contrast, we later find John Weir, chamberlain of Kelso abbey's Lanarkshire barony of Lesmahagow, unable to write, subscribing his accounts with the help of a notary.[30] At Arbroath abbey James Ogilvy of Balfour, a relative of the bailie, Lord Ogilvy, was chamberlain.[31] There were two lay chamberlains of Dunfermline abbey in the mid-sixteenth century, Alan Coutts and Thomas Toscheach.[32] In 1554 the commendator of Coldingham priory sued the recently deposed chamberlain, Hercules Barclay, for refusing to hand over his account books and those of two of his predecessors,[33] and in 1566 Bishop Patrick Hepburn, as commendator of Scone, raised an action against the chamberlain, Alexander Blair of Friartoun, for witholding money and ornaments belonging to the abbey.[34]

In December 1555 Gavin Hamilton, commendator of Kilwinning, appointed Robert Hamilton, younger, of Dalserf, as his chamberlain. The terms of the appointment, in the form of a contract, give a good idea of his duties. He uplifted, through his officers, the rents, commutation-money for services, and the kirksilver, or strictly ecclesiastical dues, pursuing in the barony court and in the king's courts if necessary those who refused to pay. He arranged for the collection of all dues, at his own expense, including the transport of the grain rent to the abbey, out of which he paid the monks their *portions* and the various monastery servants their *bolls*. He also supplied the steward of the commendator's household, should the latter be in residence. He was required to present an account to the commendator at the following Allhallowmas and to render a complete account for the first year of his office, at latest by the following Easter. His fee was 120 merks and a quantity of meal, oats and cheese. If he could prove that land had been 'unlaboured' and 'unsown', this would be allowed to him in his account. He was also allowed incidental expenses, such as payments to agricultural workers, and others incurred in taking legal actions to the king's courts.[35]

In a large barony, or in a lordship or regality which consisted of scattered baronies, subordinate officers had reponsibility for collecting the rents and dues locally and thereafter accounting for them to the chamberlain, who used their information when making up his 'great' or final accounts. For example, the surviving accounts of the bishopric of Dunkeld, 1505-1517, are largely those of subordinate officers, the serjeants and graniters of the various districts,[36] while those of the archbishopric of St Andrews in the time of Cardinal Beaton, 1538-1546, are the final accounts for these years, rendered by chamberlain and graniter (the officer responsible for the grain rents), in which the individual accounts of the subordinates are referred to but have not survived.[37] At the other end of the scale, in small baronies, arrangements were less complex, the accounts often being kept by the baron's clerk who accounted for the income, handing money over to the master himself and victual and other provisions to the steward. Even on this more intimate level, however, help was needed to bring in the rents and a check had to be kept on all outgoings.

Rents were usually paid in two instalments a year, at the terms of Whitsunday and Martinmas, and consisted of money, rent in kind, mainly grain, with certain customary payments, often in poultry and provisions. In the sixteenth-century accounts these parts of the rents — that is, money, kind and custom — are usually designated *maill, ferme* and *kane*. Some holdings paid entirely in money, some entirely in kind, but most in a mixture of the two. In the barony of Snaid belonging to Lord Hay of Yester, in 1582, some of the tenants paid entirely in money, some of their neighbours in kind:

Coitistoune — a 4 merkland and 40d; in Andrew Cunningham's hand, paying 8 merks: Comesoune — 30s land; John Smith occupies it, paying 12 bolls meal; Over Bordland — 20s land; William Haggart occupies it, paying 13 bolls meal: Nether Bordland — 20s land; Andrew Cunningham occupies it, paying £10: The Shaw — 1 merkland; John Cunningham occupies it, paying 16 merks: Gilmursoun — 1 merkland; Cuthbert Grene has it, paying £8, and paid of old 9 bolls meal by the late William Grene.[38]

The grain part of the rent was most commonly wheat, bere (barley), oats, meal and malt, and the other payments in kind, which included the *kane*, were usually a selection from capons, hens, chickens, geese, butter, cheese or animals such as cattle, goats and sheep, and, in some places, fish. The accounts for the barony of Hamilton in 1588 preserve a wide variety of rents; wheat, bere, malt (ground and unground), meal, horsecorn or oats, cows, cheese, stirks, sheep (clipped and unclipped), salmon, geese, capons, hens, chickens, eggs, one or two 'fed boars' and loads of coal. The grain, stored until made into bread and ale, was used for the landlord's household and to feed and pay domestic and farm servants. Meat and fish would be salted down for winter use. The households of great lords and ecclesiastics moved between residences on their scattered estates eating up the rents, literally, as they went. But even a stationary household, including that of a monastic community, with its servants, consumed large quantities of provisions, for we sometimes find chamberlains and stewards buying in extra supplies. In 1528 and 1530 the chamberlain of Arbroath abbey was authorised to buy in provisions for 'the place', which may mean the house of the abbot, David Beaton, who entertained King James V there in 1528 and was himself in residence for some time in 1530.[39] These additional supplies included 180 *marts*, animals for slaughter and salting or carcases already salted, over and above those received from the tenants, 800 sheep, eleven barrels of salmon, although the abbey's rents included forty-nine barrels, and over 150 chalders of victual.

Although there was an obvious need for grain and provisions, which long continued to be a large proportion of the rents, it is clear that in the sixteenth century many landlords were trying to turn as much of the rent as possible into cash. Ready money became increasingly important in the early-modern period as prices rose steadily and the life of the rural middle class — the lairds — became less localised and more geared to luxury and participation in public life. Cash was also welcomed by absentee landlords such as bishops, abbots and commendators, who waited for their chamberlains to send the rents on to them wherever they might be. It is remarkable that many quite small tenants appear to have had the money to pay the rents and that a certain amount of cash seems to have circulated among the rural population. In 1563 three friends of a Kilwinning barony tenant, James Campbell in Doucathill, who was apparently unable to find enough money for his maill, presented the chamberlain on his behalf with £17 2s 'togadir with ane Inglis pece of silver for 18s money'. The chamberlain was sceptical about the reputed value of the English coin and scribbled a memorandum in the margin of his book, 'and geif the said pece of silver be nocht wyrthe 18s I sall delyver the samen agane to Johne Younge (one of the tenant's friends) or James Campbel for 18s'.[40] The point is that the chamberlain seems determined to have cash although, presumably, he could have taken the value in grain.

There were several ways of getting money from the land. Firstly, there were the maills themselves, the 'silver' in the terminology of the account books, the money rents which were a standard if still not major part of the rents by the sixteenth century, in all parts of the Lowlands of Scotland at least. Few surviving estate accounts are complete enough to help us determine the proportion of money rent to rent in kind, but those of the barony of Lochleven for the years 1548 to 1553 actually give the maill as amounting to £290 for those six years and the ferme as £1,740, making the money part of the rent about 16 per cent.[41]

Secondly, money could be raised by selling the rents in kind, particularly the grain, often to the tenants themselves, either on the ground or from the granaries. Selling the victual rent was a common practice which is often mentioned in chamberlains' accounts. Grain was sold, for example, to tenants on the lands of Scone abbey,[42] the archbishopric of St Andrews,[43] the bishopric of Dunkeld,[44] the earl of Argyll[45] and Lord Oliphant.[46] At Scone in 1573 twenty chalders of victual were sold to the tenants, evidently from the ground, compared with twenty eight received into the granaries. In 1595 the earl of Argyll's chamberlain sold bere, meal and cheese to the tenants to the value of £1,020, noting in his book that £168 had still not been paid when he made up his accounts. In 1538 ferme and kane were sold to tenants of the archbishop of St Andrews, on lands both north and south of Forth. On Lord Oliphant's lands at the end of the century, in 1595, over £4,000 worth of the victual rent was sold. Selling victual rent to the tenants had the effect of turning most of their dues into money and, while this would appear to have given them the chance to save a little more grain for the next year's sowing, or even to re-sell the grain themselves at market prices, we should remember that if the landlord sold the grain rent in a year of dearth and high prices he was virtually levying a rent-increase. There is not enough detailed information to help us determine what sort of tenants were asked to buy the grain rent. They may well have been the more substantial ones, perhaps absentee middlemen who had leased the land.

Thirdly, money could be raised by leasing the actual rents themselves, setting them in *tack* for a fixed, annual *tack-duty,* the tacksman collecting the rents for himself from the local inhabitants and, presumably, selling the grain at market prices. In 1574 the victual rent of the barony of Torry in Aberdeenshire was leased by the commendator of Arbroath for £32 13s 4d to two individuals, one of whom was Gilbert Menzies, a bailie of Aberdeen.[47]

A fourth money element in this period was the *commutation* into cash of a variety of customary payments and labour services. Commutation, however, was often only partial, even within one barony. About mid-century, Paisley abbey tenants paid *bownsilver* in place of certain harvest work, 10s in lieu of each long carriage, but continued to perform other labour services.[48] A little farther south-west, in the barony of Kilwinning, the tenants paid *dam silver,* for upkeep of the dam on the River Garnock, but still undertook carriage service and some harvest work.[49] At Bogmuchells in Angus, Lord Ogilvy's tenants paid *custom cow silver* but still rendered a variety of other kane, including sheep, capons, geese and custom oats.[50] As early as 1500, on the other hand, a tenant of the laird of Minto in Renfrewshire paid 3s commutation for each load of custom coal.[51] The laird of Lochleven's tenants, about mid-century, paid *wedder silver* (i.e. in place of custom sheep) but rendered custom corn in kind.[52] A rental of Scone abbey dating from the 1560s gives an interesting list of commutation rates for services due from holdings which had been converted to feu-ferm:

Balgarvie: Constantine Small, heritor . . . tilling, harrowing, shearing and leading, £6 13s 4d, arriage and carriage, £6 13s 4d.
The heirs of James Rattray, heritor of a quarter thereof . . . capon 12, £6; poultry 12, £3; tilling etc., £6 13s 4d, arriage and carriage, £6 13s 4d. Mr Francis Hay, heritor . . . a hook in harvest, 20 days' work, £5 13s 4d.[53]

Where land had been set in feu-ferm, as was increasingly the case with church land, the annual dues, *feu-duty* and *augmentation,* were paid in money and the services were likely to have been commuted. On the succession of an heir double feu-duty was paid, and there were periodic *grassums* to compensate for the loss of the old-style grassum formerly payable on the renewal of a lease. It was also increasingly likely, in the case of feued land, that the *herezeld,* best animal of the herd and flock payable on the death of a husbandman, would have been commuted. Freeholders, like feuars, paid their casualties of *ward, marriage* and *relief* in cash. All these money payments would appear in the *charge of silver* in the chamberlain's accounts.

The accounts for the great Hamilton estates for 1589 list a whole range of casualties and maills, exceptional it is true, but nevertheless featuring some kinds of money income which would find its way into the coffers of lesser landlords:

Casualties	
Price of 10 bolls oats from Castlebarn	£26 13s 4d
Corn silver from William Hamilton	£10
Received from Mr John Carnegie, chamberlain of Arbroath	£57 10s
From Gavin Stevenson, of the taxation silver	£62 7s 3d
From William Muirhead, maltman, of his *rests* (arrears) of 1587 and 1588	£166 13s 4d
Price of 13 mart hides, *viz:* twelve from The Wood and one from Henry Cochrane, at 32s. each.	£20 16s
Price of 25 hides from Craignethan and Hamilton Wood, at 40s each	£50
Profit of the yards of Craignethan	£20

198 sheep skins whereof were delivered to
    William Hamilton, 13. Remainder to James
    Hamilton, skinner, at my Lady's command.

Total — £2,257 9s 8d

Charge of maills of barony of Hamilton, Cambuslang,
Carmunnock, Machanshire, Thriepwood, annual of Lanark,
Greenhill and Bothwellmuir, of Whitsunday and
Martinmas terms 1589

Hamilton, with Holliscroft	£285 11s 8d
Cambuslang and Carmunnock	£67
Machanshire, Thriepwood and annual	
of Lanark	£98 9s 10d
Maill of Greenhill	£14
Bothwelmuir	£151 8s
Feu maills of Lesmahagow	£174 3s 2d

Total £790 12s 8d

Total charge of money — £4,848 7s 9½d[54]

In these Hamilton accounts the money raised from commutations and from selling custom payments and rents in kind, which account for most of the *casualties,* amounted to almost half the money derived from the *maills.*

From the accounts of Archbishop David Beaton for 1538-1546, a selection of *casualties* shows even more of the sort of cash payments likely to be handled by chamberlains of smaller estates:

The *ward* of Lethen	£26 13s 4d
Ward of a third of Clerkinsheils	£3 9s
New infeftment of redeemed land of	
Hiltarvet (had been wadset)	£53 6s 8d
Quinquennial duplicand of feu-ferm	
of Kemback	£20
Entry into a third of mill of Monimail	
after death of tenant, William Russell	£1 6s 8d
Sale of poultry from tenants of Monymusk,	
312 at 3d each (1536-38)	£3 18s
Herezeld of Thomas Bontaveron, tenant,	
dying in Letham	£3
Relief of nether Princado	£10
Non-entry of third of Wester Pitcorthy	£66 13s 4d
For *escheat* of George Blyth, manslayer,	
bought by William Borthwick	£24
Herezeld of Alexander Strang in Kilrenny	£4
Herezeld of a woman in Logytarroch	£2[55]

Here the lord of a regality received money not only from the sale of custom dues, for renewal of leases and from herezelds of the husbandman class of tenants, but also from the heirs of his freeholders who succeeded while under age, who failed to have themselves formally entered on reaching majority or who received new charters of their lands, and from the exercise of his judicial powers in the regality court in which he was able to escheat criminals and sell their goods to others.

Income also came regularly from the mills, minerals and fishings in a barony, leased to tenant families or to outsiders, bringing in an annual mixture of money and produce. The income from mills, especially grain mills, was a prominent item in the estate accounts. Where these were leased to tenant families who often worked them for several generations, they would pay rent for them in the normal way, either in money or kind. In the barony of Kilwinning in Ayrshire the waulk mill at Groatholm paid £4 yearly, the corn mill at the Bridgend of Kilwinning, quite near the abbey, £16, and that at Sevenacres two chalders of meal.[56] The first two were worked by families named Walker and Miller respectively, who can both be traced back into the fifteenth century. If the mill was leased to an outside tacksman, he would pay an annual tack-duty, usually in cash. Over and above the rent of the mill, however, the superior of the land received *multures,* a tax on the grain ground at the barony mills, in practical terms either a quantity of grain or a fixed sum of money. A landlord was at liberty to reserve his right to the multures of land which he leased, or might grant the multures away with the land if he so wished. In the barony of Kylesmure in mid-Ayrshire, in 1528, the grain representing multures of the Haugh mill began to be delivered to the chamberlain at Mauchline at Lammas, soon after harvest had begun.[57] The payment of the multures by tenants and tacksmen of mills led to many complaints and court actions, and if they had been conveyed to a tacksman with the ground his attempts to extract them from the tenants under him often led to disputes. In 1604 the barony court of Urie was obliged to re-enact statutes previously passed by the then baron's father with regard to 'obstraiking and withaldyng of his multures and duties from his mill'.[58]

In a land rich in freshwater fish, every other landlord derived valuable income and produce from the local rivers, while sea-fishings were important in seaboard baronies. Fishings, like mills, were often set in tack, sometimes to non-resident tacksmen who paid their tack-duty to the baron and employed local people or their own servants to work the fishings. The rich fishings belonging to Arbroath abbey were largely leased in this way, bringing in an increasing revenue over the years. Fish due as rent to the abbot in 1530 from the fishings of Banff, Aberdeen, Monifieth, Montrose and Perth amounted to forty-nine barrels.[59] By 1593 the 'salmon silver' of Arbroath, set in tack to a number of lairds and others, brought in £134.[60] On the other hand fishers were sometimes directly employed and paid by landlords. The chamberlain of Melrose abbey, based at Mauchline in Kylesmure, paid five fishers in the 1520s to work a stretch of the River Ayr.[61] At the end of the century the earl of Argyll's chamberlain was still paying 'the fisher of Gairlocheid and uthir fishers'.[62]

Mineral resources were more likely to be worked by the baron and the coal and salt used by him. Tenants were not as a rule given much use of minerals although those on the Hamilton lands, whose custom payments included loads of coal, were an exception.[63] Feuars of church land were sometimes granted the use of minerals but they were usually lairds who had the necessary labour and the means of marketing the product, as, for example, Sir George Bruce at Culross, or William Douglas of Lochleven who feued the coal pits of Kelty from the abbey of Dunfermline. The laird of Lochleven employed colliers on his own lands as early as the 1540s:

Delivered to the colliers   26s
Given to the colliers   12d
To the colliers   22s
To a boy to go to the coalheuch   3d
To John Wright to give the colliers   22s
To John Wright for coals   7s 4d
To the men at the heuch   17s[64]

Unfortunately, there is nothing in the Douglas accounts to tell us how much coal was mined or how much income was derived. The coalheuch of the barony of Hamilton was 'in my lord's hands' and, presumably, worked with direct labour, towards the end of the century, but at the same time the *kane* coal from the estates amounted to 783 loads.[65] Much of this was used in the residences scattered over the estates held by Lord John Hamilton including Arbroath, where the 1593 accounts refer to payments:

To the boatmen who brought the coal from the Nes (?Bo'ness) to Arbroath   £18
To carts which led the cols   £4[66]

In the baronies of Kilwinning and Mauchline, where profitable use of the coal deposits had to wait for over two hundred years, the abbot of Kilwinning paid the colliers in meal in the first half of the century[67] and the chamberlain of Mauchline noted receipt of coal in his account book for 1528:

Item, the 29 day of Octobar, 24 horsis ledand collis, 2 peck of meyll, 12 pund cheis. Item, the last day of Octobar, 28 horsis ledand collis, 3 peck of meyll, 1 stan of cheis, and for watryn of tham 4 nechtys, 16d. Item, to the collewenner for fyfte laids of collis, 18s 8d.[68]

On church estates there were payments which came in as ecclesiastical dues and, because of the system of *commendation,* these were sometimes going into the pocket of a layman. The biggest single source of income which was properly ecclesiastical came from the *teinds,* the tenth of the parish's grain crop, nominally the property of the parson, and the *small teinds,* the tenth of all produce such as cheese, butter, eggs and the young of the herds and flocks, nominally reserved to the vicar in charge of the parish. But, since the majority of parishes and their teinds were by the sixteenth century annexed to monasteries, cathedrals and other churches, the teinds were collected on behalf of these institutions and their clergy, and were usually sold by them for cash. The collection of the teinds was done by literally riding round the parish, warning the parishioners and then collecting the teinds, or selling them, and *riding books* were kept as account books for the teinds alone.

However, the payment of the teinds was a complicated business by this period for, like the land and the rents, they were often set in tack for an annual tack-duty. Sometimes a superior would grant them away with the land. Where they were still due to be paid by the parishioners directly, they were very generally in arrears on the eve of the Reformation, after which the 'old possessors' and the new Reformed ministry of the kirk haggled over them well into the seventeenth century until the government of Charles I took the matter in hand. It is not only on church estates that teinds come into the accounts. Those held in tack by the laird of Lochleven brought in annual commutation, *teind silver,* from a number of tenants in the barony of Keillour in 1540, ranging from payments of 20s to £4 8s.[69] In the fullest set of household accounts for the laird after he had become earl of Morton, his chamberlain set out 'the particularis debursit be me at your lordschipis command, sen yor cuming to Dalkeyth to thresche the teindis in May 1595',[70] and four years later there was drawn up 'the compt of Andrew Hopburne of his intromissioun with the teind victual of the parishes of Linton and Newlands of the crop 1599, heard, received and allowed be ane noble lord, William earl of Morton, at Dalkeyth'.[71] Teinds conveyed to a lay landlord with church land were treated as an integral part of his income. In 1595, while the earl of Morton's tenants were paying *teind silver* as well as teinds in grain, those of Lord Oliphant were still paying entirely in grain, although some of it was sold back to them by the chamberlain, William Oliphant of Gask.[72]

In a different kind of situation, where what had been a church estate had become the property of a layman, as with the lands of Arbroath abbey which came into the hands of Lord John Hamilton, teinds and other ecclesiastical dues were already part of the income, although a separate account of them might be kept. The 1530 rental of Arbroath, while David Beaton was commendator, gives the money value of the teinds and kirklands of appropriated parishes as £1,936.[73] In 1574, by which time the lands belonged to Lord John Hamilton, the maills and teind silver of Dunnichen, Ochterlonie and Craquhy had been set to John Carnegie in feu-ferm for over £200 a year.[74] In 1593 the teinds and other rents of Arbroath were combined in one account.[75] Teinds, like the grain rents, were often sold back to those from whom they were due. In 1528 the chamberlain of Melrose abbey, while arranging for the teind bere of Mauchline parish to be collected, sold the teind lambs at £2 3s 4d a score to several parishioners, including 'the gudwyf of Mossgevil (Mossgiel).'[76]

A surprising amount of paper work was done in managing an estate even in the sixteenth century, although it is the papers of bigger landlords that tend to have survived. Estate accounts are only properly so-called when they show a *charge* and *discharge* side or, as we would now call them, credit and debit. Keeping track of expenses — the discharge side — was to some extent reasonably straightforward. The chamberlain examined and passed the individual accounts of subordinates, together with the bundles of receipted bills — *vouchers* — and the superior's authorisations of payments — *precepts* — all of which proved that the officers had in fact spent the money and victual which they claimed to have spent: he accounted for all money and provisions laid out by himself or delivered by him to the steward of the household and deducted all these expenses from the year's income, making allowances for arrears — *rests* — various sanctioned deductions — *defalcations* — and any accidental loss of income — *inlaik* — such as deterioration of grain in the granaries. Even a bad harvest and consequent non-payment of rent was accounted for among the inlaik, as when the bishop of Moray's chamberlain noted that 'the loch of Spynie rais up and stood on thair cornes.' The chamberlain would deduct, last of all, any money or victual due to himself since the previous accounts had been rendered.

Determining what the total income ought to be in any given year — the charge side of the accounts — was a more complicated business, demanding that the chamberlain and his clerks be familiar with how and to whom the ground was set and for what annual duties. In order to determine this, to establish how much income ought to come in, the chamberlain's clerks compiled working *rentals* of the barony, or the baronies comprising a big estate, and the information in these formed the charge side of the accounts. Many of these rentals have survived; in fact for some baronies there is a series covering several years, for these rentals were often kept for reference.

Before looking closely at the form these working rentals took, it will help if we distinguish the several kinds of sixteenth-century record commonly called 'rentals'. Firstly, the term *rental* was applied to the landlord's great rental book, the rent roll of the estate, in which, under the names of farms and holdings, the entry of tenants was recorded, giving name, date of entry, relationship to the previous holder very often, the conditions of holding and the annual dues to be paid.

Here is a typical entry in the Coupar Angus abbey rental book, which is entitled 'Registrum Assedationum, etc., B. Marie de Cupro, 1443-1538'. At Coupar Angus, where cultivation was closely supervised, there are unusually full details of the conditions of holding:

Cupar Grange

At Pentecost 1468, Cupar Grange is let to Simon Anderson, John Olyvar, Thomas Anderson, William Roger, John Foyd, William Pylmur, William Meyk, Alan Nicholson, Donald Anderson, Patrick Geky, for five years, for annual payment of 1 chalder of good barley, 24s 4d with 2 bolls of horse corn, 14 loads of fuel; and each plow shall sow 1 boll of corn, with pease corresponding, and each of them shall plant ash, osier, and sauch trees, and they shall labour every one for his own part for the recovering of the marsh, as well as for fuel as for pasturage, according to the rules given to them by the cellarers, David Blare and William Stabil. Moreover, they shall pay 12 dozen of capons yearly, with service.[77]

Individual tenants were given a copy of the entry in the rental book to keep as their title, and where the grant of the holding was for life it was customary to call the tenant's copy his *rental,* and the tenant-for-life a *rentaller*. It was also from the great rental book that the working rentals were compiled by the chamberlain's clerks. So there were at least three types of record described as *rentals:* the rental book or rent roll, the copy from it which was given to a tenant-for-life, and the working rentals compiled for accounting purposes.

These working rentals, drawn up year after year, varied in form. Sometimes they were comprehensive, containing all information necessary for the charge side of the accounts — that is, the rental of maills, fermes, kane, feu-duties and casualties. In some of these fuller rentals not only the names of the farms and holdings are given but also the names of the tenants to whom they were set. It is quite likely that such a list, showing the names of the tenants underneath the names of the farms, with the amount of rent due from each individual, denotes farms let in *shares* to a group of tenants who were each responsible for their own share of the cultivation and rent. On the other hand, where rentals simply list the farms but do not detail the individual tenants and their rents, these may relate to farms which were *jointly* set to a group of tenants, who were jointly responsible for the cultivation and total rent and who, no doubt, arranged among themselves how the rent should be paid and in what proportions, depending on how they divided up the ground among themselves for the purpose of cultivation.

A working rental of the barony of Hamilton for 1590 suggests many *shared* farms, with tenants each responsible for their own previously laid-down share of the rent:

Allantoun occupiit as followis,	£4 10s land
Payis of silver maill	£16
Quheit	10 bolls
Beir	16 bolls
Capones	8
Pultrie	5 dozen
Wedderis	4 tua quarteris
Coillis leding	3 scoir laidis

With daylie areage, cariage, entres and herezeild
Occupiit as followis

Patrik Steynstoun	11s 3d land
Payis of maill	40s
Quheit	1 boll 1 firlot
Beir	2 bolls
Capones	1.
Pultrie	7
Wedderis	2 quarteris, 16th part wedder
Coillis leding	7 laidis
Gawyne Steynstoun	11s 4d land

Payis maill in all thyngis conforme to the said Patrik.

Charles Forrest	22s 6d land
Payis of maill	£4
Of quheit	2 bolls 2 firlots
Beir	4 bolls
Capones	2
Pultrie	15
Coillis leding	15 laidis
Wedderis	1 and a half quarter[78]

There follow similar entries for four other tenants of Allantoun.

By contrast, the rental of Bogmuchells in Angus, belonging to Lord Ogilvy, suggests joint farms:

Hilend 5 merks maill, 6 custom capons, half custom wedder, 1 goose, 5s custom cow silver, 2 firlots custom oats and fodder, 3 long carriages and due service.[79]

Carriages and service may have been commuted.

In some rentals we can distinguish the *jointly held, shared* and *single-tenant* farm within one barony, by the way in which the rental is laid out. An early rental of Kilwinning barony, probably dating from before 1540, shows single-tenant and joint-tenant farms:

Clonbeth £4, for harvest work 4s, 9 capons, 9 hens, 9 loads of turfs, for dam siller 4d, . . . 9 carriages.

Sevenacres £3 6s 8d, for harvest work 4s, 12 capons, 12 hens, for dam siller 4d . . . 10 loads of turfs, 12 carriages; set to Constantine Montgomery.

Guslone £2, 6 capons, 6 hens, 8 dayswork, for dam siller 12d . . . 5 loads of turfs; set to John Dunlop, James Morland, Katherine Dunlop.[80]

Note: although the names of the tenants of the last-named farm are given, their proportions of the rent are not, suggesting a joint farm.

Besides working rentals, prepared before drawing up the annual accounts, the chamberlain and his clerks sometimes had occasion to conduct enquiries, or to consult the results of enquiries made by the bailie, into the state of occupancy of the land, and a certain number of such surveys and investigations have survived.

Sometimes they are called 'rentals' or 'accounts', either by those who compiled them or by later antiquarians and editors, but these descriptions are misleading. The reasons for compiling them were various: for the information of a guardian during the minority of an heir, in the preparation of a court case, to determine the correct annual duty of individual holdings where record of the occupier's *entry* was for some reason lost, as the result of the regular inspection of the individual *rentals* of those tenants who held for life to see that they were honouring their side of the agreement, an enquiry into a tenant's right to occupy his holding, a check that all tenants had paid their *entry silver* on taking up possession, lists of feuars and freeholders as distinct from tenants. We know that in England *survey books* of estates were kept, annotated in the margins and between the lines as additional information was added year by year. While this may not have been a formal practice in Scotland, it is clear that clerks and chamberlains and bailies compiled similar information, also covered in marginalia and notes, which was obviously amended from time to time and would doubtless be of use to the chamberlain when making up his accounts and admitting tenants, receiving their entry money and grassums, or checking their statements and those of witnesses as to their rights to their holdings.

A memorandum headed 'The earl of Huntly's accounts', dated 1616, is really an attempt to give a total money value of the rents of a number of territories, with their extent: 'Petmowny, two ploughs, £11 8s, Ochterkaig, four ploughs, £22 16s.' At the foot are queries about duties from lands that had been feued: 'the kirkland of Kinkell, of auld maill £4 13s 4d, and ye maun speir at John Innes that gat the few, umquhile earle of Huntlie, that is in Mr James Skeynis prothocoll (book), the augmentation and grassum, ane sowm togidder, in his rentall'.[81] The lands of the earl of Morton in the second half of the century provide several examples of these surveys and enquiries. In July 1586, for example, there was an examination of the rentals of the tenants-for-life, their names, holdings and dates of rentalling being noted down:

Debog and Hartwood; David Douglas, 40s land of Dabog, and 20s land of Hartwood. Rental, 16 July 1579.
Glaspen; John Douglas in Glaspen and George Douglas his son, 5 merkland of Glaspen, occupied by David Eccles. Rental, 1 August 1576.
Udingtoun; Ninian Anderson, son of the late George Anderson, 1 oxgang of Udingtoun. Rental, 31 May 1579.
Robert Wichtman was rentalled in half an oxgang, stands at debat between his sister and George Wichtman.[82]

'The tryall taken of the kyndnes' of the barony of Preston, in 1575, which we shall look at more closely in another connection, is an examination of the claims of the occupiers to customary inheritance of their holdings.[83] 'The entry of tenants in the lordship of Douglas', of 1578, is an enquiry into how many tenants were in possession of holdings without having paid their *entry silver*. The margin bears the word 'solitum' (paid) opposite the names of those tenants who had subsequently paid and had been formally *entered*. The word 'caution' denotes those who had given security for their forthcoming entry money, either as one payment or by instalments. The marginal notes are in Latin, the work of a professional clerk or notary.[84]

The chamberlain, his officers and clerks were in charge of the mechanical business of collecting the rents, usually at Martinmas and Whitsunday. The tenants probably attended personally to pay cash but may have come to an arrangement among themselves about transporting the rent in kind, animals and so on. Sometimes they were reminded that payment was due, as in the barony of Kylesmure in 1528 where an officer was paid in the month of June to 'warn' the tenants to pay their cheese and in October of the same year when a horse was bought for Jok Reid to ride round 'warning' them for their *marts*.[85] Rent was usually collected at the landlord's principal dwelling on a particular barony or part of the estate; Kilwinning feuars are found paying feu-duties at the abbey,[86] the chamberlain of the scattered lands of Newbattle abbey accepted rents and granted receipts at Edinburgh, where the commendator had a lodging, at Kipchapel in Lanarkshire and 'at the kirk of Monkland' in the same district,[87] and the laird and lady of Lochleven were both present when their chamberlain rendered his accounts 'at the Newhouse' on the shores of Lochleven.[88] On the seaboard territories of the earl of Argyll a boat was used to collect the victual rents.[88]

Notes

1 Collection of John C. Brodie (S.R.O.), GD 247/101/1a, fo. 5v
2 Eglinton muniments, GD 3/2358
3 Lochleven account book (S.R.O.), RH 9/1/2, fo. 8r
4 Breadalbane muniments, GD 112/9/5
5 Accounts of the regality of Hamilton (S.R.O.), RH 11/36/1
6 Accounts of the regality of Argyll (S.R.O.), RH 11/6/1 (Argyll regality)
7 Rental of Lord Menteith's bowgangs (S.R.O.), RH 9/3/84
8 Collection of John C. Brodie, GD 247/101/1a, fo. 4r
9 Wamphray barony court book (S.R.O.), RH 11/69/1 (Wamphray)
10 *See* Chapter 4
11 Curle Collection (S.R.O.), GD 111/2/11
12 Lothian muniments, GD 40/1/630
13 Morton muniments, GD 150/2084/1
14 Lord Forbes Collection (S.R.O.), GD 52
15 *R.P.C.*, III, 144-5
16 Eglinton muniments, GD 3/1/732, 733
17 *R.M.S.*, V, 382
18 *Registrum episcopatus Glasguensis* (Bann. Club), I, no. 526 *(Glasguensis)*
19 *R.M.S.*, IV, 2305
20 Morton muniments, GD 150/2079/1
21 Airlie muniments (S.R.O.), GD 16/30/54, fo. 25r
22 G. Chalmers, *Caledonia*, VI, 512 *(Caledonia)*
23 *R.M.S.*, IV, 1764

24 *Ibid.,* IV, 1966
25 *Ibid.,* IV, 2402
26 *Liber de Mailros* (Bann. Club), no. 598
27 Acts and decreets, xx, fo. 345v
28 Edinburgh commissariot records, register of testaments (S.R.O.), CC 8/8/3, fo. 121r (Edin. testaments)
29 R. K. Hannay, *Rentale Dunkeldense* (S.H.S.), 322 *(Dunkeldense)*
30 *Liber de Calchou (Bann. Club),* I, 483 *(Calchou)*
31 R. K. Hannay, *Rentale Sancti Andree* (S.H.S.), 166
32 *R.M.S.,* V, 342, 898
33 Acts and decreets, x, fo. 309r
34 *Ibid.,* xxxvi, fo. 408r
35 Register of deeds, old series (S.R.O.), ii, fo. 6v
36 *Dunkeldense,* xvii and *passim*
37 *Rentale Sancti Andree, passim*
38 Yester writs (S.R.O.), GD 28/836
39 Airlie muniments, GD 16/25/127
40 Collection of the Society of Antiquaries of Scotland (S.R.O.), GD 103/2/22 (S.A.S. collection)
41 Morton muniments, GD 150/147
42 Yule collection (S.R.O.), GD 90/2/10
43 *Rentale Sancti Andree,* 79, 80, 81, 83
44 *Dunkeldense,* 97
45 Argyll regality, RH 11/6/1
46 Morton muniments, GD 150/2084/1
47 Hamilton muniments (Lennoxlove), MSS 573/1
48 J. C. Lees, *The abbey of Paisley,* Appendix, clxvii *(Paisley)*
49 Eglinton muniments, GD 3/1361
50 Airlie muniments, GD 16/30/76
51 Craigans writs (S.R.O.), GD 148/58a
52 Lochleven account book, RH 9/1/2
53 Rental of Scone, RH 9/3/163
54 Rental of the lordship of Hamilton (S.R.O.), RH 11/36/1
55 *Rentale Sancti Andree, passim*
56 Eglinton muniments, GD 3/1361
57 *Mauchline account books,* 92
58 *Urie,* 5
59 Dalhousie muniments (S.R.O.), GD 45/13/300
60 Airlie muniments, GD 16/30/54
61 *Mauchline account books,* 100
62 Argyll regality, RH 11/6/1
63 Collection of Tods, Murray and Jamieson (S.R.O.), GD 237/202/4
64 Lochleven account book, RH 9/1/2
65 Tods, Murray and Jamieson, GD 237/202/4
66 Airlie muniments, GD 16/30/54
67 Eglinton muniments, GD 3/1361
68 *Mauchline account books,* 99
69 Lochleven account book, RH 9/1/2
70 Morton muniments, GD 150/2727
71 *Ibid.,* GD 150/2086
72 *Ibid.,* GD 150/2084/1
73 Dalhousie muniments, GD 45/13/300
74 Hamilton muniments, MSS 573/1
75 Airlie muniments, GD 16/30/54
76 *Mauchline account books,* 94
77 *Cupar,* I, 142
78 Tods, Murray and Jamieson, GD 237/202/4
79 Airlie muniments, GD 16/30/76
80 Eglinton muniments, GD 3/1361
81 Lord Forbes collection, GD 52/283

82 Curle collection (S.R.O.), GD 111/2/11
83 Morton muniments, GD 150/2079/2
84 Curle collection, GD 111/2/9/2
85 *Mauchline account books,* 93
86 Yule collection, GD 90/1/151b, 153
87 Tods, Murray and Jamieson, GD 237/106/2
88 Accounts of William Douglas of Lochleven (S.R.O.), RH 9/1/3
89 Argyll regality, RH 11/6/1

4

The Tenants

'. . . they say rich tenants make a rich master, for they ought, being the image of God, to have even
the part of their labour, as the master should.'
  James, sixth Lord Ogilvy, to his grandson, 1606, Airlie Muniments, GD 16/34/6.

THE inhabitant of a barony lived within a framework of the law, and his place in
society depended on the extent of his rights to the piece of land that he possessed,
not on the amount of his worldly goods. The laird might die in debt to one of his
thrifty husbandmen — some did — or buy a cow from a cottar, but he was still
'master of the ground' and of those who cultivated it. He was their master only
because they did cultivate it, however, and not in any personal sense; the Scottish
countryman was very conscious of his personal freedom.

In a sense rural society was a hierarchy. Nearest to the landlord — king, noble,
bishop, abbot, laird or whoever he might be — were the main tenants, so called
because they held directly from him and paid their rents directly to his chamberlain. The backbone of the rural tenantry, the husbandmen, had long ceased to
hold simply the husbandland (two oxgangs) from which they took their name, but
might possess anything from that amount to a whole ploughgate, about 104 Scots
acres. Alongside them were small tenants, also holding directly, who might have
anything down to a thirty-second part of a township's arable land, about a quarter
of an oxgang. The rental of the toun of Prestoun for 1579 clearly shows how
tenant holdings varied in size:

Tenants	Number of oxgangs
William Cowstein	2
Thomas McKie, yr.	1
William Martin	2
John Martin	3
John Anderson	1
John Williamson, yr.	2
Helen Gibbisoun	1
Hugh Maxwell	5
Thomas Newall	3
John Wilson	1[1]

Most tenants spent the year cultivating and harvesting their holdings but those
who were rural craftsmen, a distinct group in the community who worked for
local markets, including the smith, mason, wright, cooper, weaver, shoemaker and
tailor, divided their time between farming and the practice of their craft. A more
mobile group, also with a limited amount of time for farming, included fowlers,

fishermen, ferrymen, chapmen, messengers and sailors, who, nevertheless, needed a holding on which to grow their families' food, like the butt of land in the Seatoun of Duin in Banffshire which belonged to Andrew Goiger, a skipper there.[2] Such a tenant sometimes held a piece of land in return for fowling, fishing or operating a ferry. A tenant of Lord Ogilvy's at Bogmuchells held a croft 'with his service in the craft of fowling'.[3] In the barony of Hamilton, which boasted a few holdings owing special services, the 'cooper croft' was held in 1590 for rent and 'findand ane sufficient couper to my lord',[4] for by then it was, presumably, not always leased to a practising cooper. Rural industrial workers such as colliers, salters and quarriers also held land. Since grain and waulk mills (i.e. fulling mills) were often worked by a family for several generations, there were always plenty of hands to attend to the mill and at the same time till the mill lands that commonly went with it, and, naturally, the season of ploughing and sowing fell in with the slack time in the miller's year, although harvesting the mill lands coincided with preparation for the autumn grinding of the barony's grain crop.

There were lairds and nobles among the main tenants, with baronies of their own which they held from the king or from one of his vassals, who were at the same time tenants of other proprietors, often leasing land from bishops and monasteries. In this way the Campbells of Cessnock held land in mid-Ayrshire from Melrose abbey, Fergushill of that Ilk and Ralston of that Ilk, in Ayrshire and Renfrewshire respectively, leased land from Kilwinning abbey, Lord Semple from Paisley abbey, the Ramsays of Bamff from Scone, the Master of Ogilvy from Coupar Angus and Boyd of Penkill in Carrick from Crossraguel abbey. Finally, in this top layer of tenants who held directly came the middlemen, those with a speculator's eye on the land, burgesses and merchants, lairds, lawyers and crown servants. These leaseholders need not necessarily have lived in the neighbourhood of their holdings but farmed them from a distance, either with paid labour or by subletting them to the local inhabitants.

This brings us to the second group in the rural hierarchy, the subtenants, a numerous class whom we are apt to forget because they rarely turn up in estate rentals. Most main tenants could, with the landlord's consent, create subtenants on their holdings. The practice commended itself most to those with a limited amount of time to spend on tilling the ground — the lairds, for example, who in this way saved themselves the expense of paying agricultural labour, the non-resident middlemen, the rural craftsmen, those with itinerant occupations like the sailor and chapman, and the industrial workers. It was also practised by husbandmen with large or scattered holdings, accumulated over the years, which had grown too big for the tenant and his immediate family to cultivate by themselves. Subletting could affect a rural community in different ways. If it was done by resident tenants such as husbandmen or rural craftsmen, it might well create population increase as subtenants and their families moved in. On the other hand, subletting by outsiders demoted the inhabitants to the rank of subtenants, creating a stratification in the local population. If a merchant, for instance, leased a whole township, the inhabitants automatically became his subtenants from whom his factor then collected the rents. Needless to say, it was in the interest of the superior to control the number of subtenants or he might wake up to find the main tenant collecting more rent from the subtenants than the former was due to pay the superior himself. At Coupar Angus abbey the creation of subtenants was sometimes encouraged in order to maintain a good standard of cultivation, but the abbey was careful to reserve a certain control over them. In 1473, when the lands and woods of Calady were set for life to Neil McKeden, it was laid down that 'for the mair fredoum that al condicionis forsad be wele kepit, we hafe grantyt hym licens to bryng in tenandis and put furth at his awin discretioun, sua that the nowmer of the tennandis be nocht mynyst (diminished), bot thar be als mony at the lest as the ground wes occupyit with in the tyme of the makyn of thir letres, the profet and chetry (escheat) of tham reservyt to the abbay'.[5]

The position of the cottars, the next group to be considered, was a mixed one, or, rather, one which varied from place to place. The cottar, like the husbandman, took his name from the unit of land that he occupied, *cottagium,* cottage-land or cotland, which usually had some kind of dwelling attached to it. By our period this name had ceased to denote its physical extent but simply meant the smallish holding of someone with cottar's rights, which were more restricted than those of the husbandman. Some cottars held more than one cotland, others less. We find eight individuals occupying nine cottages and subcottages at Gilmerton in Midlothian, the subcottages probably occupied by the cottars' families and servants,[6] forty-six cotlands divided among fifty cottars at Dalkeith,[7] while up in Glenisla in Angus an eight merkland was set to five cottars, one of whom was a shepherd.[8] Occasionally, we discover the actual size of cottar holdings, as when the abbot of Coupar Angus let thirty-nine acres of Baitscheill 'in form of cottary' to fourteen men, the holdings ranging from one to six acres.[9] Where a territory was entirely set to cottars it was known as a cottoun, and in this the cottars might have had larger holdings than elsewhere.

In social position a cottar was an agricultural labourer with a tied house, working for the husbandman or directly for the landlord. Sometimes their number was regulated. When Coupar Grange was let in 1454 to the husbandmen living there, those holding a twelfth part were limited to two cottars, those with an eighth to three, while the cottars themselves were to have no labourers under them and must cultivate their own kailyards. The lands of Balbrogie, also on the Coupar Angus estates, were set to six husbandmen and six cottars, having been previously divided among sixteen of each, suggesting a move towards larger holdings, possibly even to enclosure, in which the cottars shared.[10] A husbandman was permitted to create subtenants under him 'either in cottary or husbandry', but only those subtenants who held in husbandry were required to present themselves before the landlord on their entry in order to take the oath to obey him 'in all service and rents that pertain to husbandry'.[11] For all practical purposes the cottar's landlord was the husbandman and his farm work probably sufficed for rent. At Urie cottars were fined 8d for each day that they failed to serve their masters.[12] Cottars were sometimes placed by husbandmen on newly cultivated land. When Cowbyre was let by the abbey of Coupar Angus in 1463, it was laid down that 'all the tenants each in his first year shall settle one cottar on the north part of the said grange where the lord abbot shall determine and in the third year three tenants shall be transferred to the forsaid north part, with their habitations, as their lot shall be'.[13]

But there were variations in the circumstances of the cottars. On the Grange of Balbrogie, let, as we saw, to a mixture of husbandmen and cottars, where the tenants were allowed to divide the settings among themselves, those cottars who held parts of the middle ploughgate were required 'to answer the monastery in the law of husbandmen'.[14] We can see how, from an allocation of holdings, or by persistent acquisition by an ambitious cottar of several cotlands until they formed a substantial holding, a cottar might upgrade himself in the rural hierarchy. Again, many of them clearly possessed more land than was necessary for growing their own food, having their yards besides, and some of them paid rent directly to the superior himself as distinct from labour services to the husbandmen. In fact, their cotlands were sometimes set to them by the landlord himself, his chamberlain receiving their rents. The cottars of the Green of Torphichen paid money rent for their houses and one of them, John Shaw, was allowed his house free 'for povarte'. Twenty acres set 'out' of the Mains of Torphichen were held by twenty cottars who paid rent directly to the chamberlain of the barony.[15] Fifty-eight and a half cotlands set by William Douglas of Lochleven brought him in over £45 in 1574.[16] The rather smaller cotlands of Dalkeith, many of them laid waste by the English invasions of the 1540s, were worth 6s 8d each to the earl of Morton in 1554.[17] In these circumstances the cottars had the character of main tenants, albeit with restricted rights. This was particularly true of a cottoun and, indeed, those who held the cottouns of Doleraine and Craigenitie in Glenisla were called *tenants* in the stent rolls of that barony.[18] The cottars of the late laird of Balnagowan at Ballintrad, Priesthill and elsewhere 'made account' with his chamberlain and executors when they paid over their victual rent outstanding at the time of his death, from which the chamberlain then paid the landless agricultural labourers in these townships.[19] Undoubtedly, some cottars were better off than others, almost substantial enough to merge with the husbandman class. They may have been more secure in their possession if their cotlands were set to them by the landlord himself than if they were simply 'planted' by husbandmen, but we cannot be sure of this.

Certainly, they had roofs over their heads which in a sense they could call their own, which is more than can be said for the remaining class of rural dwellers, the labourers without even customary rights in the land, who were, in fact, what we would now call wage earners. Here, we must distinguish between the general labourers and those skilled agricultural workers, such as ploughman, shepherd and grieve, who were often regularly contracted and employed from year to year by the bigger tenants, or by the landlord himself to work on the Mains of the barony, and who normally lived in like their employers' domestic servants. In testaments we often find references to fees or legacies to ploughmen, shepherds, hinds and grieves and even to 'muckmen' and 'barnmen', the last being threshers who, although they obviously must have done other farm work out of season, were skilled enough at the job of threshing to be employed for that purpose.

Around 1540 Kilwinning abbey paid 'two beyrn men' for 'wyrkyn five dayis'.[20] On the Mains of Mauchline in 1527 the chamberlain of Melrose abbey paid horse ploughmen and an ox ploughman separately and hired 'the lime man' to prepare the ground for the spring sowing.[21] Patrick McCrecken in Sanquhar owed money to three ploughmen in 1566,[22] Mirabel Kinnear to two ploughmen and a shepherd in 1563[23] and John Matheson in Broughton to two ploughmen and a muckman in 1567.[24] A town-dweller who held land at a distance or a landholder with scattered territories might employ a hind in several places to oversee the other labourers. Contracted servants, skilled or otherwise, were paid a *fee,* part money and part meal, the latter called their *boll,* and were often fed, clothed and housed as well. A *wage* in sixteenth-century parlance seems more correctly to have denoted a payment made to a servant for his subsistence while temporarily away from his normal place of employment, such as a servant travelling on his master's business. Married men in the labouring class may sometimes have been given a piece of ground from which to sustain themselves and their families in food. Both skilled workers and general farm labourers turn up in chamberlains' account books, employed perhaps on the Mains of a barony or any other part of the estate which for one reason or another was in the landlord's hands. It is impossible to tell how many of these labourers who appear in accounts were absolutely dependent on casual work and how many were members of tenant families, spared from the family holding in order to earn some extra victual or cash. Some would be the servants of tenants and cottars, others would be employed by tenants who owed the landlord labour services, such as the provision of so many sickles in harvest.

As Henryson's Country Mouse declared, a happy life depends not on how much one possesses but on how sure one is of being able to hold on to what one has:

> The sweitest lyfe, thairfoir, in this cuntrie
> Is sickerness, with small possessioun.

In trying to determine how much security these people had — tenants, sub-tenants, cottars and labourers — we need only consider the first group, the tenants, for the circumstances of the others depended very largely on theirs. Nobody could guarantee to have absolute security, for nobody but the king *owned* the land; all others *held* it from him or from someone else under him. But, as the law of land-holding stood, the tenant's security did depend greatly on the conditions on which he held his holding and so we shall look now at the ways in which this could be done.

The most common way would appear to have been by lease, or, as it was called in Scotland, by *tack*. The duration of the tack varied, even within one estate, from three, five or seven years to nineteen years or even for life. Although the material for a study of tenant organisation on church estates is plentiful and varied, it is not always of the kind from which the pattern of leases can easily be worked out. One needs a register of leases covering a fairly long period, giving the names of territories and tenants. Church estates for which we have fullest information include those of Coupar Angus abbey in Perthshire and Angus, those of Arbroath abbey in Angus and Kincardine and, to a lesser extent, those of Dunfermline abbey in Fife and those of Holyrood in Midlothian and Stirlingshire.

The rental books of Coupar Angus abbey cover two periods with a 23-year gap in the middle, from 1464 to 1516 and from 1539 to about 1560.[25] The gap is unfortunate, for it represents a period of transition, the pattern of leases in the second period being quite different from that in the first. Between mid-fifteenth and mid-sixteenth century there are 675 recorded leases. In the earlier period, that is before 1516, the greatest number of leases, 289, were of five years' duration, but eighty-seven were granted for life. While the use of patronymic surnames on the Coupar Angus lands in this earlier period makes it difficult to give round figures for the number of families enjoying continuity of possession, it seems safe to say that on the majority of settlements there was continuous possession by several families. The pattern of leases in this earlier period at Coupar Angus works out as follows:

Leases on the Coupar Angus estates, 1464-1516	*Duration of leases*	*Number*
	Life	87
	19 years	1
	15 years	1
	10 years	1
	8 years	1
	7 years	11
	6 years	4
	5 years	289
	4 years	2
	3 years	12
	2 years	6
	1 year	3
		418

The pattern on the Coupar Angus estates in the later period, from 1539 to about 1560, presents a different picture. Towards mid-century there was a definite trend towards stability in the pattern of tenancy, which may have been the policy of Abbot Donald Campbell, who was appointed in 1526. Out of 257 leases granted in this period, 150 were for life and forty were for a duration of nineteen years. Besides, of the sixty-six five-year leases granted in this period about half were renewed for life to the tenants concerned. It is interesting that Abbot Campbell granted these life-leases in the 1550s when he was also feuing much of the abbey land:

Leases on the Coupar Angus estates, 1539-c.1560	*Duration of leases*	*Number*
	Life	150
	19 years	40 (14 converted to life
	5 years	66 (32 converted to life; two converted to 19 years)
	1 year	1 (converted to life)
		257

Increased security in the 1550s did not necessarily mean that the Coupar Angus tenants looked back to the time of their fathers and grandfathers as 'the bad old days' of the short tack. The large number of five-year leases in the earlier period did not automatically mean a precarious situation for the tenant or recurrent hardship, nor did it mean that at the end of his short tack he was turned out of his holding with nowhere to go. We have been taught to believe, by John Major and those who have followed uncritically in his tradition, that the practice of granting short tacks was invariably a bad one from the tenant's point of view, giving him a sense of insecurity and discouraging him from making the most of his holding. 'Since our discussion is concerned with property and social organisation,' Major wrote in his *Quartus Sententiarum* in 1519, 'I shall raise a debateable question, namely, whether a kingdom is well ordered when its farmers and peasants do not hold their land in perpetuity, on annual payment of the rents to the owners, and I raise this matter on account of the Scots in Britain. Throughout the realm tenants are changed at the landlord's whim. I shall discuss the case of one farmer, Sortes (who) has land on lease for the space of four or five years and no more. At the expiry of the lease the landlord can evict him and this, indeed, is what happens in most cases.'[26] Simply being contemporary did not qualify John Major to give a true picture of the rural economy of his day. As for the poor state of husbandry, this probably owed as much to the immediate cause of primitive agricultural methods as to the terms of a tenant's holding although, even in this respect, it is time we paid more attention to those agricultural historians who explain that the farmtoun with its adjuncts, infield, outfield, loan, meadow, moss, commonty and shielings, was perfectly adapted to the needs of self-supporting rural communities. In judging the effects of the short tack, too much reliance has been placed on literary and secondary sources without examination of the primary material, printed and unprinted, where we find some indication of what actually happened.

Working through the Coupar Angus records, for instance, we discover that tenants moved about a good deal, or at least changed their holdings if not their dwellings, that they were allowed to allocate the portions among themselves and were even allowed to exchange holdings with other tenants. That this was not done against their will can be seen in a number of agreements with the landlord and in clauses inserted into leases. A memorandum in the abbey's rental book for 24 February 1481 reads:

James Hetoun, with permission of the lord abbot simply exchanged his tenements which were let to him for life, viz., a sixth part of *le* Arthuristane, and an eighth part thereof, which he had from Nicholas Henrysoun, in exchange for his tenement *le* Crunanswell, with Patrick Sprunt, viz., for the tenement which the said Patrick had in the Myddiltoun of Balbrogy, and the eighth part of Chapeltoun which the said Patrick had after the decease of John Olyuer; and the said James becomes bound to pay for the said tenements just as the said Patrick paid, and the said Patrick as the said James paid; and the lord abbot holds and grants this mutual exchange valid, that they may enjoy the same privileges in the exchanges as they formerly enjoyed in their proper tenements.[27]

One of the holdings which James Hetoun exchanges with Patrick Sprunt, an eighth of Arthurstane, had been acquired, it appears, by an earlier exchange. At the same time, one of the pieces he was now acquiring, an eighth of Chapeltoun, had come to Patrick Sprunt on the death of another tenant. The passage captures well the element of tenant mobility on the estates.

In November 1473 the lands of Balgersho were let to five husbandmen 'ilkane of thaim in quantitie as tha brukit of before', with the following provision at the end of the tack, 'and gyf tha thynk that tha ma sted tham bettyr in uthir placis tha sal haf our fre licens, warnand half a yer before the terme'.[28] In 1475 Agnes Brown, a widow, was granted a lease for her lifetime of the lands of Glentulach to be divided between her two sons after her death, 'conjunctly or severely as it lykis thame'.[29] There are frequent instances of tenants leasing portions which were said to have 'formerly' belonged to another person, this being stated while that person was still alive and in possession of other lands, which again suggests exchange of holdings. The fact is that many tenants held land in different places at the same time, so that the expiry of one tack did not leave them without a livelihood. All this suggests that short tacks did not necessarily mean insecurity. The rental books also show many tenant families having their tacks of particular holdings regularly renewed. Tacks of nineteen years or more were regarded as alienation of the property from the landlord's side and required the consent of the monks and attachment of the monastery's common seal; the tenants talked about getting a new 'common seal' when they meant the renewal of a long tack, and as we can see from the Tables, these increased in number in the second half of the sixteenth century. A glimpse of this continuity of possession is given in an entry for 7 April 1545 in the abbey's Book of Compositions, that is down payments for tacks and renewals:

the samyn day componit with Stevin Portar, at the request and desyre of Gibbe Portar his fader, being seik, send with Alexander Berny, for ane fyve yeir tak to Bessie Millar his moder, and to himself . . . Compositioun. £4.[30]

Gilbert Porter, here making provision for his wife and son in the event of his own death, was the third generation of his family to have an interest in the waulk mill of Keithick. His grandfather had a life lease in 1478, Gilbert's father and he himself had held half the mill on five-year leases and the young Stephen, who now succeeded his father, continued to hold it on that basis, having his tacks renewed in 1550 and 1561, representing almost a hundred years of family occupation.

Moving eastwards to the Arbroath abbey lands, in the seaboard part of Angus and Kincardineshire, information comes from an abbey Register covering the period 1329 to 1536, in which tacks begin to appear in sufficient numbers from about mid-fifteenth century:

Leases on lands of Arbroath abbey mid-fifteenth century — 1536	*Duration of leases*	*Number*
	Life	127
	19 years	87
	17 years	1
	15 years	1
	11 years	3
	10 years	2
	9 years	4
	7 years	4
	5 years	4

233

The fact that over half the Arbroath tacks were granted for life and about 37% for nineteen years suggests a fair amount of stability among the tenancies. But although tacks were renewed for these longish periods, they were less frequently granted to the same tenant families than in the case of the Coupar Angus estates. In the hundred years or so covered by the Arbroath record there is a fair turnover of tenants' names. This may, again, as at Coupar Angus, point to exchange of holdings. Less democratic trends are apparent at Arbroath, however, during the abbacy of David Beaton from 1524 onwards. In January 1526 Andrew Garden, whose family had held the lands of Dunbarrow since at least 1483, gave place there to James Beaton of Melgund, the abbot's brother.[31] This does not necessarily mean that Garden was removed from Dunbarrow, but he would become James Beaton's subtenant, with restricted rights. Members of the Lichton family had held the Bruntoun of Ethie and parts of the Mains of Ethie since 1483 and 1493 respectively. When David Beaton gave a life lease of the Bruntoun to his mistress, Marion Ogilvy, in 1528, David Lichton resigned his life lease of it and received instead half of the Mains, a relative holding the other half. He had to put down a sum of money for his half of the Mains, and the victual rent which he paid for it thereafter was double that which he had paid for the Bruntoun.[32]

Nevertheless, it is easy to exaggerate the effect of Abbot David Beaton's exercise of patronage in favour of his friends and relatives, for there were other developments on the estates which favoured the tenants. There was a tendency towards fragmentation of holdings in the sixteenth century which benefited the small people, even if the down payments which they paid for their tacks put more money in the abbot's pocket. In a number of cases lands which had earlier been leased *en bloc* were broken up when the lease expired. The lands of Kepty, for example, which were set to two Arbroath burgesses in 1433, were leased from 1485 onwards to an increasing number of small tenants holding a few acres each, until the numbers reached twenty-one in 1528.[33] In every instance leases of Kepty were for nineteen years. In 1485 the combined territories of Punderlaw, Disterland and Hospitalfield were leased to William Scott, burgess of Arbroath, for life, his son, John, getting a renewal of the lease in 1520, this time for five years only.[34] In 1525, when John's lease expired, Punderlaw and Disterland were set to thirty persons who actually cultivated them, instead of to the absentee burgess, Scott, some of these tenants holding as little as an acre of the whole, which extended to sixty acres.[35] From time to time heirs of some of these people received renewals of tacks and, interestingly enough, it was mainly to the sitting tenants that this area was feued in the 1550s.

The register of Tacks of Dunfermline abbey covers only twenty-eight years and relates to fewer than thirty territories out of the whole of the abbey's extensive estates.[36] It does show, however, that every one of the forty-three tacks recorded was granted for nineteen years. Twenty-six of the tacks went to inhabitants who probably cultivated the ground, and the remainder to members of the smaller landed families and a variety of other individuals likely to create subtenants under them.

The period covered by a similar register belonging to the bishopric of

Aberdeen is even shorter, 1549 to 1551, but it contains the texts of sixty-one tacks:

Leases on the bishopric of *Aberdeen, 1549-1551*	*Duration of leases*	Number
	19 years	8
	18 years	52
	13 years	1
		61

The unusual term of eighteen years may be explained by the fact that in the register it was sometimes stipulated that the tack should be renewed every three years until the whole term had run out.[37] Four lairds were among those receiving tacks from the bishop, but all others appear to have been the inhabitants of the lands.

The Register of Tacks of Holyrood abbey covers the years 1545 to 1567 only, but the preamble to a tack on folio three reveals that nineteen-year tacks were customary by the first half of the sixteenth century.[38]

For the secular estates of sixteenth-century Scotland there is nothing like the quantity of continuous record that survives for the church lands but, although the records are fragmentary, the glimpses we have of the tenants on the lands of nobles and lairds suggest similar circumstances to those of the church tenants. On the estates of lay landlords it is not uncommon to find a tenant family still in possession who were in arrears with their tack-duty. In a rental of the lordship of Douglas for 1578, recording the rental of tenants to family holdings, there are memoranda all down the margin as to whether or not the tenant was 'paid up', including his *entry money,* or whether he had given security, *caution,* for arrears: 'Thomas Carmichael in the Syd, to fynd cautioun for payment of all biganis (bygones) and to cum . . .'; 'John Forth, younger, sone of umquhle Alexander Forth in Drummaben, rentallit in twa oxingang of land there . . . William Forth, younger, cautioun heirfoir'.[39] Indeed, one has the impression that security of possession often depended on the apathy or absence of the landlord, who allowed the management of his estates to grind on from year to year in the hands of his officers until the chamberlain was driven to draw his attention to the accumulating arrears of rent, whereupon a list of holdings would be drawn up, giving details of who held what and since when, after which the defaulters would be reprimanded in the barony court and threatened with confiscation of goods or eviction if they failed to pay up. In 1582 the family of one of Lord Hay of Yester's tenants, Edward Crichton, were said to have held the lands of Gordonstoun in Berwick-shire for the past thirty years without paying tack-duty to his factor, yet during that time they apparently got away with wadsetting the lands and redeeming them again.[40] We also find tenants in possession who had failed to have their tacks renewed. When this was discovered, they were summoned to court on a charge of *violent occupation,* occupying the land *without tack or licence,* but it was simply the case that tenants often found it financially difficult to pay for the renewal when it fell due. Even for a small tenant the outlay was considerable. A *grassum,* down payment, was charged on the grant or renewal, usually equivalent to several years' rent, and *entry silver* was paid at the term when the tenant officially took up possession, a time normally fixed in the tack. It is clear from the Coupar Angus Book of Compositions that tenants paid in actual cash, sometimes by instalments:

Chapeltoun

Quhilk day componit with Thomas Jamesoun . . . for 19 yeris tak . . . for ane thrid pairt of the Chapeltoun at he occupiis now: Entres at Whitsunday in 44 yeris: Compositioun £40, of the quhilk £10 in hand pait and £10 gude Wodnisday, and the tothir £20 at Mydsomer nixt to cum.

Quhilk day componit with Johne Campbel for ane thrid pairt of Ovir muirtoun . . . Compositioun 10 merkis . . . of the quhilk 5 merkis gratis, for gude service to be doine, and 5 merkis in hand, pait to the supprior.

The samyn day componit with Henry Thome for renewyng of ane common seill to hyme . . . of sex acris of land . . . Compositioun £10 all pait in hand to my lord.[41]

In 1590 a tenant of the earl of Morton in Carsegowny in Kinross-shire, on paying his *grassum,* 'promesit to satisfie my lord for his entres before Whitsunday, or tyne (lose) his grassum'.[42] The remarkable thing is that, as on church lands, tenants appear to have remained in possession, sometimes for years, without having renewed their tacks. In 1582 the earl of Cassillis, presiding in the bailie court of Carrick on behalf of the king, made a second attempt to evict two of his own tenants on a charge of this kind whom he had failed to remove after dealing with them in his own barony court of Cassillis. On the same occasion he issued a second warning to others who having received their first warning three years previously were still in possession of their holdings.[43] It seems to have been easier to evict a tenant than to get him to stay out. In any case, it was probably more important that he should cultivate the ground and regularly pay rent than promptly pay grassum and entry silver.

The other form of holding to be found in all parts of the country (but chiefly in the south and west), which at first sight appears to have been more secure than the tack, was the *rental*. When a *rentaller,* as he was called, was enrolled in the landlord's rental book, he was given a copy of the entry to keep as his title, to be produced in defence of his possession if need be. Rentals were nearly always granted for life, whereas the tack might be for a shorter period, and according to the customary law of most baronies where they were to be found, rentals were usually renewed to a rentaller's nearest heir on his death. Rentalling was, in fact, a system of inheritance subject to renewal which preserved continuity of possession in a family. As an additional safeguard, rentals were often transmitted to sons or other heirs during the rentaller's lifetime. Provided he kept the conditions of his rental, the rentaller's rights were fairly incontrovertible. In 1558, while defending a rentaller from the barony of Newbattle who had held his lands for thirty-two years under two successive abbots, Mr John Spence, the advocate, argued that the man could not be removed 'becaus of the consuetude of the barony . . . ane tenand being anis rentallit . . . be vertew of his rentale hes tytle and ryt to the landis quhilkis he is rentallit in . . . ay and quhill the same be forfaltit in ane court'.[44] A similar defence of a Kilwinning tenant had been put forward in court twenty-four years earlier: 'quhat tennentis havand takkis of thar landis be rentalling in thar rentale and pais thar males and dewties with ane gratitude to everie abbot at thar interes, thai sall bruke thar malingis for lyftymes, quhilkis unbrokin as yit'; 'the use is, a tenand beand rentallit in the said rentale (i.e. landlord's rental book) usit nocht to be remufit fra thar maling for thar lyftymes, thai payand thar males and dewties with ane gratitude at the entres (i.e. in the interest) of ilk abbot.'[45]

Two surveys of holdings in the lordship of Douglas, in 1578 and 1586, tell us a lot about rentallers.[46] A number of them were actually in possession without having been formally rentalled and, of course, not having paid their entry silver. Two tenants in this position held over 100 acres each. They were not removed out of hand but were granted their rentals on giving security for payment of their 'byganis'. In the list of new rentallers their relationship to the previous holders is always noted; usually this was 'son of', but rentals were also granted to grandsons, stepsons, sons-in-law, nephews and daughters. A number of these people inherited — for in practical terms this is what was happening — during the previous rentaller's lifetime, and we therefore find a father paying the entry money of his two sons between whom the family holding was being divided, a widow paying entry on behalf of her son and another on behalf of her daughter. Some rentals were granted to an individual for his own lifetime, others to a husband and wife and for the remainder of the life of the longest liver, or to a father and his son after him.

The clearest picture of rentallers on church estates comes from the west of Scotland, from the registers of Paisley abbey and the archbishop of Glasgow. The so-called Paisley 'Rental' is a register of the entry of tenants, a *rental book,* kept in such a way as to show at a glance the succession of tenants in a particular territory.[47] It does not give the duration of holdings, simply using the phrase, *assedatur est (set to),* over and over again, but from the mention of rentalling here and there and the fact that holdings were mostly renewed on the death of tenants, it is clear that rentalling, in effect life-leases, was normal. The period which has been analysed is from 1526 to 1555 and the lands concerned lay in Renfrewshire, part of Dunbartonshire and in the barony of Monkton in Kyle, in Ayrshire:

Rentals of lands of Paisley abbey, 1526-1555	*Total number*
Holdings set to persons with same surname as previous tenant or who are definitely said to be related to him or her	193
Number of holdings set to persons who are *not evidently* related to the previous tenant	108
Total number of renewals of rentals	301

About 64% of the holdings, therefore, were probably inherited. The pattern of tenancy did not greatly vary between the different districts of the Paisley estates: 36% of those rentalled in Kyle were not evidently related to the previous tenant compared with 38% in Renfrewshire and Dunbartonshire. The majority of holdings changed hands only once during the period studied, about thirty years. In two cases the land was acquired through marriage with the heiress, two tenants had their personal rentals altered to joint holdings with their wives on marriage, while another tenant acquired land by marrying the widow of the previous tenant.

Widows were granted rentals and passed them on to their sons, and a holding was sometimes set to an heir during his father's lifetime. The phrase 'set with consent of', used repeatedly in cases where tenant and successor were not evidently related, suggests exchange of holdings, as happened elsewhere.

On the Paisley lands, as at Arbroath in the 1520s, there was an undemocratic trend in the pattern of tenancy during the abbacy of John Hamilton, later archbishop of St Andrews. On the Ayrshire lands in this period eleven dispositions went to lairds, seven of whom were Hamiltons. In the few cases where lands granted to lairds changed hands, again they invariably went to their sons. On the Renfrewshire and Dunbartonshire lands there were fifteen grants to Hamiltons. In spite of this, however, we find that many tenant families on the Paisley estates in mid-sixteenth century had possessed their holdings since at least the 1460s and 1470s.

The diocesan registers of Glasgow contain a splendid record of the entry of rentallers from the early years of the sixteenth century, giving considerable detail about occupancy of holdings and their transfer from one tenant to another over the years.[48] The following tables relate to the barony of Glasgow itself:

The rentallers of the barony of Glasgow	*Number*
Rentallers who inherited their holdings	527
Rentallers entered *with consent of* previous holder, who is *not evidently* related to them	395
Rentallers entered *on death of* previous holder, who is *not evidently* related to them	4
Circumstances of transfer not given	17
	943

Further break-down of inheritance in the barony of Glasgow	*Number*
Rentallers entered *with consent of* father, during his lifetime	202
Rentallers entered *with consent of* other relatives	40
Rentallers entered *on death of* father or other relative	186
Rentallers who acquired land *through marriage*	50
Rentallers who acquired land *through mother*	49
	527

In the barony of Glasgow, then, according to these reckonings, at least 55% of the rentallers inherited their holdings — that is, those represented by the figure 527. But tenants *not evidently* related to previous holders may, nevertheless, have been their nearest heirs, which increases the percentage of inherited holdings.

The difference in security between tack and rental, however, was more apparent than real, for they shared certain advantages. The rentaller got a copy of his title from the landlord, but so did the tack-holder and, provided he honoured its conditions and paid his tack-duty regularly, he was as secure in his possession as the rentaller. Again, rentals were granted for life but, as we have seen, so were a great many tacks. It is clear, too, that as with the rental a tack might be renewed to a son or other heir and that families often held by tack for several generations. There are even cases where a tack was renewed to a son during his father's lifetime, as we saw in the case of the Porter family at the mill of Keithick. According to Sir James Balfour, in his *Practicks,* when a rentaller died leaving wife and children, the widow enjoyed the rental for her lifetime but the heir was rentalled in his father's place, the widow being unable to put another person in it. According to the archbishop of Glasgow's rental, even if a husband alone was rentalled, his widow enjoyed it for her lifetime by a privilege known as 'St Mungo's widow'. In the Glasgow register there are many instances of the reservation of a widow's liferent, at the time of the heir's rentalling. In the same way a widow was often able to keep a tack on her husband's death, and if they had been joint-grantees of a tack she kept it by right. An entry for Whitsunday 1513 in the Coupar Angus rental book reads: 'the tak and tenement that umquhyll Robert Haw brukit is set til Jonet Andersoun his spouse . . . and falzeand of hyr til hyr sone, callit Donald Haw.'[49] Both tack and rental were recognised in the king's courts where the lawyers upheld the customary law of the baronies.

The fact that the position of tenants who held by tack and by rental was so similar in practice makes it arguable that tack and rental were simply variations on a basic type of customary tenure which in England came to be known as *copyhold.*

Notes

1 Morton muniments, GD 150/2079/3
2 *Ibid.,* GD 150/1950
3 Airlie muniments, GD 16/30/76
4 Tods, Murray and Jamieson, GD 237/202/4
5 *Cupar,* I, 198
6 Yule collection, GD 90/1/124
7 Morton muniments, GD 150/2028
8 Airlie muniments, GD 16/29/28/1
9 *Cupar,* I, 177
10 *Ibid.,* I, 123, 143
11 *Ibid.,* I, 166
12 *Urie,* 23
13 *Cupar,* I, 139
14 *Ibid.,* I, 143
15 Collection of John C. Brodie, GD 247/101/1a
16 Accounts of William Douglas of Lochleven, RH 9/1/3
17 Morton muniments, GD 150/2028
18 Airlie muniments, GD 16/29/28/1
19 Monro of Allan muniments (S.R.O.), GD 71/451
20 Eglinton muniments, GD 3/1361
21 *Mauchline account books,* 100
22 Edin. testaments, CC 8/8/1, fo. 110v
23 *Ibid.,* CC 8/8/1, fo. 61v
24 *Ibid.,* CC 8/8/1, fo. 50v
25 *Cupar,* I, II, *passim*
26 *Innes Review,* II, 65
27 *Cupar,* I, 234
28 *Ibid.,* I, 177
29 *Ibid.,* I, 224
30 *Ibid.,* I, 225, 214, 258; II, 249, 273

31 *Liber de Aberbrothoc* (Bann. Club), II, nos. 219, 612 *(Aberbrothoc)*
32 *Ibid.,* II, nos. 230, 341, 697, 698
33 *Ibid.,* II, nos 67, 286, 690
34 *Ibid.,* II, nos. 282, 557
35 *Ibid.,* II, no. 596
36 Register of tacks of Dunfermline abbey (S.R.O.), CH 6/3/1 (Dunfermline tacks)
37 *Registrum episcopatus Aberdonensis* (Mait. Club), I, 434, *(Aberdonensis)*
38 Register of tacks of Holyrood abbey (S.R.O.), CH 6/4/1 (Holyrood tacks)
39 Curle collection, GD 111/2/9/1
40 Yester writs, GD 28/836
41 *Cupar,* II, 218
42 Morton muniments, GD 150/2081
43 Carrick, RH 11/14/1
44 Acts and decreets, xviii, fo. 273r
45 *Acts of the Lords of Council in Public Affairs, 1501-54,* 413, 421
46 Curle collection, GD 111/2/9/2; GD 111/2/11
47 *Paisley,* Appendix, *passim*
48 *Glasgow registers,* I, *passim*
49 *Cupar,* I, 288

E

5

Customary and Kindly Tenure

'James Giffert, younger of Sherefhall; makand mentioun that quhair his fadir, he and his predecessouris hes bene and ar auld and kyndlie tenentis and possessouris of the eist and west mylnis of
Newbottill . . . be sindry nynetene yeris takkis set unto thame be the Abbottis . . . of Newbottill for
the tyme . . .'

Register of the Privy Council, II, 590

IN introducing the Scottish customary tenant, it will be helpful to take a look first
of all at the picture south of the Border where the *copyholders,* whose title consisted of a copy of their enrolment in the lord's court roll, accounted for most of
the customary tenants. There were three main types of copyhold. Firstly, there
was *copyhold of inheritance,* which laid down that for a fixed number of years a
holding should pass from a tenant to his heirs, with the right of renewal to the
tenant or his heirs on the expiry of the term. Secondly, *copyhold for life, or lives,*
by which the holding was granted to the tenant for life or for his own and the
lifetimes of other persons named in the copy. Thirdly, there was *copyhold for
years,* to last for a stated number of years.

It has often been said that the Scottish *rentaller* resembled the English
copyholder, but the resemblances really go further than this. There is a sense in
which all Scottish tenants who held by copy from the landlord's books, rental
book or register of tacks, were *copyholders.* The *rentaller,* whose holding according to custom usually went to the nearest heir, was very like the English
copyholder of inheritance. The tenant who received his holding for life or for his
own and the lifetimes of certain named persons, a right created in Scotland under
both tack and rental, was somewhat analogous to the English *copyholder for life,
or lives.* The tack-holder who held his land for a stated number of years, be it for
three, five or nineteen, resembled the English *copyholder for years.* I have
deliberately avoided saying that the Scottish copyholders were the equivalent of
those English ones just described, for there were differences, and it is dangerous to
transfer concepts from one legal system to another. In the Scottish *rentals* which
resemble the English *copyholds of inheritance,* for instance, it is unusual to find it
stated that the rentaller's heirs shall have right of renewal: it simply worked out
that way in most cases.

It seems possible to say, therefore, that in Scotland as in England, most
customary tenants were copyholders of one kind or another. Those not so far
accounted for were *absolute-tenants-at-will,* who had no piece of paper or parchment with which to defend their possession. These people were quite distinct from
the copyholders who, although they held at the lord's will to some extent, were

tenants-at-will with a difference. A quotation from an English lawyer, used in Dr Kerridge's book, *Agrarian Problems in the Sixteenth Century and After,* defines the difference: 'although such customary tenants (i.e. copyholders) are termed in law tenants at will, yet they are not simply so, not merely tenants at will, but only tenants at will *according to the custom of the manor,* which custom warrants his possession here for his life, and therefore it is a more certain estate than an estate at will, for the copyholder may justifie against his lord, so cannot the tenant at will'.[1] Customary law, administered in the Scottish barony courts, decided a case in the end, and not the landlord's will, for he was not above the law of his own barony, and a copyholder had written evidence of his right to possession, his tack or his rental, which he could produce in court if need be.

Not only do tack-holders and rentallers — the Scottish customary tenants — seem to have enjoyed a similar degree of security and not only are they analogous to the English copyholder, but their position even bears comparison with that of the group whom we normally think of as having the greatest security of all — the king's vassals and those who held from them in the feudal pyramid according to the common law of the land. If this seems to be taking things too far, consider these points of similarity between the tack-holder and rentaller on the one hand and the feudal vassal on the other: the formal, written basis of possession — tack, rental or charter; the fact that all these titles were equally upheld in the royal courts; the fact that when the land *descended* it did so in exactly the same way for the customary tenant and vassal — to the eldest son, then the younger sons, then to an only daughter or to daughters jointly; the provision for widows — the widowed countess with her *conjunct-fee* lands, as they were called, in which she and her late husband had been jointly infeft, the St Mungo's widow, or widow elsewhere with the liferent of her husband's rental or tack; and, on the debit side, the payments due from both customary tenant and vassal to the lord of the ground — the money payment now representing the old feudal services as well as the occasional exactions of *ward, marriage, relief* and *non-entry* in the case of the vassal and, in the case of the customary tenant, the payments of *maill* and *ferme* (money and rent in kind), as well as the occasional payments of *grassum, entry silver* and the husbandman's death-duty of *herezeld.*

The vassal scored over the customary tenant in that the former's charter settled the succession to the family property once and for all; it was granted *to him and his heirs.* The customary tenant, our copyholder, lacked this formal recognition of the customary right of inheritance which his family had long enjoyed in practice. Behind the customary law as it had come to be practised through tack and rental lay a concern that the holding should remain in the family, that it should pass from a man to his heirs as did his moveable goods. In the sixteenth-century records we become aware of a real build-up of the feeling that inheritance was the thing that mattered, the thing to get hold of and a name had come to be attached to this element in customary landholding — it was known as *kindly tenancy.*

The kindly tenant is still thought to be something of a mystery, a vulnerable member of rural society who had no legal right to his holding but whose family remained in possession one generation after another at the landlord's will. It is said that most kindly tenants were to be found on church land and that their position deteriorated in the sixteenth century as the kirklands were set in feu-ferm to those who could afford to pay for them. People spoke out in their defence at the time and they have always had a sympathetic press.

The closer we look at the kindly tenants, however, the less mysterious they become. The term *kindly* derives from the word *kin* and came to express belief in the rightness of possession by inheritance, a claim to hold the land because one was kin, usually nearest-of-kin, to the previous holder. Discussions of kindly tenancy usually stress its precarious nature, on the assumption that kindly tenants had no real comeback in the face of eviction, that they were *absolute-tenants-at-will*. Certainly, there must have been many in this position, occupying their holdings generation after generation on the kindly principle but without written rights. These were the really vulnerable people, who needed all the championship they could get. But the kindly tenant who had so much to say for himself in the sixteenth century *did* have a written, although customary, right to his holding in the form of a tack or rental, to which he laid claim by right of kinship with the previous tack-holder or rentaller. This claim he called his *kindness*.

Confusion has arisen from attempts to define kindly tenancy as a distinct *form* of tenure. Kindly tenancy was not *how* the tenant held but *why* he held. Two short examples will illustrate the point. The abbot of Dunfermline granted a *tack* of the lands of Balmule to Marion Telfer, then under age, who was said to be heir to her father who, in turn, had been heir to his uncle, the grant being 'in kindly tenancy' — a splendid example, by the way, of inheritance by means of a renewable tack.[2] Secondly, the abbot of Melrose granted a *rental* 'to George Campbell of Cessnock who and his predecessors' had been kindly tenants of the lands of Whitehauch and others, admitting him 'as rentaller and tenant'; which reminds us that kindly tenants included men as substantious as the laird of Cessnock.[3] So, one could be a kindly tack-holder, a kindly rentaller or a kindly tenant-at-will. Kindly tenancy was nothing less than the claim to customary inheritance, *however* the tenant held.

When we start to look for it there is a surprising amount of information about how kindly tenancy worked, and although the material is fragmentary there is enough to show that the principle operated in much the same way throughout the country, on church and lay lands alike. The principle was always there, in the background and taken for granted, only finding its way into the records when disputed or in danger of being violated. It was their kindly tenure, after all, that gave the customary tenants their continuity of possession, however short their tacks might be. By the sixteenth century it was every bit as vital to them as the law of inheritance was to the feudal vassal, and *in practice* was very like it.

In the first place, it kept holdings in the family. Some extracts from a rental of the barony of Preston, dating from the 1560s, provide commentary on how the principle worked.[4] It was assumed that the oldest son had the strongest claim to inheritance, 'the best kindness', so that any arrangement to split the holding among his brothers and himself required his consent:

William Kennedy of Hawtchis, occupyar of for oxgait of land thair (Preston) quhilk pertenit to Johne Andersoun, quha is decessit and suld now be the kindlie rowme (holding) of Johne Andersoun his sone. . .

Kindness passed by descent from heir to heir, through a man or woman to their children, but did not slip sideways automatically to a husband or wife through marriage:

Alesoun Gibbinson, wedo, relict of umquile Johne Costene, occupyar of ane oxgait of land thair, quhairto *scho* is kyndlie . . . [Author's italics]

What happened in practice was that a husband, usually, and a wife, very often, was accepted as tenant jointly with the spouse who already had the kindness of the holding:

Thomas Maxwell, occupyar of half ane oxgait and ane quarter oxgait of land thair, quha entrit thairto throw his wyffis kyndnes, Marioun Gibbinson, payand etc . . . (Marginal note) and Johne Maxwell, thair sone, quha is kyndlie thairto . . .

— an example of descent through a mother. Alison and Marion Gibbinson, referred to in the last two extracts, were probably sisters and joint heiresses of their father, former kindly tenant of the entire holding:

Hew Maxwell, quha hes maryit Jonat Dikson, the relict of umquhile Harbart Andersoun, occupyar (i.e. Hew) of six oxgait of land thair, of the quhilkis the barnis of the said umquhile Harbart is kyndlie . . .

— an example of the descent of kindness through the father, by-passing a stepfather.

It was remarkable what a family could do with the kindly tenancy of its holding. The kindness could be bought and sold:

Thomas Newell, occupyar of the thre oxgait of land thair quhairunto he is kyndlie to tua of thame and cofte (bought) the kyndnes of the thrid oxgait fra Joke Gibbinson . . .

A tenant might divide his kindness among his sons, in preparation for splitting up the holding among members of the family. Then, when he died, or the tack fell due for renewal, the sons would ask to be entered to those parts of the holding of which their father had assigned them the kindness. Thereafter, the sons might continue to alter the pattern on the holding by buying and selling one another's kindness to the various pieces:

Johne Gibbonson, occupyar of thre oxgait of land thair and is kyndlie unto ane of thaim and hes bocht the kyndnes of the uther tua fra Thomas Gibbonson, his brother . . .

In the barony of Kilwinning, Ayrshire, in 1551, John Watt, son of the late George Watt, 'maler and inhabytour' of the merkland of Over Smithstoun, paid nine merks for the kindness of his half-brother, John White, through whose mother the holding had come into the family.[5] This vignette of family relationships clearly demonstrates the direct descent of kindness; although George Watt had paid rent for and had inhabited Over Smithstoun, the kindness had belonged to his wife, who transmitted it to her son by a previous marriage, whose step-brother now buys it from him.

Customary tenants sometimes bequeathed their kindess in a will. By doing so a man transmitted his right to the land to another, almost bequeathed the land in effect, something which he could not legally do by will which, in the sixteenth century, governed only moveable goods. This may simply have been done to make doubly sure that arrangements previously made about the holding would be carried out after the tenant's death. One sometimes feels that moral pressure was brought to bear on a landlord in this way; Robert Simpson, referring in his will to a long span of family occupation, left his kindness of his father's steading, now occupied by his own son, John, and his grandson, to that son after his death, requesting him to come to an agreement with the landlord, the laird of Buccleuch, whom he knows will 'place him in that kyndlie rowme'.[6] Sometimes the tenant may have hoped that respect for his last wishes would give his widow additional security, for sons could not always be relied upon to be charitable to their mothers; Robert Dempstertoun left the kindness of his steading to his wife for her lifetime — a temporary transmission of his personal right, as it were — and then to their son, Lawrence, after her death.[7] Patrick McCrecken in Galloway ratified to his son, Thomas, half the kindness of his holdings, not hurting his wife's liferent.[8] In a list of legacies which included clothes and jewels, a bailie of Dalkeith left his daughter 'the right, kindness and possession' of his four oxgangs of land.[9]

Quite small tenants sometimes settled the kindness to a piece of land on a daughter and son-in-law, or son and daughter-in-law, in terms of a marriage contract. In these cases the kindness was granted to the couple jointly and to their children after them, almost as in the terms of a charter of conjunct-fee:

The quhilk day Harbart Andersoun in Prestoun clamis the kyndnes of tua oxgait in the toun of Prestoun quhilk pertenit to Johne Ahannay and now occupiit be Thomas Dikson, allegeand that be the space of 28 yeris syne he mareit the said John dochtir and that the said Johne dimittit the kyndnes of ane oxgait to the said Harbart and his spouse and pat him in possessioun thairof . . .[10]

However it evolved, by the sixteenth century kindly tenancy was a firmly established principle of customary landholding, not simply folk-law but a recognised right which could be renounced, for which compensation could be asked, and which was upheld in both local and royal courts. Since patterns of cultivation and of tenancy are closely linked, kindly tenancy may have become formulated as periodic run-rig farming faded out, for it was easier to press one's claim to a piece of land which could be pointed out as having been cultivated by one's family for generations than to put forward a purely nominal claim to hold land anywhere in the barony under a system of continual reallocation of rigs. This may partly explain why proof of continuous occupation, with regular payment of rent, was an essential element in claims to kindness in the sixteenth century, echoed in the frequently used phrase 'native kindly tenants'.

This emphasis on long occupation was the only defence possessed by kindly tenants-at-will who, when kindly tenancy first gained recognition — whenever that may have been — may have been the majority of kindly tenants. But, with a further change in cultivation patterns, admittedly a slow one — the fixing of holdings in one family and the consolidation of holdings — a parallel change came over the meaning of *kindness*, for, with the tendency of tenants to exchange their holdings in order to consolidate them, the transmission of kindness to someone other than the nearest of kin would become more common. We can see that the tenants themselves, for their own convenience, may have been eroding the meaning of *kindness* before ever it was threatened by feu-ferm. The rentals of the barony of Glasgow and Paisley, for example, are full of the exchange or taking over of holdings 'with consent of' the previous holder, a phrase which recognises the fact that in exchanging or giving over a holding a tenant was relinquishing the right to it, the *kindness*. This is the 'guidwill of the possessouris' referred to by the prebendaries of Lincluden collegiate church when they remonstrated with the provost over his programme of feuing:

My lord, it is bayth by (outwith) Goddis law and mannis to sett takkis or to few ony manis kyndlie stedyng or landis of thame quhilkis hais bene in possessioun sum 40 sum 50 yeris and utheris past memor of man till ony uthir gentill man quha nevir had kyndnes thairto nor guidwill of the possessouris . . .[11]

In mutual exchanges of holdings probably no compensation was necessary. In other cases, although it is not recorded, it may well have been paid by private bargain.

When kindness was sold or assigned to someone, a new line of kindly tenants was created in that person's family. This explains how families could claim kindly tenure of holdings which they might only recently have acquired. They need not have held them 'past memor of man', if that phrase ever meant what it said, for their claim to be valid, since the claim was based no longer on long occupation but on the fact that they had bought the kindness or had had it assigned to them. Kindness, like the property to which it was a claim, had become marketable.

Like the property itself, however, kindness was enjoyed under the control and with the approval of the lord of the ground. It was his ground that the tenants occupied, paying him their rents and services. A vacant holding might remain in his hands, as at Keillour, so that 'na man can clam ryt therto nor kyndnes therto wythout his speciale gyft . . .'[12] Tenants of the barony of Crossmichael were warned not to give the kindness of their mailings to anyone without licence or their tacks would be terminated and 'thair kyndnes to remane in my handis'. One individual was told to allow his stepmother to possess the holding 'during her wedoheid and . . . mak na assigna of this tak nor kyndnes except to ane of his brethir . . .'[13] As with subletting, landlords no doubt kept a close eye on the assignation of kindness. In the touns of Stobo and Eddleston in 1580, where a number of tenants had bought the kindness of their holdings without permission, those who were thus 'unkyndlie' had to pay double entry silver as a fine.[14] A threat of the loss of kindness was used to enforce labour services at Eglinton in 1576, when John Muling gave surety 'to entyr himselff at Iames nyxt to my lordis awane lawbar, othyrwayis renuncis his ryt and kyndnes of the landis of Bradyrwell to the said erll wyt favour and kyndnes and wythout ony uthyr process of law'.[15] On another occasion, John Fleming, an Eglinton tenant, pledged the right and kindness of his holding that he would pay the sum of £80 to the earl, while one of his neighbours who guaranteed to *relieve* him, was called upon to pledge *his* kindness in turn for the relief money.[16] In the last analysis, then, kindness and its enjoyment was at the landlord's will, however strong a claim it had become, yet action by the landlord was not arbitrary but through the mechanism of the barony court.

A landlord could, of course, influence the decision of the court or he might remind a tenant, even on his entry, that he, the lord of the ground, had the last word. In 1594 the earl of Morton 'enteris, rentallis, ressavis and admittis William Ahannay, brother germane to Michael Ahannay, sometime in Prestoun, under the sett and kindlie tenent of the landis underwritten, in kyndlie tenent to us', with the provision that should he fail to pay his rent for one full year he should not only lose his rental but renounce his kindness.[17] We can see that it could be but a small step from renunciation to being bought out of one's kindness and that a forced renunciation would facilitate eviction.

As long as the ground was continuously occupied, however, and not for any reason 'in the lord's hands', disputes over kindness as over other customary rights were referred to the barony court or to a special enquiry set up by the landlord and conducted by bailie or chamberlain, although in at least one case at Preston two tenants had referred the matter to the arbitration of friends.[18] In 1575 a number of disputes in that barony led to a formal investigaion — 'the tryall of the kyndnes' — details of which throw useful light on the subject.[19] Claims were usually made on the evidence of continuous occupation and regular payment of dues directly to the lord, of the ground:

The quhilk day comperit Andrew Strugeon and clamit 1 oxgait of land of the 2 oxgait in Torrerie occupiit by Johne McKe, for that the said Johne's predecessouris occupiit it as subtenentis to the said Andrew's fader and guidschir. And compeirit Hobbe McKie, son to the said Johne, and allegeit that the said Johne and his predecessouris hes occupiit the samyn as kyndlie tenentis past memor of man, and payit ther dewteis thairof to my lord and na utheris. And the said last allegeance is admittit . . .

Attempts to set aside the kindly principle at Preston were continually defeated in favour of the complainers. A younger grandson had tried to dispone the kindness which was not his to give away to an outsider who had offered him money. A kindly tenant pleaded that his right had been given away during his minority. Another proved that he had been turned out of his father's holding by force. From evidence other than this enquiry into their kindness it appears that the kindly tenants of Preston were *rentallers* but this fact is not mentioned in the investigation, where they were concerned only with their basic customary rights of inheritance. In the same way, the inhabitants of Inveresk, Monktonhall and Smetoun, who were also rentallers, resisted eviction in 1581 on the grounds that they had occupied their holdings for several generations, paying the maills and duties contained in their rentals.[20]

On the whole these circumstances suggest a measure of resource and opportunity such as we would expect to find behind an assertive rather than suppressed section of the community, and they tend to detract from the traditionally defenceless image of the kindly tenants. Of course, the kindly tenants-at-will were in a peculiar position, but we can only assume it was precarious because they are not, on the whole, the kindly tenants who turn up in the records; they may be those who figure in the literary and popular propaganda of the time. Those who were able to defend themselves had a good deal of pressure behind them. Not all of them were, by any means, humble tillers of the soil but included lairds and even nobles whose families had leased land from monasteries for generations, like the lairds of Cessnock from Melrose. Again, we must sometimes read between the lines of hard-luck stories as told in court where the 'kindly tenants', as they rightly called themselves, may have been the non-native leaseholders, some of them of substantial means, who had perhaps bought the kindness from the inhabitants.

To sum up: the security of the individual customary tenant, so far as he could count on it, depended on his written *copyhold* right, while the prospect of his family's continued possession of the holding, one generation after another, depended on their *kindly tenancy*. The kindly tenants of the sixteenth century certainly had a great deal to say for themselves. Without intending to undermine sympathy for them, I suggest that their outcry was as much a cry of protest as a call for help. This protest, heard again and again in the records of the period, as well as in literature and propaganda, really came from the tenants on the church estates. What made *them* so vociferous was the threat to their customary right of inheritance which came with the spread of feuing on the church lands. A feu charter settled a family's right to inherit the land once and for all; in the light of this development customary rights of inheritance were no longer good enough. There was the danger that landlords, able to raise capital on their estates by feuing, would sell the land to the highest bidders, ignoring the tenants' customary rights.

The feuing movement on the church lands has been called a 'fatal revolution' for the kindly tenants. How did they really fare? Before answering that question, we have to discover how and why feuing came about.

Notes

1 E. Kerridge, *Agrarian Problems in the Sixteenth Century and After*, 68
2 Dunfermline tacks, CH 6/3/1, fo.30r
3 C. Romanes, *Melrose regality records* (S.H.S.), III, 321, *(Melrose regality)*
4 Morton muniments, GD 150/2079/1
5 Yule collection, GD 90/1/138
6 Edin. Testaments, CC 8/8/1, fo. 63r
7 *Ibid.*, CC 8/8/1, fo. 104r
8 *Ibid.*, CC 8/8/1, fo. 110v
9 *Ibid.*, CC 8/8/1, fo. 89r
10 Morton muniments, GD 150/2079/1
11 W. McDowall, *Chronicles of Lincluden*, 137
12 Keillour, RH 11/41/1
13 W. McDowall, *op. cit.*, 108, 109
14 Newbattle muniments, GD 40/1/741
15 Eglinton muniments, GD 3/1361
16 *Ibid.*, GD 3/1361
17 Morton muniments, GD 150/1514
18 *Ibid.*, GD 150/2079/1
19 *Ibid.*, GD 150/2079/2
20 *R.P.C.* III, 396

6

The Coming of Feu-Ferm

'My Lord James, Commendatare . . . of Melrose, in presence of the said supprior and certane of the brether being present had requyrit him and the convent to sele and subscrive ane chertour of few . . . to Adam Aird . . . and the said supprior answerit . . . that . . . for unfulfilling of certane poyntis and articlis be my Lord . . . for the wele of the said abbay, the convent culd nocht . . . subscrive . . .; and eftir the said answer gevin . . . my Lord Commendatare . . . as apperit be his wult and the exteriour moving of his body grew crawbit . . .'

Melrose Regality Records, iii, pp. 155-56

THE feuing of the kirklands was one of the biggest changes affecting Scottish rural society in the sixteenth century, turning as it did hundreds of tenants into proprietors great and small. The sources of information, although they vary in usefulness, provide a wealth of detail about land and people, even preserving the names and circumstances of scores of small folk who would otherwise have been unknown to history, but without the acquaintance of whom our picture of society at the time would be incomplete.

The feuing movement had a long history and is extremely well documented. In spite of the magisterial tone of the act of the Scottish parliament of February 1458,[1] which advised the king to 'begyne and gif exempill to the laif (the others)' by setting the crown lands in feu-ferm, it is clear that many churchmen had been doing so since at least the late thirteenth century.

The best sources of information are those which contain the full texts of charters with the dates of granting, namely, the *Register of the Great Seal,* which is stuffed with crown confirmations of ecclesiastical feu charters, reciting the texts at length, and the 'Register of Abbreviates of Feu Charters of Kirklands' which, in spite of its title, also gives full details.[2] The *Register of the Privy Seal* is a frustrating source to use in that it does not give the date of granting and the texts are rather abridged. Episcopal and monastic chartularies, registers and rental books, many of them published by historical clubs and societies of the nineteenth century, sometimes contain references to feu charters, but as a rule give little detail. In the register of the bishopric of Moray, for example, which contains long lists of persons receiving feus, it is not stated whether these grantees were sitting tenants or not, an important element in the feuing picture. The accounts of the archbishopric of St Andrews refer to the collection of *augmentations,* part of the feuars' annual duties, resulting from important grants by Cardinal David Beaton in the 1540s, for which the texts of the charters themselves have not survived.[3] The printed cartulary of Inchaffray abbey contains a long list of feuars and the lands they held, but in many cases the original charters have not come to light. In

the *Melrose Regality Records* are lists of precepts of *clare constat,* dating from the
1570s and 1580s, by which the superior recognised the heirs of many small pieces
of land in Kylesmure, small holdings which were almost certainly feued in the
1550s as a result of the agreement, which has survived, between the kindly tenants
of Kylesmure and the commendator of Melrose.[4] A search for feu charters in the
private archives of landed families showed that people often kept the *instrument of
sasine* (legal evidence of having taken up posession) rather than the charter itself
which contained full information on feu-duty, conditions of holding and so on, not
always rehearsed in full in the instrument of sasine. It is possible to give undated
charters covering dates, at least, working from the name of the granter.

There are one or two supplementary sources of information on the feuing of the
kirklands. From 1564 onwards the accounts of the Treasurer of Scotland contain
lists of *compositions* paid for crown confirmation of charters and, although almost
all the grants of land referred to in these do turn up elsewhere, it has been possible
to date some undated examples from this source. Cases of dispute and complaint
as a result of feuing, which were brought before the Privy Council and Court of
Session, also add to the number of charters.

Table 1: Chronology of feu charters of kirklands

Before 1300	8
Before 1400	11
Before 1500	87
Before 1530	76
1530s	88
1540s	272
1550s	646
Undated charters, probably before 1 August 1560	123
1560s	782
1570s	432
1580s	348
Undated charters, probably after 1 August 1560	56
Undated charters which could have been granted before or after 1 August 1560	130
	3061

It will be as well to make one or two reservations about the totals in Table 1,
since round figures sometimes conceal as much as they declare. Obviously, for the
earlier period, before 1530, the chance of survival of charters is less than for the
sixteenth century. Again, land was sometimes feued more than once, either on the
cancellation of the charter or on the resignation of the first feuar for a sum of
money, so that there is a small element of double counting. Then, although it
appears that more charters were granted after than before 1560, the year of the
Reformation-settlement, we shall see later that in the case of certain bishoprics
and monasteries feuing took place mostly before the Reformation, while others
had a later programme. Estates feued mostly before 1560 include Kilwinning,
Coupar Angus, Lindores, Holyrood, Newbattle and the lands of the archbishops
of St Andrews in Angus and Kincardine; later feuing took place on the barony of
Glasgow, the bishopric lands of Brechin and on those of the abbeys of Scone,
Kinloss, Crossraguel and Dunfermline in Fife.

Nevertheless, the figures do give a general idea of the growth of the movement.
There are only eleven charters fewer in the first three decades of the sixteenth

century than appear to have survived for the whole of the fifteenth, the numbers increasing further in the 1530s and 1540s. There was another big increase in the decade just before the Reformation-rebellion, while the peak years appear to have been the 1560s. However, of the undated charters granted before 1560, more are likely to have been granted in the 1550s than earlier, which would make the amount of feuing just before and just after the Reformation about equal.

It was during the fifteenth century that feu-ferm was deliberately encouraged, by an act of parliament which ordained that 'quhat prelate, barone or frehaldare that can accorde with his tenande apone setting of feuferme of his awin lande in all or in part, our soverane lorde sall ratify and appreif the said assedacioun . . .', and by the example of the king who began to set the crown lands in feu to his tenants, particularly in Fife, Menteith and Ettrick Forest. Fifteen ecclesiastical feu charters, however, date from before the act of parliament of 1458, seven from the abbot of Dunfermline, two from the bishop of Brechin, two from the abbot of Paisley and one each from the abbots of Arbroath, Holyrood and Newbattle and the bishop of Moray. The reasons for feuing are stated in some of the charters. Richard, abbot of Dunfermline, feued the burgh rents and customs of Kirkcaldy in January 1451 to the bailies and community of that small trading settlement 'as freely as the burgesses of Dunfermline', who had received their charter in 1395.[5] In 1443 Walter, abbot of Arbroath, feued the kirklands of Brekko to John Ogilvy of Lintrathen.[6] The charter is in the form of an indenture, the terms of which demonstrate how a laird might round off his estate by feuing small pieces of adjacent land if he were in a position to put pressure on his neighbour, in this case Arbroath abbey.

The number of feu charters certainly increased after the legislation of mid-century, but it should be mentioned that of the seventy-three granted before the end of the century forty-two were by the abbot of Paisley, George Shaw, and represent the clearest case of definite feuing policy in this earlier period. A register of the feus granted by Abbot Shaw at this time, and in the early sixteenth century by his successor, has survived.[7] In 1488 the toun of Paisley, a cluster of craftsmen's and traders' houses on the River Cart, was created a burgh of barony for the abbey, and two years later the burgesses were given many small feus in the *terra burgalis*, lying on both sides of the king's highway and along 'Causayside', with one or two outlying pieces in the *terra campestris,* including the lands of Seedhill on the monastery's side of the river. Ten of these charters contained licence to build houses and premises, increasing the extent of the built-up area that is now the heart of the modern town.

Other charters dating from the second half of the fifteenth century were granted by the abbots of Arbroath, Kelso, Newbattle, Holyrood and the prioress of North Berwick, by the archbishop of St Andrews, the bishops of Moray and Dunkeld, the Dominican Friars of Edinburgh, the Carthusians and Dominicans of Perth, the dean of Glasgow cathedral as prebendary of Hamilton, and by the chaplain of St Salvator's altar in Dundee parish kirk who happened to be a canon of Dunkeld. In only three of these later fifteenth-century charters is the reason for feuing given.

A month before he got his charter of Rothiemurchus, Alexander Keyr MacIntosh entered into an agreement with the bishop of Moray in an attempt to end the 'controversy' between them, an agreement which brought him a feu of the lands under dispute.[8] The charter by Malcolm, abbot of Arbroath, to Thomas dc Tulloch in 1459, giving him in feu the lands of Tulloch and Craquhy, bluntly admits that it was done in order to end a longstanding quarrel.[9] In only one charter of this period is there a specific reference to the act of parliament 'anent feu-ferm'; this was in 1468, when the provost of Bothwell collegiate church feued the lands of Osbarnstoun to Mr Robert Hamilton, canon of Glasgow, with consent of the patrons and 'virtute etiam et vigore acti parliamenti Jacobi II Scotorum Regis et trium regni statuum'.[10]

The surviving pre-1500 feu charters of kirklands, while they show some variety of background circumstances, and would seem to some extent to be the result of outside pressures such as war conditions, the introduction of feu-ferm tenure in the royal burghs by the crown and deliberately aimed legislation, nevertheless appear on balance to owe more to local than to national circumstances, especially to bad relations between local landholders. They may at times have been nothing more than a means of 'buying off' troublesome neighbours. In 1380 the 'Wolf of Badenoch', Alexander Stewart, and the bishop of Moray had a personal confrontation about their respective rights over local inhabitants while the bishop was in the act of holding his court as lord of Badenoch. In February 1387 Alexander got a feu charter from the bishop of land in Abreachy, just two years before he set fire to Elgin cathedral.[11] The trials of the bishops of Moray and the quarrels of the abbots of Arbroath contrast with the economic and town planning of Abbot Shaw of Paisley at the end of the fifteenth century.

The great number of feu charters for the sixteenth century makes it possible to distinguish three basic reasons for the acceleration of the movement. First, the pressure of financial and economic conditions; second, the effects of political relations with England, which led to war damage and loss of income and were bound up with the unsettling effects of the growth of the Reform movement, many of whose sympathisers had English connections; third, personal and local circumstances. The reasons for feuing, as given in the preambles to charters, need not always be taken at face value, but they do tie in with what we know to have been the background to life in the sixteenth century.

There can be little doubt that the church landlords from about the beginning of King James V's personal reign were under considerable financial strain. The prelates ultimately agreed to grant the king £72,000 in four years in addition to a permanent annual subsidy of £1,400 from their benefices, ostensibly towards the endowment of a professional civil court, to be known as 'the College of Justice', and for the defence of the realm. Besides, in the frequent levies for military purposes, in James V's reign and during the regency of Mary of Guise, the church was liable for half of the national tax. It is all very well to set this against the fact that, compared with the crown's patrimony of some £17,000, the church's wealth stood at over £300,000 a year, but this ignores the wide variation in wealth within the church itself. If the bishops felt the pinch, even more so did the small monastic communities on the western marches and the Highland line.

In the preambles to twenty-four charters it is stated that the feu was granted in return for money to pay taxes. In many more cases there is mention of help 'to pay creditors', which may refer to debts incurred in borrowing money to meet the tax as well as to personal debts. Eleven charters dating from King James V's reign or from soon after his death reveal attempts to recoup 'the great tax' authorised by Pope Clement VII and lifted by the king. In 1536 James Stewart, canon of Glasgow and commendator of Dryburgh, received 280 merks from Mr Andrew Hume, brother of the laird of Wedderburn, to 'sustain' the monastery 'and to pay the tax granted to the king by the apostolic see'.[12] In 1539 the abbot of Balmerino abbey granted a feu charter to Andrew Leslie, son of the earl of Rothes, 'to pay to the king the tax granted to him by the pope'.[13] Help towards payment of taxes was one reason why the abbot of Kelso feued most of the barony of Lesmahagow to Sir James Hamilton of Finnart in 1533.[14] This reason for feuing also occurs in charters to lesser folk, as, for example, in that to Alexander Farquarson, kindly tenant in Gilmuliscroft in Kylesmure, in 1535.[15]

Even after the death of James V reference continued to be made to the need to recoup the outlay in taxes, for the church continued, nominally at least, to pay its £1,400 annually to the crown. In January 1553 William, commendator of Culross, granted a charter in return for 1,000 merks 'for repairs, to give his creditors and to pay the great tax imposed by the pope'.[16] Heads of small houses found it even more difficult to meet this expense. In 1543 Adam, commendator of Dundrennan, feued lands in the stewartry of Kirkcudbright to Mr James McGill, then an up-and-coming advocate who had already appeared in court actions on behalf of the abbey, in return for 600 merks, some of which was used to pay 'taxes imposed by the pope', because the commendator and convent could not do so themselves;[17] feuing was to prove a new purchasing device for 'thae writer chiels that buys a'thing'. Two years after James V's death the prior of Strathfillan received 300 merks from James Campbell of Lawers, partly to 'pay taxes levied during the reign of the late king'.[18]

At this slightly later period there were frequent taxes for defence purposes. In 1547 William Hamilton of Sanquhar gave the commendator of Melrose abbey money 'to pay the tax levied for war',[19] and in 1558 the provost of Lincluden received from Hugh Douglas of Dalveen £2,000 to help pay certain taxes for the defence of Scotland.[20] The perpetual tax of £1,400 a year was to be lifted from benefices in the patronage of the prelacies. Thus as late as 1567 the perpetual vicar of Bothkennar, with consent of the prioress of Eccles, to which house the church was appropriated, feued the kirklands in return for 200 merks 'to pay his share of the tax granted by the prelacies towards the defence of Scotland'.[21]

We need not imagine, of course, that money received at the granting of a feu charter was necessarily used to pay taxes or, for that matter, to meet any other commitments which a granter cared to write into the preamble. The fact is that feus were virtually bought — sometimes for vast sums of money — and the pious reasons given in charters were an attempt to make the transactions look less like the business deal they were, and also to keep on the right side of canon law, which forbade the alienation of church land except in certain apostolically sanctioned circumstances. At the same time, the ostensible reasons for feuing do reflect prevailing financial, economic and political circumstances.

High on the list of financial commitments — apart from taxation — was the repair and maintenance of the fabric of churches and monasteries, although it appears that this responsibility was often neglected in the sixteenth century. It was not entirely neglected, however. Most surviving estate records of bishoprics and monasteries suggest that at least running repairs and routine maintenance were kept going. In the 1550s the monks of Melrose complained to the unsympathetic commendator, James Stewart, about the pitiful condition of their living quarters, kitchen and offices through neglect, 'throcht inlak of the samyn the conventuale observance and ordinar ar nocht kepit', adding that, 'without the kirk be repairit this instant sommer God service will ceise in winter'.[22] The more ruinous a building was said to be, the greater excuse the superior had for accepting a large sum of money for its repair and, consequently, for granting a feu charter to the person concerned. If we are to believe the following description of Kilwinning abbey in July 1559, conditions there were as bad as at Melrose: in granting a charter the commendator received sums of money for repair and 'restoration of the said monastery, and of the houses, dormitory and refectory of the regulars of the same, being ruined from the foundation to the top'.[23] It is very doubtful if Gavin Hamilton, the commendator, intended to spend his 'sums of money' on the comfort of the brethern in the summer of 1559. In 106 charters there is mention of money which had been handed over to the granter for repair of property, a great deal of which would never get that length; the monks of Melrose, at any rate, had to take the commendator to law for breaking his promise to use the money, raised in this way from the tenants of Kylesmure, to make the place watertight.

Describing the sack of Scone abbey in June 1559, John Knox wrote: 'the multitude easily enflamed, gave the alarm, and so was that abbey and palace appointed to sackage; in doing whereof they took no long deliberation, but committed the whole to the merciment of fire; whereat no small number of us were offended, that patiently could not speak to any that were of Dundee and Saint Johnstoun.'[24] Between August 1559 and November 1566 Bishop Patrick Hepburn, as commendator of Scone, granted eighteen charters in which he acknowledged receipt of money for repairs to the damaged monastery, amounting in all to over £2,800. In addition to this he received just over £2,000 for other charters in which the actual destination of the money is not stated. It is remarkable that Hepburn had granted only one charter of Scone lands before the abbey was sacked. One cannot help thinking that John Knox would have saved himself the trouble of defending the bishop's granary on the night of the looting could he have foreseen the fortune which Hepburn was to make for himself out of the incident. It is extremely doubtful if much of the money was used to repair the property. At any rate, in 1570, in granting a pension of £16 to the aged prior of the monastery, Henry Abercrombie, the commendator recounted how the senior member of the convent had had to rebuild his own chamber and yard and make the former habitable at his own expense. One wonders how his fellow canons fared in their chambers, 'quhilkis . . . wes haillelie spoliit, ruinat and distroyit the tyme of the destructioun of our said place'.[25]

Nine charters of Newbattle abbey lands were granted in return for money to repair the monastery by Mark Kerr soon after he came into effective possession of the property just on the eve of the Reformation. In the spring and autumn of 1577 the earl of Morton took feus of large tracts of land in Peeblesshire from the archbishop of Glasgow in return for money to repair the cathedral.[26]

No doubt a variety of economic situations lie behind many charters which are silent as to the circumstances of granting. In some it is simply stated that they are granted in order to increase the rental, others in order to recoup money spent in managing the estates. In four charters granted in 1561 the bishop of Dunkeld referred to the fact that for the past three years he had been unable to collect his rents from 'his ungrateful tenants'; the charters transferred the problem to the feuars.[27] Certainly the tenants of Dunkeld seem to have been badly in arrears with their teinds at the time of the Reformation — not an unusual state of affairs elsewhere. It is possible that the bishop, Robert Crichton, who remained conservative in religion at the Reformation, was experiencing some kind of local opposition to his authority.

Problems of land management, as we can see, could be passed on to a feuar. In February 1534, for example, Abbot Robert Bellenden of Holyrood feued the lands of Little Saltcoats in the barony of Kerse in Stirlingshire to William Wotherspoon, a Linlithgow burgess, in return for £200, and because the lands had been flooded by the Rivers Carron and Forth.[28] Wotherspoon, who had paid a sum of money to the abbot's predecessor in 1527 for a nineteen-year tack of the lands, would perhaps hope to benefit from land reclamation. The problem of developing waste land was solved by the abbot of Lindores in 1565 by his granting it in feu to his kinsman, John Philp of Ormiston. The land in question was the Whitepark of Lindores, described in Philp's charter as then almost entirely uncultivated. Philp was given liberty to remove the trees and turn the area over to arable land.[29] An even bleaker picture was drawn in 1569 of the kirklands of Errol which, although they were said to have two occupants, were at the same time described as 'waste and devoid of inhabitants'. They were feued to Peter Hay of Megginch by the prior of the Perth Charterhouse.[30]

This device of using a feu in order to shift the problem of estate management from superior to proprietor is neatly put in the preamble to a charter of 'the place of the monastery of Balmerino, houses, buildings, yards, orchards and woods, with the fruits, rents, offerings, teinds and duties of the baronies of Balmerino, Pitgorno and Barry', granted in May 1565 by the commendator to John Kinnear of that ilk because the former was unable 'to lift the fruits and rents of the abbey or conduct the business, being continually in the Queen's service and because the convent are unable to do so from age and infirmity, and in order to ensure the regular collection of the fruits and the obedience of the tenants and occupiers'.[31] Kinnear paid 100 merks for his charter, with a feu-duty of 900 merks a year, obliging himself to pay the monks' portions and permit them to keep their chambers and yards.

From 1543 onwards some charters make mention of war damage by the English armies and money received from feuars which was, nominally, earmarked for repairs. As we might expect, the religious houses and churches concerned were mainly those on the invasion routes or at places where fighting took place in the 1540s: the abbeys of Melrose, Jedburgh, Kelso, Newbattle and Inchcolm, the nunneries of St Bathans and Coldstream, although the latter's prioress acted as a spy for the English, Bolton parish church and the collegiate church of Restalrig. On 27 April 1543 and 10 March 1544, shortly before he resigned office, Abbot Richard of Inchcolm feued the barony of Beath in Fife and considerable tracts of the abbey's lands in Midlothian to James Stewart, brother of Lord Avondale and father of the future Lord St Colm.[32] On each occasion Stewart gave the abbot money to repair the monastery, which had been damaged by the English in 1542. In November 1545 the dean of Restalrig, in granting a charter to his brother, Arthur Sinclair, acknowledged his help in defending the ornaments of the church during the time that the English forces had been in Edinburgh and Leith in the previous year.[33]

To some extent the formula 'for money to repair damage done by the English' was just the fashionable excuse for feuing; one wonders, after all, how much damage could have been repaired with the smallish sums of money handed over to the commendator of Coldingham by the tenant of a few husbandlands in Eyemouth or to the prioress of St Bathans by Robert Sleich, a tenant of two acres in the toun of Duns. Besides, when the depredations of the English are still being used as a pretext for disposing of large tracts of land of Kelso abbey to the earl of Moray as late as 1569, the reason does seem to be a little out of date, or the repairs somewhat overdue. It is more likely that the £4,000 handed over by the Regent was kept for the use of his nephew, the young commendator, Francis Stewart.[34] In 1547 Sir William Hamilton of Sanquhar, who administered the affairs of Melrose abbey on behalf of the young royal commendator, James Stewart, received a feu charter from the latter in return for 'his great labours' in defending the whole church of Scotland and especially the monastery in time of war; Hamilton had, nevertheless, been a member of the diplomatic mission which arranged with Henry VIII for the marriage of the young Queen Mary and Prince Edward.[35]

References to the disturbances of the civil war period are to be found in charters granted in 1568 and 1573. In one of them, issued from Dumbarton castle on 20 July 1568, Archbishop John Hamilton acknowledged receipt of money, 'tempore turbulento', from Alexander Cunningham of Craigens.[36] While it is nearly always repairs to the fabric of buildings that are mentioned in connection with war damage, many establishments must have suffered loss of income through the burning of crops and the general dislocation of agriculture, a loss which doubtless occasioned some feu charters. The extent of the damage on the Coldingham lands is seen in four surviving teind books, covering the years 1543 to 1547.[37] Above an entry for the lands of West Reston is the momorandum, 'West Restoun, considerit wyth the advice of honest men efter the Inglis armye campit in it and in the pendikkells therabout'. The following abstract from the teind books gives an idea of the extent of damage to crops around the priory:

The teinds of Coldingham priory received between 1543 and 1547	Year	Victual given in firlots
	1543	11,013
The 1546 crop shows an almost	1544	7,746
58 per cent drop on that of 1543	1545	7,044
but there was a slight recovery	1546	4,667
in 1547	1547	6,524

A large number of charters was granted by the commendator of Coldingham in the 1550s, mostly of husbandlands and cotlands and often to the sitting tenants. At the same time, there is no noticeable increase in the number of charters for Balmerino abbey in these years when it, too, suffered heavily from the English invasions.

The growth of the Reform movement must have caused ecclesiastical landowners as much concern as did the effects of the recurrent invasions. Reformation, even at its most political — indeed, in its political aspects above all — as seen in the actions of Henry VIII of England, made the Scottish hierarchy nervous lest James V should follow his uncle's example and lay hands directly on church property. Archbishop Spottiswoode quotes Lindsay of Pitscottie as saying that 'the bishops conceived in their minds that if King Henry met with our king, he would cause him to cast down the abbeys of Scotland as he had done in England. Therefore they budded (bribed) the king to bide at home and gave him three thousand pounds a year to sustain his house from their benefices.'[38] While Cardinal Beaton was in France in 1541, James V considered an invitation to meet his uncle at York,

> Bot our prelatis nor I wald never consent
> That he sulde se Kyng Harye in the face.
>
> (Sir David Lindsay, *The Tragedie of the Cardinal*)

The feu charters which the cardinal, as archbishop of St Andrews, granted to influential nobles and lairds in the critical years preceding his assassination in 1546 often allude to help 'against the Lutherans', and 'in defending the liberties of the church against Lutherans and other heretics', but they were really attempts to buy or maintain political support from those with Anglophile and Reforming sympathies. A feu charter, however, was no better guarantee of a man's future actions than a simple money bribe. Archibald, fourth earl of Argyll, to whom the cardinal granted lands in the lordship of Muckartshire, although he gave some support to the anti-English campaign at that time, eventually went over to the Reformers and was one of those who invited John Knox to return to Scotland in 1557.[39] The same change of allegiance was true of John, fourth Lord Borthwick,[40] and Patrick, fourth Lord Gray,[41] both of whom were given feus of land belonging to the archbishopric. An even greater waste of parchment was the charter granted in 1544 to the brother of Norman Leslie, one of the cardinal's assassins.[42] The charter granted in February 1547 by the commendator of Melrose to Walter Scott of Branxholm mentions 'his great labours on behalf of the catholic church in Scotland'.[43] Since Scott had recently married Janet Beaton, a kinswoman of the cardinal, it is possible that the latter had helped to negotiate the grant of land before his death.

Several charters dating from about 1560 mentioned disturbances which must refer to conditions during the politico-religious crisis of 1558-1560. In January 1559, six months before the sack of Scone, the elderly abbot of Coupar Angus, Donald Campbell, who was soon to prove amenable to the proposed changes of 1560, spoke of help which he had received from Thomas Kennedy, fiar of Coiff, against 'the insults of many lay magnates and their inferiors of the realm of Scotland opposing in those days the catholic faith and destroying many sacred places in various neighbouring parts'.[44] It is possible that the religiously conservative Robert Crichton, bishop of Dunkeld, was referring to genuine moral and financial support when he spoke in a charter of January 1566 of 'great and necessary assistance to him and on behalf of the liberty of the church', from Mr Robert Crichton of Eliok, the queen's advocate, who, shortly before then, had been employed by her in negotiations with those resisting her authority over the Darnley marriage.[45]

It is difficult to regard as other than pious jargon, however, the words 'pro summa pecunie persoluta pro ecclesiastica libertate preservanda illis periculosis Lutheranisque diebus' in a charter granted in April 1560 by William Colville, commendator of Culross, to his nephew, James Colville, since both were supporters of the Reformation, while James's brother, Robert, who witnessed the charter, was killed a month later fighting the French at the siege of Leith.[46]

In April 1560 Alexander Bannerman of Wattertoun gave Walter Reid, abbot of Kinloss, 500 merks to help compensate for the theft of 'fruits and goods of the abbey', said to have been taken 'in time of war'.[47] This was certainly not the last attack of the kind on the monastery, for in June 1560 Patrick Dunbar, sheriff of Moray, with his son, and Andrew Buk, an Aberdeen burgess who had recently feued lands from Bishop William Gordon, broke into the abbey church, domestic buildings and offices at Kinloss and carried off 'bellis, hersis, pillararis, standing chanlaris, lettronis and other brazen work' as well as several lasts of salmon from the 'fish-house' beside the River Findhorn. The following November they returned to take away grain and other goods which had been stored in the granaries since the previous harvest.[48]

Among more personal and local situations which lie behind the granting of some feu charters are a handful of cases of hardship which were the direct result of the events of the Reformation-rebellion and in two of which reference is actually made to the break-up of friaries and dispersal of the inmates. Knox says that about the time Scone abbey was burned the earl of Argyll and the Lord James Stewart rode to Stirling to intercept the troops which the Queen Regent had dispatched there 'before whose coming the rascal multitude put hands in the thieves', I should say friars', places and utterly destroyed them'.[49] On 12 September following, the prior of the Stirling Dominicans, Andrew Makneill, feued the lands of Dalgonagane to his brother, John Makneill, burgess of the Canongate, 'for eighty-five merks for sustentation of the prior after his violent ejection from the house and the demolition of the place'.[50] Seven years after the Reformation-settlement, Christian Bellenden, prioress of Sciennes Dominican nunnery near Edinburgh, then living with her relatives at Warriston, granted eighteen acres of arable land to Henry Kincaid, probably her nephew, for money given to her and the sisters of the convent 'immediately after the destruction of the place and their dispersal among friends and relatives'.[51]

Alexander Gordon, bishop of Galloway, as commendator of Tongland abbey, Adam Bothwell, bishop of Orkney, Leonard Leslie, commendator of Coupar Angus abbey, and Mr Robert Erskine, dean of Aberdeen, received money said to be used to defray expenses in connection with provision to their benefices. Alexander Gordon must have run up a considerable bill at the papal court, having been involved in provision to no fewer than four bishoprics and three commendatorships since 1544. The charter by Alan Stewart, commendator of Crossraguel abbey, in which he spoke of support from David Kennedy of Dalserroch 'in these more than perilous times', was probably a desperate attempt to secure the goodwill of a Kennedy laird at a time when the earl of Cassillis was making things difficult for him in Carrick.[52] The post-Reformation holder of the prebend of Logie in Dunblane cathedral, Robert Seton, granted a charter in 1567, with consent of his father and administrator, Walter Seton of Tullybody, in return for money to be used partly 'for his education at the schools (university)'.[53] Legal expenses sometimes figure in the preambles to charters. Mr James McGill, later Lord Clerk Register, had acted as advocate on behalf of Dundrennan abbey before the end of 1543, when the abbot granted him a charter. In 1507 the abbot of Balmerino recorded his indebtedness to Hugh Moncrieff, son of Moncrieff of that Ilk, 'for his help in his case against John Evyot of Balhousie over certain fishings in the River Tay'.[54] Some ecclesiastics and commendators must have spent a fortune in the 'guid ganging pleas' which they sustained year after year in the courts when, in addition to the advocates' fees, there were travelling expenses and lodgings in Edinburgh to be paid for when they chose to appear in person during a case, unless they were prelates with town houses in the burgh. In 1536 the bishop of Galloway, as commendator of Tongland abbey, solved a difficult local problem by giving a feu of the lands of Donjop to John Eschennan, who already had them on a nineteen-year lease, 'because the lands aftermentioned are near to the Thieves' Way by which common thieves and rebels have been in use to get access to the barony of Tongland and carry away the goods and cattle of the tenants, and for erection on the lands of a tower or house by him'.[55]

The wheel seems to have come full circle in the words of the charter granted in February 1565 by Thomas Young, prior of the Carmelite friary at South Queens-ferry, to the local laird, George Dundas of that Ilk.[56] By then the prior was being cared for in his 'great poverty and old age' by the laird's family at the castle of Dundas and, in gratitude, the prior feued him certain lands in the barony of Winch-burgh 'because George's predecessors had given the lands to the friary in free and perpetual alms'. While King James VI, who regarded lands given long before to the church as originally part of the royal patrimony, recovered the *superiority* of them by his Act of Annexation in 1587,[57] many of the descendants of those who had made territorial donations to the church in earlier times regarded themselves as still having some kind of right to recovery of the *property* of these lands. It is particularly noticeable in the case of private chapels and the parish kirklands and friaries that the lands belonging to them often returned by means of a feu charter to the patrons or descendants of the founding families. It was almost logical that this should happen. Property was given to the church *in free alms,* as the prior of Queensferry's charter states, in return, that is, for the intercessory prayers of her clergy, and, since these were no longer necessary after 1560, it is as if the longstanding contract had been cancelled, the property returning to the original donors. In one sense feuing was the long drawn out disendowment of the medieval church in Scotland.

If that were all it amounted to, however, it would scarcely merit the central place which it occupies in the social history of sixteenth-century Scotland. The fact is, as we shall see in the next chapter, that as the kirklands were secularised by feuing — coming more firmly into the hands of laymen — they did not *always* fall to the descendants of those who had been the landed classes in the so-called 'age of faith', when men are said to have given land to the church for the safety of their souls. Rather, in the sixteenth century many church lands were feued to Scots whose forebears, in the not so very remote past, had been humble peasant farmers and tillers of the soil. It is the creation of this wedge of new proprietors, drawn from the rural population below the class of laird, which is one of the most important social changes of the period. It is very significant that this should have been accompanied by a revolution of the bases of religious life and a certain devolution of political initiative in favour of the smaller landed classes and professional men.

Notes

1 *A.P.S.,* II, 49
2 R.F.C., i and ii
3 *Rentale Sancti Andree,* 118, 124, 127, 165, 197, 206
4 Morton muniments, GD 150/1455c
5 *Registrum de Dunfermelyn* (Bann. Club), no. 432 *(Dunfermelyn)*
6 *Aberbrothoc,* II, no 86
7 Paisley charters
8 *Registrum Episcopatus Moraviensis* (Bann. Club), Appendix, no. 448 *(Moraviensis)*
9 *Aberbrothoc,* II, no 83
10 *R.M.S.,* II, 985
11 *Moraviensis,* nos. 159, 168
12 *R.M.S.,* III, 2332
13 *Ibid.,* III, 2624
14 *Ibid.,* III, 1330, 1885
15 *Ibid.,* III, 2657
16 *Ibid.,* IV, 746
17 *Ibid.,* III, 3106
18 *Ibid.,* III, 2993
19 *Ibid.,* IV, 159
20 *Ibid.,* IV, 1652
21 *Ibid.,* IV, 1946
22 *Melrose regality,* III, 218
23 *Archaeological and Historical Collections at Ayr and Wigton,* I, 216 *(Kilwinning charters)*
24 J. Knox, *History of the Reformation in Scotland,* ed. W. C. Dickinson, I, 191 (J. Knox, *History)*
25 *Liber Ecclesie de Scon* (Bann. Club), 210-11 *(Liber de Scon)*

26 *R.M.S.,* IV, 2727, 2764
27 *Ibid.,* IV, 2108, 2119, 2493; V, 1211
28 *Ibid.,* III, 3016
29 *Ibid.,* IV, 2394
30 *Ibid.,* IV, 1911
31 Register House charters (S.R.O.), RH 6/1990
32 *R.M.S.,* III, 2915, 2999
33 *Ibid.,* III, 3312
34 *Ibid.,* IV, 1905
35 *Ibid.,* IV, 159
36 *Ibid.,* IV, 2411
37 Morton muniments, GD 150/1739
38 J. Spottiswoode, *History of the Affairs of Church and State,* I, 45
39 *H.M.C. Report,* IV, *(Argyll)* 484
40 *R.M.S.,* III, 2985
41 *Ibid.,* IV, 3029
42 *Ibid.,* III, 2662
43 *Ibid.,* IV, 2319
44 *Ibid.,* IV, 1380
45 *Ibid.,* IV, 2495
46 *Ibid.,* IV, 1632
47 *Ibid.,* IV, 1647
48 Acts and decreets, xxviii, fos. 50r - 50v
49 J. Knox, *History,* I, 191-92
50 *R.M.S.,* IV, 1373
51 *Ibid.,* IV, 1980
52 *Archaeological and Historical Collections of Ayr and Wigton,* XIII, 57
53 *R.M.S.,* IV, 2378
54 *Ibid.,* II, 3081
55 Register House charters, RH 6/1132
56 *R.M.S.,* IV, 1607
57 *A.P.S.,* III, 431

7

The Feuars

... and for the forsaidis landis of Craigelto and pertinentis, 40s yeirlie ... and foure dosane chikkynis ..
. and ane gude and sufficient swarme of beyis in ane skep yeirlie.'
Feu charter by the bishop of Dunkeld to John Stewart of Arntully, 1561 (R.F.C. i, fos. 85r-86r)

IT is possible to tell who a great many of the feuars were by looking at the hundreds of surviving charters. They were mainly to be found on church land, of course, because — apart from the king — the amount of feuing by secular landlords was slight, but the *kirklands,* as the estates belonging to bishops and monasteries and the lands held by collegiate and parish churches were called, accounted for much of the best farming country in Scotland and a fair proportion of rural society in the Lothians and Berwickshire, the Tweed valley, the fertile crescent of north and mid-Ayrshire, Fife, the Carse of Gowrie, the Perthshire straths, Angus, the lowlands of Aberdeenshire and Banffshire and the Laich of Moray.

Table 2, in which the feuars are divided into social groups, was compiled from details in over 2,700 feu charters, dating from the late fifteenth and sixteenth centuries.

Table 2: Social distribution of the feuars

Group	No. of feuars	Percentage of whole
1. Nobles	52 ⎫	3
Kinsmen of above	33 ⎭	
2. Known lairds; persons designated *of*	541 ⎫	29
Kinsmen of above	222 ⎭	
3. Burgesses; indwellers in burghs	222 ⎫	8
Kinsmen of above	12 ⎭	
4. Persons designated *in* or who are known to have been below the class of laird	1,128 ⎫	44
Kinsmen of above	69 ⎭	
5. Clergy, before and after the Reformation	61 ⎫	
6. Lawyers	14 ⎬	3
7. Crown officials and servants, not otherwise designated	9 ⎭	
8. Name only given; doubtful cases	344	13
	2,707	

The figures given should be taken as a guide to group representation rather than as a final count. The nobles can be identified with certainty. It is not surprising to find that they represent a very small percentage of the total feuars, since they were only a tiny fraction of the population. What is more surprising about them is to find that grants to them account for only just over three per cent of the charters found. No matter how few the nobles were in numbers, there was presumably nothing to stop church landlords from granting them any number of charters. Admittedly, charters to noblemen often contained a large number of territories, including whole baronies, and, what is perhaps more important, many of the commendators who were granting the charters were themselves drawn from noble families who thus profited from the feu duties. Yet, even allowing for all this, it must be asked why commendators did not grant more charters to near kinsmen. We can only suppose that advantage was to be had from doing otherwise. When we think of feuing from the grantees' point of view, as a kind of investment, it may have been the lairds and bigger tenants who had the wherewithal to speculate, rather than the younger sons and relatives of the nobility. From the granter's point of view the offer of a good *grassum* from a substantial tenant must sometimes have outweighed the desire to give one's kinsman a feu on easy terms.

The noblemen who received charters consisted of one duke, twenty-five earls and twenty-six lords. In the following lists the figure in brackets indicates the number of holders of a particular title receiving charters over the period:

Duke: Chatelherault (6 charters).
Earls: Argyll (3), Glencairn (1), Morton (1), Sutherland (2), Huntly (2), Montrose (1), Errol (2), Marischal (1), Bothwell (1), Cassillis (3), Rothes (2), Moray (1), Crawford (2), Caithness (1), Atholl (1), Orkney (1) (54 charters).
Lords: Borthwick (1), Drummond (1), Erskine (3), Fleming (2), Lovat (1), Gray (1), Yester (1), Herries (1), Boyd (1), Lindsay (1), Glamis (1), Ogilvy (3), Livingston (2), Maxwell (1), Oliphant (1), Ruthven (1), Semple (1), Seton (1), Ochiltree (1) (47 charters).

The second group of feuars in the table, those designated *of*, with their kinsmen, contains within itself a variety of lesser groups. Basically, the designation denotes that the person was, when he took a feu of kirklands, already the proprietor of some land, held from the king or some other superior. The sons of such a person were prospective members of the same social group, but more distant relations might receive, by the feu charter, their first piece of heritable property. In this way a laird's relations might receive from a church landlord more land than the laird himself and his predecessors had held from the king. In most cases, however, it happened that the kinsmen of Group 2 were sons. A number of families in Group 2 were, of course, the descendants of the younger sons of noble houses and could, therefore, be classed as kinsmen of Group 1, but many of these cadet branches had been established long enough to be reckoned units on their own in terms of economic resources, though this may have been less true of them with regard to social and military interdependence. An English observer in the 1560s remarked that the Kennedy lairds of south Ayrshire, such as Blairquhan and Bargany, were 'nothing inferior in living to the earl of Cassillis except that he is their chief and of a surname'. Of 541 lairds and proprietors in Group 2, 140 are to be found in the Register of the Great Seal before 1500 and were, therefore, of fairly long standing. Group 2 also includes the medieval baronage such as the Roses of Kilravock, the Arbuthnots of Arbuthnot, the Inneses of Innes and the Blairs of Blair although, interestingly enough, these older families do not figure prominently as feuars.

The burgesses, Group 3, some of whom feued land in rural areas, come from the royal burghs, the episcopal cities and burghs of barony created for landholders, and also include three *indwellers* in Leith. Groups 5, 6 and 7 are self-explanatory. The lawyers do not include men like McGill of Nether Rankeillor, Lord Clerk Register, or Bellenden of Auchnoule, Lord Justice Clerk, whose families had built up estates before feuing church land and who are, therefore, classed with Group 2. The clergy include twenty-two canons, fifteen non-graduate priests entitled *sir,* four at least of whom were chaplains, one monk of Newbattle who got his charter in 1557 and six ministers of the Reformed church.

The most significant total in the table, Group 4, is that of persons who, from the context of their charters or what is otherwise known of them, appear to have been below the class of laird as this term is commonly understood. All but a handful of these people are designated as *in* a locality, which has been taken to mean that they had no heritable tenure of the land they occupied and of which most of them now received feu charters. The status of those allocated to this group who are not specifically designated *in* has been judged from their earlier appearance in rentals, from testaments where these have survived and from other external sources. Group 8 consists of those feuars about whom we are told nothing but their names and about whom too little is otherwise known to make it possible to group them more precisely. Admittedly, they include people who shared their names with local lairds and even nobles, but in these cases we should remember the many servants and small tenants who, in the late medieval period, took their lord's name or, like him, took it from the locality, and who now used their feu charters as a means of striking out for themselves as proprietors. Many of those in Group 8, however, were undoubtedly of small substance. We can hardly doubt that the Patersons, Thomsons, Millers, Williamsons and Smiths of rural society were fairly humble folk.

Although there must have been a common element in the social and economic background of feuars in the same group, there would be some variety in their resources. Among the twenty-six small tenants of Coldingham priory who have been classed as Group 4 feuars, we find some who were local craftsmen and traders serving the needs of the rural community, who later subfeued their hold-ings in order to relieve themselves of the burden of cultivation, and others who were entirely dependent on the cotlands and husbandlands which they took in feu in the 1550s. Some of these small tenants also held land from neighbouring lairds and some were even able to derive a little income from subletting property to others, like Thomas Gray in Eyemouth who rented a house and granary to an Edinburgh merchant.[1] On the estates of Scone abbey in Perthshire, where with one or two exceptions the land was virtually turned over to the tenants in feu-ferm, there must have been considerable differences in the resources of the small feuars, many of whom paid highly for their charters. Nor does the designation *of* automatically mean a man held much land or possessed many of this world's goods; when we come across a feuar called 'of Middle Dubheid', there seems to be something in Alan Breck Stewart's jibe that some people had little more than the name of a farm midden after their surnames.

The figures and percentages in the Table of Feuars suggest that the opportunity to become the proprietor of a piece of church land came the way of most sections of Scottish society and was not monopolised by those whom we might suppose to have had most social and financial pressure behind them. The picture drawn by Sir David Lindsay of the 'gearking gentillman' who took the tenants' holdings in feu was by no means universally true. Indeed, if we add together the feuars of Groups 4 and 8, the result suggests that about half the feuars were below the class of laird or proprietor.

This conclusion provokes the interesting related question, 'how much land was granted to the occupants?'. If about half the feuars were small people, they are likely to have been the sitting tenants, or occupants, which suggests that feuing might have progressed in many areas without much dislocation of the pattern of possession — without a 'revolution'.

Before looking more closely at the local picture we must clarify in our minds the two basic types of feuar, the *occupant,* or sitting tenant, and the *non-occupant,* or outsider. The *occupant,* so designated in his charter, might be the person who cultivated the land himself or with the help of his servants and subtenants; in this category were the husbandmen and bigger tenants whose forebears had long lived on the land as rentallers or tack-holders. These occupants will be referred to as *resident* in the following analysis. At the same time, the occupant might be a laird, merchant or other person who, though not necessarily living in the locality or personally supervising the cultivation, nevertheless had had a tack of the land prior to feuing it. The grant of a feu to such a person, who had been the main tenant of the property, did not mean a change of immediate landlord for the inhabitants, who had been his subtenants, although there was always the risk of a passed-on rent increase after feuing. This second class of occupant, who will be referred to as *non-resident* in the analysis, reveals that the interest of middlemen in church land existed in all parts of the country before feuing accelerated. Then there is the other basic type of feuar, the *non-occupant,* the outsider who took the feu 'over the head' of the sitting tenant or on the resignation of the latter's kindness.

Table 3 shows the percentage of grants to occupants in a number of areas representing the main church estates in the more populous parts of the country, for which there are sufficient extant charters to make the survey worthwhile. The geographical areas concerned are shown in Map 1. The percentages of grants to occupants have been calculated by taking separately *not* the charters but the units of land, great and small, mentioned in the body of the charters and noting whether or not these were granted to occupants, so that the spread of feuing can be followed over the land surface, as it were. In the small number of cases where land changed hands after being first feued, this has been discounted except when feus were later resigned *in bulk* by a substantial non-occupant feuar in favour of the local tenants, an important development which did take place here and there, one which we shall look at more closely in another place. Table 3 also shows a breakdown of the individual feuars, dividing them into *occupant* and *non-occupant,* the former being subdivided into *resident* and *non-resident.*

It begins to look as if, in the business of feuing, the small man did reasonably well for himself, better in some places, certainly, than others. Of the feuars on those estates listed below, more than 63 per cent were sitting tenants, no less than

Table 3: Amount of land granted to occupants

Areas	Percentage of grants to Occupants	Number of Feuars		
		Occupants		*Non-occupants*
		Resident	*Non-Resident*	
Kinloss: barony of Kinloss	34	19	2	17
Kinloss: barony of Strathisla	51	36	3	13
Pluscarden: baronies of Pluscarden and Urquhart	18	1	1	10
Aberdeen bishopric	45	14	14	35
Brechin: Angus	13	7	—	28
Arbroath: Angus	36	28	7	23
St Andrews archbishopric: Angus and Kincardine	15	3	4	16
Dunblane: Perthshire	28	6	—	22
Dunkeld: barony of Dunkeld	56	38	8	25
Coupar Angus: Perthshire and Angus	57	34	3	30
Scone: Perthshire	77	91	6	19
Lindores: North Fife	42	6	2	10
Balmerino: North Fife	60	14	2	13
St Andrews archbishopric: North Fife	56	108	1	19
St Andrews priory: North Fife	6	6	2	22
Dunfermline: Fife	67	58	24	29
Culross: South Fife	35	12	5	35
Newbattle: Lanarkshire	43	13	1	16
Holyrood: Broughton and Kerse	29	7	6	19
Newbattle: Midlothian	28	8	4	24
Dunfermline: Midlothian	62	7	6	3
Coldingham: Berwickshire	72	28	—	8
Kelso: Roxburghshire	23	6	—	10
Jedburgh: Roxburghshire	9	1	3	4
Melrose: Roxburghshire	64	82	2	20
Kelso: Lesmahagow	46	21	1	2
Crossraguel: South Ayrshire	13	7	1	9
Melrose: mid-Ayrshire	53	66	2	25
Kilwinning: North Ayrshire	52	71	5	20
Paisley: Renfrewshire	80	124	8	17
Glasgow: barony of Glasgow	80	35	13	3

87 per cent of whom were resident occupants. A further analysis, in Table 4, of the social groupings of those resident occupants confirms the general impression; over 60 per cent of them were Group 4.

Map 1: Percentages of kirklands feued to the *occupants*.

Table 4: Social groupings of the resident occupants

Areas	Groups							
	1	2	3	4	5	6	7	8
Barony of Kinloss	—	—	1	9	—	—	—	9
Barony of Strathisla	—	—	—	27	—	—	—	9
Baronies of Pluscarden and Urquhart	—	—	—	—	—	—	—	1
Aberdeen bishopric lands	—	1	—	11	2	—	—	—
Brechin: Angus	—	—	—	7	—	—	—	—
Arbroath: Angus	—	2	6	5	—	—	—	15
St Andrews: Angus and Kincardine	—	1	—	2	—	—	—	—
Dunblane: Perthshire	—	6	—	—	—	—	—	—
Barony of Dunkeld	—	6	—	24	—	—	—	8
Coupar Angus: Perthshire and Angus	—	5	—	24	—	—	—	5
Scone: Perthshire	—	—	—	35	—	—	—	56
Lindores: North Fife	—	1	—	5	—	—	—	—
Balmerino: North Fife	—	—	—	14	—	—	—	—
St Andrews: North Fife	—	—	—	108	—	—	—	—
St Andrews priory: North Fife	—	1	—	5	—	—	—	—
Dunfermline: Fife	—	7	9	55	—	—	—	1
Culross: South Fife	—	2	1	2	—	1	—	1
Newbattle: Lanarkshire	—	1	—	12	—	—	—	—
Holyrood: Broughton and Kerse	—	1	—	6	—	—	—	—
Newbattle: Midlothian	—	—	—	8	—	—	—	—
Dunfermline: Midlothian	—	—	—	7	—	—	—	—
Coldingham: Berwickshire	—	2	—	26	—	—	—	—
Kelso: Roxburghshire	—	2	—	4	—	—	—	—
Jedburgh: Roxburghshire	—	—	—	1	—	—	—	—
Melrose: Roxburghshire	—	1	—	81	—	—	—	—
Kelso: Lesmahagow	—	6	—	15	—	—	—	—
Crossraguel: South Ayrshire	—	3	—	4	—	—	—	—
Melrose: mid-Ayrshire	—	15	—	32	—	—	—	19
Kilwinning: North Ayrshire	—	7	—	18	1	—	1	44
Paisley: Renfrewshire	—	3	42	19	—	—	—	60
Glasgow: barony of Glasgow	—	—	—	33	1	—	—	1

It may be objected that the number of resident occupants is inflated because of the exceptionally high numbers of tenants who obtained feus in certain localities, such as Lessudden and Newstead (Melrose)[2] and at the South Ferrytoun of Portincraig (St Andrews archbishopric).[3] However, the inclusion of these numbers in the reckoning is perfectly valid. Since some superiors feued heavily populated settlements to outsiders *en bloc,* the examples of Newstead and similar touns where feus went to the sitting tenants deserve all the more to be taken into account. It is significant that while the tenants of the Tweedside touns belonging to Melrose abbey, such as Newstead, Lessudden, Gattonside and Newtoun, became proprietors of their holdings, the settlement which clung to the walls of Dryburgh abbey, almost within sight of Newtoun and Lessudden, should have been granted almost in entirety to the brother of the laird of Powfoulis.[4] It is as relevant to take account of small feuars in one locality as to count them when they are spread over a whole estate.

It is worthwhile now to follow the pattern of feuing in some of the localities listed in Tables 3 and 4 and on Map 1, for they cover very different parts of the country and a variety of local conditions.

1. The baronies of Kinloss and Strathisla

The lands and peoples of the baronies of Kinloss and Strathisla, which together made up most of the estates of Kinloss abbey, differed in certain respects. Kinloss, in Moray, was a seaboard barony lying along the shores of the bays of Findhorn and Burghead. The principle settlements at Hempriggs, Cowtfald, East Grange, Burgie, Struthers, Kinloss (a burgh of barony) and West Grange lay in a rough semi-circle from east to west. Findhorn, at the mouth of its river, was a small fishertoun. The burgh of Kinloss, clustered about the monastery, was only a few miles distant from the royal burgh of Forres.

Strathisla, in the neighbouring sheriffdom of Banff, beyond the lands of Pluscarden priory and those of the bishop of Moray, lay in the fertile valley of the River Isla and of its two little tributaries at that point, the burns of Aultmore and Paithnick. The Grange of Strathisla at the heart of the barony held the Mains, the tower which was the centre of the administration and the parish kirk of Keith, a *mensal* church of the bishop of Moray. The land was cultivated by numerous tenants in a pattern of small holdings, on what would appear to have been the fixed-runrig system, even the lower slopes of Knock, Gallow and Lurg Hills being under cultivation.

Feu charters by the abbots and commendators of Kinloss, relating to both baronies, span the period from the paternalist government of Abbot Thomas Chrystal (1504-35), who died at the tower of Strathisla, to the lay commendatorship of Edward Bruce, who became Lord Kinloss in 1604. As many as 100 of the 104 extant charters, however, were granted by Walter Reid, who became abbot in 1553 while still a university student at Paris and who took over the administration in 1558 on the death of his uncle, Robert Reid, commendator of Kinloss and bishop of Orkney. It was Walter Reid, therefore, who effectively feued the abbey lands, so that if there is any policy behind the pattern of feuing it is his.

The feuars of the baronies of Kinloss and Strathisla

a. *Barony of Kinloss*

Occupant feuars		Non-occupant feuars	
Resident Group 3	1	Group 2	10
Group 4	9	Group 3	3
Group 6	9	Group 4	2
Non-resident Group 4	1	Group 5	2
Group 5	1		
	21		17

b. *Barony of Strathisla*

Occupant feuars		Non-occupant feuars	
Resident Group 4	27	Group 1	1
Group 6	9	Group 2	5
Non-resident group 2	3	Group 3	2
		Group 4	2
	39	Group 6	3
			13

Note: Doubtful cases of occupancy (Kinloss): Group 8–2
Case where feuar was occupant of only part of the lands he feued (Strathisla): Group 8–1

The initial alienations of abbey land by Walter Reid in the spring and autumn of 1559 must have given the tenants cause for anxiety, since eight out of eleven grants were in favour of outsiders. These included a huge grant of most of the barony of Strathisla to Euphemia Dundas, the young abbot's mother, for £2,000 feu-duty.[5] The 1560s saw the alienation of whole territories, some to the tenants and some to outsiders such as Mr Alexander Dunbar, dean of Moray,[6] John Anderson, a canon of Kirkwall cathedral,[7] and an Edinburgh burgess, Alexander Acheson.[8] Between May and September 1569, however, there were thirty-one charters of land in Strathisla, the majority of which went to the sitting tenants who cultivated them. In January 1570 Alexander, Lord Saltoun, acquired the Mains of Strathisla, the two mills and the tower on resignation of Adam Dundas, brother of the laird of Fingask, to whom they had earlier been resigned by the abbot's mother.[9] In the 1570s a number of tenants again come into the picture, although there were also grants in this later phase of feuing to the brother of Lord Saltoun,[10] to Michael Balfour, fiar of Montquhanny in Fife,[11] and to one or two Dunbar and Dundas lairds.[12] In spite of big grants to some outsiders, however, it is clear that the tenants do feature quite prominently in the feuing of the Kinloss estates.

Fewer tenants of Kinloss barony received charters than in the barony of Strathisla, where the tenants did rather better for themselves. The arable land around the touns of Kinloss barony was feued in a variety of ways, sometimes *en bloc* to outsiders and sometimes in small pieces to tenants. The charters often reveal the previous pattern of tenancy and actually name the inhabitants who now became feuar's subtenants. Robert Bruce, brother of the laird of Green, had a charter in 1580 of several tenements around the toun of Kinloss itself, to which were added a house occupied by David Guthrie who cultivated one of the holdings in Bruce's feu, another house occupied by John Irvine and a third, with a yard, occupied by Adam Elder, former prior of the monastery.[13] When Adam Dundas of Knock acquired three acres of the Killand near Kinloss, these included four 'outlandis' formerly belonging to four of the monks but which Dundas appears to have previously held in tack, subletting them to local people.[14]

The extent of a toun would no doubt influence the way in which it was feued, as a unit or in small pieces. The touns of Cowtfald and Hempriggs must have been fairly extensive; even the modern farms of these names cover a fair area on the map. The toun of Cowtfald was feued in 1574 in eight small parts among six tenants.[15] The toun of Hempriggs was feued in five parts over a period of sixteen years, having been first feued to and then resigned in favour of the local tenants by Alexander Acheson of Gosford, who no doubt made a profit in doing so.[16] Newtoun was granted to two tenants and to Adam Dundas, who already held a third in tack.[17] A number of territories in the barony of Kinloss were feued to non-resident occupants who already held them in tack, thus avoiding a change of immediate landlord for the local inhabitants. One such place, Struthers, already leased to John Anderson, canon of Kirkwall, was said to be held by him and two 'cow tenants or cottars' who had newly cultivated the land.[18] Windyhills had been set in tack and was later feued to the precentor of Elgin cathedral.[19]

In the terms of the charters there are occasional glimpses of the family circumstances of those occupants who feued their holdings. David Duncan in Kinloss, James Dick there and James Reid, a smith, all feued their family holdings during their father's lifetimes.[20] Thomas, Nicholas and Gilbert Watson in Cowtfald feued parts of the family holding, their father keeping the life-lease of the whole.[21] David Anderson took a feu of the third part of Newtoun of which his brother James was the occupant; David may, in fact, have been his brother's heir.[22] Another third of Newtoun was feued by Thomas Hill in East Grange, whose mother was the occupant and who reserved the liferent.[23] John Anderson, canon of Kirkwall, resigned his tack of the lands of Struthers in 1565 for a joint feu charter to himself and his wife, Janet Gibson, whom he married soon after the Reformation.[14]

The fact remains that while more than half of the feuars of Kinloss barony were occupants, only about 34 per cent of the land surface feued passed into their possession. The pattern was more favourable to the sitting tenants of the distant barony of Strathisla. A remarkable number of the place-names of sixteenth-century Strathisla still appear on the modern map in an area which has so far remained free of both industrialisation and afforestation. The arable land surrounding the scattered settlements was leased to and cultivated by tenant families, with their cottars and subtenants, in varying numbers of oxgangs. For instance, in October 1559 the abbot gave a nineteen-year tack to Andrew Paton and his wife, Agnes Langmure, 'and thair cotteris and slotenentis all and haill the sex oxingang of the landis of Burroleyis quhilkis now the saidis Andro and Agnes his spous occupiis, togidder with the new landis callit the Corbie Craig . . .'[25] Sometimes the holdings are designated in acreage. Details in a number of charters reveal how tenant families had graduallly acquired holdings in neighbouring territories, these being united in their feu charters, e.g.

Alexander Gordon and Bessie Hay, his wife	2 oxgangs of New Fortry 4 oxgangs of the outset of Fortry[26]
John Wilson in Fortry	4 oxgangs in Nether Fortry 1 oxgang in Over Fortry Part of Auldtoun[27]
Thomas Christie	Quarter of Alehoustack Half of Inchdenny[28]

Two non-occupant feuars of Strathisla, Lord Saltoun and George Adamson, son of a prominent Edinburgh burgess, need special mention since their feus affected the economic life of the local community. In January 1570 Alexander, Lord Saltoun, feued the mains of Strathisla, which may have been previously cultivated with direct labour, and which consisted of nine territories, with pasturage on the Aultmore and the use of the Wood of Craigward. Saltoun's charter also conveyed the tower of Strathisla itself and the Overmill. In the following year Lord Saltoun received from the bishop of Moray a nineteen-year tack of the teinds of the neighbouring parishes of Keith and Rothiemay.[29] Also in 1570 George Adamson received a charter of the Nethermill of Strathisla and with it the multures due from the lands of Knock, Millegan, Janetscheill, Braco, Haughs,

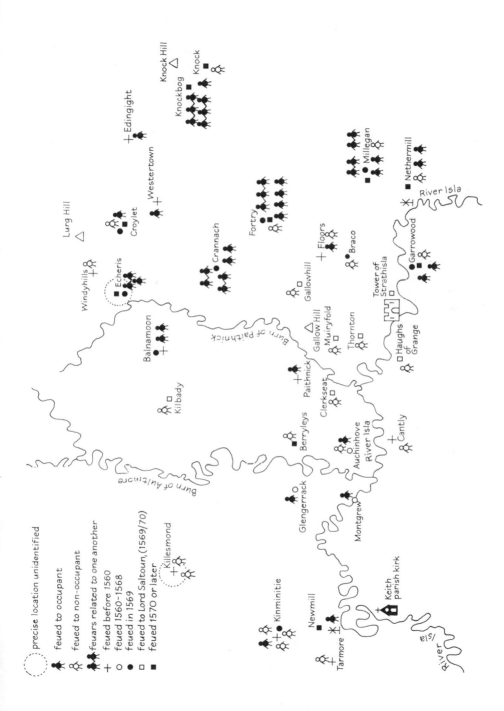

Map 2: The feuing of Strathisla.

Thornton, Boglogy, Floors, Fortry, Crannach, Echeris, Windyhills, Edingight and the Grange of Strathisla.[30] We can see how complicated the economics of life could become in a locality where the inhabitants paid their feu-duty to the chamberlain of Kinloss abbey — or, if they were subtenants of a feuar, their mails and fermes to a middleman who had taken the feus of their holdings — their multures to the factor of an Edinburgh merchant and their teinds to the officer of Lord Saltoun, the bishop of Moray's tacksman. In 1559, in the initial stages of feuing Strathisla, Abbot Walter Reid had granted his mother, Euphemia Dundas, a huge charter conveying most of the barony, but it would appear that she resigned many of the lands at a later stage, not without protest, however. A number of lands named in her charter of 1559 were later feued to local tenants, and to George Adamson, already mentioned. This device of an outsider feuing land and subsequently resigning it to the inhabitants may have been a profit-making property speculation; it happened in other parts of the country and we shall be looking at it more closely in another contenxt presently.

In Strathisla two-thirds of the feuars were occupants, 91 per cent of them were resident. Their charters account for just over half the land feued, most of it lying in the eastern region of the barony. A number of the tenant-feuars were related to one another either by blood or marriage, cultivating the farms among themselves as a family. On the lands of Knock, for example, when it came to feuing, the lands were sometimes granted in liferent to the feuars' fathers who were still involved in the cultivation of the farm:

Fourteen oxgangs of Knock feued in 1569[31]

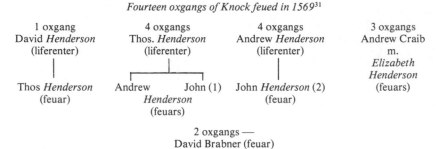

1 oxgang	4 oxgangs	4 oxgangs	3 oxgangs
David *Henderson* (liferenter)	Thos. *Henderson* (liferenter)	Andrew *Henderson* (liferenter)	Andrew Craib m. *Elizabeth Henderson* (feuars)
Thos *Henderson* (feuar)	Andrew John (1) *Henderson* (feuars)	John *Henderson* (2) (feuar)	

2 oxgangs —
David Brabner (feuar)

There was a similar pattern of relationships among the occupant feuars of Millegan, which almost bordered on the Mains of Strathisla:

Millegan feued in 1569, except for the Nethertown which was granted to Innes of Paithnick in 1577[32]

2 oxgangs	2 oxgangs	6 oxgangs	2 oxgangs
David *Forsyth* (liferenter) Adam *Forsyth* (feuar)	David *Forsyth* (feuar) (may have been brother of Adam Forsyth)	William *Murray* (feuar)	George *Murray* (feuar)
	8 oxgangs William Ruddach (feuar) m. Margaret Langmure	2 oxgangs William Fordyce in Corskellie (feuar)	

While some tenant families took feus of their shares of these farmtouns, in other places tenants became feuars side by side with middlemen, creating a mixed pattern of landholding. At Croylet, for example, four oxgangs went to John Craig, the occupant, while Wester Croylet was granted to Thomas Innes, son of the laird of Edingight, three tenants being named in his charter.[33] At Garrowood the feuars were the son of the laird of Paithnick, Alexander Abernethy and Katherine Wilson, widow of a tenant, who feued what was called the 'mydhalf', for which she paid a new-style entirely money feu-duty of over £2.[34]

The feuing pattern on the farmtouns of Strathisla, carried out in mid-sixteenth century, created a pattern of small proprietors which survived well into the following century. The Secretary's Register of Sasines (land register), which survives for Banffshire from 1599, reflects the pattern of economic and social life in Strathisla, particularly on the lands east of the Paithnick Burn where the *portioners*, the sons and grandsons of the original feuars, and their families, intermarried, borrowed and loaned money to one another and wadset, excambed, subfeued and alienated their holdings.[35] By mid-seventeenth century Strathisla was peppered with the little tower houses of the portioners and bonnet lairds. The buying up of small feus by big landowners in the later seventeenth century was characterisitc of many parts of the country, often in those places where feuing of a church estate to the tenants in the sixteenth century had created many small proprietors. The story is told of how Alexander Duff of Braco, ancestor of the earls Fife who ultimately came into possession of much of Banffshire, stood on a hillside in Strathisla watching the smoke go up from the towers of all the little lairdships and remarked 'that he would make the smoke of these houses to go through the one vent by and by'.[36]

2. Church lands in Perthshire and East Angus

The feuars on the barony of Dunkeld

Occupant feuars		Non-Occupant feuars	
Resident Group 2	6	Group 1	3
Group 4	24	Group 2	11
Group 8	8	Group 3	2
Non-resident Group 1	1	Group 5	1
Group 2	1	Group 6	2
Group 3	5	Group 7	2
Group 6	1	Group 8	4
	46		25

Of the thirty-eight resident occupants in the barony of Dunkeld, where 56 per cent of the feus went to tenants, six were lairds, while twenty-four are designated as *in* the lands which they cultivated and feued, these being mainly the neighbouring territories of Caputh and Dalgarthill and, farther up the River Tay, those of Dalguise and Dowally. The non-resident occupants, previously holding the land in tack, were Alexander Abercrombie of that Ilk, David, third son of Lord Ogilvy, Mr Robert Crichton, advocate, Alexander Macky and John Moncur, citizens of Dunkeld, and three Edinburgh burgesses. The non-occupants, or outsiders, were the earls of Atholl and Montrose and the wife of the earl of Errol, eleven lairds, or their relatives, two burgesses, two crown servants and one who can probably be identified with the son of Bishop Patrick Hepburn of Moray.

The feuars on the lands of Dunblane bishopric

Occupant feuars		Non-occupant feuars	
Resident Group 2	6	Group 1	2
	6	Group 2	14
		Group 3	1
		Group 5	1
		Group 8	4
			22

On the Dunblane lands the number of occupant feuars was small and even the resident occupants included the bishop's kinsmen, the Chisholms, who had previously held the lands of Cromlix before feuing them. A number of outsiders acquired property in and around Dunblane itself, although the earl of Montrose received a big grant of land lying between Muthill and Braco.[37] James Stirling of Keir, who married the daughter of Bishop William Chisolm, had a substantial grant of lands in the stewartry of Strathearn.[38] The feuars of Dunblane were heavily represented among the lairds and their relatives.

The feuing pattern on the lands of Coupar Angus and Scone abbeys, however, favoured many tenants. In the case of Coupar Angus it is possible to fill in the pre-feuing pattern of tenancy and to discover that the forebears of many feuars had been in possession of their holdings for several generations. On the Scone lands there is no equivalent accessible record from which to construct the pre-feuing picture, but there is also likely to have been a good deal of tenant continuity in this area, where 77 per cent of the feus went to the sitting tenants. The two monasteries stood only about twelve miles apart and, as can be seen from Map 3, their lands lay mainly between the Tay estuary and the southern ends of Strathardle and Glenshee. The greatest concentration of Scone lands lay to the east of the Tay estuary on the high land overlooking the Carse of Gowrie, with the most distant of the Coupar Angus granges lying in the Carse itself. On the east bank of the Tay the Coupar Angus lands of Wolfhill were only about a mile away from Scone's Craigmakerran. In the case of each abbey the majority of the feu charters were granted by one individual: Abbot Donald Campbell of Coupar Angus between 1558 and 1560, and Bishop Patrick Hepburn as commendator of Scone, mainly between 1559 and 1566. In the case of the aged Abbot Campbell, the desire to raise money in the face of a likely emergency probably motivated his extensive feuing of the abbey lands. Bishop Patrick Hepburn began to feu the Scone lands immediately after the sack of the monastery in June 1559. Although most Coupar Angus charters were granted between 1558 and 1560, suggesting some precipitation of the process, there does seem to have been a trend towards stabilisation in the pattern of tack-holding between 1539 and 1560, when over seventy nineteen-year and five-year tacks were renewed for life; in other words, practical alienation of the land did not have to wait for feuing. For a number of tenants a feu charter was the final step in getting permanent possession of their holdings.

(C) – Coupar Angus
(S) – Scone

Forter (C) ●

Cammock ●

Clintlaw ●
● Airlie

● Persie (C)

Balmyle (C) ●

● Drimmie (C)

Cally (C) ●

● Tullifergus (C)
● Polcalk (C)

Blacklaw (C) ●

Grange of Aberbothrie (C) ●
Milthorn (C) ●
● Coupar Grange (C)
● Balbrogie (C)
● W, Denhead (C) ● Arthurstane (C)
COUPAR ANGUS ABBEY
● Kemphill (C)
● Kethick (C)
● Balgersho (C)

● Coltward (C)

● Wolfhill (C)
● Campsie (C)

● Byres (S)
● Craigmakerran (S)

Newmills (S) ●
Barclayhills (S) ●
Innerbuist (S) ●
● North Friartoun (S)
● Bauchland (S)
● South Friartoun (S)
● Over Fingask (S)

● Ardgilzean (S)
● Lethendy (S)
● Carsegrange (C)

● Sherifftoun (S)
● Balboughty (S)
PERTH □ SCONE ABBEY
Arnbathie (S) ●
● Nether Durdie (S)
● Hole of Clien (S)

FIRTH OF TAY

Map 3: The lands of Coupar Angus and Scone abbeys.

The feuars of Coupar Angus abbey

Occupant feuars			Non-Occupant feuars	
Resident Group 2	5		Group 1	6
Group 4	24		Group 2	16
Group 8	5		Group 3	1
Non-resident Group 1	1		Group 4	3
Group 2	2		Group 8	4
	37			30

Note: Two individuals feued lands, only part of which they had previously occupied.

The outsiders who feued land previously leased to tenants included six members of noble houses and sixteen lairds or their sons. It is noticeable that a higher proportion of the abbey's lands in Perthshire than in Angus was feued to outsiders. Here and there farms which had been set in tack to several tenants were consolidated in one feu to an outsider, who was then responsible for renewal of the subtenants' tacks. Coupargrange, before being feued to John Campbell of Skipinch, had been set to tenants in twelfth parts. We do not know whether Campbell of Skipinch compensated those tenants who had recently received life-leases — some of them having put down considerable grassums for them — when he received his charter of the whole of Coupargrange on 8 January 1560, since there is certainly no mention of the occupants in his charter.[39] The lands of Monks Cally were feued in January 1559 to James Hering of Glasclune only eight years after nineteen-year tacks had been given to three tenants.[40] The family of one of these tenants, William Reid, had been on the land since 1513.[41] It may be said that the cost of a feu charter was beyond the pockets of tenants who had recently paid for the renewal of tacks; the grassum for a tack of a quarter of Cally rose from £2 13s 4d in 1512 to £20 in 1543.[42] Hering's charter conveyed to him 'all the services which the occupants of the lands were wont to make'.

The sitting tenants of Coupar Angus, however, did manage to acquire 57 per cent of the lands feued, some touns and granges being feued in the shares in which they were already held in tack. Unlike Coupargrange to the north-west of the abbey and the grange of Kincreich in Glenisla, which were granted in their entirety to outsiders, the grange of Balbrogie was feued to eight individuals, only two of whom were non-occupants. One of the tenant families receiving feus, the Hendersons, had been in Balbrogie since 1468.[43] A quarter of Easter Balbrogie was feued in 1558 to Robert Montgomery, whose previous nineteen-year tack was dated 1547, when the holding was said to have been 'bruikit befoir' by Andrew Allan.[44] Interestingly, Allan is called Montgomery's subtenant in the feu charter of 1558, showing that although Allan had been replaced as tack-holder by Montgomery eleven years before, he had actually gone on living in the holding, Montgomery, who does not have a local name, was presumably a non-resident tack-holder.

Cowbyre was feued in three portions to occupants: William Burt, John Perry and Walter Leslie.[45] Burt's grandfather had had a five-year tack of a third of Cowbyre in 1507 and his father a life-tack in 1550, when he was cultivating his holding with the help of cottars.[46] John Perry's charter, on the other hand, is a good example of the recovery of a holding which had temporarily been out of a family's possession. After the death of John's father, William Perry, who may be identified with one of the abbey's apprentice carpenters at the beginning of the century, the holding passed in 1550 to John Henderson and was later feued to Andrew Baxter who, in 1561, resigned it to John Perry himself.[47] For the grange in the Carse of Gowrie, which extended to fifty-two acres, there are surviving charters to seven people, two of whom were non-occupants, John Campbell of Murthly and Peter Hay of Megginch.[48] The tenants who feued their holdings there were Thomas Turnbull, whose family had held tacks in Carsegrange since the beginning of the century, Thomas himself receiving a life-tack in 1554,[49] Alexander Jackson in Waterybutts, one of a number of Jacksons to hold parts of Carsegrange and whose life-tack of 1554 was converted to a feu about five years later,[50] Andrew Powry, who cultivated four acres which he had leased for life in 1546.[51] James Galloway, whose father had a life-tack,[52] and Thomas Cook, who held an eighth part.[53]

The feuing picture on the Coupar Angus lands is a mixed one and to some extent incomplete. On the whole it suggests an eleventh-hour policy which, in theory, ought to have consolidated the trend towards stabilisation of the pattern of tenure apparent from the 1520s onwards. In practice, however, the comparatively sudden decision to feu the estates may have caught a number of tenants unprepared and unable to pay for a feu charter, with the result that, while in some areas feuing led to the entrenchment of tenant families of longstanding, in others holdings passed to middlemen. As to the incompleteness of the picture, this is because some territories on the estates are not represented in the surviving charters; there is only one charter, for example, for the grange of Aberbothrie and two charters only of Baitscheill conveying two acres, although it was said to contain thirty-nine acres 'set in cottary' in 1475. When all is said, however, it is surprising that, given the circumstances of the late 1550s, the whole of the Coupar Angus estates did not simply pass into the hands of the aged abbot's relatives, cadets and branches of the powerful house of Argyll.

The feuars of Scone abbey

Occupants			*Non-Occupant feuars*	
Resident Group 4	35		Group 1	1
Group 8	56		Group 2	12
Non-resident Group 2	6		Group 3	2
	97		Group 4	2
			Group 8	2
				19

Doubtful occupancy	
Group 4	1
Group 8	3
	4

Thirty-five feuars of Scone are described as *in* the lands they feued, while only the names are given of another fifty-six resident occupants, evidently tenants of small substance. The six lairds and their relatives who took feus of land which they already held in tack were Hugh Mitchell of Kinkell,[54] George Drummond who later took his designation from the lands of Blair which he feued,[55] George Ramsay of Bamff in Alyth parish,[56] James Hepburn, doubtless a relative of the commendator,[57] Andrew Rattray of Ballinhard,[58] and Patrick Stewart of Stewkis;[59] the substance of these people no doubt varied a good deal.

The non-occupants included William, master of Ruthven, later first earl of Gowrie,[60] Adam Hepburn of Bonhard,[61] James Hepburn of Rollandstoun,[62] James Spence, son of Spence of Kilspindie,[63] David Ogilvy of Templehall,[64] Sir Thomas Erskine of Brechin,[65] William Chalmer of Drumlochie,[66] Patrick Blair, brother of the laird of Balthiock,[67] James Hering of Wester Gormock,[68] John Lindsay of Evlick,[69] David Murray of Tibbermure,[70] John Ogilvy, son of the laird of Inchmartin,[71] and Janet Williamson, widow of Patrick Blair of Lethindy.[72] Two small tenants feued land occupied by others: John Duncan in the Mote of Errol, who acquired two acres in Clien, where the widow of the former occupant was still in possession,[73] and Laurence Fairy, a wright in Scone.[74]

As we saw elsewhere, Patrick Hepburn began immediately after the sack of the monastery to feu the Scone estates systematically by means of 131 charters which, in the case of the majority of farmtouns, simply converted the existing tenancies into feu-ferms. Thirty-one of those charters alone brought him in almost £5,000 in grassums, suggesting that he must have made himself a fortune out of the whole operation, which lasted from 1559 almost until his death in 1573.

Most of the occupant feuars of Scone were residents, many of them belonging to the husbandman class. We often find farmtouns being cultivated by a group of relatives as, for example, at Bauchrie, feued to John, William and George Soutar;[75] Kinnochtrie, held by John, Robert and Thomas Small and by Robert Petillo, whose mother, Janet Small, had a liferent of his holding;[76] Sherifftoun and Shepherdland, shared between Ranald and John Robertson;[77] and Invergowrie, feued to Patrick and John Black and William and John Morris.[78] Tenants' shares of the farms were commonly eighth, quarter and third parts. Some single tenant farms, occupied by husbandmen whose families had probably acquired them piecemeal over the years, were feued to them in entirety, as at Muretoun of Creuchies, feued to the tenant, David Rattray;[79] Balbuthie, feued to Thomas Elder, whose widowed mother retained her liferent;[80] Braidwell, feued to James Henderson;[81] Brighouse, feued to John Wedder;[82] Dargo to William Charteris;[83] Limpotts to Patrick Snell;[84] Parkhead to John Ireland;[85] Pawinshill to John Brown;[86] and Futhrunis to William Small.[87]

Apparently, the feuing of the Scone estates benefited many tenant families, bringing widespread security of tenure. The testaments of thirteen occupant feuars have survived and, with one exception, show that these people were able to pay their grassums, feu-duties and augmentations and still remain solvent.

3. Church lands in Fife

Moving across into Fife we find that, with one exception, the percentage of feus granted to tenants was reasonably high — an interesting fact in a part of Scotland characterised by the holdings of small lairds and crown tenants, now increased with those of the feuars and *portioners*. The exception to this pattern is St Andrews priory, probably the richest monastic house in Scotland. Neither the commendator, James Stewart, later Regent, nor Robert Stewart, bishop of Caithness, who between them granted all but one of the charters, gave many feus to tenants. Only three people are actually called occupants: Mr David Balfour, non-resident occupant of Gregstoun,[88] Cuthbert Cranston, son of the laird of Thirlestanemains, who feued the distant lands of Wester Morestoun in Renfrewshire belonging to the priory,[89] and David Balfour of Balledmonth, who had possessed the kirklands of Forgund as subtenant of the commendator's mother, Margaret Erskine, before feuing them.[90] Only five people, the conditions of whose occupancy are difficult to determine, may have been husbandmen. All other feuars of St Andrews priory were non-occupants, mainly influential lairds and St Andrews burgesses, while three were servants of James Stewart, the commendator, including his chamberlain David Orme who had three priory charters and two from the abbot of Lindores.[91]

On the Fife lands of the archbishops of St Andrews, however, the picture was quite different.

The feuars of the archbishopric of St Andrerws in Fife

Occupant feuars		Non-Occupant feuars	
Resident Group 4	108	Group 1	1
Non-resident Group 3	1	Group 2	12
	109	Group 3	2
		Group 5	2
		Group 8	2
			19

Fifty-six per cent of the archbishops' feuars, in north-east Fife, were occupants. Certain farms were set in feu in small portions to the tenants who cultivated them: to three tenants at Boarhills, four at Craigfoodie, two at Cunnoquhie, six at Kincaple, six at Letham, eight at Radernie and seventy-eight at the South Ferrytoun of Portincraig. Alexander Winchester, citizen of St Andrews, although a non-resident tack-holder, is described with his father as 'naturalis at antiqui tenentis', having held the lease for so long.[92]

The feuars of Balmerino abbey

Occupant feuars		Non-Occupant feuars	
Resident Group 4	14	Group 2	6
Non-resident Group 2	2	Group 3	1
	16	Group 4	4
		Group 8	2
			13

On the comparatively small estate of Balmerino abbey on the south bank of the Tay, two tenants received feus at Scarbank, four at Dewcherone, two at Bottomcraig and five at Coultra. Non-resident occupants included Learmonth of Balcomie,[93] and David Balfour of Balbuthie[94] who occupied parts of Newgrange and six other lands before feuing them in 1569. The outsiders included the neighbouring lairds of Kinnear,[95] Nauchton,[96] Lochleven[97] and Creich.[98]

The feuars of Lindores abbey

Occupant feuars		Non-Occupant feuars	
Resident Group 2	1	Group 1	1
Group 4	5	Group 2	6
Non-resident Group 2	2	Group 3	1
	8	Group 8	2
			10

Five sitting tenants of the Grange of Lindores received feus there, but so did Mr James McGill of Nether Rankeillor, the Clerk Register, who had a grant of fifty-six oxgangs.[99] Other outsiders on this small estate included members of the abbot's family, the Philps,[100] the earl of Rothes[101] and a Newburgh burgess, John Calve.

The feuars of Dunfermline abbey in Fife

Occupant feuars		Non-Occupant feuars	
Resident Group 2	7	Group 1	2
Group 3	9	Group 2	23
Group 4	55	Group 3	2
Non-resident Group 2	8	Group 7	1
Group 5	1	Group 8	1
Group 8	2		29
	82		

The tenants of Dunfermline abbey's Fife lands come well into the picture, but not until an influential middleman, Mr Robert Richardson, Treasurer of the realm, had made a profit for himself out of the situation. In 1563 Richardson got three charters from the commendator of Dunfermline, Robert Pitcairn, which conveyed to him no fewer than seventy-seven farms and scattered holdings,[103] although in 1566 pressure in the civil court by certain tenants resulted in a royal letter to Pitcairn commanding him to 'set the whole landis to the old kindly possessouris'.[104] In fact, the abbey's register shows that from September 1565 onwards Richardson had been systematically resigning land all over the Fife estates in favour of the tenants, for which he would no doubt receive compensation.[105] Altogether, he resigned sixty-six separate pieces in favour of the same number of tenants. The texts of charters to sixty of these people are extant and in effect they almost cancel the earlier grants to Richardson. Clearly, it became policy to turn most of the estates over to the tenants in feu-ferm. An agreement signed by the commendator in February 1580, providing for the infeftment of kindly tenant John Kellock in the lands of Masterton, contains the phrase 'as all fews ar sett to the remanent tenentis of the lordschip of Dunfermling'.[106] Non-occupant feuars were certainly in the minority.

The picture on the lands of Culross abbey, which lay in what is now administratively Fife but was then in the sheriffdom of Perth, is of feus going to local proprietors and their sons, to inhabitants of the burgh of Culross and one or two Edinburgh burgesses who were prepared to invest in the local mineral resources.

The feuars of Culross abbey

Occupant feuars		Non-occupant feuars	
Resident Group 2	2	Group 1	1
Group 3	1	Group 2	14
Group 4	2	Group 3	4
Group 6	1	Group 8	16
Group 8	6		35
Non-resident group 2	3		
Group 3	1		
Group 5	1		
	17		

Note: Group 8 feuars may include burgesses or indwellers in Culross, not specifically designated as such.

4. Berwickshire and the Borders

The feuars on the barony of Coldingham

Occupant feuars		Non-occupant feaurs	
Resident Group 1	2	Group 1	1
Group 4	26	Group 2	3
	28	Group 4	2
		Group 8	2
			8

The feuing of the barony of Coldingham, belonging to that priory, is characterised by charters of small pieces of land in and around the touns of Coldingham and Eyemouth, including the commonty of Eyemouth which may have been taken under cultivation in an attempt to compensate for the war damage in the barony in the 1540s. It may have been that the devastated lands of the priory were not coveted by bigger feuars. King James V had obtained from the pope a blanket licence to feu lands belonging to those monasteries held by his sons *in commendam,* and it is worth noticing in this connection that John Stewart, commendator of Coldingham, feued much of the priory's lands in the decade before the Reformation, at the same time as his brother, James, as commendator of Melrose, was feuing the barony of Kylesmure in Ayrshire as the result of an agreement with the tenants there.

The feuars of Jedburgh abbey

Occupant feuars		Non-occupant feuars	
Resident Group 4	1	Group 2	4
Non-resident Group 2	1		4
Group 3	2		
	4		

There is only a very small number of extant charters for Jedburgh abbey. Lancie Ainslie in Oxnamtounhead is the only feuar who can with certainty be called a resident occupant of the lands he feued.[107] The other two occupants were non-resident tack-holders, burgesses of Jedburgh, and a fourth was William Douglas of Bonjedburgh.[108]

In the case of Kelso abbey there is a difference between the pattern of feuing in the abbey's lands in Roxburghshire and that in the barony of Lesmahagow in Lanarkshire. In Roxburghshire, where only 23 per cent of the feus went to occupants, there were only six residents but ten outsiders who feued the bulk of the lands among them.

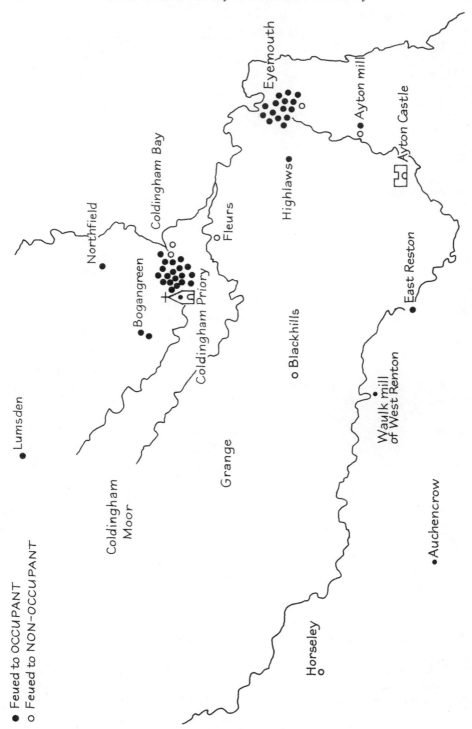

Map 4: The feuing of the barony of Coldingham.

Kelso abbey feuars in Roxburghshire

Occupant feuars		Non-occupant feuars	
Resident Group 2	2	Group 1	1
Group 4	4	Group 2	4
	6	Group 3	1
		Group 7	1
		Group 8	3
			10

In the abbey's Lanarkshire barony of Lesmahagow the situation was more favourable to the tenants, where the only non-occupant feuars were Sir James Hamilton of Finnart, whose charter of 1532 which conveyed the castle of Craignethan and twenty-two neighbouring lands keeps the actual percentage of land granted to occupants down to 46 per cent,[109] and David Collace, son of the laird of Balnamoon, who got a charter of eight territories in 1576.[110] Of the twenty-one occupants, only one was non-resident.

The feuars of the barony of Lesmahagow

Occupant feuars		Non-occupant feuars	
Resident Group 2	6	Group 2	2
Group 4	15		2
Non-resident Group 2	1		
	22		

The high proportion of feus granted to occupants of Melrose abbey's lands in Roxburghshire is surprising, considering how often this part of the property changed hands in the unsettled political conditions of the later 1560s. On 24 October 1566 the commendator, Michael Balfour, promised to give the earl of Bothwell a charter of all those Melrose lands 'not already set in feu'.[111] On 4 March 1568, after Bothwell's fall, Balfour gave the Regent Moray 5,000 merks for Bothwell's escheat and thereafter feued the forfeited lands to Alexander Balfour of Denmylne.[112] On 11 June 1568 Denmylne resigned into the commendator's hands the lands of Newstead in favour of the 'kyndlie tenentis therof alanerlie. Provyding always that in cais he dispone not the samen to the kyndlie tenentis or that thai cannot aggrie therupoun . . . anent the fewis therof and fulfillis not the aggreance, that the said Alexander salbe reponit agane be the said comendatar to his ryt of the samyn lyk as if this present resignatioun had nevir bene maid.'[113] The commendator and tenants did reach agreement, however, for in 1586 feus of the lands of Newstead were confirmed by the crown to thirty-two tenants.[114] Other lands of Melrose feued to the occupants on the resignation of a middleman were those of Lessudden, which were first feued to Arthur Sinclair in 1540 and resigned in 1556 by Mr Henry Sinclair, who had inherited them, after which they were feued to a number of tenants.[115] The final pattern on the Melrose lands in Roxburgh was as follows:

Melrose abbey's feuars in Roxburghshire

Occupant feuars		Non-occupant feuars	
Resident Group 2	1	Group 1	2
Group 4	81	Group 2	13
Non-Resident Group 3	1	Group 3	1
Group 4	1	Group 4	2
	84	Group 8	2
			20

5. Feuing on kirklands in the West of Scotland

The feuing of Melrose abbey's Ayrshire barony of Kylesmure began in earnest as the result of an agreement of May 1555 between the commendator and the kindly tenants, who account for the majority of occupant feuars. These people included small tenants who farmed their own land and lairds whose families had long been settled in this part of the upper Ayr valley — the 'Lollard country'. The land was feued at times in very small pieces in an area which was sufficiently highly populated to warrant the erection of a new parish around Muirkirk after the Reformation.

The feuars of Kylesmure

Occupant feuars		Non-occupant feuars	
Resident Group 2	15	Group 2	16
Group 4	32	Group 3	1
Group 8	19	Group 4	3
Non-resident Group 2	2	Group 5	1
	68	Group 8	4
			25

The barony of Glasgow, the lands of Paisley abbey in Renfrewshire and the barony of Kilwinning covered much of the low-lying land on each bank of the River Clyde, a few miles from its estuary, and the Cunninghame district of Ayrshire, south of the hilly border land between Ayrshire and Renfrewshire. The background to the feuing of all these areas is one of remarkable continuity of tenure among the rentallers, as tenants of all three church estates were called.

The feuars of the barony of Glasgow

Occupant feuars		Non-occupant feuars	
Resident Group 4	33	Group 1	1
Group 5	1	Group 2	1
Group 8	1	Group 5	1
Non-resident Group 1	1		3
Group 2	6		
Group 3	3		
Group 5	3		
	48		

Note: Lord Boyd feued lands in some of which he had previously been rentalled and others of which he was not the occupant. This was also true of John Hay, son of the parson of Renfrew.

Although the extant charters do not account for the whole barony of Glasgow, most of the bigger settlements are represented. About 80 per cent of the feus went to the rentallers. There were only three non-occupant feuars, Robert, Lord Boyd,[116] Thomas Crawford of Jordanhill[117] and John Hay, son of the parson of Renfrew.[118] In June 1579 Lord Boyd received a charter of the Whiteinch meadow and Newpark 'except those parts long since and now cultivated by the tenants and rentallers of East Partick'. A year later he feued the lands of Badlay, Molanys, Provost's Hauch and Cuninglaw in which he had been jointly rentalled with his wife in 1535 as the result of a contract, possibly a marriage contract, between himself and his father-in-law, George Colquhoun, who had previously held them. Boyd's case shows how non-resident occupants, such as noblemen and lairds, might acquire rentals in the same way as humbler tenants. According to his will drawn up before his death in 1590, Lord Boyd sublet his feu lands.[119] Several lairds feued land which they and their subtenants occupied, including James Foulis of Colinton, near Edinburgh, whose family had acquired the lands of Ramshorn and others through marriage with the Heriot family who had held them since at least 1518.[120] Three of the non-resident occupants who feued land between 1579 and 1581 were Archibald Wilson, burgess of Glasgow,[121] George Elphinston of Blythswood, who in 1579 received a charter of Gorbals and Bridgend which his forbears had rented since 1522,[122] and James Shields, burgess of Renfrew, whose family can be traced at West Schiell (whence they gradually took their surname, discarding the use of the patronymic) from 1525, and whose mother and her second husband actually lived on the holding which James feued.[123]

In the case of the thirty-three rentallers who became feuars, it is interesting to discover at times how they came to acquire and build up the holdings which they feued. Sometimes holdings were feued between relatives who already shared the farm, as with John and Robert Otterburn at Cowstoun.[124] Occasionally someone feued a holding which had been temporarily out of his family's possession. This happened to John Stirling at Gartinkirk, part of whose family holding had passed to the Provands in 1529, by marriage, and another part of it to William Gray, who returned it in 1549, 'which rental and kindness was bought by John Stirling, elder, by a contract'. John Stirling's great-great-grandson feued the land in 1581.[125] Sir James Hill, ex-chaplain, recovered his family's holding in Govan from his parents-in-law in 1564, on his post-Reformation marriage. Sixteen years later it was feued to his son, Thomas.[126]

Of the lands in the barony of Glasgow which were feued *en bloc,* eight were granted to non-resident occupants whose families had held them in rental for some time and whose feu charters need not have caused much local dislocation. The number of tenant-feuars on the farms of the barony varies from place to place, usually from two to eight. This may reflect the previous pattern of tenancy, but we must always allow for the fact that the charters of small feuars may have been lost trace of, or may never have been confirmed by the crown. The Tables in Appendix A illustrate the pre- and post-feuing pattern of tenure on the barony. The general picture is one of continuity even although feuing came comparatively late to the archbishop's lands, very largely in and around 1580. Crawford of Jordanhill appears to be the only example of land speculation, backed in his case by political pressure from the Regent Morton. It is not surprising that the cathedral chapter objected to his proposed charter, saying 'that they were unwilling to enter a preparative consenting to the few of the landis and rowmis being of the patrimony of the said Archebischoprik quhilkis ar possessit be auld and kyndlie rentalit tenentis'.[127]

The feuars of Paisley abbey in Renfrewshire

Occupant feuars		Non-occupant feuars	
Resident Group 2	3	Group 1	3
Group 3	42	Group 2	6
Group 4	19	Group 5	2
Group 8	60	Group 8	6
	124		17

```
Non-resident Group 1      2
           Group 2      5
           Group 5      1
                       ───
                       132
```

Note: Discounting the fifteenth-century charters to 42 burgesses of the newly created burgh of Paisley, the ratio of occupants to non-occupants becomes 90 to 17.

The lands of Paisley abbey stretched from the lordship of Kilpatrick on the right bank of the Clyde, a little to the north-west of the barony of Glasgow, across the Clyde into Renfrewshire, along the left bank of the Black Cart, with the greatest concentration of territories lying between that river and the White Cart on which stood the monastery and the settlement which became a burgh of barony in 1488, then south-westwards into Lochwinnoch parish on the Ayrshire border, with a group known collectively as the lordship of Glen. The abbey's barony of Monkton in Kyle is not included in this survey.

The feuing of the Paisley lands falls into two periods and concerns two distinct areas: the property in and around Paisley itself, feued soon after the erection of the burgh, and the more outlying parts of the estates feued in mid-sixteenth century. About 80 per cent of the feus went to sitting tenants. The resident occupants include forty-two burgesses, eighteen persons designated *in* the lands they feued and three small lairds who feued land near to that which they held heritably and which they already cultivated with their own servants and sub-tenants.

The non-occupants were three members of noble houses, Andrew, Master of Semple,[128] Michael, brother of Lord Elphinston[129] and David Erskine, commendator of Dryburgh;[130] six lairds and two ecclesiastics — Gavin Hamilton, commendator of Kilwinning,[131] and sir Thomas Dickson, vicar of Torphichen.[132] The names only of some feuars are given; we know that one of them, Robert Aschindor, was the abbey janitor.[133]

By the end of the fifteenth century the village which had grown up beside the monastery, inhabited by artisans, agricultural labourers and the abbey servants, straggling as it did along the king's highway leading to the bridge over the River Cart and on to Glasgow, had increased in size and activity sufficiently to merit its being granted burghal status like Arbroath, Newburgh and Dunfermline. The charter creating the burgh was granted by King James IV in 1488 but, five years before, Abbot George Shaw had asked papal permission to set the lands of the toun of Paisley in feu-ferm. On 2 June 1490 a feu contract was drawn up between abbot and burgesses, forty-two of whom then received individual charters.[134]

Under the abbacy of John Hamilton (later also archbishop of St Andrews), from 1525 to 1571, and the commendatorships of Lord Claud Hamilton and William Erskine later in the sixteenth century, feu charters to some extent reinforced a trend apparent in the Paisley rental, which we have already looked at, towards the replacement of tenants by lairds and other influential outsiders. For example, in March 1561 Archbishop John Hamilton, as abbot, granted a charter of the lands of Barns, Culboy Easter and Wester to Gavin Hamilton, the commendator of Kilwinning, in liferent, and to his son in feu-ferm. Parts of Barns had long been set to members of the Knock family, Thomas Knock being a tenant as early as 1460 and John Knock, the last of the family to be named as a rentaller, being entered to his father's holding in 1554.[135] In 1580 commendator William Erskine made a large grant of land in the lordship of Kilpatrick, previously set to a number of tenants, to David Erskine, commendator of Dryburgh, whose feu charter names twenty occupants whose families can be traced back in some cases to the rental of 1460. There had been Stewarts at Barroger since 1465, but these lands were feued to John Blair of that Ilk in 1582, when they were said to be occupied by 'John Stewart and others of his name'.[136]

Happily, there is a brighter side to the feuing of the Paisley lands in that seventy-five tenants took feus of their holdings under the later commendators. As can be seen from the breakdown of the tenancy/feuing pattern in Appendix A, the ancestors of a number of these feuars were in possession from the early sixteenth century at least, and a glance through the still earlier rentals shows that a fair number of their families were tenants in the same lands from the second half of the fifteenth century. The lands of Meikleriggs were feued in 1581 to three tenants, Robert and John Slater and Robert Wilson, whose families appear there in 1502 and 1508 respectively.[137] Robert Slater, his father and his brother cultivated the farm between them when it was taken in feu. The Orr family had held Jaffraytack since at least 1460, eventually feuing it in 1556.[138] In spite of the menace from outsiders, therefore, some Paisley tenants benefited from the coming of feu-ferm, obtaining heritable possession of holdings which they, as kindly tenants, had passed from one generation to another by customary right.

The feuars of Kilwinning abbey
(Baronies of Kilwinning and Beith)

Occupant feuars		Non-occupant feuars	
Resident Group 2	7	Group 1	2
Group 4	18	Group 2	16
Group 5	1	Group 4	1
Group 7	1	Group 5	1
Group 8	44		20
Non-resident Group 2	1		
Group 3	2		
Group 4	2		
	76		

The Kilwinning lands lay mainly in the baronies of Kilwinning and Beith, with a grange in Kilmarnock parish and a handful of farms in what is now the parish of Darvel. The pattern of feuing in the baronies of Kilwinning and Beith, separated as they were by Dalry parish, differed noticeably.

The environs of the monastery itself resembled those of Paisley abbey: standing beside the king's highway, in this case the main route south-westwards, surrounded by a small built-up area clinging to the precincts and inhabited by the same sort of people, agricultural labourers, traders, craftsmen, one or two notaries, a miller, a king's messenger and the monastery's servants, domestic and administrative. Although Kilwinning did not become a burgh of barony at this time, when this status was being conferred on similar communities, nevertheless in 1473 King James III granted the abbot and monks power to hold chamberlain courts on their lands, and there are references in the records to a market and miller's crosses.[139] The close proximity of the royal burgh of Irvine probably prevented the creation of another burgh in the district.

In addition to the central part of the township, clustered about the abbey, there were intensively cultivated settlements at Corsehill, Easter and Wester Bridgend, at either end of the bridge over the River Garnock, Nethermains, Overmains, Kilrig or Oxenward, and at Byres. The tenants of Kilwinning abbey must have been perpetually aware of their landlord in this low-lying part of the country, for the twin western towers of the massive abbey kirk were visible from most of the settlements and farmtouns mentioned in the charters. There are indications that the barony of Kilwinning was highly populated, upwards of fifty farms being named in the rentals, often set to tenants in very small holdings. These farms lay most thickly in the flat, somewhat marshy part of the barony between the abbey and the boundary with Stevenston parish, also along the valley of the Garnock on which stood the grain and waulk mills, and between that river and the Lugton, on the boundary with the barony of Eglinton. In the barony of Beith the abbey tenants lived mostly on the Grange on the opposite, southern side of Kilbirnie and Barr lochs from Paisley abbey's lordship of Glen.

Fifty-two per cent of the feus were granted to occupants, which suggests, at first glance, that the tenants were just able to hold their own with outsiders. A closer look at the feus, however, shows that a higher proportion of land in the barony of Beith than in that of Kilwinning went to outsiders and that, with regard to Kilwinning itself, those parts of the barony feued to the occupants were the best arable lands, while the middlemen tended to feu small pieces in and around the toun of Kilwinning itself, with meadowland along the Garnock. In any case, where outsiders were to be found there were also tenant-feuars. One prominent outsider, Robert Hamilton, younger of Dalserf, the abbey chamberlain, feued a number of houses and yards around the monastery.[140] The largest grant of land to a non-occupant, *en bloc,* was the charter to the duke of Chatelherault in 1553 of the lands of Monkcastle.[141] Sixteen of the outsiders were lairds and their relatives, many of them Hamiltons, benefiting from the abbacy of Alexander Hamilton in the 1540s and the commendatorship of Gavin Hamilton of Raploch in the 1550s and 1560s.

The forty-four feuars whose names only are given all feued very small holdings which they occupied. The remaining resident occupants were eighteen tenants designated *in* the lands which they feued, the families of many of whom had been in possession for several generations, William Kirkpatrick, a former monk and first minister of Kilwinning who feued his chamber and yard in the abbey precincts,[142] and Thomas Ezat, messenger-at-arms, who had a charter of his house and garden in the Abbey Green and of several neighbouring yards.[143]

Gavin Hamilton granted a number of feus to his relatives, including Margaret Hamilton of Broomhill, his mistress, who became his wife after the Reformation.[144] Alexander Cunningham, son of the earl of Glencairn, who was still under age when he became commendator in 1571 on the death of Gavin Hamilton during the civil war, also granted land to his family, sometimes cancelling the charters of forfeited Hamilton feuars.[145]

Clearly, a fair number of Kilwinning tenants were able to feu their holdings, a great many doing so between 1557 and 1560, suggesting an eleventh-hour feuing policy by Gavin Hamilton, who was a careful, middle-of-the-way man as far as the Reformation-settlement was concerned.

Whatever the variety of local conditions and patterns of feuing, it is interesting to find that over 63 per cent of the feus recorded in surviving charters were granted to sitting tenants, over 60 per cent of whom were below the class of laird or proprietor and were now receiving their first piece of heritable property. Feuing did much to entrench the tenant class in many of those parts of Scotland which had been church estates. One feels that the 'owner-occupied' look of a town like Tayport may have had distant origins in Archbishop John Hamilton's charter to the seventy-eight householders of the then South Ferrytoun of Portincraig.[146] The social effects of this sixteenth-century boom in proprietorship will be more closely considered in a later Chapter. The way it appears to have suffered a recession, as small feus were swallowed up in the seventeenth and eighteenth centuries, is another story altogether.

Notes

1 Edin. testaments, CC 8/8/3, fo. 226v
2 *Melrose Regality,* III, 236-37, 357-63
3 *R.M.S.,* V, 2332
4 *Ibid.,* V, 173
5 J. Grant and W. Leslie, *Survey of the Province of Moray,* 74
6 *R.M.S.,* IV, 1947
7 *Ibid.,* IV, 1660, 1915, 1977
8 R.F.C., i, fo. 135r
9 *R.M.S.,* IV, 1961
10 *Ibid.,* IV, 2588, 3007
11 *Ibid.,* IV, 2731
12 *Ibid.,* IV, 2542, 2918; V, 988, 1046, 1276, 1301; R.F.C., ii, fo. 118r
13 *Ibid.,* ii, fo. 109r
14 *R.M.S.,* IV, 2918
15 *Ibid.,* IV, 2469, 2663; V, 1095, 1096, 1097; *R.S.S.,* VII, 129; R.F.C., ii, fo. 227r
16 *R.M.S.,* IV, 2223, 2542; V, 573, 1301
17 R.F.C., ii, fos. 118r, 258r, 269r
18 *R.M.S.,* IV, 1660
19 *Ibid.,* IV, 2566
20 R.F.C., ii, fos. 185r, 209r
21 *Ibid.,* ii, fo. 227r; *R.M.S.,* V, 1096; *R.S.S.,* VII, 129
22 R.F.C., ii, fo. 258r
23 *Ibid.,* ii, fo. 269r
24 *R.M.S.,* IV, 1660
25 J. Stuart, *Records of the Monastery of Kinloss,* 151
26 R.F.C., ii, fo. 112r
27 *R.M.S.,* IV, 2667
28 R.F.C., ii, fo. 268r
29 J.F.S. Gordon, *Book of the Chronicles of Keith,* 7
30 R.F.C., ii, fo. 34r
31 *Ibid.,* ii, fo. 13r; *R.M.S.,* IV, 2614, 2615, 2616, 2618, 2622
32 *Ibid.,* IV, 2619, 2620, 2621, 2689, 3036; R.F.C., ii, fo. 45r

33 *Ibid.,* ii, fos. 23r, 244r
34 *Ibid.,* ii, fo. 44r
35 Secretary's Register of Sasines for Banff (S.R.O.), RS 15/1, *passim*
36 *N.S.A.,* XIII, 216
37 Inventory of Montrose Writs (S.R.O.), transcript only, GD 220 Vol 1, 100
38 *R.M.S.,* V, 2210
39 *Ibid.,* IV, 1735
40 *Ibid.,* IV, 1699
41 *Cupar,* I, 289
42 *Ibid.,* I, 286; II, 221
43 *Ibid.,* I, 143
44 *Ibid.,* II, 52; R.S.S., lii, fo. 162r
45 *R.M.S.,* IV, 2039, 2376; R.F.C., i, fo. 59r
46 *Cupar,* I, 263
47 *Ibid.,* I, 310; II, 96; R.F.C., i, fo. 54r
48 *Ibid.,* i, fo. 128r; R.S.S., liii, fo. 3v
49 *Cupar,* II, 112; R.F.C., i, fo. 270r
50 *Cupar,* II, 50, 104; *R.M.S.,* IV, 1788
51 *Cupar,* II, 34; *R.M.S.,* IV, 1791
52 *Cupar,* II, 121; R.F.C., i, fo. 270r
53 R.S.S., liii, fo. 14r
54 *R.M.S.,* V, 2229
55 *Ibid.,* V, 1231; Douglas collection (S.R.O.), GD 98/414; R.F.C., i, fo. 177r
56 Inventory of Ramsay of Bamff muniments (S.R.O.), GD 83, p. 137
57 R.F.C., ii, fo. 294r
58 *Ibid.,* i, fo. 63r
59 *Ibid.,* i, fo. 229r
60 *Ibid.,* i, fo. 204r
61 *R.M.S.,* V, 681
62 R.F.C., i, fo. 296r
63 *R.M.S.,* IV, 1602
64 R.F.C., ii, fo. 258r
65 *R.M.S.,* IV, 1983
66 *Ibid.,* IV, 1473
67 R.F.C., ii, fo. 264r
68 *Ibid.,* i, fo. 37r
69 *R.M.S.,* IV, 1708
70 *Ibid.,* V, 982
71 *Ibid.,* V, 926
72 *Ibid.,* V, 948
73 *Ibid.,* V, 1778
74 R.F.C., ii, fo. 322r
75 *R.M.S.,* V, 775, 973, 1117
76 *Ibid.,* V, 929, 932; R.F.C., i, fo. 243r
77 *Ibid.,* i, fo. 57r
78 *Ibid.,* i, fo. 96r; ii, fo. 255r; *R.M.S.,* V, 939, 955
79 R.F.C., i, fo. 56r
80 *Ibid.,* i, fos. 48r, 53r
81 *R.M.S.,* V, 947
82 R.F.C., ii, fo. 263r
83 *Ibid.,* i, fo. 66r
84 *Ibid.,* ii, fo. 291r
85 *Ibid.,* i, fo. 59r
86 *Ibid.,* i, fos. 61r-62r
87 *Ibid.,* ii, fo. 262r
88 *R.M.S.,* IV, 41
89 *Ibid.,* IV, 1693
90 *Ibid.,* IV, 2709
91 *Ibid.,* IV, 1458, 2105
92 *Ibid.,* V, 585

93 R.F.C., ii, fo. 201r
94 *R.M.S.*, IV, 2102
95 R.F.C., ii, fo. 235r; Register House Charters, RH 6/1990
96 Erroll charters (formerly GD 175/444) (S.R.O.), RH 1/6, microfilm
97 Morton muniments, GD 150/36/2
98• *R.M.S.*, V, 150
99 R.F.C., i, fos. 36r-37r
100 *Ibid.*, i, fo. 264r; *R.M.S.*, IV, 2394; V, 35
101 R.F.C., i, fos. 80r, 140r
102 *R.M.S.*, IV, 2326
103 *Ibid.*, IV, 1475, 1476, 1477
104 Acts and decreets, xxxv, fo. 294r
105 Dunfermline tacks, CH 6/3/1, fos. 81v-IIIr
106 Pitreavie papers (S.R.O.), GD 91/39
107 *R.M.S.*, V, 1303
108 *Ibid.*, III, 2780
109 *Ibid.*, V, 2008
110 Closeburn Writs (S.R.O.), GD 19/1/19
111 Register of deeds, old series, viii, fo. 427r
112 *Ibid.*, ix, fo. 262r; *R.M.S.*, IV, 1819
113 Morton muniments, GD 150/1462
114 R.S.S., liv, fo. 153v
115 *Melrose Regality*, III, 232-37
116 *R.M.S.*, IV, 2937; V, 509
117 *Ibid.*, IV, 2199
118 *Ibid.*, V, 90
119 Edin. testaments, CC 8/8/21, fo. 238r
120 *Glasgow registers*, I, 76, 128, 161, 186; *R.M.S.*, V, 465
121 R.F.C., ii, fo. 206
122 *R.M.S.*, IV, 2938; *Glasgow registers*, I, 82
123 *Ibid.*, I, 74; *R.M.S.*, V, 659
124 *Ibid.*, V, 1018
125 *Glasgow registers*, I, 93, 103, 143; *R.M.S.*, V, 522
126 *Glasgow registers*, I, 158, 182; *R.M.S.*, V, 581
127 *R.P.C.*, II, 110
128 R.F.C., ii, fo. 163r
129 *R.M.S.*, V, 302
130 *Ibid.*, V, 128
131 *Ibid.*, IV, 234
132 S.A.S. collection, GD 103/1/55
133 R.S.S., l, fo. 31r
134 *Paisley*, 154-58
135 *Ibid.*, Appendix, cxlvi
136 *Ibid.*, Appendix, lvi; R.F.C., ii, fo. 229r
137 *Paisley*, Appendix, cxx, cxxii; *R.M.S.*, V, 264, 300; R.F.C., ii, fo. 185r
138 *Paisley*, Appendix, lxxxviii, *R.M.S.*, IV, 2778
139 Eglinton muniments, GD 3/1/727
140 *Ibid.*, GD 3/1352
141 *R.M.S.*, V, 1132
142 R.F.C., ii, fo. 54r
143 *Ibid.*, ii, fo. 129r
144 *R.M.S.*, IV, 2633
145 *Ibid.*, IV, 2374, 2489, 2747; V, 94, 341; *R.S.S.*, VI, 1195
146 *R.M.S.*, V, 2332

8

The Property

'. . . ane yard, barn, upper chamber and garden and ane little hous pulled down and the knowe thereof.'

Feu charter to John Gregory in South Ferrytoun of Portincraig: Register House Charters, RH 6/2437

THE hundreds of feu charters, stereotyped legal documents though they may be, contain a bonus of graphic detail about the pattern of holdings, the methods of cultivation and land use in general. They reveal what a wide variety of property was actually set in feu-ferm: arable land, sometimes accompanied by pasture rights, buildings and premises, mills, brewhouses, orchards, woods and fishings. Land might be designated according to *old extent* — the five merkland or five poundland. It might be delineated according to its geographical extent — in acres, husbandlands, oxgangs or in small portions such as roods, rigs or even butts. Sometimes it was indicated whether the land had been recently cultivated, or was lying waste, and there are many examples of the use of local field names, derived from their ownership, use or physical appearance.

Many grants were of the arable land in and around a settlement; 'the toun lands of', or, in cases where the place was feued as a unit, 'the toun *and* lands of'. In some cases a settlement and its arable land clung around a monastery, as at Scone, Dryburgh, Kilwinning, Kinloss, Coldingham, Newbattle and Lindores. Elsewhere considerable touns had flourished in fertile spots in the open country, as at Lessudden and Newstead (Melrose), Punderlaw (Arbroath), Inveresk and Monktounhall (Dunfermline) and Kincaple and Raderny (St Andrews archbishopric). Others were definitely fostered, such as Keithick which began as a cottartoun and in 1492 was created a burgh of barony for Coupar Angus abbey. Over and above these were the countless farms scattered over the arable countryside.

Different types of property might be packaged together in one feu. In 1580 Ninian Bruce, brother of Bruce of Powfoulis, received a feu of fifty-nine acres in the toun of Dryburgh, occupied by sixteen tenants, a house built in the Byregreen, another one on the east side of the toun of Dryburgh next to the waulk mill and one next to the market cross of the toun, five separate yards, one of which was next to the monastery's 'mantill wall', a new yard on the south side of the mill dam, one next to that of a canon of Dryburgh, a yard with three wells built in it on the west of the cloister wall, with the right to operate a ferry on the River Tweed.[1]

The Mains of most baronies, where these were feued, were granted as complete units; this certainly happened with the Mains of Ethie (Arbroath), Farnell (Brechin), Crossraguel, Kinghorn-Easter (Dunfermline), Aberlady (Dunkeld), Haddington nunnery, Holywood, Inchaffray, Restenneth (Jedburgh), Strathisla (Kinloss), Mauchline (Melrose) and Whithorn, all of which went to non-occupant feuars. There were one or two exceptions to this pattern; the Overmains and Nethermains of Kilwinning, long leased to tenants, were feued among sixteen occupants, those of Creuchies and Clien belonging to Scone abbey to twelve tenants and the Mains of Lesmahagow in Kelso abbey's Lanarkshire barony to nineteen.

Many abbey granges, or at least lands which had earlier been granges, were feued. The pattern on those of Coupar Angus varied, as we have already seen, with seven surviving charters of Balbrogie and five for Carsegrange, whereas the whole grange of Kincreich was granted to Thomas Kennedy of Coif.[2] On the grange of Lindores forty-two oxgangs were feued among six tenants, while fifty-six went to Mr James McGill, the Clerk Register, in whose charter the names of another eight tenants are mentioned. The grange of Culross, lying only a mile or two from the abbey, was divided by the sixteenth century into West, Middle, East and Byre granges, the last three being feued as units between 1549 and 1558. Newbattle abbey's lands of Prestongrange were feued in 1559 to Alexander Hume, son of the laird of Coldenknowes, and consisted of eighty-two acres, with the manor and coal heuchs.[3] Hume also had a charter of the abbey's Newtoungrange.[4]

There is often detailed information on the local patterns of cultivation, worked out over the years, with the enumeration of small pieces of land then being consolidated into one feu. Two charters of ground around the burgh of Cullen in Banffshire, belonging to the collegiate church there, list and name separately thirty-two individual crofts lying in 'the Langruiddis', 'the Seyruiddis (Sea roods)' and 'the field crofts'.[5] When Alexander Hamilton in Preston got a charter of the lands and toun of Preston from the commendator of Newbattle, these were said to consist of twelve acres altogether, divided into six different 'lots'.[6] Sometimes land is actually said to be 'in run rig', usually where tenants were feuing their own fixed-run-rig holdings, as at Caputh, Dalguise, Dalgarthill and Dowally in the barony of Dunkeld. The charter of one Dunkeld tenant, John Haggart, speaks of 'the middle part of that quarter', run-rig, of the lands of Wester Caputh occupied by John and his mother, and three rigs of another middle part, 'the Craggy rig in the Querrell-hoill, the Cruikit rig liand contigue adjacent therto in the same sched, and the Braid rig liand in the east and west sydis of the Cobill gait', suggesting that the holdings of some tenants were still fairly scattered.[7] Thomas Innes feued 'six parts of Wester Crolaittis in runrig' in the barony of Strathisla, where small feuars can be found at the end of the century exchanging land units in an attempt to consolidate their holdings.[8] Andrew Hoppringle feued land near the toun of Blainslie (Melrose) 'in run rig'[9] and John Jordan six 'buttis' of land, run-rig, near Newbattle.[10] Three feuars divided between them the lands of Brochtounscheillis belonging to Stobo parish kirk, 'lying in run-rig', on which they undertook to build within three years 'ane stane hous with lime ... to keep thair geir frae thevis and reaveris'.[11] There is a reference to *rundale* at Inveresk in Midlothian, in 1556.[12]

Many examples occur of local names for crofts, yards, fields and meadows, some of them of agricultural origin and others derived from their connection with a monastery or church: 'the *pettie commone* aikeris', 'the *terraris* medo', 'the *elimosinaris* field', 'the crofts of St Thomas the Apostle' at Dunkeld, 'the vicartoun' at Girvan parish kirk in Ayrshire, 'two acres called the kirk-door-keyis' at Leuchars parish kirk in Fife, 'the *cellaris* medo' at Lindores abbey, 'St Michael's acres' in the canonry of Ross and 'the prioriscroft' at Paisley.

Occasionally there is reference to the physical features of the land: 'the shady half', 'the sunny half', 'the shadow pleuch of the sunny side'. There is mention of *corn lands* and *bere lands*. A number of charters include pieces of waste land, or of land not previously cultivated; in Coldingham barony the lands of Horsely had been 'uncultivated many years' and the mill lands of Coldstream, feued in 1579, were said to have been 'destroyed in the war with the English'. In 1570 the lands of Elcho nunnery were described as being 'devoid of inhabitants'. To feu land like this would most likely mean paying a small feu-duty, with the prospect of returns from reclaimed and recultivated land. There are some charters of reclaimed land, notably in the bishopric of Caithness between 1556 and 1575, while the lands of Ballinknock were said to be 'newly improved' and the mill of Migdale and its croft newly cultivated.

According to Sir James Balfour, it was against the law for the 'place' of a monastery, its yards and buildings, to be set in feu-ferm, since this prejudiced the rights of the king as patron of the *prelacies,* the greater benefices such as bishoprics, abbeys and priories.[13] Nevertheless, there are many charters of land and buildings around monastic precincts and even one or two feus of the *place* and dwelling quarters. In 1582 Esme Stuart, as commendator of Arbroath, granted to lord Ogilvy the tower of the abbey with some yards and the dovecot.[14] There are one or two feus of the 'barn croft' of Balmerino, right beside the abbey.[15] At Sweetheart abbey Cuthbert Brown was granted a merkland called 'Under-the-wall', lying on the north of the abbey wall, reserving a strip three feet wide to the abbot and monks for a right-of-way.[16]

The word *orchard* often occurs in the legal jargon of the charters, but there are some cases where it may be taken literally; the earl of Rothes, for example, feued the orchard and east yard of Lindores, with the stanks, hedges and walls surrounding them and the 'use of the fruit growing therein',[17] James Anderson, burgess of Perth, feued Scone abbey's orchard 'in the Drumhar above the upper mill of Perth',[18] and John Abercrombie the lands of Throsk belonging to Cambuskenneth abbey, containing the orchard, for which his feu-duty included 1,000 apples and pears.[19] James Beaton of Creich feued the orchard and 'plowme yaird' of Balmerino.[20]

Some feuars acquired what can only be described as a *site,* on which they doubtless planned to build or which they intended to turn over to cultivation. John Gregory, a tenant in the South Ferrytoun of Portincraig, got a variety of property there, including 'ane yard, barn, upper chamber and garden and ane little house, pulled down, and the knowe thereof'.[21] Robert Mathieson got from the priory of Pittenweem a piece of waste ground, thirty-six feet long and eighteen feet wide, under the priory wall, with the 'to-fall' built against it next to the Water Wynd.[22] Robert Ashindor had a feu of the site on which Paisley abbey's smithy had formerly stood.[23]

Grants of mills accompany innumerable charters of arable land. In some cases these were feued to the families who operated them, becoming their heritable possession, at other times mills went to outsiders. The corn mill and waulk mill of Kilwinning were feued to the men who had long leased them, John Miller[24] and William Walker.[25] A share in the mill of Badlay in the barony of Glasgow was included in the feu charters of twenty-one rentallers there. The brewhouse, sometimes called 'the common brewhouse' or 'alehouse', is mentioned almost as often as the mill. Many of these were conveyed as part of the pertinents of the feu and, presumably, were sources of income, many being operated on a monopoly basis with the barony lands thirled to them, as in the case of the mill.

Fishings were often extremely lucrative, to judge by the high feu-duties demanded. These were sometimes feued by burgesses who then sublet their rights to the local people. Gilbert Collison, burgess of Aberdeen, paid £104 commutation for twenty barrels of salmon, with £1 augmentation, for half the fishings of 'raik and stellis' on the River Dee and the teinds of certain other fishings, all of which he and his predecessors had held on lease 'for a long time'.[26] Alexander Knowles, an Aberdeen merchant, paid £38 feu-duty for fishings on the River Don.[27] There are feu charters of fishings in the Rivers Stinchar, Girvan, Nith, Ayr, Dee (Galloway), Deveron, Teith, Tay, Eden, Ericht, Findhorn, Spey, Ness and Lossie. Archbishop David Beaton gave a feu of fishings in Lochleven to Douglas of Lochleven in 1544.[28] Grants of fishings accompany a number of feus in Orkney and Caithness. In 1546 David Crichton of Nauchton had a charter of all the fishings of Balmerino abbey.[29]

When Adam Dundas of Knock got his feu charter of the lands of Findhorn in 1571 it included the liberty to fish in the sea there and the right of 'ferryboat' in the bay.[30] John Grant of Culcabock acquired ferry rights, similarly, with a grant of land beside the River Spey.[31] The widow of Patrick Scott, a tenant of the bishop of Dunkeld at Caputh, and her son John Scott were given a feu of 'the boatland of Caputh' at a point on the river now crossed by a bridge, together with some fishings.[32] David Wood, fiar of Craig, with his son, received a charter of 'the ferryboat and passage of Montrose' and fishings called 'St Thomas's net' on the River North Esk, paying £6 for the ferry rights and £10 for the fishings.[33]

Any attempt to estimate the amount of church land feued by the end of the sixteenth century, against that still held in tack and rental, must be inconclusive. In the case of most sizeable estates some of the lands mentioned in the early seventeenth-century charters, which created them secular lordships, are missing in the earlier feu charters. For example, eight known territories do not appear in the case of Holyrood, sixteen in that of Kinloss, twenty-one in the case of Kilwinning, fifteen in that of Dunfermline abbey's lands in Midlothian, ten in the case of

Scone, thirty-four in Paisley, twenty-nine in Newbattle, thirty-six in the barony of Glasgow and fifty-six in the case of Arbroath.

Admittedly, many of these 'missing' lands are crofts and small pieces which may not have been individually designated in the feu charters but appear in those of the erection of temporal lordships, which are very detailed. Besides, the loss of charters must be taken into account. The impression is that the majority of church estates were mostly feued before the Act of Annexation of 1587, which transferred the superiority of church land to the crown. When feuing was begun on an estate it was not necessarily carried through as a comprehensive programme but was often sporadic and piecemeal. Information in the Books of Assumption, compiled in the 1560s for government information, often shows feu-ferm and other tenures existing side by side, as in the following part of the rental of lands in Fife belonging to Lindores abbey:[34]

Lands	How held
The grange, eight ploughgates	feu-ferm
Berryhoill, four ploughgates	feu-ferm
Ormistoun, two ploughgates	feu-ferm
Haltounhill, two ploughgates	life-tack
Lumquhat, two ploughgates	feu-ferm
Toft of Woodhead, with Southwood	feu-ferm
Eastwood, with the teinds	feu-ferm
The brewhouse of Grange	feu-ferm
The burgh maills (of Newburgh)	feu-ferm
Tenants of Newburgh	feu-ferm
Tenement in St Andrews	feu-ferm
Deracht land of Creich	19-year tack
Toft of Cullesse (Collessie)	feu-ferm
Toft of Kinlocht	19-year tack
Brewhouse of Ochtermochtrie	feu-ferm
Toft of Old Lindores	19-year tack
Cluny-easter	feu-ferm
Lodging in Falkland	feu-ferm
Craigend	feu-ferm
Marie croft	19-year tack
Craig mill	feu-ferm
The 'Clayis', with parts of meadow land	feu-ferm
Reid inch, with yards	feu-ferm
Thirty-one acres in the Hauch	'set for maill'
Brodlands and meadows	'set yearly, at two merks per acre'
The Almerycruik	feu-ferm
The acres under the Wood	'set for maill yearly'
Cow inch and the 'hillok park', the east yard and fishings	feu-ferm

At about the same time thirty-three lands belonging to the priory of St Andrews were shown to be feued, as against twenty-one still leased.[35] The rental of the bishopric of St Andrews, as it appears in the Books of Assumption, speaks of 'certain lands set in feu-ferm',[36] suggesting that others had not been feued, although an early programme is suggested by the fact that by September 1545 feuing had progressed sufficiently on the archbishop's lands to warrant the drawing up of a new rental book.[37] Some church estates, on the other hand, appear to have been entirely feued. All those comprising the estates of Inchcolm abbey are listed with the memorandum, 'thir landis ar all set in few and confeirmit.'[38] A statement in court by an Inchaffray tenant in 1556, that 'the commendatar hes fewit all the haill lordschip of Inchaffray,' shows that the change there had taken place comparatively early.[39]

Basically, the feu charter conveyed the right to and use of the *property* of the land from granter to grantee, the former keeping the *superiority* and the right to receive feu-duty. When the commendator of Dunfermline, having redeemed from his brother, Mr John Pitcairn, the eighth part of the lands of Masterton, resigned them in favour of John Kellock, the kindly tenant, so that the latter might be put in possession of them, in feu-ferm, he stated, in the usual legal formula,'...be the tennor of thir presentis we for us, our airis and assignis renuncis ... all heretable ryt ... propertie and possessioun quhilk we have ...'[40] The circumstances at Masterton demanded this separate deed of renunciation of the property but, in effect, every feu charter was just that. While, in theory, granter and grantee (superior and feuar) exchanged use of the property in return for feu-duty, nevertheless the granter could, in drawing up the charter, place any obligations, restrictions or privileges he cared on the feuar.

Some of the obligations in feu-ferm charters were similar to those required from tack-holders and rentallers, including duties such as carriage service, preservation of boundaries and attendance at the head courts of the barony or regality. Where the tenant became the feuar, these obligations would simply be carried over. The tenants of Dowally, Dalgarthill and Caputh in the barony of Dunkeld, who had their holdings converted to feus in the 1570s, were obliged, in addtition to their feu-duties, to perform one carriage, providing a horse and servant, and fifteen to twenty loads of peat. William Borrie, feuar of Little Dalmernock, in the same barony, was asked for twenty loads of peat and 'ane schort and ane lang day work with ane horss'.[41] John Melville in Coldingham, who feued several cotlands there including the one on which he lived, had to give twelve days' work, four in 'turf tyme', four at hay-making and four at harvest, with the usual arriage and carriage.[42] Where the feuar was an outsider, presumably his subtenants rendered these services.

Some new obligations were written into feu charters, however, not necessarily previously required from the tenants, but part of the bargain between superior and feuar. In this way, for example, some superiors transferred the burden of estate management on to the feuar's shoulders. George Gordon of Blairdinnie, in getting a feu of the Haugh of Bogy from the bishop of Aberdeen, was required to build two *outsetts* near the castlehill of Drymminmure to guard the marches of Clatt.[43] David Boswell of Glassmonth was obliged to make improvements to the lands of Cullelo in the regality of Dunfermline.[44] John Cairns, who received the feu of some ruined houses in St Andrews from the commendator of the priory, undertook to repair and rebuild them to the value of £40 within four years.[45] When Thomas Alexander feued the kirklands of Stobo parish kirk, he and his heirs were required to live there, to build houses and plant trees.[46]

Many superiors, on the other hand, included well-defined reservations to themselves of rights in and use of the property. Although there are many general grants of mineral rights and feus of coal pits and salt pans themselves, there are at the same time as many reservations of these to the granters. The abbot and monks of Paisley, in feuing half the lands of Nether Gallowhill to John White, the tenant, reserved to themselves the use of all stone quarried in the locality; John and his father, as it happened, were quarriers working for the abbey.[47] The commendator of Melrose reserved the use of coal mined on land feued to Hamilton of Sanquhar, during any time when the commendator happened to be living in his castle of Mauchline.[48] In another charter of land near Mauchline, this time to Adam Cunningham in Ayr, the commendator allowed Cunningham to use coal found on the land 'without undue interference or damage to the soil', a ban on any serious development of the coal pits.[49] Alexander Erskine was forbidden by the commendator of Inchmahome priory to sell or use wood for the benefit of himself or his subtenants.[50] Ten stones of all lime found on the lands of Wester Kinghorn were reserved to Dunfermline abbey[51] and the same superior reserved every ninth load of coal from Natoun at Musselburgh and all coal mined on the lands of Lathanis in Fife.[52]

On the commonty of Eyemouth, several pieces of which were feued to inhabitants of that toun, William Hume in Whitrig was obliged to preserve a 'way' on three sides of the portion feued to him so that 'kartis and wainis' could easily pass to and from the priory of Coldingham.[53] An interesting reservation occurs in a charter of the prior of Monymusk in 1580, where a house standing behind the 'place' was set aside for a school 'for the instruction of the youth at the church of Monymusk'.[54]

More common than reservations, however, are the definitions of the rights and privileges granted to feuars with their property. No doubt the word 'permission' when it appears in charters signifies an agreement between superior and feuar. After all, people paid highly for feus and expected value for money, more than simply heritable possession. There can be no doubt that many feuars, even small ones, saw economic possibilities in the acquisition of the land and were prepared to put down large sums of money for their charters.

Some feus held out the possibility of income and profit, such as those of coal pits and salt pans. There are five feus of salt pans at Culross: one granted to Robert Colville in 1540,[55] one to Gilbert Primrose in 1581, another to Walter Callander in the same year,[56] two to John Porterfield in 1586[57] and two to Alexander Craw in 1587.[58] The pan acquired by Primrose was under construction at the time and was resigned to him by another Culross burgess. The feu to Alexander Craw included a piece of waste ground and two buildings for stabling and storing grain. Colville's charter describes the salt pan which he had built 'from the foundation' on a piece of waste ground. In Februaury 1540 he was granted the pan, the land on which it was built and five roods of land round about, with liberty to build storehouses and a stable and to dig coal and use it for salt-making. He was also given permission to open up new coal pits if necessary. Colville was, of course, the commendator's brother, hence the extensive privileges and provision for expansion.

The grant of the lands of Boirdie to the brother of Robert Callander of Maner in 1581 included the use of 'fishings, salt pans, mines and the service of tenants'.[59] On 31 January 1575 the three 'heretible feuaris and fermoraris' of Lurg near Culross were given all the commendator's 'rights, titill and possessioun' of these lands because 'thai have a part of thair ground wastit and underminit be onskilfull collieris and workmen and likelie to be dailie mair and mair waistit and undyr-minit and deteriorat, sua that thai sall nocht be abill to pay to us and our successouris thair farmes and dewties'. This seems to be a transfer of mineral rights which the commendator had reserved in an earlier charter, illustrating the difficulties which might arise when the use of mineral resources was not conveyed with the land. Probably, however, the agreement was simply a device to get the coal pits of Lurg, and the services of the colliers, into the feuars' hands.

On Dunfermline abbey lands the practice varied with regard to the feuars' use of minerals. For example, the abbey reserved a certain amount of coal from the lands of North Lathanis, Natoun and Wester Kinghorn, but on the other hand granted feus of actual coal pits at Kelty, Woolmet and Wallyford and Carberry to Douglas of Lochleven,[60] James Richardson of Smetoun[61] and Mr Hugh Rigg of Carberry.[62] The charter to Douglas of Lochleven of the mines of Kelty heuch contains a licence to sell the coal for his own profit. Coal pits belonging to Newbattle abbey were also feued, those of Newtongrange to Alexander Hume, son of the laird of Coldenknowes,[63] and those of Prestongrange to John Blacadder of Tulliallan.[64]

Mines are mentioned in a charter by the abbot of Kilwinning to Thomas Niven of the lands of Monkredding in 1539 and the working of them probably contributed to the family's prosperity in later generations.[65] John Stewart of Arntully was given liberty to make new coal heuchs on the lands of Dalmarnock in the lordship of Dunkeld.[66] Three feuars of Pittenweem priory, Andrew Wood, Hugh Moncrieff and Andrew Simpson, all received licence to use the minerals on their feu lands.[67] On the whole feuars of industrial property such as coal pits and salt pans tended to be middlemen, rather than tenants, or, if they were tenants, were men of local consequence and reasonable means. Whereas the miller and his family could feu the mill and continue to operate it among themselves, or the profits from a mill be fragmented among a number of tenants, as at Badlay in the barony of Glasgow, it took someone with financial resources to operate coal mines, to organise their maintenance and labour and to market their output — or use it up in a large household. So that it was primarily the lairds who feued industrial property, becoming the new masters of a monastery's colliers and salters.

Permission to build, or repair existing structures, was granted to all kinds of feuars. In September 1564 the future Sir James Balfour of Pittendreich, then 'Mr' James Balfour, feued from Archbishopp John Hamilton of St Andrews the manor and place of Monimail with the green in front of it, the building being then said to be so waste and ruinous that it could not be repaired without great expense — a common excuse for feuing.[68] Balfour rebuilt the tower of the archbishops of St Andrews and put his initials and coat of arms on the parapet in 1578. In January 1559 John Campbell, son of an Ayr burgess, was given a third of the lands of Chapelton by Abbot Donald Campbell of Coupar Angus with permission to build the dwelling house and improve the surrounding policies.[69] Liberty to build on feued land was also granted to Francis Douglas at Reidspittal in East Lothian, belonging to the collegiate church of Dunglass,[70] to the earl of Cassillis who was allowed space in which to build a kitchen and stable on to a newly constructed house which had belonged to a prebendary of Maybole collegiate church,[71] to the sheriff of Cromarty, who agreed to rebuild the house of the prebendary of Kirkmichael in Rosemarkie,[72] and to William Tweedie, burgess of Edinburgh, who was given land belonging to the parish kirk of Linton beside the River Lyne on which to build a house and barn.[73]

There are one or two instances of permission to build mills. In 1576 Robert Leslie of Dewglie feued the kirklands of Athie and Murehead from the bishop of Ross, with licence to build a mill there, although he was still required to pay his own dues to the mill of Rosemarkie.[74] Robert Campbell of Kinzeancleuch, in Kyle, received a charter of the millstead of the Haugh mill of Mauchline, with permission to construct a waulk mill on it.[75] James Hamilton, brother of the laird of Haggs, was permitted to build a waulk mill at Coutts in the barony of Monkland belonging to Newbattle abbey.[76] James Hoppringle had a charter of the Mains of Coldstream and the mill, 'waistit and destroyit', with licence to rebuild it.[77] When the feu of a mill went to an outsider, this had an effect on the status of the previous tenant, who was commonly the miller himself. When Thomas Crawford of Jordanhill, for instance, received a feu of the mill of Partick, this even included the miller's house, then occupied by John Paton.[78] Andrew Wilson who feued the waulk mill of Culross was given power to arrange for its working, a very open-ended licence.[79] The Over mill of Balmerino was granted to John Kinnear, a local laird, 'with power over all husbandmen and cottars thirled to the mill'.[80]

Similarly, some feuars were empowered to build brewhouses. Alexander Leslie received a feu of a croft belonging to Coupar Angus abbey, called Boghill, on which he was permitted to build an alehouse, with a piece of ground on the north of the market cross at Keithick on which to build a house.[81] Andrew Powry, feuar of the same abbey, was allowed to put a common brewhouse on four acres of the lands of Carsegrange.[82]

Grants of pasture are as common as those of mills and brewhouses, either of pasture attached to certain lands or on moors and commonties. The extent varied considerably, from the right to pasture animals anywhere in the barony of Spittal where there were no crops, granted by the bishop of Aberdeen to his mistress, Janet Knowles,[83] to pasture for six cows granted to William Fendure, a tenant of Balmerino, with six acres of land in Scarbank.[84] Most grants are of common pasture rights but sometimes limits were set, both on the amount of grazing and on the number of animals. John Fethy, who had a charter of the mill of Foddismill with kilns and granaries also received eight *sowmes* of grass in pasture on the grange of Abercrombie belonging to Culross abbey.[85] David Liddell in West Barns was given pasture there for eight oxen and two horses by the provost of Dunbar collegiate church.[86] David Herd was granted a croft in the toun of Easthouses belonging to Newbattle, with pasture for twenty sheep and twenty cows and liberty to cast peats.[87] On occasion pasture might be reserved in a charter;

granting the kirktoun of Daviot to Alexander Leslie of Pitcaple, the bishop of Aberdeen reserved to the tenants the common pasture in the kirk glebe of Daviot and the right to cast peats there.[88]

A miscellany of other privileges is to be found in the charters: the right to cut trees for building purposes, grants of tolls and market customs, or the right to claim wreck from the sea, granted in 1581 to Mr Peter Young by the commendator of Arbroath[89] and in 1563 to George Dunbar by the bishop of Caithness.[90] In 1564 Patrick Hepburn, as commendator of Scone, gave a feu charter to John Smith, 'smith in Denmylne', in Forfar, of the 'smiddie and smiddie croft' with 'the haill thirle of the irne werk of owre landis of Angus usit and wont', a profitable monopoly.[91]

Clearly, the grant of certain rights and privileges with feus of arable land and other property had the effect of either settling resources and facilities in a family's heritable possession or gave to outsiders and middlemen a share in and supervision of local rights and amenities which were essential to the rural economy but which they as feuars could now exploit in their own interests.

The pattern of feuing on the lands of parish kirks and rural chapels differed in some ways from the feuing of property belonging to the bishoprics and monastic houses. For one thing, the feuing of the parish kirklands tended to come later; about 71 per cent of parish kirk charters date from after the Reformation-settlement of 1560, and the percentage of these feus granted to occupants, 25 per cent, is small compared with that on the great church estates. However, many small crofts and pieces of land attached to parish kirks and chapels, said to be 'occupied' by vicars, curates, chaplains and their servants, could be feued without interfering much with the rights of sitting tenants, unlike the situation on arable land elsewhere. It is important to note at this point the kind of people who feued parish kirklands and chapel lands:

Table 5: The feuars of parochial kirklands

Group	Number of feuars	Percentage of whole
1 Nobles and their relatives	15	c.4%
2 Known lairds and persons designated *of*, with their relatives	127	c.38
3 Burgesses and their relatives	58	c.18
4 Persons designated *in*, or who are known to have been below the class of laird, with their relatives	43	c.13
5 Clergy, with their relatives	23	c.7
6 Lawyers	4	c.1
7 Crown servants, not otherwise designated	2	—
8 Persons whose names only are given, and doubtful cases	58	c.18
	330	

Almost a quarter of the charters were given to persons who shared the granter's surname or were said to be related to him. Many feuars were local lairds or others with influence in the parish, some of whom already held the land in tack. In a case where the feuar's own land marched with the lands of the parish kirk, he would be prepared to pay for the land that would round off his estate. Just over half the burgesses in Table 5 feued land attached to churches in their home burghs; they do not come much into the picture in the landward area as far as the parish kirklands are concerned. There were one or two exceptions, however — townsmen with influence in a nearby rural parish. Alexander Mowat, burgess of Irvine, who feued the parish kirklands of Dreghorn, probably belonged to the family of Mowat of Busbie who were prominent in that parish.[92] John Wardlaw in Leith, who feued the parish kirklands of Garvock in Kincardineshire, was probably a relative of the vicar, Mr John Wardlaw. William Tweedie, an Edinburgh burgess, who feued the vicarage kirklands of West Linton, was in all likelihood from the family of Tweedie of Drummelzier.[94] James Williamson, bailie of Dalkeith, who received a substantial charter of the lands belonging to the altar of St Thomas in Douglas parish kirk, no doubt had behind him the influence of the earl of Morton, who granted the charter as tutor of the young earl of Angus, patron of the chaplainry.[95] The extent to which local influence determined the pattern of feuing on parish kirklands is suggested by the fact that there are only thirteen charters of churches in lay patronage. This suggests that local landowners were reluctant to allow alienation of lands in which they had a direct interest, unless the charter went to a relative or friend. The rights of a patron were especially strong in the case of altarages and private chapels, since the chaplain was considered as *holding* the lands or, more correctly, the rents derived from them, in return for religious service, while the patron still regarded the lands themselves as his patrimony. Eighteen charters of land attached to altars and private chapels were granted to relatives of the patrons.

The charters represent parishes from all over the country with the exceptions of the sheriffdoms of Selkirk, Sutherland and Caithness. They show how lands gifted over the years to the parish churches varied in extent from parish to parish and were sometimes quite extensive. The vicarage kirklands of Liberton contained twenty-two acres of arable land,[96] those of the parsonage of Strabrock in Linlithgowshire, eleven acres,[97] and the vicarage kirklands of Binning in the same sheriffdom thirty acres.[98] Those of Dunscore in Dumfriesshire extended to ten acres,[99] those of Leuchars to thirteen acres,[100] those of Stevenston in Ayrshire to over twenty-four acres[101] and those of Restalrig near Edinburgh to forty-four.[102] A charter of the parish kirklands of Kilchuslane in Kintyre lists ten separate territories.[103]

In some parishes the kirklands were small scattered pieces, donated at various times and by many donors, and were sometimes consolidated into one feu. The vicarage kirklands of Liberton, for example, contained twelve acres called the *Priesthill*, nine acres lying at the Bridgend of Craigmillar and an acre and a husbandland in the town of Gilmerton 'on the back of the Mains thereof'. Those of the vicarage of Inverness included two roods in the burgh, an acre in a field called the *Shipland* and a croft in the town of Essie.[104] The perpetual vicar of Stevenston in Ayrshire feued five acres called the *kirklandfens*, three acres next to it in the north, one and a half acres called the *kilakir* (kilnacre), six roods of land in the *holme,* six roods called the *priesthill*, three acres at Corsinkell, a piece of land lying on the south of the church, six acres of West Dubbs and an acre called the *priestsfauld,* all to the heir of the local laird, James Campbell of Stevenston.

At other times, small pieces of land were feued to those who occupied them, and crofts and bits of waste land to those who had a definite purpose in mind for them. A piece of land annexed to the parsonage of Chirnside called 'the Chirnside acre' was feued to sir Adam Learmonth, who occupied it.[105] A piece called 'the parson's isle' at Melport, with the fishing belonging to the parson, was feued to John Campbell of Inverlever, who already held it in tack.[106] The vicar of Kinneil feued 'the vicar's croft' to George Crawford in Kinneil, who already leased it, and the vicar of North Berwick a croft next to North Berwick Mains to the occupant, Alexander Carrick, a burgess there.[107]

As in charters of other church land, those of the parish kirklands often carried certain privileges. Pasture rights, transferred from parson or vicar to feuar, are mentioned in charters of the kirks of Abercorn, Cambusnethan, Carrington, Cumnock, Dreghorn, Gogar, Largs, Methlick, Monimail, Oldhamstocks, Stobo, Strathaven and West Linton. The grant of the glebe and manse of Carriden to Patrick Crombie in 1545 included pasture for 'one horse, two cows, one brood sow, brood geese' and common pasture on the commonty.[108] There were grants of mills with the parish kirklands of Kincardine in Aberdeenshire, Dull and Dowally in Perthshire, and fishing rights with those of Cargill, Leuchars and Lessudden. David Hamilton of Fingalton received the moss adjacent to 'the vicar's flat' of Tranent.[109] In 1580 Neil Campbell, parson and vicar of Craignish, made James Campbell, or McNeil, probably his son, bailie of his kirklands by means of a feu charter.[110]

An important element in the feuing of the parish kirklands was the alienation, or reservation, of the manse and glebe, the dwelling place and arable-cum-pasture land nominally set aside for the priest in charge of the parish in pre-Reformation times and the minister afterwards. Manse and glebe, however, went not so much with the job as with the benefice, so that neither pre-Reformation curate nor, at first, post-Reformation minister had a legal claim to his possession. The number of working parish priests who were also benefice-holders was probably small on the eve of the Reformation. Where the parsonage and vicarage revenues were appropriated and the vicar was non-resident, the curate who was actually in charge of the parish might be given the use of manse and glebe as part of his fee, or in terms of an agreement with the parson or vicar. But it was the man who held the benefice, or the religious establishment to which the parish was appropriated, who had the legal right to the manse and glebe and who feued it. This alienation of the manse and statutory four acres or so of glebe land was forbidden both by provincial councils of the pre-Reformation church and by parliament itself in the later sixteenth century, but neither could put a stop to the practice. Nearly all feus of parochial kirklands granted directly by appropriating institutions were of entire

J

kirklands; some specifically mention manse and glebe and in only seven examples are these definitely reserved. Nineteen feus by cathedral and other higher clergy include the glebe, and in forty-nine cases it was alienated by the parsons and vicars themselves.

Fifteen glebes were feued before the Reformation. In March 1545, for example, Patrick Crombie, already mentioned, received from sir Archibald Wotherspoon, the perpetual vicar, a charter of the manse and glebe of Carriden in West Lothian, which was said to consist of three acres arable land in the easter manse, an acre in Wester Carriden, an orchard called 'the delf' running to the sea and 'the house, manse and yard of Carriden'. In the winter of 1543 sir John Jackson, perpetual vicar of Swinton, feued to John Swinton of that Ilk the kirklands 'with the glebe belonging to the vicarage because these were laid waste by the English and the vicar and his predecessors have derived nothing from them'.[111] In the spring of 1560 Mr Patrick Vaus, parson of the appropriated parish of Wigtown, gave a charter of the kirklands and glebe to Alexander Vaus of Barnbarroch.[112]

After the Reformation — one of the most important achievements of which was the recovery of a resident parish ministery — parliament endorsed the earlier enactments of the provincial church councils forbidding the feuing of manses and glebes. In June 1563 it was laid down that ministers must be given possession of the manse and glebe and that if there were no suitable dwelling, one must be built at the expense of the parson, vicar or feuar and sufficient land for a glebe attached to it.[113] In fact, the feuing of the manse and glebe, like the feuing of the parish kirklands in general, accelerated after the Reformation. Charters were granted not only by the surviving pre-Reformation benefice-holders in an attempt to narrow the gap between long-established tack-duty, derived from leases, and the rising cost of living which now included the annual payment of the *third* of their benefices to the crown, but also by ministers who had come into possession of benefices, who used feuing as a means of supplementing their sometimes inadequate stipends, and by lay presentees to benefices.

In fifty-six cases, however, manse and glebe were reserved for the use of the vicar, minister or reader of a particular parish, and details in the reservation clauses of charters throw light on their living accommodation provided for the man in charge of the parish and on how much land over and above the statutory four acres he enjoyed.

The feuing of parochial kirklands could affect those tenants who lived on and cultivated them and lairds and others who held them in tack. Charters occasionally give a list of occupants, many of whom would be non-resident tack-holders, since by the sixteenth century the bulk of the parish kirklands seem to have been set in tack. At the same time, the term 'occupant' may refer to the actual cultivators of the kirktouns and arable land around a church. There were five occupants of the kirklands of Auchinleck,[114] for example, nine on the kirklands of Kilmalcolm,[115] eight on those of Ancrum,[116] eleven at West Kilbride where two of them shared the glebe with the reader of the kirk,[117] ten at Kilbirnie, including the laird of Glengarnock,[118] four at Dreghorn,[119] and seven at Kilbarchan.[120] In some places the glebe itself had been set in tack prior to feuing, as at Ballantrae, Dunlop, Sanquhar, Dalgety and Dunscore. At Renfrew three acres next the kirk were 'labourit' by Patrick Hay, while some of the parsonage lands of that parish were leased to some citizens of Glasgow.[121]

Perhaps dislocation in the pattern of landholding and tenancy was mitigated in the case of the parish kirklands by the fact that much of the interest shown in feuing of this kind of property was local. Even where feuars were non-occupants, they tended to live near or have connections with the neighbourhood, particularly the lairds. In any case, the feu charters that have come to light represent less than a third of the parishes in Scotland and only a fraction of the hundreds of altars and private chapels.

Notes

1 *R.M.S.*, V, 173
2 *Ibid.*, IV, 1380
3 R.F.C., i, fo. 144r
4 *Ibid.*, i, fo. 141r
5 *R.M.S.*, V, 582
6 R.S.S., liii, fo. 101v
7 *R.M.S.*, IV, 2240
8 R.F.C., ii, fo. 244r
9 *R.M.S.*, V, 1229
10 *Ibid.*, V, 1248
11 R.F.C., i, fo. 115
12 *R.M.S.*, V, 1190
13 J. Balfour, *Practiks*, i, 171
14 *R.M.S.*, V, 453
15 *Ibid.*, IV, 3013; R.F.C., ii, fo. 209r
16 *Ibid.*, i, fo. 102r
17 *Ibid.*, i, fo. 81r
18 Records of King James VI Hospital, Perth (S.R.O.), GD 79/5/44
19 *R.M.S.*, V, 1292
20 *Ibid.*, V, 150
21 Register House Charters, RH 6/2437
22 *R.M.S.*, V, 2317
23 R.S.S., l, fo. 31r
24 *R.M.S.*, V, 77
25 *Ibid.*, V, 819
26 *Ibid.*, IV, 2550
27 *Ibid.*, V, 830
28 *Ibid.*, V, 1145
29 Erroll Charters, formerly GD 175/444, see microfilm, RH 1/6
30 *R.M.S.*, IV, 2918
31 *Moraviensis*, 31
32 *R.M.S.*, V, 1080
33 *Ibid.*, V, 140
34 Books of Assumption (S.R.O.), i, fo. 36r
35 *Ibid.*, i, fo. 12r
36 *Ibid.*, i, fo. 1r
37 *Rentale Sancti Andree*, xxviii, 204
38 Books of Assumption, i, fos. 13r-v
39 Acts and decreets, xii, fo. 472r
40 Pitreavie papers, (S.R.O.), GD 91/39
41 *R.M.S.*, V, 1212
42 *Ibid.*, IV, 2430
43 *Ibid.*, V, 1035
44 *Ibid.*, V, 798

45 *Laing charters,* no. 468
46 Yester writs, GD 28/537
47 *R.M.S.,* IV, 2077
48 *Ibid.,* IV, 159
49 Fraser charters (S.R.O.), GD 86/174
50 *R.M.S.,* IV, 1027
51 R.F.C., ii, fo. 234r
52 *Ibid.,* i, fo. 246r; *R.M.S.,* IV, 1837
53 R.F.C., ii, fo. 206r
54 *R.M.S.,* V, 1267
55 *Laing charters,* no. 442
56 *R.M.S.,* V, 1043, 913
57 *Ibid.,* V, 1270
58 *Ibid.,* V, 1284
59 *Ibid.,* V, 913
60 Kinross House papers (S.R.O.), GD 29/862
61 *R.M.S.,* IV, 2659
62 *Ibid.,* III, 2941
63 R.F.C., i, fo. 141r
64 *Ibid.,* i, fo. 142r
65 *R.M.S.,* III, 3245
66 R.F.C., i, fo. 86r
67 Pittenweem writs (S.R.O.), GD 62/1
68 Leven and Melville muniments, GD 26/3/468
69 *R.M.S.,* IV, 1779
70 R.F.C., i, fo. 213r
71 *Crossraguel charters,* I, 70-1
72 *R.M.S.,* V, 716
73 R.F.C., i, fo. 83r
74 *R.M.S.,* V, 2112
75 R.F.C., i, fo. 301r
76 *R.M.S.,* V, 2331
77 R.F.C., i, fo. 307
78 *R.M.S.,* IV, 2199
79 R.F.C., ii, fo. 331r
80 *Ibid.,* ii, fo. 77r
81 *Ibid.,* ii, fo. 222r
82 *R.M.S.,* IV, 1791
83 *Ibid.,* V, 829
84 R.F.C., ii, fo. 277
85 *Laing charters,* no. 507
86 *R.M.S.,* IV, 2227
87 R.F.C., ii, fo. 258r
88 *Ibid.,* ii, fo. 57r
89 *R.M.S.,* V, 190
90 R.F.C., ii, fo. 100r
91 *R.M.S.,* V, 931
92 R.F.C., ii, fo. 210r
93 *Ibid.,* ii, fo. 63r
94 *Ibid.,* i, fo. 83r
95 *R.M.S.,* IV, 2180
96 R.F.C., i, fo. 139r
97 *R.M.S.,* V, 814
98 R.F.C., i, fo. 283r
99 *R.M.S.,* IV, 104, 2321; R.F.C., ii, fo. 115r
100 *R.M.S.,* IV, 2691
101 *Ibid.,* IV, 2482
102 R.F.C., ii, fo. 124r
103 *R.M.S.,* V, 41
104 *Ibid.,* IV, 2482

105 R.F.C., ii, fo. 68r
106 Register House Charters, RH 6/1691
107 *R.M.S.*, IV, 431, 1612
108 R.F.C., i, fo. 29r
109 *Ibid.*, i, fo. 181r
110 *R.M.S.*, V, 131
111 Swinton charters (S.R.O.), GD 12/117
112 R.F.C., i, fo. 183r
113 *A.P.S.*, II, 539
114 *R.M.S.*, V, 196
115 R.F.C., ii, fo. 22r
116 *Ibid.*, i, fo. 223r
117 *Ibid.*, ii, fo. 160r
118 Lindsay papers (S.R.O.), GD 20/534
119 Eglinton muniments, GD 3/1/165
120 *R.M.S.*, IV, 2412
121 *R.S.S.*, VI, 226

9

Changing Social Patterns

'the middle part of that quarter runrig of the lands of Wester Caputh occupied by John and his mother, and three rigs of another middle part, *viz:* the Craggy rig in the Quarrell hole, the Cruikit rig lying adjacent thereto in the same shed, and the Braid rig lying on the east and west sides of the Cobill gait.'

Details in a feu charter to John Haggart in the barony of Dunkeld, 1574 *(R.M.S.,* IV, 2240)

A programme of feuing in a locality altered the structure of society in relation to their interest in the land which, as we saw at the beginning, was what decided a person's place in the rural hierarchy. Heritable proprietors — the feuars — came into being where there had been only tenants before, varying in number from place to place according to whether holdings were amalgamated, fragmented or feued in existing units. Where the feuars were outsiders, the occupants, who had previously paid their rents directly to the superior's chamberlain and officers, became the feuar's subtenants, paying their rents to him. If, with the superior's consent, the new proprietor sub-feued the land, yet another middleman would come into the picture, between the principal feuar and the tenants, unless the land was sub-feued to the local people themselves.

As far as actual population shift was concerned, this might happen where the feuar brought in new tenants, as he was sometimes empowered to do, fragmenting the holdings of his subtenants in order to increase his income from the land, or where he removed tenants in order to cultivate the land with paid labour or with his own servants. It was more likely, however, that a feuar would prefer to continue to uplift the rents of numerous tenants, especially if their services were conveyed with the land, rather than pay agricultural workers.

Sometimes sizeable settlements were extensively feued to the occupants. These included not only the bigger of the farmtouns scattered over the countryside but also those clustered about mill, ferry, kirk, coal heuch, salt pan or monastery itself, or around the administrative buildings of an outlying barony, or on the Mains. The inhabitants of these settlements, which now became communities of owner-occupiers, would often consist, as we have seen, of a mixture of farmers, fishermen, craftsmen, traders, colliers, salters and quarrymen.

This is what happened, for instance, at the South Ferrytoun of Portincraig, now Tayport. It happened, too, on the lands lying immediately to the south and east of the precincts of Kilwinning abbey, at Overmains, Nethermains, Longford, Bridgend and Corshill, which with the passage of time and growth of population became the heart of the modern town of Kilwinning. A glance through the abbey's earliest surviving rental book, probably dating from before 1540, shows that feuing simply made permanent a pattern of landholding created by rentalling early in the sixteenth century.[1] Similarly, the touns of Coldingham and Eyemouth were feued to many occupants in husbandlands and cotlands. A number of feuar-touns were created on the lands of Melrose abbey in the Tweed valley, notably at Newstead, Newtoun, Gattonside and Lessudden, in an area where modern planning is creating an even more intensively populated community. Many feuar-touns survived into the seventeenth century.

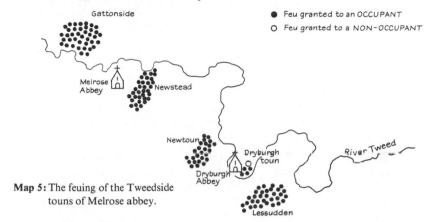

Map 5: The feuing of the Tweedside touns of Melrose abbey.

On the farms of the open countryside two basic patterns emerged from feuing: the perpetuation of existing units, as single-tenant, shared or jointly-held farms, and the consolidation of small holdings into single feus, which does not always mean that the holdings were territorially consolidated but that they became one legal entity in the feu charter.

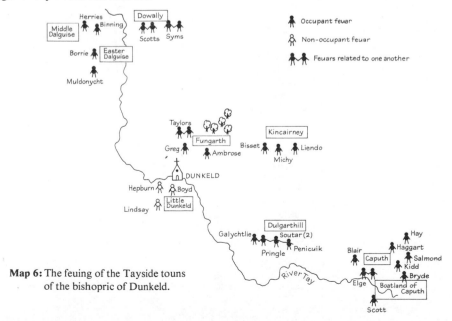

Map 6: The feuing of the Tayside touns of the bishopric of Dunkeld.

A good example of the perpetuation of holdings is to be found in the string of farmtouns in the barony of Dunkeld, lying along the west bank of the River Tay: Caputh, Dalgarthill, Fungarth, Dowally and easter and middle Dalguise, all of which were feued to the tenants in varying numbers of oxgangs. Further east, in the valley of the River Isla, lay the lands of Coupar Angus abbey, some of which were marked by small feus, such as Keithick, Carsegrange and Balbrogie. Keithick was feued in portions ranging from two to six acres with one grant of an 'eighth part'. At Balbrogie the Overtoun was feued in two halves and the remainder in eighths and quarters. Carsegrange was divided into eighths, quarters and small acreages, Chapeltoun and Cowbyre each into third parts. In Inchaffray abbey's barony of Madderty the lands of Craigtoun, Wester Craig, Balmaclone, Ballyclone, Ardbennie and Williamstoun were similarly feued in small pieces to tenants. Certain parts of north-east Fife were characterised by small feus reflecting the previous pattern of tacks, as at Craigfoodie, Kincaple, Letham and Raderny belonging to the archbishops of St Andrews, and on one or two parts of the estates of Balmerino and Lindores abbeys, including Cultray, Dewcherone, Disblair and the grange of Lindores. The feuing of the farmtouns of Melrose abbey's barony of Kylesmure in mid-Ayrshire, although it did not create the biggish feuar-touns of Tweedside, nevertheless created many small proprietors as the kindly tenants received feus of their holdings 'quhilkis thai bruik now presentlie and ar in rentale of', as the agreement between themselves and the commendator put it.[2] Small feus were also a feature of the barony of Glasgow and, in the north of Scotland, in the barony of Strathisla in Banffshire and on the bishopric lands in Moray.

The farms of Scone abbey in Perthshire were mainly feued in the existing portions held by tenant families. The following examples show the pattern in its many variations:

		Number of feuars	
Lands	Pattern of feus	Occupants	Non-occupants
Ardgilzean	1 third and 2 sixths	3	—
Balcormock	1 eighth, 2 quarters and 1 third	3	1
Bauchrie, West	4 quarters	4	—
Bauchrie, East	*En bloc*	1	—
Clien, Mains of	4 eighths and 2 quarters	5	—
Clien	$1\frac{1}{2}$ acres, 2 pieces of 2 acres, 1 piece of 4 acres	4	—
Clien, Hole of	*En bloc*	—	1
Durdie, Nether	2 quarters and a half	2	1
Innerbuist	1 eighth and 3 quarters	4	—
Gourdie, West	2 halves	2	—
Gourdie, Middle	2 halves	2	—
Sherifftoun with Shepherdland	3 quarters 3 quarters	3 3	— —
Kinnochtrie	2 eighths, 2 quarters and a portion containing 3 eighths (N.B. This appears to add up to more than 8 eighths)	5	—
Invergowrie, West	2 quarters, 1 eighth and a portion containing an eighth and a quarter	4	—

Invergowrie, East	*En bloc*	*Doubtful*	
Liff, Kirktoun of	2 quarters and 4 eighths	5	1
Blair, Weltoun of	3 third parts	3	—
Blair, Kirktoun of	2 thirds (N.B. No charter found for remaining third)	2	—
Blair, Lochend of	2 halves	2	—
Creuchies, Mains of	3 thirds	3	—
Creuchies, Weltoun of	3 thirds	3	—
Creuchies, Haltoun of	*En bloc*	1	—
Creuchies, Muretoun of	*En bloc*	1	—

The charters of Blair, Creuchies and Clien illustrate the dispersed settlements characteristic of a Scottish barony; the Kirktoun, Weltoun, Lochend of Blair and the Mains, Haltoun, Weltoun and Muretoun of Creuchies.

Although small feuars are to be found in all parts of the country, they appear to have been most common in the Perthshire valleys just south of the Highland Line, in lands belonging to Inchaffray abbey, the bishopric of Dunkeld and the abbeys of Coupar Angus and Scone; in north-east Fife; in the barony of Coldingham; the Melrose lands on Tweedside and in Kylesmure; in the barony of Glasgow and parts of the estates of Paisley and Kilwinning; and in Banffshire and the Laich of Moray. They appear, in fact, and long continued, in the most fertile parts.

We should remember, however, that in order to reflect the previous pattern of tenancy the land need not be feued in small pieces, for many sitting tenants who became proprietors had previously held whole farms which they laboured with the help of their families and servants, a feature which particularly characterised the farms of Scone, Coupar Angus and the barony of Glasgow. In any case, the number of areas in which small feus were to be found would be increased if many more charters to small feuars had survived; it is reasonable to suppose that the numerous single charters of eighth and twelfth parts of farms, which survive from all parts of the country, were originally accompanied by others which represented the remaining portions of the farms.

The other basic pattern created by feuing was the consolidation of holdings by charters which united them into single pieces of heritable property. Frequently, these consolidating charters were granted to outsiders, non-occupant feuars. In this way, for example, most of Holyrood's barony of Kerse, in Stirlingshire, was feued to the duke of Chatelherault in 1552,[3] the year in which he also got a substantial grant of Kilwinning abbey lands.[4] Coupargrange, which between 1542 and 1558 was leased to fourteen tenants for nineteen years and to seven tenants for life, was feued to John Campbell of Skipinch, *en bloc,* in 1560.[5] Also on the Coupar Angus estates, the lands of Drymmies, feued in 1567 to the earl of Atholl as the final step in a process of consolidation, had earlier been leased to seven tenants.[6] Cambock, in Angus, was set to three tenants before being feued to the earl of Argyll in 1560.[7] The lands of North Ferry, Culback, Wester Persie, Ethie and Auchmithie, all of which had been held by several Arbroath abbey tenants in the first half of the sixteenth century, were each granted to a non-occupant feuar. In the west of Scotland, on the estates of Paisley abbey, the same thing happened on the lands of Arkilston, Auchintoshan, Barscaven, Cochnoch, Culboy, Drumgrane and Drumtochir.[8] It would be tedious to cite further examples of this development which, of course, demoted the inhabitants of the farmtouns to the position of subtenants of the new feuar, to who they would now pay their rents.

But non-occupant feuars were not always complete outsiders. They might even be local inhabitants whose charters united holdings, only some of which they had previously occupied, others perhaps being held by their neighbours. This meant that a husbandman's neighbours might become his subtenants, causing a stratification among local people who had hitherto been on roughly equal terms, socially and economically. In Kilwinning barony, for example, Thomas Niven, who shared the lands of Monkredding with several other tenants before 1540, took the whole of the lands of Monkredding in feu between 1539 and 1545.[9] Fifteen years later the other tenants appear in an abbey rental as occupants still, and presumably by then Niven's subtenants.[10] In the barony of Strathisla Alexander Gordon feued not only the two oxgangs of Fortrie which he occupied himself, but also four oxgangs held by his neighbours, Patrick Neill and William Thomson.[11]

Consolidating charters, however, sometimes simply turned into one unit of heritable property a handful of scattered holdings which a tenant family had previously held by separate tacks. In fact, it is often the texts of their consolidating feu charters that reveal just how many small pieces they had acquired, as in the case of the following feuars around the town of Kinloss:[12]

Feuar	*Holdings feued*
Ninian Spence	3 acres called Dynneisacres; 2 acres called Newlandhead
Thomas Christie	A quarter of Alehoustak; half of Inchdenny
Robert Gray and his wife	2 acres in the Killand (Kiln land); 2 acres in St Johnswell; a small house and garden
David Duncan, son of John Duncan in Kinloss	A tenandry of land occupied by him and his father; 6 acres in the Cellarer's Cruik, Mill Cruik and Slaterland; a quarter of Alehoustak and Woodland; an acre called Whiteacre.

The portions consolidated might be extremely small; Andrew Robertson and his son, at Cunnoquhie in the lordship of Monimail, received a charter of a sixteenth and a thirty-second part of these lands. Neighbouring farms might be feued just as they had previously been shared as, for example, at Auchincreich and Burnskeith in Kylesmure:[13]

Auchincreich	*Burnskeith*
Half a merk to sir Mark Slewman	3s 4d worth to sir Mark Slewman
3s 4d to William Slewman	—
Half a merk to Edward MacKynnel	Half a merk to Edward MacKynnel
3s 4d worth to Heleis MacKynnel	3s 4d worth to Heleis MacKynnel
Half a merk to John Gaw	—

On the Newbattle estates the lands of Prestongrange were feued to six individuals, their charters uniting some very small portions indeed.

The feuing of Prestongrange[14]			
Feuar	*Langshot*	*Millhill*	*Hawklaws*
Alexander Hume, son of laird of Coldenknowes	63 acres	12 acres	7 acres
Richard Trollope	2 dales; 1 rig; 1 acre	5 acres (listed separately)	—
John Jardine	2½ acres; 6 butts to west of Langshot	—	—
John Bannatyne, burgess of Edinburgh	4 acres	—	—
James MacCartnay	—	2 crofts; 2 rigs; 1 rig; 4 butts	—

In many places what can only be called a mixed pattern of landholding emerged from feuing where, although an influential outsider took part of the lands in feu, some tenants were able to obtain charters of their own holdings. This kind of situation is well illustrated, for example, on the lands of Knock in Strathisla, where thirteen separate holdings were concerned. Some time before 1572 eleven of them were feued to Adam Dundas, brother of the laird of Fingask, while the remaining two continued to be held by two tenants, David and Thomas Henderson.[15] In 1572, however, Dundas resigned seven of the holdings in favour of William Abernethy of Byrnes and four in favour of the sitting tenants.[16] At the same time the two Hendersons took feus of their own holdings.[17] In Perthshire, on the Coupar Angus lands, at Campsy, the lands of Over Campsy were granted in 1578 to John Craigo, whose family had held them since 1483, but Nether Campsy went to the earl of Atholl.[18] Robert Turnbull, tenant of a quarter of the lands of Arthurstane, feued his holding in 1559, while the other three quarters were again granted to Atholl.[19]

How was it that some tenants appear to have had sufficient bargaining power, and money, to enable them to feu their holdings in the face of the land-hunger of neighbouring lairds and even nobles? Those who managed to acquire them only after they had been feued and then resigned to them by middlemen would pay dearly for them. It has been suggested that, although in some areas the tenant farmers did manage to feu their holdings, feuing was a golden opportunity to acquire land for those with capital behind them, such as burgesses, merchants and professional men. If the kirklands might have been expected to go to the highest bidders, why did the big buyers not come forward in greater numbers? The fact remains, from the evidence of the charters, that in most places feuars came from all social groups and, indeed, a great many of them from among those who in the matter of wealth were below the lairds, merchants and professional men.

On the lands of Holyrood abbey lying between Edinburgh and Corstorphine, feuars included not only Lord Fleming,[20] Sir James Forrester of Corstorphine,[21] Douglas of Borg[22] and the brother of Carmichael of Meadowflat,[23] but also local tenants such as John Liston in Sauchton,[24] John Learmonth in Sauchton,[25] James Watson in Sauchtonhall[26] and Andrew Bartholemew in Caldcotts.[27] The six

Edinburgh burgesses who did feu land from the commendator of Holyrood mainly acquired crofts and premises around the abbey itself. There were rich merchants in Glasgow, yet 80 per cent of the feus went to the rentallers. The lands of Balboughty, Sherifftoun, Lethendy, Ardgilzean, Clien and Innerbuist, belonging to Scone abbey, all of which were feued among tenants, lay on the doorstep not only of the Perth burgesses but of families like the Murrays and Ruthvens, the latter the abbey bailies. It is a mistake to expect the peasant farmers to have had a better chance of obtaining feus in remote parts, the merchants preferring land nearer the burghs, or at least in the heartland of Scotland, for professional and commercial classes feued land almost anywhere, when they did feu it, since they lived on the rents of subtenants, collecting the dues through a factor, and did not have to be in close touch with the locality. When burgesses feued land at a distance it was often because they had a personal link with the superior, the granter of the charter. Acheson of Gosford, an Edinburgh burgess who had already bought himself a secular estate in East Lothian, feued land in the regality of Kinloss, being related through his wife, Helen Reid, to Walter Reid, commendator of that abbey.[18] In any case, much of the best arable land which was worth feuing lay at a distance from the burghs.

In considering the economic resources of feuars there is a danger in detaching the professional and commercial classes of the sixteenth century from the rest of society — lairds on the one hand and peasant farmers on the other — a danger pointed out when discussing Table 2, *The social distribution of the feuars*. Most Scots, whatever their occupation might be, were to some extent connected with and dependent on the land in a basically agricultural society. There were many burgesses who grew crops and owned animals, something which their testaments make perfectly clear. Besides, many burgesses, including prosperous merchants and master craftsmen, were the town-dwelling relatives of nobles and lairds. George Elphinston, bailie of Glasgow, part-owner of several ships' cargoes, who feued the lands of Blythswood and left goods to the value of almost £3,000, referred in his will to 'Alexander, master of Elphinston, my chief'.[29] The professional classes, too, had landed connections. In the case of the crown servants, when we consider how ill-paid were their salaries, eked out by gifts of customs and feudal casualties, it is doubtful if many of them could have become rich as a result of office-holding alone. High-ranking officials in the central administration, like James McGill, the Clerk Register, came from families who had acquired lands over the previous generation or two before feuing church property. The fifty-six oxgangs of the grange of Lindores which McGill feued lay only a few miles from his own estate of Nether Rankeillor. The Justice Clerk, Sir John Bellenden, and his relatives, got land belonging to the Dominican nunnery of Sciennes near Edinburgh because they were related to the prioress, Christian Bellenden, and land in Holyrood abbey's barony of Broughton through their kinship with Abbot Robert Bellenden, but previous to all this the family had held the estate of Auchnoule. In statistical terms burgesses, lawyers and crown servants together represent only 9 per cent of all feuars. The really significant contrast in social representation among the feuars is that between Groups 2 and 4, between those, that is, who already held land heritably and those who were acquiring it for the first time. It was the high percentage of the latter that created so many small feus, driving a wedge of new, small proprietors into Scottish rural society, swelling the ranks of *portioners* and *bonnet lairds* for a generation or two to come.

The spread of feuing often entrenched families, great and small, in localities where they were already resident or influential, at other times it might spread their property interests into new districts. It is not surprising to find land belonging to the bishoprics of Aberdeen and Moray often feued to Gordons, Dunbars and Inneses, or that belonging to Arbroath, Culross, Inchaffray, Jedburgh, Scone and Crossraguel going to Ogilvys, Colvilles, Drummonds and Murrays, Humes, Ruthvens and Kennedys, respectively, for all these families were influential in these areas. Charters of land in Kylesmure went not only to small kindly tenants but also to a handful of Campbells, offshoots of the house of Argyll who had long been settled in that part of Ayrshire.

We find great tenants as well as small ones making sure that land in which they had long had an interest came into the family to stay by means of a feu charter. On the Arbroath estates Lord Ogilvy's charter of Little Kenny in the barony of Kingoldrum, which he feued in 1563 for a very small augmentation, described the lands as already occupied by him and his subtenants, 'and possessed by his predecessors for a hundred years'.[30] Slightly earlier, in 1558, the lands of Meikle Kenny had been feued to an abbey tenant, James Ochterlony of Kellie, whose castle stood near Arbroath itself.[31] Other Arbroath tenants in the laird class feued lands which their families had long held, John Carnegie, son of Carnegie of Kinnaird, who feued Mugdrum, George Meldrum of Fyvie, who had a charter of Scottstoun in Kincardineshire, and James Garden, son of Patrick Garden of that Ilk, who feued the lands of Corstoun in Dunnichen parish. Feuing a piece of church property might be a way of acquiring an estate for a younger son. The Carnegies of Kinnaird built up considerable property interests around Arbroath as the sixteenth century wore on; in 1550 Sir Robert Carnegie of Kinnaird, senator of the College of Justice, feued the barony of Ethie to the north-east of the abbey,[32] including the castle which was a residence of the abbots, while his son, John, put down £6,000 for charters conveying the Seatoun of Arbroath, the lands of Dunnichen, Craichie and others lying nearer the burgh.[33] The barony of Ethie with its castle, having passed to Carnegie's descendants, became the principal seat of the earls of Southesk in the seventeenth century.

The Cunninghame district of Ayrshire was peppered with the tower houses of small lairds, a number of whom, as tenants of Kilwinning abbey, received charters of land which their forbears had long occupied. In this way John Fergushill of that Ilk feued the lands of Nether Auchentiber,[34] Adam Montgomery, son of Montgomery of Braidstone, those of Marshelland in Beith barony,[35] Hugh Ralston of that Ilk the lands of Woodside and Turnerland in the same barony,[36] and Patrick Montgomery the lands of Sevenacres which his father had held before him.[37]

What is just as interesting is the way in which the influence of some families spread geographically as a result of feuing, with a charter granted by a relative who was the superior of an ecclesiastical estate. A splendid example of this is found in the earls of Argyll, who received large grants of church land in Perthshire, Clackmannanshire, Fife and Angus. Archibald, second earl, the father of the future abbot of Coupar Angus, Donald Campbell, received from the bishop of Dunkeld a charter of the kirklands of Dollar, previously held by his father and Duncan Campbell of Glenorchy, which included the bishop's castle of Gloom, later known as Castle Campbell.[38] Twelve years later he acquired the lands of Balgonar in Fife, belonging to the collegiate church of St Salvator in St Andrews.[39] In the 1540s the fourth earl, who supported Cardinal Beaton for a time, received a charter from him of the barony of Muckhartshire, actually in Perthshire but neighbouring the lands of Dollar in Clackmannanshire.[40] On the eve of the Reformation, when Abbot Donald Campbell was feuing the Coupar Angus estates, the fifth earl got a charter of seven territories in Glenisla in Angus and five in Perthshire.[41] In 1566 Bishop Alexander Campbell of Brechin feued to the same earl the Mains of Farnell which, like those of Dollar, included the bishop's castle, and made the earl hereditary bailie of the bishopric lands.[42] In 1579, Colin, sixth earl, who had married the widow of the Regent Moray, acquired more land in Fife from the commendator of Dunfermline.[43]

In the 1550s James, duke of Chatelherault, head of the house of Hamilton, received charters of lands belonging to the abbeys of Kelso, Cambuskenneth, Holyrood, Kilwinning and Saddell.[44] Admittedly, in the case of the first three, the lands fitted in geographically with his hereditary possessions in Lanarkshire, Linlithgowshire and Stirlingshire. In 1553 he gave the Hamilton commendator of Kilwinning £1,000 for a charter of lands in that barony including the lands and tower of Monkcastle and the lands of Dalgarven. His charter makes no mention of the occupants, but a list of parishioners drawn up a few years later names twenty-five inhabitants and there were doubtless more.[45] In 1556 he got a charter of the Mains of Saddell in Kintyre from the Hamilton bishop of the Isles.

It was not only the great nobles, however, whose influence spread in this way. The Justice Clerk of the later sixteenth century, Bellenden of Auchnoule, and his family, descended from the parish clerk of the Canongate and related to a pre-Reformation abbot and post-Reformation commendator of Holyrood, as well as to the prioress of Sciennes nunnery, not only feued land in the hinterland of Edinburgh, as we have already seen, but later acquired property as far afield as Orkney. The Justice Clerk's nephew, Adam Bothwell, bishop of Orkney, created and granted the *tenandry* of Birsay to Sir John himself, that of Stenness to Patrick Bellenden and that of Westray to his kinsman by marriage, Gilbert Balfour.[46] The Bruces of Wester Kennet in Fife, one of whom became commendator of Kinloss abbey and finally Lord Kinloss, acquired land in the barony of Strathisla in Banffshire just before the Reformation.[47] Bishop Robert Crichton of Dunkeld granted the lands of Drummellie and the Mains of Cluny, including the castle, to his namesake Mr Robert Crichton of Eliok, advocate, father of 'the Admirable Crichton', the family originally coming from Dumfriesshire.[48]

The spread of family or individual property interest, like the mobility of people in general and the extent of their geographical influence, was often greater than we might suppose. This came about not only by feuing, however, but by all the other ways of acquiring and exchanging land; by marriage, excambion, outright purchase or the gift of an escheat. The Dunbars from Cumnock in Ayrshire had already moved into Moray before feuing church land there. Stewart of Beath, who acquired land in Fife through his relative the abbot of Inchcolm, was the brother of Lord Ochiltree who had exchanged a lordship in Lanarkshire for one in Ayrshire. Yet, on balance, most feuars from among the nobles and lairds tended to feu land in their home country, where they already had influence, just as most burgesses feued property in their home towns. It was as much with the influential local lairds as with the distant speculators that the tenants had to contend in acquiring feus of their own holdings. It is interesting to see how they fared having acquired them.

Notes

1 Eglinton muniments, GD 3/1361
2 Morton muniments, GD 150/1455c
3 *R.M.S.*, IV, 885
4 *Ibid.*, V, 1132
5 *Cupar*, II, *passim; R.M.S.*, IV, 1735
6 *Ibid.*, IV, 1809; *Cupar*, I, *passim*, II, 132
7 R.F.C., i, fo. 230r; *Cupar*, II, 156-59
8 See Appendix A
9 *R.M.S.*, III, 3245
10 Acts and decreets, xxii, fo. 114r
11 R.F.C., ii, fo. 112r
12 *Ibid.*, ii, fos. 185r, 268r; *R.M.S.*, IV, 2988; V, 1193
13 *Ibid.*, V, 1721; R.F.C., ii, fos. 239r-240r
14 *Ibid.*, i, fos. 144r, 225r; *R.M.S.*, IV, 1943, 2275; V, 1247, 1248
15-17 *Ibid.*, IV, 2588, 2614, 2615, 2616, 2618, 2622
18 *Laing charters*, no. 973; *Cupar*, I, 242, *R.M.S.*, IV, 1809
19 *Ibid.*, IV, 2263; V, 2248
20 Wigtown charters (S.R.O.), GD 101/236
21 R.F.C., i, fo. 227r
22 *R.M.S.*, III, 1846
23 *Ibid.*, V, 1240
24 R.S.S., lii, fo. 49v
25 *R.M.S.*, V, 409
26 R.F.C., ii, fo. 279r
27 *Ibid.*, ii, fo. 321r
28 *Ibid.*, i, fos. 135r, 299r
29 Edin. testaments, CC 8/8/17, fo. 158r
30 *R.M.S.*, IV, 1740
31 Airlie muniments, GD 16/14/18
32 Northesk muniments, GD 130 Box 1, 3
33 *R.M.S.*, IV, 1636, 2516; *Ibid.*, V, 107, 558, 631, 1257
34 *Ibid.*, IV, 2803
35 *Laing charters*, no. 691
36 *Kilwinning charters*, 193-6
37 *R.M.S.*, V, 852
38 *Ibid.*, II, 2354
39 *Ibid.*, II, 2971
40 *Rentale Sancti Andree*, 206; Adv. MSS (N.L.S.), 17/1/3
41 R.F.C., i, fo. 230r
42 *R.M.S.*, IV, 1764
43 *Ibid.*, V, 74
44 *Ibid.*, IV, 883, 886, 885; V, 1132; *H.M.C. Report*, 158, 222

45 Acts and decreets, xxii, fos. 113v-117v, 167v-168v
46 *R.S.S.*, V, Pt. II, 2554; R.F.C., i, fo. 197r
47 *R.M.S.*, IV, 2268
48 R.F.C., i, fo. 9r; *R.M.S.*, IV, 2495

10

Portioners and Bonnet Lairds

'A King's name is good enough for me, though I bear it plain and have the name of no farm midden to clap to the hind end of it.'

Alan Breck Stewart, in Stevenson's *Kidnapped*

THE basic effects of becoming a proprietor, although not necessarily the most apparent, were the change in the feuar's legal status and the opportunity which security of inheritance gave him to improve his holding and circumstances.

The main legal obligation he had was the regular payment of feu-duty and what was called the *augmentation,* a distinct element in the annual dues representing the increase in rent resulting from the feuing of the land. But in addition to these, certain other payments, laid down in the charter, reflected the new legal relationship, that between superior and proprietor, and were intended to compensate the superior for the loss of income formerly derived from *grassums* paid for the renewal of tacks and rentals and from those casualties levied from tenants from time to time, such as *herezelds.* The new-style payments included *periodic grassums,* paid every three, five or seven years, and the payment of *double feu-duty* on the entry of an heir, making up for loss of the herezeld and equivalent to the feudal casualty of *relief.* On the lands of Inchaffray abbey, where very many tenants became feuars, a money equivalent of the former herezeld was paid, while the kindly tenants of Kylesmure who became feuars rendered the money equivalent of the *sasine ox,* probably to mark the taking up of possession by the heir, in place of the tenant's old *entry silver.*[1]

Superior and feuar were mutually obliged to produce the feu charter or sasine for the inspection of the other party, and some superiors were ordered by the courts to hand over title deeds to feuars or their heirs. The Register of Acts and Decreets of the civil court contains a number of such cases; the commendators of Holyrood, Kilwinning and Coldingham, the prioress of Haddington and the vicar of Drymen all demanded the production of charters granted by their predecessors in order to establish the correct amount of feu-duty payable. A case involving the bishop of Ross was complicated by the fact that the lands had been confiscated from the original feuar and then disponed to a third party by the person to whom they had been granted in the second instance.[2] In the Kilwinning case the judges accepted the feuar's explanation that he had given his wife the charter for safekeeping, but that at her death their son had made off with it.[3] Six actions for the production of title deeds, however, were raised by the feuars themselves. John

Cockburn of Ormiston complained in 1561 that although he had been given a charter by the commendator of Kelso, the latter had delayed to *infeft* him in the property, in spite of a decreet of court.[4] Elizabeth, grand-daughter of Ninian, Lord Ross, explained that she could not find her grandfather's feu charter and that the abbot of Paisley had refused to grant her a copy from 'the register buikis of the abbay'.[5] John Forrester, feuar of Balmerino, demanded the return of his *evidents* from the abbot,[6] and Margaret Balcanquell and her son brought a similar action against the same monastery.[7] Margaret Ogilvy, sister and heiress of John Ogilvy of Durne, sued Mr Alexander Anderson, subprincipal of Aberdeen university, for refusing to give her the feu charter granted to her brother by the late bishop of Aberdeen. The case was brought in February 1561, Anderson explaining that he had left the charter with his belongings in his chamber in the university 'when he last cam frae hame' and that since then 'the said college and housis thereof ar brokin up', and he could not guarantee to be able to find it.[8]

Many actions for reduction (i.e. legal cancellation) of charters appear in the civil court record, the background circumstances outlining the legal framework within which the feuar used his rights and privileges. Some cases were over failure to pay feu-duty. In March 1560 the bishop of Moray, as commendator of Scone abbey, attempted to have reduced a charter of land in the barony of Scone because the heirs mentioned in the *entail* part of the feu charter had acted on an agreement among themselves to change places in the order of succession;[9] unlike splitting the *kindness,* 'breaking the *entail*' had dire results. Some actions arose out of family tussles over the property; in 1564 James Weir, heir of Thomas Weir of Blackwood, tried to have annulled an infeftment given to a relative on the grounds of an 'alleged resignation' by himself, which he roundly denied having made.[10] Some reductions were the result of violation of a clause in the charter forbidding subfeuing.

Provisions in many charters, however, suggest that the terms were often drawn up for the benefit of the feuars, many of whom seem to have had a certain amount of bargaining power. Interesting in this connection is the large number of charters given to a grantee in *liferent* and to a named relative, usually the heir, in feu-ferm, an arrangement made in over 200 charters:

	Feu charters containing liferent provision	
Liferent to	*feu-ferm to*	*Number of charters*
Father	Son	152
Father	Daughter	1
Father	Stepson	3
Father	Son-in-law	1
Grandfather	Grandson	2
Uncle	Nephew	2
Uncle	Niece	1
Brother	Brother	3
Mother	Son	24
Widowed mother	Son	27
Mother	Daughter	2
Widowed mother	Daughter	2

Granted to occupants	114
Granted to non-occupants	39
Occupancy doubtful	67
	220

The arrangement echoes the customary practice of renewing rentals and tacks during the holder's lifetime in order to reinforce continuity, although the barony of Glasgow, where the renewal of rentals before the death of the rentaller had been common, is not represented at all among these liferent dispositions. Four of the sons who got feu charters on this basis were illegitimate and would not have inherited land otherwise. Five of them were second sons, some of whom may, nevertheless, have been surviving heirs through the death of an elder brother. The lands of Petoucher on the Dunfermline estates, leased for nineteen years to David Boswall of Glassmonth, were feued in 1557, reserving the liferent to him and his wife with the provision that after their deaths half the land would be feued to their son, William, and a quarter each to his brothers, David and Alexander; an arrangement rather like that which might have been made under the old customary laws of inheritance, where the father's kindness was divided up.[11] A sixteenth part of Raderny in Fife was feued by Archbishop John Hamilton to a sitting tenant, Thomas Stevenson, whose mother still occupied it, Stevenson keeping the liferent and the feu going to George Wilson and Margaret Stevenson, his wife, probably Thomas's daughter and son-in-law, showing how this small holding passed through three generations.[12] Charters were granted to two widows and their daughters: Matilda Sturrock, a tenant of Arbroath abbey, and her daughter, Marion Guthrie, the lands being entailed to the heirs of Matilda Sturrock, the mother, rather like a carry-over from the old kindly principle;[13] and, at Stravithie in Fife, to Elizabeth Monypenny, widow of Andrew Wood, she and her own mother sharing the liferent, while the feu went to Andrew Wood, her son.[14] A number of the charters granted to mothers in liferent and to their sons in feu were the means by which some pre-Reformation clerics provided for their illegitimate children. In 1557 one-and-three-quarters husbandlands in the town of Lessudden were granted to the occupants, Marion Cochrane in liferent and her daughter, Christian Stoddart, and her husband, Robert Bryden, in feu-ferm, showing how charters were framed to suit the family circumstances of even quite small people.[15]

We might wonder how the smallest feuars fared, having paid for their charters, and facing the heavy annual payments. Some of them were alienating their land within a generation, while others prospered as substantial portioners and bonnet lairds well into the seventeenth and, in some cases, even into the early eighteenth century. Evidence of the circumstances of these new proprietors is uneven. It tends to be fullest in the case of the bigger feuars, but interesting glimpses of the smaller folk are to be found in rentals and other estate papers, the records of the law courts and in testaments. For those feuars whose forbears had long lived in the locality and whose influence did not extend beyond travelling distance, the feu charter at least meant legal security and brought the prospect of better circumstances a little nearer. It did not, of course, usher in Utopia for those who had to reap their living from the land by their own labours, for poverty and debt had still to be kept from the door and, no matter how greatly feuing was said to improve the *policy,* the primitive methods of agriculture with their smallish returns continued as before.

Some small feuars had, in fact, built up their property gradually, which may have given them a better chance of survival. John Craigo, a Coupar Angus tenant who feued the lands of Over Campsy, or Wolfhill, is a good example. Campsy lies beside the River Tay only about two miles from Craigmakerran, feued to tenants of Scone and, although in the barony of Keithick, it was one of the most southerly of the Coupar Angus territories. In the first half of the fifteenth century Campsy was leased to several tenants who, among other duties, supplied the fishing tackle for the abbey's fishermen who worked that stretch of the Tay, with a quantity of victual for the fishermen and the abbey forester who operated in the locality. At Whitsunday 1471 the lands were leased to four tenants who were each made responsible for keeping part of the wood. At the same time they also became directly responsible for working the fishings in place of the paid fishermen. They were allowed a total of sixty oxen and cows and the forester-general four cows and a horse, 'and he shall remain with the rest of the cottars at the head of the wood, and no one shall burn any of the wood except it be from the ditch nearer the ploughed land.' The tenants kept the fishing boat in repair, it being provided by the abbey, and were forbidden to sell the fish without the abbot's licence. This tack was granted for a year as an experiment, 'and thereafter during the abbot's pleasure'.[16] Three years later the arrangement was still working. In 1479, when it was renewed for another trial period of a year, the tenants were told to take into cultivation land at Blair 'and of the forest within the walls as much as they can'. There was to be only one cottar in the town, Andrew Dawson, and 'another for carrying the fish brought to the monastery at their expense'.[17]

In 1483 a John Craigo appears for the first time at Campsy as one of four tenants who received a five-year tack with conditions 'as before', except the additional obligation to build a wall round the forest in two years; possibly, with land intake going on, the limits of the forest area had to be redefined.[18] In 1494 the land outside the forest walls was leased, two parts to John Bell for six years, and a third part for five years to John Craigo, 'with that part next the Lymekyl', with liberty to have six cows inside the forest area 'along with the cattle of the monastery'.[19] In 1508 the lease of Campsy was renewed for five years to John Craigo and the Bells, father and son, except the riverside meadow stretching from Campsy to Stobhall. Details were given of the fishing tackle which the tenants were to 'sustain' and with which they were to fish 'diligently day and nicht', at all times of the year, all fishing gear to be ready for use 'within eight dais eftir their corne be led in'.[20]

In 1513 John Craigo increased his own holding, taking a five-year lease of 'the thryd onder the wod and the quarter bown the wod of Campsy'.[21] At the same time he and sir Alexander Spence witnessed, in the abbey kirk, the ratification of an agreement between another tenant, David Pullour, and his son about the former's liferent of a tack.[22] In 1532, there is a note in the abbey rental book 'Elizabeth Bell, relict of John Craigo, John Craigo her son, and Jonat Jak his spouse, in three fourths of Wolfhill.'[23] John, younger, kept possession of the family's holding and in December 1578 received a feu charter of it from Leonard

Leslie, the commendator.[24] John Craigo's farming background was one of changing land use, continual acquisition, land intake and varied obligations towards the landlord, as well as a tradition of continuous possession, and what was true of him, about whom we know so much, was probably also true of countless tenants whom we sometimes picture as cultivating the land in a static, monotonous environment. For people like these the coming of feu-ferm was simply yet another change, although an expensive one, and a change which not only legalised their customary security but gave them increased liberty to develop their property. John Craigo's charter not only conveyed Over Campsy, or Wolfhill, but also five acres of Boghall, part of the moss of Monkmyre, lying further north, and certain customs from the Fair held every Friday before the monastery gates. He was also given a piece of waste ground in the burgh of Keithick, next to the monastery, measuring twenty-four feet by sixteen feet, on the north side of the market cross and cuckstool, on which to build a house. Yet, while John Craigo was adding to his possessions and acquiring property in the little trading centre of Keithick, the lands of Nether Campsy, held by his fellow tenants of the farmer-cum-fisher community on the River Tay, were granted to the earl of Atholl who was also given the right to teinds of the whole of Campsy, including John Craigo's feu lands.[25]

On the other side of the country a small tenant of the barony of Kilwinning, Thomas Niven, whom we have met before, became even more prosperous and influential than John Craigo of Wolfhill. In the little rental book dating from the first half of the sixteenth century the lands of Monkredding, only about two miles north-east of the abbey, were set to three tenants, Thomas Niven, John Adam and Giles Jamieson, the last-named probably a widow with the liferent of her husband's rental.[26] Between 1539 and 1545 Thomas Niven took the whole of Monkredding and neighbouring lands in feu; on 20 July 1539 he and his wife received a feu charter of the 20s land of East Monkredding 'cultivated by them',[27] four years later, in 1543, Thomas feued the lands of Guslone and Bannach, lying roughly north-east and south-west of Monkredding,[28] and in April 1545 a third charter brought him West Monkredding, Gaitmureland and three holdings in the toun of Kilwinning itself at Corshill, Corseholm and Nethermains.[29] His annual feu-duty for all these lands amounted to £7 14s. In 1546 he is found resigning some *templelands* at the Bridgend of Kilwinning, which he must have acquired at an earlier stage, in favour of Hugh Montgomery of Smithston.[30] If the laird of Smithston compensated him for his resignation, this would help to defray the cost of crown confirmation of his three charters which he obtained in the same year.

Thomas's son, Andrew Niven, had succeeded to his father's lands by February 1560. Some involvement in the public affairs of the time is suggested by Andrew's signature on the Band of Ayr of 1562, in defence of the Reformed religion, with the signatures of the lairds of Cunninghamhead and Auchinharvie and that of John Fergushill of that Ilk, a near neighbour.[31] As a small laird, Niven of Monkredding leased land from the neighbouring earl of Eglinton, witnessed a number of the earl's legal transactions and, in 1568, was curator of the young Master of Eglinton.[32] Andrew's wife, Janet Montgomery, was no doubt related to a branch of the earl's house. In the Kilwinning barony court, in 1585, Niven raised an action for removal of tenants from the lands of Bannach and Gaitmureland and during his defence produced his sasines as heir to his father, dated 1557 and 1560.[33] A list of parishioners of about 1560 names a number of his sub-tenants, three at Guslone, five at Monkredding, one at Gaitmureland and five at Bannach.[34] Andrew Niven died in 1597, leaving an inventory of over £2,000 and *free gear* (remaining moveables after his debts had been deducted) of over £1,840. The wife of the Master of Eglinton owed him £276.[35] His inventory, although it lists only a few animals and a small amount of grain, mentions 500 loads of coal 'about the house and in the same' valued at £9 'the hundreth', amounting to £145, probably the main reason for the Nivens' prosperity. In all likelihood it was Andrew who began building the typical laird's house which still stands, much added to, at Monkredding; he made his will 'at the dwelling place of Monkredding in 1597. Timothy Pont, who saw the house when it was occupied by Andrew's grandson and namesake in the early seventeenth century, described it as 'a proper dwelling, weill planted, yeilding in all the ground thereof colles and belongs to Andrew Niven laird thereof'.[36] The family remained in possession as feuars for 159 years, until 1698, when the estate was sold to near neighbours, the Cunninghams of Clonbeith, whose family had also become feuars of Kilwinning abbey, in the 1530s.[37]

It is not often possible to chart the fortunes of small feuars like John Craigo and the Nivens but sometimes, in the family papers of bigger landowners who either acquired the superiority of former church estates or bought up small feus in the seventeenth and eighteenth centuries, there are deeds and other papers which do throw light on the circumstances of smaller people. For example, some of Andrew Niven's neighbours in the barony of Kilwinning appear in the Eglinton archives. In April 1546 John Garven, whose family was one of five on the lands of Auchinmaid to receive feu charters of their holdings, formally resigned his right to the abbot in favour of his son, Luke Garven, whose charter was granted some sixteen months later.[38] Auchinmaid, lying in the upland, northern part of the barony, suitable for pastoral farming, had previously been set to the tenants jointly for payment of 112 stones of cheese and thirteen stirks. Luke Garven's feu-duty was set at forty-four stones of cheese and four and a half stirks, with another stone of cheese as augmentation, all payments probably commuted. For some reason his *precept of sasine,* entitling him formally to take up possession, was delayed for seven months, but there was no need to hurry the formalities, since Luke and his father were in occupation and farming the land as tenants.[39] Crown confirmation of the charter was not obtained until 1585, in the lifetime of Luke's grandson, John Garven,[40] who had succeeded his father in 1572, in which year he also wadset the land to an Irvine burgess in order to raise money.[41] Two years later a relative, Stephen Garven, was making arrangements with the burgess to redeem the land.[42] Three generations had held the lands of Auchinmaid as feuars within twenty-five years. The descendants of two other feuars of Auchinmaid, John Gemmill and John Mure, were still in possession in the first decade of the seventeenth century,[43] while the grandson of a fourth feuar there, James White, succeeded in 1617.[44] In fact, the descendants of twenty Kilwinning feuars who got their charters in the late 1550s appear in possession between 1600 and 1609, in the Secretary's Register of Sasines, and a number of them survived even longer.[45]

In contrast, we find John Morris of the same barony, probably the grandson of William Morris in Dalgaw who feued his holding in 1557,[46] alienating the land to the earl of Eglinton in 1582 who, in turn, granted it to his second son.[47] Another local family who eventually sold their feu were the Youngs at Nethermains. John Young feued 13s 4d of Nethermains in 1557[48] but, twenty-eight years later, his son Laurence got permission from the commendator to sell the lands 'to any person'.[49] Within the next eight years he appears to have twice wadset them. It was probably Laurence's son, by then described as 'a shoemaker in Ireland', who, at the turn of the century, resigned all his rights to this part of Nethermains to the earl of Eglinton.[50] All these developments illustrate the land speculation of the nearby burgesses of Irvine, who had money to lend to the struggling rural proprietors, the efforts of the earls of Eglinton, on the eve of their acquisition of the lordship of Kilwinning, to engross the church land on their doorstep of which they had never received a single charter, and the trend towards emigration from this part of Scotland to Ireland in the seventeenth century.

In the barony of Strathisla in Banffshire the sons and grandsons of Kinloss abbey's feuars are to be found wadsetting and exchanging their lands in the early seventeenth century in order to add to or to consolidate their portions.[51] Many of these small proprietors, related to one another by blood and marriage, regularly stood surety for one another or witnessed one another's transactions. In mid-seventeenth century, small tower houses began to appear in Strathisla, the names of many of the feuars' families being perpetuated in the district.[52] William Longmore, benefactor of the burgh of Keith in the later nineteenth century, was able to trace his descent from the Langmures who feued parts of Strathisla in the sixteenth century. In the 1790s the Rev. Francis Forbes wrote in the *First Statistical Account* of the parish of Grange: 'being thus feued out among a great number of small proprietors at the Reformation, continued in that situation except some few changes till towards the end of the last century when Alexander Duff of Braco got possession of the greater part of these small feus.'[53]

Detailed information on the circumstances of many of the new proprietors is to be found in their testaments, although this kind of material has to be used with certain reservations. In the first place, it is concerned only with moveable wealth, at a time when a man's substance was assessed not so much according to the market value of his goods and gear as from the rental of his land, a matter on which the testaments do not give much information. Secondly, even in the case of moveable goods themselves, we have no way of knowing how many of these had been given away among family and friends before an inventory was drawn up, nor are we told the value of the *heirship goods* which were exempt from the catalogue but were generally supposed to be the best and most valuable of their kinds. Allowing for an all-over margin of incompleteness, however, the value of the *free gear* of a number of feuars is a helpful figure for comparative purposes, indicating how a man succeeded or failed in managing his affairs, which in turn depended on a measure, or lack, of economic resources and favourable, or adverse, circumstances. The amount of free gear, that is moveable wealth after deduction of debts owing at the time of death, left by thirty-four small feuars — from Group 4 — is shown in the following Table. They are all almost certainly resident occupants. The amounts have been given to the nearest pound *Scots*:

Table 6: Moveable wealth of feuars in Group 4[54]

Feuar	Free gear to nearest £ Scots
John Watson in Balgey (Scone)	14
Andrew Oswald in Falkirk (Holyrood)	64
Andrew Donaldson in Templeton of Balgrugo (Coupar Angus)	107
Walter Drew in Burngray (Glasgow)	118
Stephen Hunter of Williamlaw (Newbattle)	137
Thomas Cook in Newbigging of Carsegrange (Coupar Angus)	141
John Porter in Stanbyres (Kelso)	151
John Learmonth in Sauchton (Holyrood)	156
Alexander Easton in Heads (Torphichen)	162
David Herd in Easthouses (Newbattle)	182
Alexander Morris in Goukstoun (St Andrews priory)	238
David Matthew in Kilburns (Balmerino)	241
John Weir in Clanochdykes (Kelso)	250
John Haggart in Wester Caputh (Dunkeld)	256
John Pery (Coupar Angus)	288
Alexander Jackson in Waterybutts (Coupar Angus)	302
John Cas in Monktounhall (Dunfermline/Musselburgh)	323
John Dick in Gartmore (East Wemyss parish kirk)	352
Robert Martin in Gibliston (Pittenweem priory)	352
Laurence Cockburn in kirkland of Bolton (Bolton parish kirk)	392
Thomas Thomson in Monktounhall (Dunfermline)	414
James Geddie in Urquhart (Pluscarden priory)	430
Arthur Straton in Kirkside (St Andrews priory)	439
William Dick in Ledcassy (Scone)	459
Humphrey Richard, Maybole (Melrose)	552
John Jackson in Killelong (Holywood)	581
Thomas Turnbull in Bogmill (Coupar Angus)	588
David Edgar, portioner of Gulyhill (Holywood)	716
David Bissat, portioner of Balbrogie (Coupar Angus)	840
William Soutar in Bauchrie (Scone)	855
Alexander Ogston in kirkland of Fettercairn (St Andrews priory)	923
John Watson, portioner, Sauchtonhall (Holyrood)	.1,106
William Small of Foddranes (Scone)	1,939

In some cases a large debt due by the feuar himself accounts for a small amount of free gear. The inventory of John Watson in Balgey, for instance, first on the above list, amounted to £1,483 16s 8d, but he owed others a total of £1,531 17s 2d; there is a long list of borrowings by him. On the other hand, some feuars were due a fair amount from other people, which adds in the end to the total of free gear, although their inventories may have been comparatively small. This was true of Robert Martin in Gibliston, whose inventory consisted entirely of household goods worth only £4, but to whom others owed £347. No debts were recorded against William Small of Foddranes, who was comfortably off for a proprietor in this group. Six of these feuars had over twenty oxen on their lands and ten of them had more than fifty sheep. William Small, who had feued the lands of Foddranes in 1560, had forty-one oxen there at the time of his death in 1584.[55]

The family of Drew, formerly rentallers of the archbishop of Glasgow, had been in possession of parts of Davidston since 1521.[56] In 1558 a Walter Drew was rentalled in the family holding on the death of his father and it is probably his testament which is recorded here, in 1581.[57] Three months after his death his son Walter was rentalled in the holding, taking it in feu soon afterwards.[58] In the charter, Walter, younger, the feuar, is designated as the archbishop's tenant in Burnbrae which lay next to Davidston and where he had probably lived during his father's lifetime. His father's testament, probably reflecting the circumstances of many Glasgow rentallers, contained an inventory of £165, including four oxen, twenty-two sheep and £10 of household goods.

David Herd in Easthouses died in 1584, only four years after receiving a charter from the commendator of Newbattle of property in Easthouses including some ruined premises, a croft of land with some pasture and liberty to cut peats. He was given permission to rebuild the ruined houses.[59] At the time of his death his inventory amounted to only £10, but most of the debts due to him were of 'lent siller', totalling £146. He had ten merksworth of household goods and his stock consisted of ten sheep, a stirk, a cow, a grey horse and 'ane auld cruikit black naig'. The feu no doubt passed from his immediate family since he left no sons, only a daughter whom he commended to his executors, leaving £100 with which she was to be 'nureist, cled, fed and upbrot' by them.

Andrew Oswald, feuar of the lands of Huik in the barony of Kerse in Stirlingshire, who died in Flanders in September 1581, leaving a widow and two daughters, may previously have alienated his feu, since in July 1581 the lands were in the hands of John Kincaid of Warriston who had feued other Holyrood territory.[60] James Watson, a resident occupant in Sauchtonhall, who feued three separate portions there in January 1569, also held thirty-two acres from the laird of Reidhall and had inherited property in Edinburgh, leaving his right to a *land* in the Fishmarket there to his third son, Isaac Watson, and his right to 'the laird of Corstorphine's *lands*' to his second son, Robert; the latter may have been houses in the burgh which he rented to Forrester of Corstorphine. Watson seems to have been reasonably prosperous, with an inventory of over £1,160, a landward small farmer with property interests in Edinburgh.[61] The Watsons of Sauchton became considerable landowners by the nineteenth century.

David Edgar, who drew up his will at 'his dwelling place of Gullyhill', had originally received his feu charter in conjunction with his brother, sir William Edgar, a chaplain, in 1556.[62] Three years later David was granted more land in the barony of Holywood.[63] His inventory amounted to £387 13s 4d and the money which others had borrowed from him to over £328. In spite of lending money, he still possessed £40 in 'readie siller' and ten gold crowns.[64]

For these small feuars security rather than prosperity was the outcome of their feu charters, a security and increased rights in the use of the land of which their families would begin to feel the benefit in the comparatively settled years of the early seventeenth century.

Moving away from the small feuars who had previously been tenants, we come to proprietors of kirklands among small landed families who had been independently established in Scottish rural society for several generations, but were neither offshoots of the bigger lairds nor cadet branches of noble houses: the Reids and Airds in Kylesmure, feuars of Melrose abbey, the Browns in Dumfriesshire and Kirkcudbrightshire, feuars of Sweetheart abbey, who benefited from two successive abbacies by members of the family, the Welshes and Edgars in the same district, feuars of Holywood, Dundrennan and Lincluden. All over the country we find self-made proprietors on church land who *arrived* at this position in the social hierarchy without the backing of influential relatives among the lairds or nobles and whose descendants went on to become even more influential and prosperous: Andrew Lamb of South Tarrie, feuar of Arbroath, from a Leith merchant family whose services to Cardinal Beaton first got them leases and then feus of Arbroath property,[65] Alan Coutts, chamberlain and feuar of Dunfermline abbey land,[66] John Welwood of Garvock, also feuar of Dunfermline.[67]

Then we find the relatives of lairds and bigger landholders striking out for themselves as independent proprietors, by means of a charter of church land: Blackadders in Clackmannanshire, Carnegies and Guthries in Angus, Chisholms in Perthshire, Crawfords in Renfrewshire and in the barony of Glasgow. In February 1559 Thomas Crawford, son of Laurence Crawford of Kilbirnie, then styled 'of Camphills', received a charter from the chaplain of Our Lady at Drumry of the five-pound lands of Jordanhill in the barony of Renfrew which his father had mortified to the chapel — a roundabout way of the laird's family getting the lands back on the eve of the Reformation. As Crawford of Jordanhill, Thomas added to his property over the years, in the barony of Glasgow, in Renfrewshire and north Ayrshire.[68]

Members of cadet branches of noble families carved estates for themselves out of grants of kirklands: Boyds, Campbells, Gordons, Hamiltons, Homes, Kennedys and Montgomeries, some of whom were already tenants of the ecclesiastical landlords concerned. Some of them had even been resident on the land they leased and then feued: Adam Boyd, great-grandson of the third Lord Boyd, styled '*in* Penkill' in his feu charter which he got from the post-Reformation commendator of Crossraguel abbey, although his forbears had built up for themselves a considerable holding on the abbey estates.[69] The feuar-laird of Penkill died in 1572 and was succeeded by his grandson, who died in 1596.[70] Details in their respective testaments suggest a changed way of life by the end of the century. Whereas Adam, senior, left an inventory of only £267 9s 4d, his grandson's amounted to £921, which included household goods to the value of £100. At the same time, Adam, younger, was over £300 in debt to other people as compared with the £48 owed by his grandafather, the original feuar. It was probably the younger laird who built much of the earlier part of Penkill castle which his son, Thomas, born posthumously, added to in the seventeenth century.

Another member of a long-established tenant family to feu his lands in south-west Scotland, who was descended from a noble house, was Robert Campbell *in* Kinzeancleuch in Kyle, member of a branch of the Argyll family who had settled in Ayrshire. His charter, granted by Michael Balfour, commendator of Melrose, in April 1562, a few months before Campbell signed the Band of Ayr, conveyed the 31s land of Overhauch 'called Kinzeancleuch', the waulk mill next to Kinzeancleuch wood, a tenement and yard in the toun of Mauchline and a number of other pieces of land, some occupied by Campbell and his cottars and some by other tenants.[71] In 1565 he had a grant of fishings in the River Ayr.[72]

While it would seem that most burgesses who became feuars were interested in property in and around the burghs, there were some who acquired landward property and a few who built up considerable estates as a result. A short comparative Table of the free gear left by some of these urban-based new proprietors of church land illustrates their superior financial resources to those of the tenant-feuars in Table 6:

Table 7: Moveable wealth of burgess-feuars of
landward church property

	Free gear to nearest £ Scots
George Johnston, or MacGregor, Perth	35
(Charterhouse and Dull parish kirk)	
Andrew Edgar, Dumfries (Holywood)	212
William Kinloch, Dundee (Brechin)	354
Peter Algeo, Paisley (Paisley)	457
James Barton, shipmaster, Leith (Inchcolm)	904
Archibald Lyon, Glasgow (Glasgow)	1,101
John Logan, Leith (Inchcolm)	1,159
George Herbertson, Glasgow (Glasgow)	2,065
Thomas Henderson, Edinburgh (Newbattle)	2,563
George Elphinston, Glasgow (Erskine parish kirk)	3,426
Michael Gilbert, goldsmith, Edinburgh (Restalrig collegiate church)	22,568

The cases of Michael Gilbert and George Johnston, at top and bottom of the scale as far as wealth is concerned, are interesting reminders that financial resources did not automatically lead to land speculation, for only one charter to Gilbert, the goldsmith, has come to light and no fewer than five to Johnston, a skinner and much humbler craftsman.[73] The career of Michael Gilbert, a prominent Edinburgh goldsmith who died in 1590, has been over-shadowed by that of George Heriot who followed King James VI to England, but he was influential in his day. The son of an advocate and brother-in-law of Mr Peter Young, the king's tutor, Gilbert had close associations with the legal profession, his three daughters being married to prominent advocates, Thomas Bannatyne, John Preston and Henry McCalzean; much of the money-lending which accompanied the endless lawsuits of the nobility must have come his way. The only charter of kirklands in his favour which has been discovered is that granted to him in 1560 by the dean of Restalrig collegiate church of two ruinous tenements of land lying next to the burgh of Dalkeith. It is significant that a man with Gilbert's capital should have invested so little of it in church property which was coming onto the market in the Lothians, preferring to indulge in money-lending on a large scale, to the king and to many other individuals. At his death the king and the treasurer-depute jointly owed him 3,000 merks, and a long list of prominent people were in his debt. He did hold some non-church property including land at Ravelston, which he feued from the burgh of Edinburgh.[74]

At the other end of the scale is George Johnston, or MacGregor, a skinner in Perth, whose five charters included lands outside the burgh. In February 1562 he received half the kirklands of the parish church of Dull, with some pasture and liberty to cut peat and turfs for building. In December 1566 he feued the lands of Bynyemoir, which he already held in tack, lying in the lordship of Glendochart on the Perthshire/Argyllshire border, from the prior of the Charterhouse in Perth. Craftsman though he was, Johnston was influential enough to be made a bailie in the crown-controlled burgh election of April 1566 as a result of which Lord Ruthven became provost. In 1577 he was one of eight persons 'thocht maist meit and indifferent' to sit with the Lords Auditors of the Exchequer in revising the burgh accounts after the exposure of a corruption case. In spite of his influence, however, Johnston fell on bad times financially, and when he died in October 1581 he left an inventory of only £13 6s 8d which consisted entirely of household goods.[75]

Some burgesses, particularly the merchants, would have been prosperous, by contemporary standards, without feuing church land, others were comparatively poor after having done so. George Elphinston, burgess of Glasgow, acquired an estate almost in the modern sense. In 1563 the parson of Erskine, David Stewart, canon of Glasgow cathedral, feued the £3 land of Blythswood lying to the north-east of the city to Elphinston who, although a kinsman of Lord Elphinston, was, like his father before him, a citizen of Glasgow.[76] A prominent merchant and bailie, he became known as Elphinston of Blythswood, leaving an inventory of moveables at his death in 1585 of almost £3,000. Much of his wealth lay in his share of the cargoes of two ships and in the silver work that he owned, although over £600 in ready money lay in his booth in the city.[77] Without surviving accounts it is difficult to say how much the acquisition of a landward estate added to the wealth and prosperity of a man like Elphinston.

Of the 225 burgesses and their relatives who feued church property only a handful acquired sufficient to put them in the category of new landowners or to suggest that they were seriously speculating in land. Apart from Elphinston of Blythswood, Gilbert Balfour of Westray in Orkney, burgess of Edinburgh, is a good example.[78] Andrew Buk, burgess of Aberdeen, had four charters from Bishop William Gordon and one from the chaplains of St Nicholas' church, by which he gained possession of the mill and mill lands of Murthill, the lands of Corthymure with their smithy and mill crofts and of certain fishings in the River Dee.[79] Mr Thomas Menzies, also an Aberdeen burgess, acquired the lands of Fordyce and Hallyards near Portsoy in Banffshire, but they were feued to him on the resignation of his wife, who had possessed the *kindness* as heir of her father.[80] James Adamson, an Edinburgh burgess, feued the lands of Cowthopill, extending to 150 acres, from the commendator of Newbattle, for which he paid an annual feu-duty of £20.[81] Walter Haliburton, burgess of Dundee, had a charter of four merklands of the toun of Merton in his native Berwickshire from the commendator of Dryburgh, having previously held them on a nineteen-year tack.[82] The great majority of burgesses, however, feued plots of land, yards and premises in burghs, which would perhaps bring a merchant improved warehouse facilities or add to the rents which many of them already drew from the subtenants of burgh 'lands', but not necessarily add greatly to their incomes or give them a step up the social ladder.

Turning to the clergy who became feuars, some of them acquired sufficient property to put them in the landholding class in the second half of the sixteenth century. Mr William Bailie, canon of Glasgow, whose rich prebend brought him the title of 'my lord of Provand' before the Reformation, feued extensive territory in north Ayrshire from the dean and chapter of Glasgow, paying 1,000 merks for his charter.[83] He himself granted his prebendal lands of Provand to Thomas Bailie of Ravenscraig but, the latter having died in considerable debt, the property appears to have returned to Bailie himself before his death in 1593. Active in the affairs of Glasgow university in the 1550s and, later, prominent in Edinburgh as a judge in the Court of Session, Bailie's manner of life was that of a secular landholder influential in public affairs. When he died he had in his possession £1,300 in ready money.[84]

Mr Alexander Dunbar, himself the son of a dean of Moray, succeeded to that dignity in 1559. Having conformed at the Reformation, he married, in 1562, Katherine Reid, sister of Walter Reid, abbot of Kinloss. In terms of the marriage contract the commendator promised to give his sister 500 merks *tocher* and to infeft her in the lands of West Grange. In 1566 Dunbar and his wife received a charter from his brother-in-law of the lands of Meikle Burgie in the barony of Kinloss, and in the following years added to his property.[85] The Dunbars lived in the dean's manse at Elgin, where their daughter was tragically killed in an attack during the Dunbar/Innes feud, but either the dean or his son Robert, who inherited his father's estate of Burgie, built a house there which was completed in 1602.[86]

Six ministers of the Reformed kirk received feu charters but, presumably, the land would change hands if they were translated to distant parishes as tended to happen, unless the minister was able to arrange for collection of rents from his subtenants. It would be interesting to try to discover what happened to land feued to clerics before the Reformation; perhaps, like some merchants and crown servants, they were indulging in speculation, later resigning the lands for financial profit, rather than intending to turn themselves into landed proprietors.

An interesting development following on the feuing of church lands is the number of tower houses and castles which were built or enlarged by the feuars or their heirs in the sixteenth and early seventeenth centuries, a number of which are still standing on what were formerly church estates. Sometimes a feuar took over an existing building: an episcopal castle as at Farnell (Brechin), Skibo (Caithness), Monimail (St Andrews) and Castle Gloom, Cramond Tower and Cluny Castle (Dunkeld); an abbot's residence such as Ethie (Arbroath) and Rossend (Dunfermline); or a building connected with monastic estate management, as at Monkcastle (Kilwinning) or Hassendean and Mauchline (Melrose).

Gloom Castle, renamed Castle Campbell, feued by the bishop of Dunkeld to the earl of Argyll, commands a magnificent view south towards the Firth of Forth. When the second earl came into possession of it at the end of the fifteenth century, it consisted of little more than an oblong tower to which was added, in the sixteenth century, an enclosure with improved living quarters connected to the tower by a new turnpike, while the courtyard facade of the east range of these new buildings has a domestic, almost Renaissance appearance, with a loggia, or open-sided arcade, resembling that at Falkland palace.[87] Cramond tower, of which very little remains, was granted to Archibald Douglas of Kilspindie in 1574,[88] and the bishop of Caithness's castle of Skibo, the shell of which still stands on the shores of the Dornoch Firth, was feued to the earl of Sutherland, with huge tracts of the bishop's lands, in February 1581.[89]

The Carnegies of Kinnaird, having come into possession of Ethie castle in 1555, considerably altered and enlarged it. The castle of Rossend, as it came to be called, stood on land belonging to Dunfermline abbey and was included in a charter which Abbot George Durie granted to his son, Peter Durie, in 1552.[90] An armorial panel bearing the Durie arms and the date 1554, now placed above the modern porch, may relate to building activities by the younger Durie. Of the tower of Hassendean, granted by the abbot of Melrose to Walter Scott of Branxholm in 1568, nothing now remains.[91] At Mauchline in Ayrshire, the building known as 'the castle' was associated with the headquarters of the administration of Melrose abbey's barony of Kylesmure and, according to surviving account books of the chamberlain, was being repaired internally in the 1520s.[92] In 1565 Matthew Campbell of Loudon was given a feu charter of the office of bailie of Kylesmure with a grant of land which included the Mains and castle of Mauchline.[93] The present tower dates from the fifteenth century but some alterations to the windows, giving the building a more domestic appearance, seem to be of a later period.[94] The tower of Monkcastle, which stood midway between Kilwinning abbey and its barony of Beith, in Cunninghame, was described by Timothy Pont in mid-seventeenth century as 'a pretty fair building weill planted, the inheritance of Hamilton, earl of Abercorn'. In 1553 the castle, with parts of the nearby lands of Dalgarven, Auchinkist and Birklands, was feued by Gavin Hamilton, the commendator, to the duke of Chatelherault, who eventually passed it on to his son, Lord Claud Hamilton. The building, the ruins of which stand near to the modern mansion of the same name, has little of a castellated character about it.[95]

Here and there, tenants who feued the lands which they occupied, built or rebuilt houses, particularly in the latter part of the sixteenth century, though it was sometimes left to their heirs to do so in the later years of King James VI's reign. Mention has already been made of Monkredding House, built by the Nivens in the barony of Kilwinning. In July 1545 John Guthrie, who had had a tack of the lands of Colliston from David Beaton as abbot of Arbroath eleven years previously, received a feu charter of his lands.[96] Parts of Colliston castle date from his lifetime, and his arms, with those of his wife, the date 1553 and the words 'Laus Deo', are carved on one of the turrets. A later member of the family who added to the house in the early seventeenth century set the royal arms above the doorway, with the date 1621.[97] In the parish of Dailly stands Brunston castle, which was in existence in 1569 when William Kennedy and his formidable wife 'Black Bessie Kennedy' feued the lands. Messrs McGibbon and Ross were of the opinion that the building dated from a period after Kennedy's lifetime, but it is mentioned in his feu charter.[98] The impressive tower of Craignethan castle in the barony of Lesmahagow had already been built by Sir James Hamilton of Finnart, the king's Master of Works, when he received charters of the castle and surrounding lands between 1532 and 1534.[99] Newbyres castle, near Gorebridge in Midlothian, was built by the Borthwicks of Glengelt, whose coat of arms appears on the tower, the lands having been feued by the abbot of Newbattle in 1543 to Michael Borthwick of Glengelt who already held them in tack.[100]

Mr Thomas Menzies, burgess of Aberdeen, built the castle of Fordyce in Banffshire, near the modern village of Portsoy, on land which, as we have seen, he acquired through his wife. An inscription on the castle referring to its erection is dated 1592. Mr Hugh Rig, advocate, who built Carberry tower near Musselburgh, had already had a nineteen-year tack of the lands of Carberry when he feued them from the abbot of Dunfermline in 1543, paying £500 for his charter.[101] In November 1560 David Balfour of Balledmonth received from the commendator of St Andrews priory a charter of the kirklands of Forgan in Fife, of which he had earlier had a tack, after the resignation of Margaret Erskine, the commendator's mother.[102] The building which Balfour erected some time later is more correctly described as a house than a castle, although it is now entirely ruinous. A fireplace was removed from it at one time and built into the gable of a barn at Kirkton Barns farm nearby; it carried a panel with the Balfour and Crichton arms, the initials of David Balfour and his wife, Katherine Crichton, and the date 1585.[103] That the Balfours did live in a house here is suggested by a charter granted by David and dated 'at Kirktoun' on 20 May 1594.[104] There are a few examples of houses built by middlemen, people who came from a variety of backgrounds. David Kennedy of Pennyglen, a Carrick laird, feued the lands of Baltersan near Crossraguel abbey in 1569.[105] Although the lairds of Row, with whom his family were connected, had lived there earlier in the century, which presupposes a dwelling of some kind, the typical tower house of Baltersan, the remains of which still stand, was probably built or altered in the second half of the century.[106] Terpersie castle in Aberdeenshire was built by the Gordons of Lessmoir, the lands having been granted to the laird's son, Mr William Gordon, in 1556.[107] In 1602 a castle was built on the estate of Burgie which was feued by the dean of Moray and his wife in 1566. William Adamson, the Edinburgh merchant who, in 1542, feued the lands of Craigcrook near Corstorphine from a prebendary of St Giles Church, probably began building the attractive residence which was much more of a house than a fortalice and to which additions were made in the seventeenth century. Craigcrook remained in the possession of his family until 1659.[108] One of the most striking illustrations of how church property could be thoroughly secularised must surely be at the nunnery of North Berwick, where the prioress's kinsman, Alexander Hume, who feued many of the nunnery lands, actually built a private tower house onto the walls of the monastic buildings.[109]

While heritable tenure, improved social and economic standing and increased use of the land were some of the advantages of taking land in feu, there was another, darker side to the picture for those feuars who found the new situation a financial strain and for those tenants who were unable to feu their holdings.

Notes

1 *Melrose Regality*, III, 165-6
2 Acts and decreets, v, fo. 209v
3 *Ibid.*, xvi, fo. 338r
4 *Ibid.*, xxii, fo. 86r
5 *Ibid.*, xxiii, fo. 444r
6 *Ibid.*, xv, pt. i, fo. 3v
7 *Ibid.*, xvi, fo. 437v
8 *Ibid.*, xx, fo. 29r
9 *Ibid.*, xx, fo. 158r
10 *Ibid.*, xxviii, fo. 225r
11 *R.M.S.*, V, 847
12 R.S.S., lii, fo. 45r
13 *Ibid.*, liii, fo. 23r
14 *R.M.S.*, V, 802
15 Scott of Raeburn muniments (S.R.O.), GD 104/5
16 *Cupar*, I, 220-21
17 *Ibid.*, I, 222, 227
18 *Ibid.*, I, 237
19 *Ibid.*, I, 242
20 *Ibid.*, I, 274
21 *Ibid.*, I, 290
22 *Ibid.*
23 *Ibid.*, I, 314
24 *Laing charters*, no. 973
25 *R.M.S.*, IV, 1809
26 Eglinton muniments, GD 3/1361
27 *R.M.S.*, III, 3245
28 *Ibid.*
29 *Ibid.*
30 Balir muniments (S.R.O.), GD 167, Box 8/3
31 John Knox, *History*, II, 56
32 Eglinton muniments, GD 3/1/588, 204, 504
33 Collection of Shepherd and Wedderburn (S.R.O.), GD 242/72/1/1
34 Acts and decreets, xxii, fos. 114r-v
35 Edin. testaments, CC8/8/33, 20 April 1599
36 G. Robertson, *Particular description of Ayrshire*, 331
37 *Ibid.*, 224
38 Eglinton muniments, GD 3/1/748
39 *Ibid.*, GD 3/1/753
40 *Ibid.*, GD 3/1/754
41 *Ibid.*, GD 3/1/756
42 Register of deeds, Old Series, xiii, fo. 30r
43 Register of Sasines for Ayrshire, RS 11/4, fo. 30r
44 Eglinton muniments, GD 3/2/82/2 (Inventory)
45 Register of Sasines for Ayrshire, RS 11

46 *R.M.S.*, V, 858
47 Eglinton muniments, GD 3/2/87/3 (Inventory); GD 3/1/835
48 *Ibid.*, GD 3/1/789
49 *Ibid.*, GD 3/1/790
50 *Ibid.*, GD 3/1/800
51 Secretary's register of sasines, Banff, RS 15/1, *passim*
52 J.F.S. Gordon, *op. cit., passim*
53 *O.S.A.*, ix, 555
54 The testaments of these people can be located in the manuscript registers in the Scottish Record Office by using the printed indexes published by the Scottish Record Society.
55 Edin. testaments, CC 8/8/25, fo. 168r
56 *Glasgow Registers*, I, *passim*
57 Edin. testaments, CC 8/8/10, fo. 303r
58 *R.M.S.*, V, 619
59 Edin. testaments, CC 8/8/14, fo. 305r; R.F.C., ii, fo. 258r
60 Edin. testaments, CC 8/8/11, fo. 163r
61 *Ibid.*, CC 8/8/14, fo. 39v
62 *R.M.S.*, V, 194
63 *Ibid.*
64 Edin. testaments, CC 8/8/22, fo. 90v
65 *R.M.S.*, IV, 2288; *Aberbrothoc*, II, nos. 644, 779; *Rentale Sancti Andree*, 122; G. Donaldson, *Thirds of Benefices* (S.H.S.), 279 (*Thirds of Benefices*)
66 *R.M.S.*, IV, 2969; V, 185, 898; Register House charters, RH6/1769; Yester writs, GD 28/7/738b; R.F.C., i, fo. 83r
67 *R.M.S.*, V, 736
68 *Ibid.*, IV, 2063, 2199, 2858; V, 260; R.F.C., i, fo. 130r
69 *R.M.S.*, IV, 2143
70 Edin. testaments, CC 8/8/3, fo. 259v; CC 8/8/29, fo. 460v
71 *R.M.S.*, IV, 1854
72 R.F.C., i, fo. 302r
73 *R.M.S.*, V, 612; IV, 1729, 1730, 2579, 3035; V, 726
74 Edin. testaments, CC 8/1/23, fo. 269r
75 *Ibid.*, CC 8/8/26, fo. 307v
76 *R.M.S.*, IV, 1785
77 Edin. testaments, CC 8/8/17, fo. 158v
78 *R.M.S.*, IV, 1668
79 *Ibid.*, IV, 1725
80 Dunecht writs (S.R.O.), GD 42/51
81 R.F.C., ii, fo. 307r
82 *R.M.S.*, IV, 1882
83 *Protocol books of the burgh of Glasgow*, II, 96
84 Edin. testaments, CC 8/8/26, fo. 26v
85 *R.M.S.*, IV, 1947
86 J. G. Murray, *The Book of Burgie*, 9-18
87 *Royal Comm. Report on Fife, Kinross and Clackmannan*, no. 615 (*Royal Comm. Report*)
88 *R.M.S.*, IV, 2318
89 Register House charters, RH 6/1999
90 *Royal Comm. Report*, no 72; *Dunfermelyn*, no. 554.
91 *R.M.S.*, IV, 2319
92 *Mauchline account books*, 90-1
93 *R.M.S.*, IV, 1760
94 D. McGibbon and T. Ross, *Castellated and Domestic Architecture of Scotland*, III, 202
95 *Ibid.*, IV, 121
96 *R.M.S.*, V, 1104
97 McGibbon and Ross, *op. cit.*, IV, 51
98 *R.M.S.*, IV, 2952; McGibbon and Ross, *op. cit.*, IV, 119
99 *R.M.S.*, V, 2008
100 McGibbon and Ross, *op. cit.*, III, 539
101 *Ibid.*, III, 606; *R.M.S.*, III, 2941
102 *Ibid.*, IV, 2709

103 *Royal Comm. Report*, no. 267
104 *Laing charters*, no. 1278
105 *R.M.S.*, IV, 2211
106 McGibbon and Ross, *op. cit.*, III, 502-4
107 *R.M.S.*, V, 877; McGibbon and Ross, *op. cit.*, III, 25
108 *Ibid.*, IV, 2
109 *R.M.S.*, IV, 1919

11

The Dark Side

'Anent the supplication gevin in be Jonet Stobo and Thomas Fergussone hir sone . . . aganis . . .
Alexander . . . commendator of the abbay of Inchechaffra . . . thai for thair pure maling aggreit with
him that thai suld haif thair said tak in few and heretage . . . quhilk on na wys he will do, bot gifis
thaim evill wordis . . . and causis his servandis to ding the said Thomas within this burt of Edinburgh
upoune Mounday the 20 day of Januar instant, he beand suittand befoir the lordis of consale . . .'
Register of Acts and Decreets, 1555, xii, fo. 472r.

AN adverse aspect of becoming a feuar was the expense involved. Obtaining a feu
charter meant not only initial financial outlay but also the continuing burden of
the annual feu-duty which, for a feuar who had previously been a tenant, meant a
rent increase, as well as the periodic payments we have already looked at. It is not
surprising that many years elapsed before some of the feuars were able to afford
crown confirmation of their charters; in many cases it was second or even third
generation feuars who paid for confirmation.

It is impossible to calculate the complete expenditure of the average feuar.
Firstly, not all charters mention the down payment, let alone state the amount of
it. Again, a feuar may have incurred expenses of the kind that would not be
recorded in the charter, and are not to be found elsewhere, such as compensation
to an occupant for the resignation of his rights to a holding. Expenses, all or some
of which might theoretically fall on feuars, included fees for drawing up and
registration of a feu-contract with the superior prior to the grant of the charter,
compensation to an occupant, the grassum or down payment for the charter and
payment to the convent of a monastery or to such other persons as gave their
consent to the transaction, the notary's fee for writing the instrument of sasine
which gave possession, and for entering the text of it in his protocol book, the
various fees for confirmation of the charter which was a lengthy and involved
process, including fees to the writers of the *decree* issued by the papally appointed
commissioners who sanctioned confirmation, a long document which recited all
relevant writs, and the other fees charged at the Roman Curia for papal confirmation, the composition paid for crown confirmation after 1560, as a result of an
agreement between feuar and the treasurer, and his specially appointed *compositors,* and the numerous payments due to other government officials, ranging
from the *drink siller* of all the clerks involved as the document passed through
various offices — signet, privy seal and chancery — to the cost of attaching the
great seal of Scotland to the charter itself.

The amount of the initial down payment was settled between superior and feuar
and may or may not have been written into the text of the formal feu-contract. A
complaint brought against the commendator of Scone in June 1566 by the widow

of John Acheson, burgess of Edinburgh, who with his wife 'and . . . ane air eftir thame' had had a life-lease of the lands of Polkmylne in Perthshire, underlines the bargaining character of these agreements:

'. . . thai travellit with Patrick Bischop of Moray commendatare of the said abbay of Scone, for the few of the twa thrid partis of the landis of Polkmylne forsaidis, quhairof thai hef auld takkis, and yit to rin for thair lyfetymes, as said is, and offerit him in compositioun threttie merkis for ilk merk of maill howbeit the extremetie of the law gevis bot twenty merkis for ilk land in heretage, without payment of few maill out of the samyn; yit nochtwithstanding all thir premissis he nocht onlie aganis the tennour of the saidis actis (that kirk-landis should be feued to the tennentis) bot upoun privat affectioun, hes set the saidis landis in few to his naturall sone, Adame Hepburne, utterand and declarand planelie thairt-hrow that the saidis complenaris sal haif na favour bot extremitie and troubill of him . . .'[1]

A tenant of Inchaffray abbey, who attempted to sue the commendator for breach of his agreement to feu the land to him and his widowed mother, explained to the lords of Session that only a year before he had received a nineteen-year tack of the lands, paying 'large gressum thairfor', and that when it had been agreed that he and his mother should have the tack converted to a feu charter, the commendator had set the down payment at £16 but had *allowed* them £5 2s because their tack had only run for a year. In refusing to infeft them, the commendator had not only threatened them himself but sent his servants to Edinburgh to prevent the tenant's taking the matter to court, and they, over-stepping their commission, attacked him on the High Street, 'within this burt of Edinburgh upoune Mounday the 20 day of Januar instant, he beand suittand befoir the lordis of consale . . .'[2]

In 1555 it was agreed between the commendator of Melrose and the tenants of Kylesmure that they should pay 'for everie markland in intreis (i.e. *entry*, or down payment) and compositioun thereof the sowme of threttie-five merkis . . .', which was five merks more per merkland than the tenants of Scone offered to pay ten years later. When Michael Balfour, commendator of Melrose, granted a general charter of the lands of Newstead to the tenants in September 1564, he charged thirty-three of them a total of 2,650 merks, about eighty merks each on average, some paying more than others according to the amount of land they held.[3] In addition, the tenants of Kylesmure paid a merk for each merkland to the monks of Melrose for their consent to the charter.

Circumstances determined whether or not a feuar received infeftment and was formally put in possession of the land before paying his down payment. Where he had previously been the tenant and was already in possession, he may have been required to pay within a specified time, or as soon as possible. At Coupar Angus abbey there are intervals of one and sometimes two years between the grant of a charter and recording of the payment of the initial grassum, as the down payment was often called. One of the longest intervals is in the case of Agnes Fleming, a widow, and her son, William Burt, who had a charter of a third of Cowbyre in January 1559 and 'componit' with the abbot on 13 May 1562, paying £100 for their charter.[4] John Park, occupant of part of the lands of Dubbs and Dalgaw, in Kilwinning barony, received a charter of his holdings on 2 July 1557[5] and paid 100 merks for 'the fee and heritage' four months later. The notarial instrument recording his payment to the chamberlain on the afternoon of 13 November speaks of his having already received *sasine*.[6] The vicar of Stobo, sir Ninian Douglas, in raising an action in the courts in January 1561, insisted that he had a right to the charter by which he had granted the lands of Broughtonshiels to three persons, 'unto the tyme the saidis personis had fulfillit thair conditioun and promeis maid be thame to him for the sett of the said few' — presumably referring to a delay in paying the grassum.[7]

A down payment was occasionally refunded on the breakdown of an agreement between superior and prospective feuar. Patrick Hepburn, as bishop of Moray, had to borrow 600 merks to refund the grassum paid for a charter to which he failed to get the consent of the cathedral chapter, obliging himself to feu the land instead to the man from whom he had borrowed the money with 'his own round seal onlie', a glimpse of the pressure that could sometimes be put on the granters of charters.[8] On another occasion he promised to repay John Ogilvy, son of the laird of Inchmartin, 160 merks, which Ogilvy had given him for a charter of quarter of the lands of Nether Durdie, if he failed to obtain the consent of the monks of Scone.[9]

The down payment, with its attendant expenses, must have fallen heavily on the pockets of tenants who had recently paid for the renewal of a tack, a situation which affected some of the tenant-feuars of Coupar Angus. Thomas Turnbull paid £66 13s 4d for a life-lease of the Bogmill of Carsegrange in May 1554,[10] received his feu charter in December 1558[11] and paid £126 13s 4d *composition* for it in June 1559, a total of £193 6s 8d in five years.[12] John Pery paid £40 in December 1544 for a nineteen-year tack of Ledcassy and £10 'thereftir' to have this converted into a life-lease.[13] In June 1559 he put down £100 for a feu charter of the lands, a total of £150 over fifteen years.[14] Turnbull and Pery were fairly small tenants, yet they apparently had money to lay down for their feus and we may well ask where it came from. But there are indications that tenants borrowed money to pay for their charters. Instances of feuars' wadsetting land which they had recently feued suggest one way of raising money to pay off that borrowed for a down payment. In 1584 Abbot Alexander Hamilton of Kilwinning feued the lands of Doura, then occupied by John Docheon, to Robert Cunningham of Montgreenan, a local laird.[15] In 1553, however, Docheon himself took the lands in feu on Cunningham's resignation, which may have involved payment of compensation by Docheon in addition to his grassum.[16] In May 1555 he entered into an obligation to Patrick Hamilton of Bogside by which, in return for 130 merks, he promised to infeft Hamilton and his wife in the lands of Doura — in other words, he wadset them.[17] But, since his son, Gilbert Docheon, appears at Doura in a rental for the 1570s[18] and died in possession of the lands in 1611,[19] the property was clearly redeemed by the family who had managed to ride out their financial difficulties.

Details in one or two charters suggest borrowing by feuars, from relatives and others, in order to meet their expenses. John Howieson, an Edinburgh burgess, gave money to sir Patrick Mowbray, chaplain of an altarage in Cramond parish kirk, for a feu of lands in the toun of Kirk-Cramond to John Howieson, his namesake and nephew, son of the late founder of the altarage.[20] On the other side of the country, John Peebles, elder, in Morishill in the barony of Beith, and Hugh Homill there, together put down money for a feu charter to John Peebles, younger, burgess of Irvine, and his wife, Christian Homill; one father-in-law paid £53 6s 8d at the sealing of the charter and the other £80, half at the time of the infeftment and the rest later.[21] In 1565 the younger Peebles wadset six territories, which he had feued, to Robert Hamilton, the chamberlain of Kilwinning, in return for 500 merks 'in gold and silver' received by Peebles and his wife 'in their necessity'.[22] Other feuars received charters on payment of money on their behalf; the earl of Huntly paying for Leslie of Bolquhan,[23] Henry Philp, 'marshal of Lindores', for James Philp, a relative,[24] and John Gordon, an Aberdeen burgess, for Gordon of Cluny.[25] In 1574 Blaise Colt, burgess of Perth, received a charter of the lands of Leonardley, belonging to the Charterhouse, in return for 400 merks and £133 6s 8d 'by mandate of Andrew Colt, burgess of Perth, last tenant, by his benevolence'.[26] Stephen Kincaid in Coats, who had a lease of fifty-seven acres in the barony of Broughton from Holyrood abbey, got into a complicated financial tangle when he feued them in 1558, over borrowing the 200 merks which he put down for his charter, actually borrowing from two people in the process.[17]

As to the amount of the down payments, precise figures are given in only 170 out of over 3,000 charters, the amounts ranging from £6 13s 4d to £10,000. An analysis of the figures has failed to reveal an average rate compared with current rent, something which must have depended on local circumstances such as the quality of the land, its market value, competition for the feu, or on the bargaining acumen of the parties concerned. Feuars sometimes paid identical grassums for land which differed in extent and for which the feu-duty varied considerably. Indeed, the economic situation behind the charters is seldom revealed, making it difficult to draw comparisons. A short table of down payments gives some idea of the range:

£s Scots	Number of charters
1,000 and over	26
800 and over	2
600 and over	5
400 and over	14
300 and over	11
200 and over	30
100 and over	41
60 and over	16
30 and over	12
20 and over	7
10 and over	4
under 10	2
	170

Sometimes we can detect the circumstances behind the largest payments. In 1572, for instance, the earl of Cassillis, rival of Gordon of Lochinvar for the lands of Glenluce abbey, paid £10,000 for a charter which brought him the bulk of the abbey lands.[28] Five years earlier Lochinvar had himself put down £666 13s 4d for a substantial grant of the lands of Tongland abbey.[29] James Arthur, son of William Arthur of Cairns, citizen of St Andrews, who gave the post-Reformation archbishop, Patrick Adamson, over £3,000 for a charter of the lands of

Middlefoodie in 1577,[30] was probably the bishop's 'guid brother' mentioned by James Melville as having been killed in a riot in St Andrews in 1589.[31] Other feuars who made a down payment of over £3,000 included the son of Carnegie of Kinnaird for the barony of Ethie and lands of Dunnichen, on the Arbroath estates, paying that amount each for two charters,[32] Douglas of Drumlanrig, who had big grants of land belonging to Lincluden collegiate church,[33] and Stewart of Cardonald, whose brother, the post-Reformation commendator of Crossraguel, needed all the help he could get, financial or otherwise, in his struggle with the earl of Cassillis over possession of the abbey lands.[34] The £100 to £300 bracket, which contains most of the feuars whose down payments are known, represents people of all sorts and conditions, from substantial lairds like Douglas of Lochleven to a number of smaller kindly tenants on the estates of Scone and Coupar Angus.

The comparatively small grassums at the other end of the scale were, nevertheless, large enough for many tenants: £40 for four oxgangs of arable land and part of the Wood of Haltoun of Fintray by William Harvie, the occupant, a tenant of Lindores,[35] and the same amount for eight oxgangs, called the *sunny quarter* of Disblair, by John Thomson, one of Harvie's neighbours.[35] Several tenants of Scone paid £20 for a few acres of arable land, but only a little more was paid by Hamilton of Kirkley for the tower of Haggs in Stirlingshire, six acres of land and the hill on which the tower was built.[37] The grant of a cottage-land and croft at Lindores cost John Condie £10,[38] as did the grant of one acre to Robert Finlayson, a tenant of Scone.[39]

The next lump sum that fell to be paid was that for confirmation of the charter. The act of parliament of 1564, which stated that crown confirmation of feu charters would from then on be as 'sure' as the confirmation formerly obtained from the pope, was followed about three months later by a proclamation to the effect that all unconfirmed charters must be presented to the commissioners sitting in the Treasurer's chamber during the months of April, May and June following.[40] Between the beginning of 1565 and June 1566 the Treasurer accounted for £9,000 received from confirmation of feus of kirklands.

As in the case of the down payments, it is difficult to decide how the amounts for confirmation were arrived at. These would seem to have been determined by the Lords Compositors in agreement with the Treasurer, who was ultimately accountable for them. No doubt, as Sir David Lindsay inferred, some people got favourable terms when applying for confirmation:

> By buds (bribes) may he obteine favouris,
> Of Treasurers and compositouris.

An occasional marginal note in the Treasurer's accounts and at the end of entries in the Register of Signatures, stating 'gratis' or 'deletur de consensu', suggests that this could happen.

While compositions for crown confirmation ranged from £1 to £666 they are, on the whole, lower than the down payments to granters of the feu charters. The following Table is compiled from figures in the Treasurer's accounts:[41]

£s Scots	Number of confirmations
1,000 and over	—
800 and over	—
600 and over	1
400 and over	1
300 and over	1
200 and over	4
100 and over	9
60 and over	13
30 and over	38
20 and over	54
10 and over	74
under 10	102
	297

The same composition might be paid by persons of varying social standing and for lands of different extent. The largest recorded for crown confirmation was £666, paid by Dunbar of Cumnock for fishings in the River Spey. Where a feuar paid for confirmation in his own lifetime he would face considerable outlay, but down payment and confirmation were often spread over two or more generations of feuars.

Feu-duty was a continuing expense which might be paid in money, partly in money and partly in kind, or, in one or two cases, in kind alone. In many cases the feuar was given the option of payment in kind or commutation. Payment in money alone was not confined to the bigger feuars such as nobles and lairds but was also required from many small feuars who had previously been tenants. The basic feu-duty was often the equivalent of the current rent, but was sometimes slightly higher, and there was invariably a distinct element called the *augmentation,* the device by which the granters of feu charters obeyed the letter of canon law, which required that the augmentation be separately specified in the charter.

In over 1,800 charters feu-duty is specified entirely in money, the highest numbers of these charters coming from the bishops of Aberdeen (42), Dunkeld (57), Glasgow (49), Moray (79), Ross (37) and the abbots and commendators of Arbroath (31), Inchaffray (45), Kilwinning (46), Kinloss (69), Newbattle (45) and Scone (66). All the recorded charters of Jedburgh abbey, the nunnery of Coldstream and the bishops of Galloway, and all but eight of the huge number of Melrose charters stipulate money feu-duties alone.

The fixing of a 'resonabill augmentatioun', as demanded by the Merchant in Lindsay's *Thrie Estaitis,* was an important matter affecting the occupants of the kirklands. On the one hand, these rent increases must have prevented many of them from taking their holdings in feu and, on the other, there was the possibility that these increases might be passed on to them by the middlemen who feued the lands 'over their heads', a situation they could not control. As with the down payments and compositions for crown confirmation, there would seem to be no average rate of augmentation. It is even difficult to detect local patterns, although augmentations are noticeably higher at, for example, Culross and Scone than on the lands of Coupar Angus and Kinloss, where the increases were, on the whole, small. In the barony of Glasgow the augmentations were so small as to be nominal. Scone, on the other hand, was high, the ratio of augmentation to 'old rent' ranging from a quarter to a fifth, though Patrick Hepburn, the commendator, did set smaller augmentations on his bishopric lands of Moray. Kilwinning abbey lands show a ratio of augmentation to old rent of from one third to one sixth.

In striking a bargain with the feuar, the superior may have opted for a large down payment, which benefited him personally, with a small, continuing augmentation which, like the basic feu-duty, would gradually represent less and less to his successors as time went on. Or, the granter may have agreed to a smallish augmentation, but laid down that periodic grassums were to be paid every five or seven years; this did not apply to the barony of Glasgow where, although the augmentations were nominal, periodic grassums are never mentioned, the feuing policy being apparently beneficial to the tenant-feuars in every way. Exceptionally large augmentations were sometimes demanded from those feuars who were in a position to pass on a rent increase to their subtenants. Campbell of Loudon, for instance, had to pay an augmentation of half the current rent for land belonging to Kilwinning abbey, which lay in his own district,[42] and the earl of Cassillis the same rate of augmentation for the twenty merklands of Largs, Knockraver, Lagdalduf and Monkland in Carrick, belonging to Melrose abbey, which he and his subtenants already occupied.[43] The inhabitants may have escaped a passed-on rent increase where the middleman was a relative or friend of the granter and likely to get his feu on easy terms. The charter by Gavin Hamilton, commendator of Kilwinning, to his son, Gavin, in 1566, set an augmentation of only 6s 8d on a basic feu-duty of £27 16s 8d.[44] Similarly, when the chaplain of St Katherine's chapel at Kilbarchan feued the considerable chapel lands to the brother of his patron, Chalmers of Gadgirth, with whom he was on friendly terms, the feu-duty was fixed at £10 'old rent' and a mere 3s 4d augmentation.[45]

Feu-duty was usually paid in two instalments a year, like other rents, at the terms of Whitsunday and Martinmas, and was probably paid to the chamberlain along with all kinds of rents and dues. In the Kelso abbey accounts, however, there is some evidence that special arrangements were made for the separate collection of feu-duties; 'and spendit to my Lordis commissioneris and servitouris being in Lesmahagow in December *in anno computi* for resaving of the few silver of Kylesmure'.[46] This shows, incidentally, how the 'office expenses' of the Melrose estates to which Kylesmure belonged were met from the income of those of Kelso, James Stewart being commendator of both monasteries at the time. The non-payment of feu-duty for two or more terms could mean an action in court for cancellation of the charter, but regular payment was often difficult to enforce. In a case between the bishop of Galloway and James McClellan, the feuar and his late father were said to be in arrears of feu-duty for nineteen years but were allowed to keep the lands on James's promise to pay thirteen years' duty, amounting to £65, that is from Whitsunday 1542 when the bishop had been admitted to the temporalities of his see.[47]

In ninety-eight charters the money feu-duty was accompanied by the payment

of fixed sums to the monks or 'master of the petty commons' of the monastery concerned. These were not part of the down payment but were continuing payments,
made each year with the feu-duty, except in the case of Melrose where payment to
the monks accompanied duplication of the feu-duty paid on the entry of an heir. At
Scone these payments must have brought in about £20 a year to the remaining
members of the convent.

In quite a number of charters to tenant-feuars various customary dues and commutations for services were carried over from the pre-feuing situation: *dyke siller,
dam siller* and *teiling siller* at Kilwinning, *rin-mart siller* at Arbroath and Kinloss,
fed-oxin siller at Dunfermline and *bond siller* at Melrose. In addition to those
charters in which feu-duty was specified entirely in money, there were 113 in which
a miscellany of dues and payments in kind were converted into a single, new money
payment. Only twenty-six charters out of a total of over 3,000 asked for feu-duty
entirely in kind — except, that is, for augmentation which was paid in money. In
eighty-four charters, however, feuars, although asked for payment partly in kind,
were given the option of commuting this into cash. In the majority of charters the
feu-duty was paid in a mixture of money and grain, to the advantage of the superiors
who could sell off the latter at current market prices, as they did with the tenants'
grain rents.

In addition to the heavy financial commitments of the feuars, there was on this
darker side the vulnerable position of those tenants whose possession was
threatened by outside speculators, and who were unprotected against the adverse
effects of some of the terms in the feuars' charters. Some of these tenants are on
record as having put up a fight to retain their customary rights in the face of change
and dislocation in the pattern of rural life. Many more may have suffered without
the power to protest.

The framers of the 1458 act of parliament 'anent feu-ferm', who saw the whole
business of feuing as an agreement between church landlords and their tenants,
were not unaware of the opportunities for speculation that existed, and so a
handful of acts were later passed by parliament and privy council in an attempt to
protect the kindly tenants. The provincial council of the church which met in the
spring of 1559 deplored the setting of kirklands in long tacks and feu-ferm to
others than 'the ancient, native tenants, occupiers and tillers of the land', adding,
with inevitable realism, that if this should happen and these outside feuars wished
to resign their lands, 'then it shall be unlawful for the said . . . prelates . . . to admit
or receive into possession of the said feus or tacks other tenants who are of greater
or higher degree than the resigning tenants are, so long as they are sufficient
occupants of these lands and are able to make payment.'[48] Evidence suggests that
speculators made use of the letter of this law in order to feu and then resign land in
favour of local, small tenants, making themselves a profit out of the transaction. We
have already met the case of Mr Robert Richardson the Treasurer, at Dunfermline, who feued and then resigned to the tenants over sixty separate holdings. At
Lessudden, on the Melrose estates, the same thing happened in 1556 when holdings
there were feued to thirty-two occupants on the resignation of Mr Henry Sinclair,

dean of Glasgow.[49] A case at Wester Bauchrie, on the Scone estates, provides financial details of what was almost certainly a piece of land speculation by the Justice-Clerk, Sir John Bellenden. In May 1562 a contract was registered, drawn up between Bellenden on the one hand and four kindly tenants of Wester Bauchrie on the other, John and William Soutar, John Dickson and Alexander McKie.[50] It narrates that the Justice-Clerk had taken in feu, 'owir thair heidis', the lands of Wester Bauchrie, in liferent to himself and in feu to his son, Louis, of which lands they each occupied a quarter as kindly tenants, 'and havyng na uthir stedingis to leif upone'. The tenants had promised to pay Bellenden such sums of money 'as he disbursit' upon his charter if he would resign the lands in their favour. 'Quhilk desire the said Sir John gladly accordit unto,' and renounced his rights in return for their promise to pay him £1,066 13s 4d in three instalments. Since Bellenden had actually given the commendator, Patrick Hepburn, £1,000 for his charter, he was thus making himself a profit of £66 13s 4d. The whole transaction may simply have been a device by which Bellenden loaned these tenants the money to pay for their charters, the profit representing the interest. There must often have been a situation in which a middleman could jump in and acquire feus in an area where there was local demand for them and subsequently make himself a profit by resigning them to local tenants for sums of money which exceeded his own original outlay. This may explain why some bigger feuars resigned lands which they had only recently feued, profit-making being their only motive in acquiring the land in the first place. For example, Alexander Balfour of Denmylne received the charter which included the lands of Newstead on 2 April 1568, had it confirmed by the crown on 7 June and resigned the lands to the tenants four days later.[51]

How much concern was shown for the occupants and subtenants in the terms of the charters? Occupants, subtenants and even cottars are quite often mentioned in those clauses in which pieces of land are delineated, often simply in order to identify the units of land, or to define a feuar's powers over the inhabitants, or, more rarely, to reserve certain rights and usages or to forbid the tenants' removal. Sometimes occupants are named individually, giving us an idea of the number of households in a locality. The kirklands and glebe of Kilbirnie in Ayrshire, for example, were said to be occupied by nine tenants and by the laird of Glengarnock whose subtenants, presumably, lived on and cultivated the lands.[52] There were nine tenants, also, in the vicarage kirklands of Eaglesham, ten on seven ploughgates of the Grange of Lindores feued to Mr James McGill[53] and, on the thirty-eight acres of the toun of Dryburgh, twenty-one individuals, their names being given and the amount of land held by each.[54]

Occasionally in the charters there is mention of the fact that an occupant had resigned his rights to an outsider, a small feuar who replaced him or a bigger feuar who might put in a new subtenant. When James Boyd of Kipps got a feu of the mill of Carstairs from the archbishop of Glasgow, the mill was resigned to him by Duncan Livingston, burgess of Edinburgh, a non-resident tack-holder, and the mill lands by a local man, Laurence Young, 'last rentaller'.[55] Charters sometimes went into detail about the powers of the feuar over the occupants. John Kinnear of that Ilk, in receiving a feu of the Overmill of Balmerino, acquired power over 'all husbandmen and cottars thirled to the mill', who paid him thereafter one peck for every six firlots of wheat ground.[56] Occupants of the kirklands of Dipple were asked to perform carriage and military service, if necessary, to the feuar, James Innes of Towquhis.[57] William Stewart, feuar of Paisley abbey, was granted the *bonservice* of tenants in various places, consisting of tilling, harrowing, *bone shearing* and corn leading, which shows how the services of the occupants might be conveyed with land.[58]

At the same time, certain rights and usages might be reserved to the inhabitants, even though they were now a feuar's subtenants. For example, in a charter to Alexander Leslie of Pitcaple, the bishop of Aberdeen reserved to the tenants common pasture in the kirk glebe of Daviot and liberty to cast peats there.[59] Going a step further, some charters expressly forbade the feuar to remove tenants or disturb them in the possession of their holdings. A charter to Stewart of Arntully of the lands of Dalmarnock belonging to a chaplainry in Dunkeld cathedral laid down that 'the present tenants' were to be 'in nowise removit', while another charter to him stated that 'it sall nocht be lessoum to thame to remove whatsomever puir tenentis . . . fra the saidis landis.'[60] In February 1559 Alexander Somerville of Tarbrax entered into an obligation to Archbishop John Hamilton not to raise the rents or evict the tenants of the lands of Polduff and not to lift any maills or fermes from the tenants during his lifetime, 'nochtwythstanding the discharge maid to me during my lyftime be the said reverand fader . . . of all feirmis, caneis, mells and deuteis with augmentatioun of the rentall contenit in the said . . . chartour'.[61] Not only was this feuar, for some reason, to be duty-free for his lifetime but so were the subtenants.

However, the other side to the picture is seen in those charters which gave the feuar the right to 'input' and 'output' tenants. Mr Robert Richardson, who played the middleman on the Dunfermline estates so successfully, obtained from the commendator in May 1573 a formal cancellation of a previous obligation not to remove tenants of his feu lands, 'tuiching the rasing and hychtting of the tenentis (rents) . . . removing of the saidis tenentis furt of the samen, selling, wadsetting or putting away of ony part thereof . . .'[62] In July 1581 a complaint against rack-renting and eviction was brought to the privy council on behalf of 'poor inhabitants of the touns of Inveresk and Monktounhall', lands held in feu by Richardson's son.[63]

We shall probably never know how much eviction of occupants and rack-renting accompanied the feuing of kirklands over the years. There is sufficient information, however, in the Register of Acts and Decreets of the civil court and in the *Register of the Privy Council* to give some idea of the injustices, disputes and hardship which might occur, and to show how the courts handled these cases. On looking at the cases, however, we must remember that the most vulnerable people were those who could ill afford the expense of litigation. At the same time, it is surprising how few such actions have been recorded. Even when cases arising from feuing do appear, they have an exasperating habit of disappearing from the court record before a decision had been reached. Above all, there is no way of estimating, without the kind of local records which have so rarely survived, how many evictions were carried out without a complaint's reaching the courts.

Fifty volumes of the Register of Acts and Decreets have been searched, covering the years 1549 to 1572. Over twenty cases were concerned with the position and rights of occupants; fourteen of them were outright actions for removal by a feuar, two were actions raised by kindly tenants who had had their holdings feued over their heads, and one, also raised by the tenants, was a complaint against rack-renting. The number of cases tended to increase as time went on, so that the period after 1572 may produce an even higher number. The first four printed volumes of the Privy Council Register contain five cases of complaint by kindly tenants against the feuing of their holdings to an outsider, two instances of rival claims to land that had been feued, one complaint of rack-renting which, as it happens, is the prelude to the case as it appears in the Register of Acts and Decreets, and one case where feuars were charged with having falsely obtained charters.

The judges seem to have dispensed the law with reasonable fairness — if one can forgive them for continuing the cases interminably — severity lying in the law itself, rather than in the Lords of Council and Session. Defenders lost their cases for non-compearance alone, no matter how good a chance they might have had of succeeding had they been able to put forward their side of the story. It must have been impossible for many small tenants to think of travelling to Edinburgh, or to pay a procurator to appear in court on their behalf, and we feel sorry for the Inchaffray tenant who, having got himself all the way to the capital, found himself forcibly prevented from making his appearance in court.

In six of the actions for removal the defenders were ordered by the judges to remove since they failed to compear in court when summoned. The stated reason for an action of removing was usually so that the feuar might occupy the land 'with his own proper goods' or 'as his own proper heritage'. In deciding what this really means, we are faced with the term *occupant,* as we were faced with it in the feu charters themselves. An occupant may have been a *non-resident tack-holder* drawing the rents of the *resident-occupants* whom the feuar now regarded as *his* subtenants. The non-resident tack-holder, therefore, stood in the way of the feuar's enjoyment of the property, that is, the rents of the subtenants. In some cases, therefore, we find this occupant protesting that his tack, granted before the date of the feuar's charter, held good until the date of its expiry. Thus Gavin Kneland, Cuthbert Craig and James Wood, occupants of the lands of Gartsherrie in Newbattle abbey's barony of Monkland in Lanarkshire, replied to an action for removal raised against them by Alexander Hume, feuar of the lands, that they had tacks from the abbot 'styll to ryn'. When Hume's procurator alleged that they had resigned these tacks, they still insisted that the resignations were not intended to be operative until the expiry date of the tacks. For good measure, Kneland objected that the *warning* to remove should have been directed not at himself but to his mother who, as liferentrix of the lands, was principal tenant, protected in her possession by the act of parliament in favour of the widows and families of men killed at Pinkie, as his father had been. Unfortunately, like so many other interesting cases, this one disappeared from the Register before a decision was reached.[64]

In taking over his lands, a feuar might have intended to introduce his own tenants and stock, in which case the occupants whom he wished to remove may well have been the resident occupants as well as the non-resident tack-holders. In 1569 Mark Kerr, younger, called for the removal from the lands of Easthouses of 'Agnes Turnbull, widow of Thomas Hume in Dalkeith . . . herself, servants, cottars, hynds and goods', that is, for the removal not only of her interest in the land but also the presence of those who cultivated it under her and those who supervised the cultivation, the hinds, together with the stock on it — a complete clearance.[65] In 1558, in raising an action for removal from the kirklands of Kilrenny, John Beaton of Balfour called for the removal of Alexander Kinnimont and his servants, 'to the effect that the said John ma entir therto . . . brouk and labour the samen with his awin guidis, or sett thame to tenentis as he sall think best'; the replacement of subtenants to be by those put in by the feuar.[66]

On two occasions the Lords came down in favour of occupants threatened with eviction. Adam Hepburn of Bonhard, son of the bishop of Moray, tried to remove the occupants of land in the regality of Scone, which had been feued to him and subsequently renounced during his minority, only to be confronted in court with the charters granted to the tenants of Craigmakerran after his renunciation.[67] The tenants and occupiers of the barony of Urquhart belonging to Pluscarden priory succeeded in annulling an action raised against them by certain feuars on the grounds that the sheriff, at whose instance they had been summoned, was disqualified from acting in the affair since he had obtained feus of a great part of the lordship of Pluscarden and also because they had received their 'rights' since March 1559, 'it being inhibitit to all juges . . . to proceid upone ony warningis maid be ony persounis havand obtenit ony sic fewis efter the said day'.[68] It is encouraging to find that things were not as bleak as might have been expected for the tenants of Pluscarden, where hardly any of them received feus of their holdings.

The harsh effect of rigid application of the law is seen, however, in the case of a handful of tenants, all related to one another, from the barony of Beith. The action was brought by Andrew Hamilton of Ardoch against David Fletcher and John and William Convell, tenants in Crummock, James Clerk in Rouchbank, whose grandmother lived with him, and Gilbert Fletcher in Bogside, ordering them to 'flit and remove'.[69] In the event the first four had to go because they were unable to produce written evidence in court of their right of possession. Gilbert Fletcher alone was able to produce his rental. The kindly tenants who complained to the privy council about their holdings being feued over their heads included the widow of a burgess, three lairds and a handful of smaller tenants. We have already met the widow, Janet Fisher, whose husband, John Acheson, burgess of Edinburgh, had been killed at Pinkie in 1547, and who complained that the commendator of Scone had refused the offer for a feu made to him by herself and her son for the lands of Polkmylne, but had instead feued them to his own son. The Lords took steps to prevent the confirmation of Adam Hepburn's charter.[70]

David Tyrie of Drumkilbo had bought the kindness of the 'stedyng of Petelpye' from a tenant, Thomas Abercrombie, and had afterwards reached agreement with the same commendator about a feu charter, only to find a few years later that Hepburn had granted the charter to another 'contrair the actis of parliament anent late-set feus and the said Bischopis awin promeis and fayth'. The Lords ordained the Treasurer to keep a look-out for the charter at 'the confirmation of the lait set fewis' and not to let it 'pass the seals'.[71] Another laird, John Kinnear of that Ilk, had had a tack for the previous twenty years of the Priestoun of Tealing when he complained in January 1565 that it was about to be feued over his head to the local laird, Maxwell of Tealing, who intended to get crown confirmation immediately, 'quhilk being obtainit wil be the occasioun of inymitie and discord'. The Lords postponed the confirmation of Maxwell's charter until both parties had fully stated their cases, but the case was still being 'continued' when it disappears from the record in the summer of 1566.[72]

As early as February 1534 John Curry, Andrew Wilson, John Wilson, James Wilson and Alan Cunningham, tenants of Kilwinning abbey, pleading their rights as rentallers, complained that their possession of the lands of Gardrum and Skirrumlands in Kilmarnock parish was being threatened by a charter granted by the abbot to James Hamilton of Cambuskeith; the outcome of their complaint is not recorded.[73] Another action which completely disappeared was that of James Gifford, younger, of Sheriffhall, who complained in November 1567 of his having been evicted from the 'kindly' use of the mill of Newbattle, the commendator, Mark Kerr, having feued it over his head to his own wife and family.[74]

In cases of feuars against subtenants, usually for non-payment of rent, the subtenants were sometimes able to drag the case out, evading payment for a considerable time. In June 1555 Lord Innermeath, who had taken the kirklands of Easter Lunan in feu, raised an action against Hercules Guthrie, the tenant, for non-payment of fermes, complaining that Guthrie would not admit how much he ought to pay for the land which 'pertenis to him (Innermeath) and the setting and rasing theroff aucht and suld be at his dispositioun'. The Lords required Guthrie's procurator to produce his tack from the abbot of Arbroath, but five months later Guthrie was pleading that because of 'the greit troublis which have been in the cuntrie of Angus' where he lived, he had put his tack for safe-keeping in the hands of William Mureson 'in the castle of Toquhone in the north-land'. Given time to recover it and produce it in court, his next excuse was that Mureson had given it to Gavin Baldovy 'who is now in France', whereupon letters were issued against Baldovy to produce the elusive document. The next time the case appeared was in July 1562, when Innermeath was suing Guthrie for failure to pay his maills, after which the case disappears.[75]

There are one or two instances of rival claims to land which had been feued. The judges found in favour of William Lothian, a citizen of Glasgow, who had had a feu charter in 1544 from Mr Mark Douglas, chaplain in Calder parish church, of a 'foretenement' in Glasgow, claimed by a later chaplain, sir John Watson.[76] Rival claims might occur where one party had failed to obtain crown confirmation: this seems to have been the case when the Lords found in favour of

Thomas Scott of Haining, authorising the confirmation of his charter for which he had already applied, against John Scott, minister of Selkirk, who, when a great part of the Melrose lands had been feued to the earl of Bothwell, had taken in feu 'for his own security' the half of the toun lands of Elistoun, of which he and his predecessors had been kindly tenants, but of which he apparently did not get crown confirmation.[77]

Until 1572, at least, cases of personal dispute and evidence of hardship as the result of feuing are rarer in the official records than might have been expected, although this does not mean that these effects were not felt locally without reaching the courts. The examples that have been cited demonstrate what could happen: the removal of occupants by a feuar in order to make way for new sub-tenants or direct labour; the attempt to terminate the tack of an occupant who, although perhaps not resident, had been the local landlord for some time, as, indeed, his father might have been before him, so that his going would mean a break in continuity; the feuing of land to a superior's friends and relatives; the rigid application of the law which could result in the eviction of occupants who were unable to produce the written evidence of their customary rights, or to travel to court to defend themselves, or to pay an advocate to appear on their behalf; the effects of the intervention of land speculators; the demotion of the inhabitants to the rank of subtenants under a middleman (although we must remember that this could happen even to whole townships before feuing came along); stratification of the social standing of neighbours where some tenants became feuars and others did not, or where a tenant feued his neighbour's holding with his own, as some-times happened; dislocation of the economic pattern where an outsider took a feu of a mill, brewhouse or ferry, hitherto operated by a tenant family, with a view to making a profit.

We must be careful, however, how we interpret the evidence of hardship caused by feuing, especially the evidence of the civil court records, for all we have there, in most cases, are the judges' final decisions and the briefest of information about the background to the cases. The feuar, as we have seen, was not always aiming at the small man in an action for removal, but sometimes at the outsider who already held the land in tack — at a rival middleman, in fact. Moreover, if that outsider's family had at one time acquired the kindness of the land and had held their tacks for several generations, he will be found describing himself in his defence, quite rightly, as the kindly tenant.

With all these reservations and bearing in mind just how many smaller people became new proprietors, portioners and bonnet lairds by the turn of the century, it begins to look as if the feuing of the kirklands was not quite the 'fatal revolution' in Scottish rural society it has been called.

Notes

1 *R.P.C.*, I, 465
2 Acts and decreets, xii, fo. 472r
3 *Melrose regality*, III, 358
4 R.F.C., i, fo. 59r; *Cupar*, II, 273

5 Yule collection GD 90/1/15/6
6 *Ibid.,* GD 90/1/153
7 Acts and decreets, xxi, fo. 285r
8 Register of deeds, old series, ix, fo. 24
9 *Ibid.,* xi, fo. 180
10 *Cupar,* II, 252
11 R.F.C., i, fo. 270r
12 *Cupar,* II, 270
13 *Ibid.,* II, 224, 270
14 *R.M.S.,* IV, 2376
15 Yule collection, GD 90/1/130
16 *Ibid.,* GD 90/1/146
17 Register of deeds, old series, i, fo. 188v
18 Eglinton muniments, GD 3/1362
19 Glasgow testaments, CC 9/7/8, fo. 69v
20 *R.M.S.,* IV, 2860
21 Register of deeds, old series, iii, pt. iii, fo. 462v
22 *Ibid.,* viii, fo. 170v
23 Register House charters, RH 6/1757
24 *R.M.S.,* IV, 2394
25 *Ibid.,* V, 254
26 *Ibid.,* IV, 2367
27 R.S.S., lii, fo. 7v; Register of deeds, old series, iii, pt. i, fo. 352v
28 *R.M.S.,* IV, 2202
29 *Ibid.,* IV, 1743
30 *Ibid.,* IV, 2703
31 J. Melville, *Autobiography and Diary,* 273
32 *R.M.S.,* V, 1257
33 *Ibid.,* IV, 1653
34 *Crossraguel charters,* I, 158
35 *R.M.S.,* V, 529
36 *Ibid.,* V, 1274
37 *Ibid.,* III, 2937
38 *Ibid.,* V, 2320
39 *Ibid.,* V, 951
40 R. K. Hannay, 'Church lands at the Reformation', in *S.H.R.,* XVI, 60
41 *Treasurer's Accounts,* XII, pp. 65-6, 107, 195-6, 268-70
42 *R.M.S.,* IV, 1760
43 *Melrose Regality,* III, 226
44 *R.M.S.,* IV, 2633
45 *Ibid.,* IV, 1600
46 *Calchou,* II, 480
47 Acts and decreets, xii, fo. 83r
48 D. Patrick, *Statutes of the Scottish Church* (S.H.S.), 179-81
49 *Melrose Regality,* III, 232 ff
50 Register of deeds, old series, v, fo. 164r
51 *R.M.S.,* IV, 1819; Morton muniments, GD 150/1462
52 Crawford muniments (S.R.O.), GD 20/534
53 R.F.C., i, fos. 36r-37r
54 National Library of Scotland charters, CH 724
55 *R.M.S.,* IV, 2881
56 R.F.C., ii, fo. 77r
57 *Ibid.,* i, fo. 133r
58 *R.M.S.,* V, 471
59 R.F.C., ii, fo. 57r
60 *Ibid.,* i, fos. 85r-86r
61 Advocates MSS (N.L.S.), 17/1/3, fo. 47r
62 Register of deeds, old series, xii, fo. 63r
63 *R.S.S.,* III, 396
64 Acts and decreets, xx, fol. 243r, 294r-295r

65 *Ibid.*, xlii, fo. 38r
66 *Ibid.*, xviii, fo. 154r
67 *Ibid.*, xxxi, fo. 26r
68 *Ibid.*, xxiv, fo. 394r
69 *Ibid.*, xxxvii, fo. 16v
70 *R.P.C.*, I, 465
71 *Ibid.*, I, 304
72 *Ibid.*, I, 320, 456
73 A.D.C.S., iv, fo. 413r
74 *R.P.C.*, I, 590
75 Acts and decreets, xii, fo. 34r, 260r; xxiv, fo. 341r
76 *Ibid.*, xii, fo. 255v
77 *R.P.C.*, II, 558

12

Rural Social Life

Silk 'pasmentis', silk traces, belting worsted, silk points, combs, 'certane builkis', purses and clasps, papers of pins, 'pennaris and inkhornis', little locks, chessmen and 'tabill men', spectacles with their cases, cording silk, steel glasses, candle shears, 'nicht bonnetis', salt cellars and 'uthir small waris'.
From contents of a chapman's pack: Edinburgh testaments, CC 8/8/1, fo 187v.

THIS chapter is not concerned with social customs or with what the rural population did with its lesiure time, of which it had very little, but with how a common way of life, dependent on the land, held all sections of rural society together, making them dependent on one another, laird and farmer, craftsman and cottar, men, women and children.

The land itself was all-important, the food and shelter which it provided were the priorities of life. Some people had more food and more substantial and comfortable houses than others but the grain, fish and flesh, the stone, timber, turf and thatch that all needed came locally from land and river. Although the members of the barony communities had varying degrees of interest in the land, or in some cases none at all, all were concerned with cultivating it or with organising its cultivation. The pattern of life followed the rhythm of the seasons. For much of the year the community worked from sunrise to dusk, turning out of doors daily for the business of cultivation, as people now turn out daily for industrial and commercial work. Some work, such as harvesting — one of the peak periods of activity in the year — involved the labours of women and children, as did the herding and tending of the poultry and smaller animals and the preparation and carrying of food to the workers, who ate in field and barnyard. Even small children were posted as scarecrows, or 'watchcorns'. There was a daily, seasonal and annual routine in which the whole family was involved. Not only had they to ensure that their own land was sown and harvested, the crop ground and stored, the stock pastured or sheltered, marked, clipped, milked or slaughtered in due season, but they were often bound to work for the landlord as well. In the winter months, during the worst weather, when farm work slackened off and the *marts* had been slaughtered and salted, there was the repair of buildings and dykes and the preparation of farm tools and implements for the coming spring. For the women, spinning time could be increased and clothes made and mended. For the rural craftsman, freed from farming for a time and with his customers more accessible, business flourished and even the miller and smith made household implements and small items to trade to the chapmen when better weather brought them round again.

169

Most work was communal; the ploughing and preparation of the ground for the seed, haymaking and harvesting, threshing, grinding the grain, the slaughtering of animals at Martinmas, all involved a mixture of farmers and their families, skilled workers and a host of regularly employed and temporarily hired labourers. However, there are indications that with bigger, fixed-runrig holdings, a tendency towards consolidation and the spread of feu-ferm, creating many small proprietors, some farmers may have cultivated their land in a less communal fashion. The number of plough animals a farmer owned may indicate how many he was able to contribute to the community's plough team, but may also suggest that he had his own team on his single-tenant farm, or feu. It may be that *feuars-portioner,* of whom there were a great many on church land, continued to plough in community fashion. However, details in testaments do suggest that some farmers had sufficient oxen for a team if they did cultivate their holdings independently, and we often find quite small farmers paying for 'plough graith' and for the 'laying of plough irons'. For example, David Robertson, portioner of a quarter of Sherifftoun in Perthshire, employed a 'plewch boy' and bequeathed to his grandson his 'eight oxen, plough, plough graith, harrow and harrow graith, wain and wain graith'.[1] Andrew Paterson in West Shiel in the barony of Glasgow owned a plough and graith to the value of over £26.[2] Apart from the plough itself, there are references to other farm implements, entirely the property of the farmers concerned and doubtless used by them in the independent cultivation of their properties and holdings. In 1560, Patrick Robertson in Finmouth owned linen sowing sheets, harrows and sleds[3] and, in 1567, James Calderwood had two 'furnished ploughs' worth 30s each, 'two furnished wains' worth over £5 and two harrows.[4]

On this labouring majority of the rural population depended the minority who did not actually till the ground themselves. They lived mainly on the rents from land that was *set* and on the produce from land reserved to themselves, on which they employed tenants and hired workers in ploughing, harrowing, sowing, haymaking, *leading* crops, coal and other necessities, as well as dykemaking, sheepshearing and herding. The landlord was 'lord of the ground', but in the last analysis the maintenance of rural life depended on the mutual obligation of lord and vassal, owner and occupier, superior and feuar to provide the land and render its fruits. Any attempt to over-demand by the one or to withhold by the other upset the balance. And, of course, landlord and farmer were dependent on the forces of nature in a way that most people today, being town-dwellers, can scarcely imagine. A bad season and poor harvest meant not only a price-rise, as it still does, but in days when diet was largely confined to what was grown locally it meant famine, something which was never far away in the sixteenth century.

The contact between tenants and landlords, most of whom, after all, were lairds, bonnet lairds and feuars, was probably closer in the sixteenth century than it was ever to be again, if for no other reason than that landlord and tenant still spoke the same language, vernacular Scots. Absenteeism, at least among the smaller lairds and feuars, was probably the exception, at any rate for long periods. The contrast in the standard of the domestic circumstances of landlord and tenant was probably less marked than it was later to become; a tower house might be bigger and safer than the farmer's steading but it afforded little more *private* accommodation for the householder and his family, in proportion to the number of people living in it. The paternalist feeling, which might extend to physical protection of the tenants by the landlord, was still strong, even in the Lowlands. A laird's children might be fostered in a cottar house, and as the sixteenth century progressed the sons of lairds, tenants and craftsmen would learn side by side in the parish school.

Laird and farmer had a robust respect for each other, and a weather-eye on whether the other was doing his job. No amount of Scottish respect for surname and kinship, be it even with the laird, created a race of subservient peasant-farmers. There is a sense in which John Knox, in claiming that his forbears had loyally served the earls of Bothwell, was establishing a clean family record, while Hume of Wedderburn, echoing the attitude of lesser folk in saying that 'if his chief should turn him out at the fore door he would come in again at the back door', was not only expressing personal loyalty but a right to be there, in his lord's service. The Scottish tenant who spoke up for himself in the barony court was rarely obsequious.

The landowners themselves were remarkably close to the farming process, frequently supervising the affairs of their estates in person. Even if the laird was away from home, 'the lady' was often involved, although some may have cared to be less involved than Agnes Leslie, wife of the laird of Lochleven, who travelled 'over the Mounth' into Banffshire to supervise operations in 1580. The chamberlain's accounts for the lordship of Auchterhouse for that year contain many references to her: 'deliverit to the lady, £54'; 'for a leg of beef for the lady's coming, 50s'; 'in hervest to the lady for a quart of wine, 8s'; 'for the lady's *disjone* and supper coming from Banff, £3'; 'for freight of the lady and *dailis,* 16s 8d'; 'for two new shoes to the lady's nag, harrowing, 2s'; 'deliverit to the bake-house at the lady's command, when she was there in mucking time, when she held house from 16 April to 7 May, 8 bolls 1 firlot meal'.[5] Like her mother-in-law, Margaret Erskine, before her, Agnes was present with the laird when the estate accounts were rendered at the Newhouse on the shores of Lochleven.[6]

Since livelihood had to be wrung from the land and was at the mercy of forces outwith the farmer's control, bad weather and poor harvests, disease in man and beast, the aim in life and the desired standard of living — if such things were consciously thought about — was sufficiency rather than surplus. The great thing was to have enough and, with the tenants' share of the crop at about one-third, this could not always be guaranteed. Any surplus that accrued was not usually spent, as we might now spend it, on luxuries, but was literally ploughed back into the ground. Money bequeathed to families and dependents was often earmarked 'to be laid out upon land' or to purchase 'annualrents' from land, which would bring in an annual income.

But, although the farmers' main concern was sufficiency rather than surplus, this is not to say that farming was at a mere subsistence level, or that tenants were unable to save a little victual or sell an animal or two to a neighbour, both of which they did. Even if the value of household goods, the *utencils and domicils* of testamentary inventories, respresented mere fractions of valued moveables, the most important of which were stock, grain and farming tools, the lairds and more substantial owner-occupiers might manage a reasonable level of comfort, by contemporary standards, and might even own a few luxuries. A surprising number of them, as well as some tenants, handled and even saved money, and when the lairds borrowed it was often from someone lower down the rural hierarchy. Rural craftsmen and farmers sold goods and produce in the nearest burgh market and bought in return raw materials and ready-made commodities.

Much detailed information about the daily circumstances of rural life is to be found in the Registers of Testaments of which forty-eight volumes cover the sixteenth century, from the 1560s onwards. As mentioned earlier, there are reservations to be made in using this source material. There are no registers for certain areas, including Aberdeenshire, Argyll, Caithness, Dumfries, Inverness, Moray, Ross and Orkney and Shetland, but, of course, the testaments of persons from these areas were registered in the Commissariot Court of Edinburgh, whose jurisdiction covered the whole country. Besides, surviving testaments tend to be those of the rather better-off rural dwellers, lairds, portioners and the bigger tenant-farmers; examples of those of cottars and rural craftsmen are comparatively few and of labourers almost non-existent, so that the picture of society which is derived from them is unbalanced. Testaments take account of moveable wealth only, not of heritable property which in this period mattered more. Even with regard to moveable wealth there are qualifications to be made: goods and gear might be dispersed among family and friends before death and so be wanting from the inventory. Those goods which are listed do not include the *heirship goods,* the best of everything, stock, furniture and personal belongings, which were reserved to the heir to prevent his inheriting an empty house and farm. Yet, even when all these reservations have been made, and allowing for an equal margin of deficiency all round, the testaments contain much valuable information. Indeed, for the sixteenth century there is no comparable source material for the history of social life.

Standards of domestic comfort are reflected in the valuations of household goods, but it is significant of the place assigned to these in the scale of moveable wealth that they are in most cases simply valued as a whole and only occasionally listed item by item. When they are listed they usually consist of necessities such as beds, seating, storage and cooking vessels and the furniture of the fireplace where the cooking was done. These were the only furniture which a rural family would have considered worth acquiring, unless they were exceptionally affluent, and they were often bequeathed — even 'ane kist wantand the lid' was worth having. After all, a *quot,* in effect estate-duty, was charged when the testament was registered, calculated on the value of that part of the moveable estate called the *deid's pairt,* left after all debts had been accounted for and the appropriate division of the remainder had been made between wife and children. The household goods, about which we would like to know so much, were probably the very things on which a family would grudge paying the quot. From the viewpoint of our modern, over-upholstered domestic interiors, the inside of a Scottish peasant farmer's or small laird's house seems spartan indeed. It certainly appeared so to contemporary travellers looking hopelessly for a clean and reasonably comfortable hostelry. But this does not necessarily mean that the rural population felt as miserable as they looked to foreign observers, so long as they had a good fire, enough to eat and plenty of clothes and bed coverings. The bulk of the rural population were the then 'working class' — to use an anachronism — concerned with survival. Perhaps not until comparatively modern times, when the single-tenant, self-employed farmer became the norm and mass-produced goods became plentiful, did country cottages and farmhouses contain furniture which was non-essential.

Interesting comparisons can be made, however, where household items *are* separately listed. The value appears to have largely depended on the kind of material of which the object was made and on its essential usefulness, something which can be said of the possessions of all sections of the community. Silver vessels, for example, were often valued separately even when all other goods were lumped together, and the descending scale of values for the others was usually brass and iron cooking vessels, the wooden furniture, beginning with the beds, the pewter dishes, the household linen and clothes, furred, velvet and woollen. Luxury items are sometimes valued surprisingly low, perhaps because local people did not know their outside value but more likely because, unless made of precious metals and materials, they were thought to be less marketable. James Calderwood's brewing cauldron was worth £10, his set of virginals, an uncommon luxury for an indweller in the small trading town of Dalkeith, only £4.[7] In looking at Table 8, which shows the value of household goods in the homes of a cross-section of the rural community, from lairds to cottars, it is useful to have an idea of what one might possess that could be valued at, for example, £40.

The £40 worth of household goods belonging to Patrick Robertson in Finmouth in 1560 consisted of

4 standing beds, 5 feather beds, 8 bolsters, 24 cods (pillows), 6 pairs of blankets, 2 pairs of linen curtains, probably for beds, 2 counters, or trestle-type tables, 12 table cloths, 24 serviettes, 6 washing cloths, a Flanders kist, a kist for meal, an iron chimney, a basin, a dozen pewter plates, a dozen pewter trenchers, 3 quart stoups, 3 tin pint stoups, 3 silver spoons, an iron pot of 3 gallons capacity, 2 brass pans of 1 gallon capacity, 6 *chandellars*, 6 'great trees of ash sawn for cuppillis', 3 chairs, 2 forms and 2 spits, with 12 sacks, 3 canvases containing 12 ells each, 2 sowing sheets, 6 harrows and 6 sleds

—a reasonably comfortable house for a tenant-farmer.[8]

Fewer items but superior furniture and cooking vessels, including 2 *aumbries* worth £4 10s each, 2 kists at £4 each, a cauldron valued at £10 and 2 furnished beds at £8, brought Janet Bouston's list to over £50.[9] The vicar of Cranston, sir John Greenlaw, owned a bed, a table, 17 assorted pewter dishes, 2 'luggit pewter dishes', a kist and 3 cushions of striped velvet which came to only about £14, whereas his books were valued at £26 13s 4d.[10]

As might be expected, the valued household goods of the individuals in Table 8 show the greater and smaller lairds, the feuars and portioners, the tenants and cottars in descending order. However, the figures tell only part of the story about a man's real standard of living, about how solvent or indebted he was. The full

Table 8: Value of household goods as given in testaments

Name	Value of goods			Year of death
Sir James Hume of Coldenknowes	£2,000	0	0	1596
John Campbell of Calder	666	13	4	1591
Sir James Forrester of Corstorphine	666	13	4	1589
Alexander Hume of Huttonhall	500	0	0	1594
Robert Beaton of Creich	333	6	8	1567
John Stewart of Ardgowan	333	6	8	1597
Robert Arbuthnot of that Ilk	266	13	4	1579
Sir James Stirling of Keir	266	13	4	1589
Roger Kirkpatrick of Closeburn	240	0	0	1583
John Brown of Carsluith	200	0	0	1581
George Drummond of Blair	200	0	0	1595
William Scott of Abbotshall	200	0	0	1599
John Blackadder of Tulliallan	166	13	4	1579
Alexander Abercrombie of that Ilk	133	6	8	1581
Robert Colville of Cleish	133	6	8	1584
George Crawford of Leffnoris	133	6	8	1579
George Haliburton of Kincaple	133	6	8	1596
Robert Aysoun, portioner of Arthurstane	100	0	0	1597
Alexander Balfour of Denmylne	100	0	0	1587
David Barclay of Collairnie	100	0	0	1587
Adam Boyd of Penkill, yr.	100	0	0	1596
George Hepburn, portioner of Athelstane	100	0	0	1597
Thomas Small, portioner of Kinnochtrie	100	0	0	1592
Jerome Spens of Alves	100	0	0	1586
Gilbert Balfour of Westray	66	13	4	1576
Alexander Brodie of that Ilk	66	13	4	1583
Hugh Rose of Kilravock	66	13	4	1597
John Erskine of Dun	50	0	0	1599
William Barclay of Pearston	40	0	0	1584
George Barron, portioner of Auldliston	40	0	0	1592
Adam Boyd of Penkill, elder	40	0	0	1572
Andrew Donaldson in Templeton of Balgrugo	40	0	0	1572
Patrick Robertson in Finmouth	40	0	0	1560
William Dick in Ledcassy	26	13	4	1585
David White, cottar, Brechin parish	24	0	0	(wife died in) 1582
John Cas in Monktounhall	20	0	0	1584
Thomas Cok in Newbigging	20	0	0	1591
John Henderson, portioner in Over Balbrogie	20	0	0	1587
Andrew Hood, cottar, in Balgey	20	0	0	1582
Patrick Anderson in Ardgilzean	10	0	0	1569
John Boswell, portioner of Stenton	10	0	0	1597
Walter Drew, elder, in Burnbray	10	0	0	1580
Robert Brown, hind, Linlithgow parish	10	0	0	1581
Archibald Bailie of Auldstoun	6	13	4	1592

details of the testament of Sir James Hume of Coldenknowes, for instance, who possessed over £2,000 worth of household goods, reveal that he died 'in the red', as we would now say, to the amount of over £3,000, £1,000 of which he owed to an Edinburgh flesher alone! The portioners, that is, the small proprietors, begin to appear in the Table around the £100 mark, with the lairds above this and the tenants and cottars below. On a closer examination of their testaments, however, some small people appear to have been in more comfortable circumstances than might have been expected.

For example, David White from Brechin parish, whose household goods were valued at only £24, was a cottar who was able to lend money to other people, including a citizen of Brechin who owed him £100. His stock included thirty sheep and a mare valued at £9, and his inventory amounted to over £117. While neighbours owed him over £300, he himself was owing only about £16. He paid someone to pasture his sheep, a rural tailor to make his clothes and a weaver and waulker 'for ther labouris'. He paid rent directly to the earl of Mar, in money, victual and poultry.[11]

Alexander Hume of Huttonhall's debts amounted to more than the £4,250 of his household goods, but his rents, unpaid at the time of his death and amounting to over £5,000, were what he lived on.[12] Quite apart from his standard of living, Gilbert Balfour of Westray, belonging to an influential family and holding land in south-east Scotland and in Orkney, should have been comfortably-off. His silverwork amounted to more than his household goods, his whole inventory to only about £700. Like the laird of Huttonhall, however, he lived on his rents, but about £4,000 was owing to him at the time of his death and he had pawned his silver goblets.[13]

Luxury goods usually took the form of silver vessels, valuable for the metal which could be sold or melted down, and were usually in the hands of the rural upper and middle classes, the nobles and lairds. Silver spoons, cups, basins, mazers and saltcellars turn up in a number of testaments and were sometimes bequeathed to members of a family. John Blackadder of Tulliallan, a rich man in many ways, who also referred to 'the golden chain that I daylie use', left his £120 worth of silver vessels among his sons and daughters.[14] Even a much smaller laird, if of ancient lineage, Roger Kirkpatrick of Closeburn, owned eighteen silver spoons, [15] and Thomas Tulloch of Fluris, a feuar of Kinloss abbey, whose debts exceeded his moveable estate, owned twenty-two spoons, besides a silver-gilt mazer.[16]

Some lairds bought clothes to the extent of indulgence, running up bills with Edinburgh and Glasgow tailors during their visits to town. Thomas Bailie of Ravenscraig, who also died in considerable debt, seems to have taken to living in Edinburgh, where he owed a stabler a year's 'stabill maill', but was also in debt to a Glasgow tailor.[17] Roger Kirkpatrick of Closeburn owed £38 to an Edinburgh tailor,[18] and Walter Scott of Branxholm £35 and £41 to two others;[19] in contemporary terms these represent either fairly longstanding accounts or garments of rich materials.

If smaller farmers and tenants possessed few luxuries, they evidently had enough grain and animals to help out neighbours who were short. The testaments of these folk often contain references to money owing for small quantities of victual, wool, hides, sheep and oxen purchased from neighbours. In the barony of Urie, those who were unable to provide their custom payments, such as poultry and provisions, were ordered to buy them 'in the cuntray', that is locally, or pay high commutation prices.[20] While the poor were caught stealing grain from the mill of Urie, an act had to be passed in the barony court with consent of all the tenants 'baith husbandmen and cottars' that none of them must sell peat or other fuel without special licence.[21] At Keillour two neighbours brought to court their dispute about the sale of an ox but the assize, in trying to sort out the wrangle, decided that 'the parteis hes bene troubilsum to uthir' — both had been at fault.[22]

Many bargains, arranged verbally and insufficiently witnessed, must have caused endless bad relations.

However dependent on the land rural life might be, so that for small proprietors and tenant-farmers luxury meant a little surplus grain, fuel or some animals which they could afford to sell, money did come into the picture, an increasingly common commodity which all classes handled, which some were even able to save.

We have already seen some of the ways in which the landlords tried to realise cash from their estates: by turning custom payments and services into cash commutations, by selling the victual rent to tenants, by setting the rents themselves in tack, for tack-duty, by feuing the property, particularly church land, for which they afterwards received a money down payment and an annual feu-duty which was nearly always in cash. The biggest of the lairds and the nobles, who maintained large households with many retainers and servants, still had need of rents in kind, but the greatest of the church landlords, many of them absentees, were anxious for cash.

The feuars and tenant-farmers, both with subtenants under them, probably also had a certain money income, on a smaller scale than the lairds, as well as the services of the subtenants in tilling the land. They, too, had ways of raising money: selling stock and grain, pasturing animals for neighbours for which they received payment, selling wool and hides to rural craftsmen. There were more 'wage-earners' — more correctly, *feed* workers — among the rural population than might be supposed, who were earning money: servants, including boys and girls, skilled rural workers and labourers. Servants' fees, taken over the second half of the century, as found in wills, ranged from £1 6s 8d to £3 annually for men, and from 14s to £2 for women, apart from food and board and *bounteth*. The ploughman was, and long remained, the highest-paid rural worker, earning anything up to £6 a year, with his *boll,* or grain payment. Even seasonal labourers, some of whom were probably from local tenant families, hired at haymaking and harvest for work on the landlord's own ground, might be paid partly in money. At Mauchline in Ayrshire in the 1520s, the chamberlain of Melrose abbey paid men shearing and stacking the corn 4d a day; perhaps they spent it at the local Fair which began two days after the harvest ended.[23] In 1540 the laird of Lochleven paid shearers, dyke builders, fowlers and colliers in money as well as kind, paid 22s to 'Andro Arnot for leading stanes' and 22s in *arles* to a man hired in Perth.[24] Lord John Hamilton's chamberlain, in 1593, paid the haymakers in a mixture of meal and money, amounting to over £22.[25] Money was sometimes earned for driving sheep and cattle, for ferrying them or for running errands; the Mauchline chamberlain regularly paid a band of local men to 'run' on his business and to buy provisions in places as far apart as Irvine and Dunfermline, Edinburgh and Dunscore.[26] However they came by it, the testaments show that all kinds of people had some money in their possession at the time of their deaths, or had loaned it to others during their lifetimes.

Table 9: Ready money as given in testamentary inventories

Name	Amount			Year of death
John Grant of Freuchie	£6,666	13	4	1585
John Kennedy of Ardmillan	3,333	6	8	1577
Mr Nicol Elphinstone of Shank	2,666	10	0	1578
Alexander Abercrombie of that ilk	1,600	0	0	1581
Robert Arbuthnot of that ilk	1,064	0	0	1579
Florence Martin of Gibbliston	820	8	0	1568
Thomas MacDowall of Makerstoun	595	6	0	1571
Robert Drummond in Dunblane	480	0	0	1591
Walter Urquhart of Cromartie, sheriff	382	0	0	1586
John Blackadder of Tulliallan	347	1	0	1579
George Maxwell of Garnshelloch	300	0	0	1566
Alexander Cochrane of Balbachlaw	260	0	0	1567
Alexander McClellan of Gelstoun	200	0	0	1575
John Milne in Dollerwray	100	0	0	(wife) 1566
James Hering of Glasclune	93	0	0	1579
Hugh Rose of Kilravock	76	0	0	1597
Robert Hamilton of Bathgate	74	8	0	1567
Sir James Stirling of Keir	66	13	4	1589
Alan Provand in Auchinloch	63	6	8	1590
John Fullerton of Dreghorn	53	6	8	1586
Robert Colville of Cleish	48	0	0	1584
Alan Coutts, chamberlain of Dunfermline	48	0	0	1596
David Edgar, portioner of Gullihill	40	0	0	1590
John Wilson, pupil, son of Patrick W. in	32	0	0	1590
Sanquhar	(and 10 gold crowns)			
Mr David Campbell of Denehead	28	0	0	1584
Euphemia Bonar, widow, in Hardens	21	0	0	1567
David Hering in Kirktoun of Bathgate	20	0	0	(wife) 1547
Sir William Edgar, brother of David E.,	20	0	0	1579
portioner of Gullihill	(and 20 gold crowns)			
James Colvin in Tranent	19	0	0	1563
James Calderwood in Dalkeith	10	5	0	1567
Alexander Balfour of Denmylne	5	0	0	1587
James McKene in Knockowat	5	0	0	1567
James Carrington in Traperne ('Traprain')	5	0	0	1567

Table 9 contains a sample of those whose inventories included some 'reddie silver'. In some cases the money was in the hands of others for safekeeping; Robert Drummond's £480 was 'in the hands of George Henry in ane purse in ane bonnat case',[27] and the laird of Ardmillan's 5,000 merks was in the hands of John Campbell, a relative of the laird's wife, Marion Campbell, widow of the laird of Corsewell.[28] John Grant of Freuchie must have been one of the richest men in Scotland, the nobles apart.[29] Although there were many people who had greater numbers of stock and greater rents, some individuals owed Grant large sums of money: the earl of Atholl 300 merks, Colin MacKenzie of Kintail 1,300 merks, Campbell of Calder £333 6s 8d, and two Dundee burgesses £40 for 'salmond and uthir merchandice bought by them'. Grant's inventory included 10,000 merks 'reddie silver' and 20,000 merks 'in ane box'. John Fullerton of Dreghorn's £53 6s 8d was 'in the hands of his wife . . . gottin in of the Martinmas debt of the crop and year 1585', the year before he died, so that we know that his cash in hand came from the arrears of his tenants' maills.[30]

Perhaps it is surprising to find small farmers like Thomas Carrington and James McKene with money at all. Carrington and his wife had held on to their 40s even although they owed the landlord almost two years' rent.[31] A small farmer did not need money, however, to be comfortably-off by contemporary standards, any more than he needed an elaborately furnished house. James McKene in Knockowat is a good example.[32] His entire moveable estate amounted to £650, and while others owed him over £112 he himself owed only £47. He had only a little grain left by the end of the summer but he did have a large number of stock: forty-eight cows, sixteen oxen, nineteen stots, 120 sheep and forty lambs, and was evidently engaged in horsebreeding, having horses, mares and foals to the value of £64 13s 4d. At the same time, he was a year and a half in arrears with his rent to the laird of Penkill.

Life was basically localised; horizons were as distant as a man had good reason to go, on foot or horseback, to kirk, mill and market, to the first and last of which his wife would also go, and to meetings of the barony and sheriff courts. Only occasionally would his *carriage service* take him very far away from home, and work was within walking distance. If we had met a sixteenth-century Scot in Antwerp and had asked him which *country* he came from, he might as readily have replied Gowrie or Teviotdale as Scotland. The legal framework of the barony, the pattern of agriculture as determined by soil and weather, the local demand for and supply of craftsman-made goods, the difficulties of travel and communications all reinforced the 'local' character of life and bred habits of self-reliance and at the same time of communal activity, spontaneous beyond anything that we in our day of public services and contrived 'community involvement' can possibly imagine.

The smallest unit was the immediate family, and this might be quite small at any given time. Mothers may have borne children with almost annual regularity, but infant and child mortality were high. Besides, children left home at an early age to become servants and apprentices and, in fact, many of them had been fostered or boarded outwith the family house even earlier. James Melville, minister of Anstruther and nephew of Andrew Melville, tells us in his diary that after being weaned he was 'put in ane cottar hous'.[33] The minister of Kilwinning, William Kirkpatrick, who reared his family of three in what had formerly been his 'chamber' as a monk of Kilwinning abbey, boarded some of them with a family in Byres at the other end of the town.[34] Thomas Ferguson of Thraiff in Carrick boarded his son with John Whiteford in Irvine,[35] and the laird of Craigends in Renfrewshire owed one, John Fleming, £8 at the time of his death 'for barneis burding'.[36] This is not the expenses of boarding an apprentice, which were sustained by a master in terms of the indenture. Many children while at home must have had a step-parent, for re-marriage on the death of a partner was common practice, for a woman in order to provide herself with added legal protection — that she be 'cled with ane husband', as the phrase went — and for a man in order to have someone to run his house and rear his motherless children until they left home. While many widows appear in estate rentals, whose liferent provision may have enabled them to decline re-marriage, it was normal for them to re-marry and for their husbands to be *entered* to the holding as tenants. A well-provided-for widow in a rural community was just as marriageable as a widowed noblewoman in the politico-financial marriage market of the royal court. For the peasantry, as for noble and laird, marriage was an economic necessity as well as a social institution and an ordinance of the church. George Dundas of that Ilk commended his wife in his testament in 1599, 'seeing it cannot be denyit be na honest man but that be the marriage of Dame Katherine Oliphant my secund wife, now my spous, not onlie I gat ane honorabill partie, being the dochter of the Lord Oliphant and the widow of the Knight of Kellie, but also I have had be hir ane gret rent and leving be the commoditie thereof, and be hir guid service, consall and travell tane upoun hir for me in the affairs tending to the help of my hous . . . .'[37] If a farm had been in the possession of a family for a long time and was divided into portions, children would return home to marry in their turn and sons and daughters-in-law, or daughters and sons-in-law, would set up house for themselves — and would cultivate their own part of the farm.

The most important concerns when the head of the family died, whatever his place in the rural hierarchy, were maintenance of the family unit and continuity of its possession of the land; 'willing that my hous and leving sall stand and continewe hereftir as it has done be the mercie of God in tyme bygane', as Patrick, Lord Lindsay, put it.[38] It was best if, for the time being at least, the widow and the heir could continue to live together, something which at times might be difficult, especially if the eldest son was by now married. Robert Colville of Cleish, who indited a rambling confession of his faith and a longwinded sermon for the benefit of his family and friends before making his will, was fully aware of the problem: 'since it often happenis . . . to fall furth thrawardlie and unhappilie betwix the moder and the sonne, I haif thot guid to remember my sone first to be obedient unto his moder and in nawayis trubill and molest hir in theis thingis that scho hes suirtie of . . . . Next I pray my wyf to remember to beir wyth the young imperfectionis of youth . . . . And gif it sall pleis God to moif my wyfis hairt to marie ane uthyr husband efter my deceis I will pray hir to do thairin with adwyse of hir sonne.'[39] Walter Urquhart, laird of Cromartie, wished his wife and son, Henry, to keep one household between them until 'newcorne tyme', on the expenses of the whole house,[40] while Patrick Stewart of Ballaquhan asked that his wife and their son remain 'in household' together for at least seven years 'and furder as lang as thai can agrie'.[41] Sir James Stirling of Keir, like the laird of Cleish, had an exhortation for his son, Archibald, asking him to keep household with his mother 'and my wyf to be gyde of the haill leving and hous salang as she levis and Archibald to use her counsal, for that is his greit weill. I pray Archibald nocht to be careit away by (i.e. from) his moderis counsall be na bodie for scho is his loveing freind'. If, however, they were unable to live together and set up separate houses, the furnishings of the house at Cadder, near Glasgow, where Sir James died, and of their house in Stirling were to go to his wife. The daughter of the bishop of Dunblane, Jane Chisholm sounds a managing woman and one wonders how much of the will she had dictated.[42] Roger Kirkpatrick of Closeburn wished that all his children and servants remain in the house until the coming Whitsunday, asking his son, Thomas, to be kind to them.[43]

For tenant families continuity of possession, which in their case was dependent on customary law, was probably as important as keeping the family together as an economic unit. The various ways of ensuring this are reflected in testaments. Patrick MacCreckan in Galloway left his holding to his wife, Margaret MacCulloch, according to the terms of their joint-tack, to his son, Archibald, the 'possession and kindness' of half the lands of Glenclere and others, as set out in Archibald's marriage contract, and to his son, Thomas, he left half the kindness of the lands of Senquhan, Little Toung and Balshangie, 'not hurting his wife's liferent'.[44] Robert Simpson, a tenant of the laird of Buccleuch, whom we have already met, left the kindness of his father's steading in Kirkwood to his own son and grandson, who then occupied it, and the use of the lands of Braidwood, of which he had a tack with five years still to run, to his wife, to be shared with their son, William.[45] Even a small proprietor like James Stewart of Bonskind felt it advisable to have his son *entered* with the superior during his own lifetime.[46] Unfortunately these arrangements were not always honoured; William Cunningham of Craigends at the time of his death was still in possession of £10 which had been placed in his hands for the benefit of 'Alesounis bairnis in Yoker', either to give them or 'put thaim in thair faderis stedying'.[47]

For members of the family not in a position to inherit land, money was sometimes set aside for the purpose of acquiring it, or heirs were asked to settle part of the family holding on them. George Maxwell of Garnshelloch left legacies to his brothers and a sister, to be 'put out' (i.e. spent) by his 'Maister', Sir John Maxwell of Terregles, and at his discretion 'laid upoun land'.[48] Sir Andrew Kerr of Hirsell asked his eldest son, Walter, to provide Sir Andrew's brother, Robert, with 'ane pleuchgait of land for the uphauld of his bairnis',[49] illustrating the predicament of the relatives of the lairds and nobles, who might have a personal kind of dependence on them, riding in their 'following', but with little or no independent means of livelihood in the form of land. Thomas Kirkpatrick, heir of the laird of Closeburn, was left to give his younger brother a nineteen-year tack of land from his own inheritance.[50]

Next to the business of continued possession of lands and steadings came the upbringing of children and provision for them, in particular the provision of marriage portions for the daughters, matters which affected families great and small. Wives were commonly made not only executors but also tutors of their children and guardians of them in the everyday sense, at least during the mother's widowhood. That last proviso was clearly underlined by many husbands; John Dickson, a tenant-turned-feuar in the regality of Scone abbey, urged his children to be faithful and obedient 'servants' to their mother 'and scho to enterteyne thame honestlie as ane faythfull moder', surrendering her office of executor if she married again.[52] Nicolas Murray, wife of Robert Maxwell of Trustanes in Dumfriesshire, was made executor and tutor to her children so long as she remained unmarried 'or undefylit or brutit (rumoured) with ane lemane or luif unmarat'.[52] Such provisions prevented a stepfather's control over stepchildren and their gear. Sometimes a father felt it advisable to enlist the support of an influential relative, or the man whom he thought of as his 'Maister' in the sense of head of his surname or lord of the ground. Patrick Stewart of Ballaquhan left 100 merks to the earl of Atholl, 'his maister', asking him to be 'good to his wife and bairns',[53] and George Maxwell of Garnshelloch made Sir John Maxwell of Terregles tutor to his children, hoping that he would be a father to them 'as he wes to me befoir'.[54]

The death of a father was sometimes the occasion for placing children, not already living away from home, in the 'governance' of a friend or relative. In 1583 Alexander Brodie of Brodie left his children to the care of their maternal relatives, even although their mother was alive and had charge of two younger children.[55] George was to be 'received, instructit and governed by the advice of William Hay of Dalgety' and Thomas by that of David Hay of Pennick. His daughter, Margaret, was 'to remane in servitude with Lilias Hay, young lady of Kilravock', and to be sustained in clothes and other necessaries by the Lady of Park, her grandmother, and her own mother, Margaret Hay; Kilravock was, of course, only a few miles from her home at Brodie. David Hird in Easthouses seems to have died a widower, making James Hunter in Newbattle and Troilus Lawson in Edinburgh his executors and instructing them to use £100 which he left them for the benefit of his daughter, Margaret, 'to be nureist, cled, fed and upbrot by them'.[56]

The family papers of the landed classes are full of marriage contracts, and quite a number of those of daughters of the tenant class are to be found in protocol books of notaries; there is even one in which a monk of Newbattle abbey tochered his niece, about to marry his servant, with a few animals and the use of his yard next to the monastery.[57] The amount of tocher varied according to the resources of the family and might be eked out with a few of the *bonds* which continually changed hands in the period, almost like a currency. In making their wills, fathers often set aside a sum of money as the tocher of a daughter, or daughters, as yet unmarried, and according to many testaments tochers were frequently unpaid years after a marriage. William Durie of Meadowend, a fairly small proprietor, left 400 merks to his youngest daughter, Sarah, 'to help her to her marriage'.[58] Quite often it fell to a brother to eventually tocher his sister according to a father's instructions; Lord Herries, for instance, ordained his son, Robert, to pay his sister, Grizel, £1,000 when she reached the age of fourteen, together with 1,000 merks then in the hands of Mr Mark Kerr, and 500 merks, in the hands of George Herries, 'to marie hir with', a comfortable settlement.[59] Robert Colville of Cleish left his son, Robert, to 'tak burden', that is in a marriage contract, with his sister, Elizabeth, 'to marie sic ane that feiris the Lord, according to hir degrie and estate', and to pay her tocher of 4,000 merks, 'and gif it sal happin my said dochter to leid ane simpill (single) lyf and nocht to be movit in hir hairt to tak ane husband, in that cais my sone sall intertene hir in all necessaris during hir lyftyme according to hir estate.'[60] A 'simpill lyf' was not the sort of choice a peasant farmer's daughter was likely to have and was exceptional enough even in a laird's family in the sixteenth century.

In order to make a convenient provision, children were sometimes given a sum of money in place of the *bairnis pairt* of their father's moveables that would have come to them automatically by law, and a wife might be given a cash substitute for her 'third'. The laird of Brodie's daughter, for example, received £133 'for furtherance of hir to sum honest lyf', and her four sisters and brother were also given sums of money, all in satisfaction of their *bairns' pairt,*[61] while the daughter of Kennedy of Ardmillan received 1,000 merks in place of her *bairn's pairt.*[62]

Besides provision and arrangements for a family's future security, the many bequests to members of the family, detailed in testaments, show the kind of possessions which were most valued by the rural communities: stock, including cattle, sheep and oxen, and, quite often, the young of these animals, victual and seed, essential furniture such as beds and kists, and cooking vessels. Clothes were often bequeathed too, which, as far as the humbler rural folk were concerned, were fashionable as long as they held together; George Maxwell of Garnshelloch even left his sister 'my goun to mak hir ane kirtle'.[63] The bequests of the smaller tenants tended to be in *kind,* although some of them managed gifts of money. Patrick Heriot in Winchburgh, Linlithgowshire, left three of his sons an ox each, another a cow, an ox and a mare, and the oldest son an ox and £26.[64] John MacCartnay, a small feuar of Sweetheart abbey, left his wife a white and grey nag, a young ox, a cow, six sheep and 'James MacCartnay's kist'.[65]

There are many instances of bequests to natural children, who were debarred by the law from inheriting. John, Lord Herries, who died in 1583, left his natural son, James, to the care of his lawful son, William, to be the latter's servant, asking William to keep an eye on him 'because I have found him to be of an evil inclination'.[66] Alexander Yule in Garmiltoun, East Lothian, not only left £20 to his two natural sons and £40 to a natural daughter, but gave their mother two pairs of sheets, two stones of wool, cloth that remained over from the making of his own grey gown and 'two of the best ky in the Merse', as though she were having to set up a home for her children, having possibly been under his direct protection until then.[67] Many men and women remembered their servants, with small sums of money, grain and clothes. Some masters went a little further in arranging for a servant's future. William Cunningham of Craigends in Renfrewshire left his servant, John Gilchrist, 10 merks a year till 'my sone be auchtene yeires of age', after which, if he chose to remain in service, he was to have all 'expenses', and also bequeathed to him a skin coat and canvas doublet.[68] Mr Andrew Home, parson of Lauder, left his servant, John Crewar, his kindness to the teinds of the lands of Windycleuch[69] and Sir Andrew Kerr of Hirsell left £40 each to three servants 'to help thame to stedyngis and (i.e. so long as) thay be gud servandis to the hous'.[70] Domestic servants, like the landless labourers, were dependent on the generosity of those who employed them, very often having no sort of right in the land themselves.

Supplying the needs of the rural community, both landlords and tenants, were the rural craftsmen: weaver, waulker and tailor, saddler, smith, wright and cooper, cordiner and soutar, who made and mended shoes, brewster, who was often a woman, and other women who sewed and bleached linen. Spinning was a home-based occupation of all women, but yarn was then taken to the *wobstar* to be woven, or he travelled round the farmtouns and villages for the purpose. The cordiners and soutars, besides making and mending shoes, sometimes supplied or dressed skins which, in the tighter craft circles of a burgh, would have had the skinners up in arms. John Fleming in the parish of Lenzie paid a cordiner for 'graything of hydis',[71] and John Panton in Dalkeith gave a soutar 25s 'for hydis'.[72] The smith not only shod horses, charging separately for removing old shoes and for making and fitting new ones, but supplied iron and made and repaired ploughs. The laird of Craigends paid a smith, John Black, for shoeing horses and for supplying 'plough irons',[73] Mr John Hutton in the parish of Muckhart paid £5 for horse-shoes and 'pleugh graith',[74] and Robert Hamilton of Bathgate bought 30s worth of iron from a local smith.[75] A smith in the parish of Stevenston, in Ayrshire, also supplied the laird of Craigends with lime. The testament of Thomas Kadie, cordiner in Coldingham, who feued his holding, gives some idea of the circumstances of a rural craftsman.[76] His inventory, which amounted to £326 6s 8d, included 30 bolls of bere in his barnyard, valued at £100, 12 bolls of oats, valued at £33, a horse worth £12 6s 8d, four oxen, valued at £12 each, and seven *daker* of 'barkit ledder (leather),' which was worth £140. Besides the feu of his holding, where he lived, he held land from Lumsden of Blanerne, to whom he paid a rent in kind of 10 bolls bere, the equivalent of 50 merks. A number of people had borrowed money from him but he managed to leave *free gear,* that is, moveable estate with all debts deducted, of well over £300. In the comparatively flexible craft situation of the countryside, where individual craftsmen may have been a fair distance apart and without much competition, these men may have overlapped their areas of work and exploited sidelines in a way that would not have been tolerated in a burgh.

There were points of contact with the outside world for the largely self-sufficient rural communities. Members of many landward families had become town-dwellers: lesser craftsmen, traders and servants from the small farmers and tenants, and merchants, lawyers, royal officials and the greater craftsmen, such as the goldsmiths, from among the lairds and noble families. The line between town and country was much less distinct than it is today for, apart from personal con-tacts with their rural origins, many townsmen were still farmers, pasturing their stock on the burgh muir and harvesting their shares of the burgh lands and land even further off. The richest merchants acquired estates or married into lairds' families, passing into the landed classes themselves but maintaining their com-mercial interests in the burghs. Only Edinburgh, the capital, was big enough to contain people with no real rural contacts and yet they, simply by living there, were dependent on the countryside from which came the capital's grain, fish, flesh and coal, from the good farming country of the Lothians and the coal pits of the Forth estuary. Many burghs were so small as to be merely large villages, and with their long *tofts,* byres and other shelters for stock they presented a reasonably rural appearance themselves. The only outstanding buildings in them were the burgh kirk and the tolbooth, smaller, perhaps, than the castles and monasteries of the countryside.

N

Countryfolk were used to coming into town if it was within reasonable striking distance. They came chiefly to market, where the magistrates made special regulations for landward craftsmen and farmers bringing in their produce for sale. Where an ecclesiastical landlord also possessed a burgh, as in the case of Canongate, Dunfermline, Arbroath, Paisley, Glasgow and St Andrews, the tenants came to town to attend the regality court, held in the burgh tolbooth.[77] The bishop of Aberdeen's tenants performed foot and horse carriage service to Aberdeen, or paid commutation of 20s and 10s respectively. Rural craftsmen bought raw materials from the burgh merchants who stocked these in large quantities, such as iron and steel and finer cloths. Individual country people while in town bought ready-made items, of which the merchants had a surprising variety, including belts, gloves, purses and bags, bonnets — like the 'black bonnet and tippet' which cost the miller of Swinton 26s from a Haddington merchant[78] — and, surely, some of the sugar, spices and confections, listed among the cloth and hardware which were to be found in the merchants' booths.

Merchants were sometimes to be found in sizeable settlements which happened to be on a busy highway; the chamberlain of Melrose abbey at Mauchline, a sizeable township lying on the important road from Ayrshire into Lanarkshire and centre of the barony of Kylesmure, bought iron from a merchant there which the local smith made into a rake, spits, trugs and a new lock for the barn door.[79] Robert Beaton of Creich, who died in 1567, although he spent much time at court and patronised the Edinburgh tailors, bought wine and other merchandise to the value of £49 from a merchant in Dundee and ran up accounts with a flesher, carpenter, cordiner, smith and baxter in Falkland, bought tar from a merchant in Cupar and planks of wood from Andrew Stoup, burgess of Perth. He was at the time of his death repairing his house at Dunbog, employing Alexander Piggot from Dundee to slate and point it.[80]

The names of debtors in merchants' testaments give some idea of the social and geographical spread of their customers. Usually the Edinburgh merchant's net was spread the widest, but he would often draw clients from the district from which he had come and where he still had relatives. James Borthwick, burgess of Edinburgh, probably originated from the place of that name in Midlothian; his customers who owed him money for merchandise at the time of his death included Matthew Borthwick in Borthwick, James Brown, Lord Borthwick's servant, John Borthwick in Brig of Hailes, 'Old Lady Borthwick's maiden', John Hepburn, brother of the laird of Fortune, William Henryson in Stow, George Shiell in Soutra Hill, William Dodds in Dalkeith, Alexander Forrester at Brig of Hailes, James Bellenden in Lasswade, George Newton in Drem, George Seton in Tranent and John Cranston in Gilmerton, as well as a number of people in Edinburgh.[81] Similarly, David Beveridge, a prosperous Edinburgh merchant, bore a name common around Kinross and on the estate of Douglas of Lochleven; a number of his customers came from that part of the country, Kinross, Kinnestoun, Cupar, Falkland and Powmill, and from there up into Perthshire, Abernethy, Ballyclone (in Madderty parish), and Perth itself.[82] On the other hand, a merchant in an outlying burgh tended to get his customers from nearer home, like Thomas

Richardson, merchant in Haddington, who had factors in Dieppe and Flanders, whose customers came from the countryside around: Longformacus, Chirnside, Chowslie, Carfrae, Garvald, Blacadder mill, Swinton mill, Barns of Fortune, Cockburnspath, Cranshaws, Fogo, where the smith's wife bought wool cards from him, Mellerstain, Horndean, Whittinghame, Langton and 'James Paterson in Whitsun for pirnit (striped) canvas'.[82]

To the more outlying parts of the countryside went the chapmen, cadgers and 'travelling merchants' with their cloth, haberdashery and small household articles and, of course, their news and gossip. The cadgers collected and sold country produce and country-made goods; the cadger who owed Thomas Kadie, the Coldingham cordiner, £3 6s 8d possibly carried round and sold shoes.[84] Chapmen bought small goods from merchants and resold them to the country people. Some of them travelled a fair distance; one from Galloway owed David Beveridge, the Edinburgh merchant, £9.[85] Thomas Peebles, burgess of Dundee, was owed money by three chapmen, amounting to over £10,[86] and John Danesoun, also of Edinburgh, did business with 'the chopman that travellis to John Hardie', suggesting that some chapmen may have travelled for particular merchants[87] — in fact, this may have been what the designation 'travelling merchant' as distinct from 'chapman' meant. James Fluker, traveller, living in Lasswade, went as far afield as Sanquhar selling his wares and, although his customers owed him over £200 when he died in 1581, he managed to leave *free gear* of £226 11s. On his holding at home he had sown oats, bere, peas and wheat, had a cow, two horses, which he no doubt used on his journeys, and household goods and clothes valued at £10.[88] Less prosperous was John Forfar, 'creelman' in Romanno Grange, whose inventory consisted entirely of seven sheep which he had left in pasture with neighbours; the value of these and the debts due to him, amounting to £16 7s 2d, were all he was worth when he died.[89]

Notes

1 Edin. testaments, CC 8/8/19, fo. 109v
2 *Ibid.*, CC 8/8/30, fo. 184v
3 *Ibid.*, CC 8/8/1, fo. 39v
4 *Ibid.*, CC 8/8/1, fo. 3v
5 Morton muniments, GD 150/2080
6 Accounts of William Douglas of Lochleven, RH 9/1/3
7 Edin. testaments, CC 8/8/1, fo. 3v
8 *Ibid.*, CC 8/8/1, fo. 49v
9 *Ibid.*, CC 8/8/1, fo. 163v
10 *Ibid.*, CC 8/8/1, fo. 95r
11 *Ibid.*, CC 8/8/12, fo. 120r
12 *Ibid.*, CC 8/8/26, fo. 79r
13 *Ibid.*, CC 8/8/5, fo. 39r
14 *Ibid.*, CC 8/8/8, fo. 37r
15 *Ibid.*, CC 8/8/13, fo. 263r
16 *Ibid.*, CC 8/8/7, fo. 364r
17 *Ibid.*, CC 8/8/14, fo. 225v
18 *Ibid.*, CC 8/8/13, fo. 263v
19 *Ibid.*, CC 8/8/3, fo. 164v
20 *Urie,* 9

21 *Ibid.*, 27
22 Keillor, RH 11/41/1
23 *Mauchline account books*, 99
24 Lochleven account book, RH 9/1/2
25 Airlie muniments, GD 16/30/54
26 *Mauchline account books*, 93, 100
27 Edin. testaments, CC 8/8/25, fo. 32v
28 *Ibid.*, CC 8/8/6, fo. 180v
29 *Ibid.*, CC 8/8/17, fo. 177v
30 *Ibid.*, CC 8/8/17, fo. 105r
31 *Ibid.*, CC 8/8/1, fo. 24r
32 *Ibid.*, CC 8/8/1, fo. 28r
33 James Melville, *Diary*, 13
34 Edin. testaments, CC 8/8/9, 26 July 1581
35 *Ibid.*, CC 8/8/28, fo. 267v
36 *Ibid.*, CC 8/8/1, fo. 122r
37 *Ibid.*, CC 8/8/34, 21 January 1600
38 *Ibid.*, CC 8/8/23, fo. 130v
39 *Ibid.*, CC 8/8/16, fo. 63r
40 *Ibid.*, CC 8/8/20, fo. 200r
41 *Ibid.*, CC 8/8/17, fo. 91v
42 *Ibid.*, CC 8/8/23, fo. 172r
43 *Ibid.*, CC 8/8/13, fo. 263r
44 *Ibid.*, CC 8/8/1, fo. 110r
45 *Ibid.*, CC 8/8/1, fo. 62v
46 *Ibid.*, CC 8/8/1, fo. 57r
47 *Ibid.*, CC 8/8/1, fo. 122r
48 *Ibid.*, CC 8/8/1, fo. 41v
49 *Ibid.*, CC 8/8/2, fo. 359r
50 *Ibid.*, CC 8/8/13, fo. 263v
51 *Ibid.*, CC 8/8/33, fo. 77v
52 *Ibid.*, CC 8/8/13, fo. 365r
53 *Ibid.*, CC 8/8/17, fo. 91v
54 *Ibid.*, CC 8/8/1, fo. 41v
55 *Ibid.*, CC 8/8/12, fo. 326v
56 *Ibid.*, CC 8/8/14, fo. 305v
57 Protocol book of Thomas Stevin (S.R.O.), B 30/1/5, fo. 93v
58 Edin. testaments, CC 8/8/22, fo. 242r
59 *Ibid.*, CC 8/8/12, fo. 201r
60 *Ibid.*, CC 8/8/16, fo. 63v
61 *Ibid.*, CC 8/8/12, fo. 326v
62 *Ibid.*, CC 8/8/18, fo. 208v
63 *Ibid.*, CC 8/8/1, fo. 41v
64 *Ibid.*, CC 8/8/1, fo. 138r
65 *Ibid.*, CC 8/8/22, fo. 311v
66 *Ibid.*, CC 8/8/12, fo. 201r
67 *Ibid.*, CC 8/8/1, fo. 55r
68 *Ibid.*, CC 8/8/1, fo. 122r
69 *Ibid.*, CC 8/8/1, fo. 117v
70 *Ibid.*, CC 8/8/2, fo. 359r
71 *Ibid.*, CC 8/8/25, fo. 22r
72 *Ibid.*, CC 8/8/15, fo. 270r
73 *Ibid.*, CC 8/8/1, fo. 122r
74 *Ibid.*, CC 8/8/17, fo. 226r
75 *Ibid.*, CC 8/8/1, fo. 77r
76 *Ibid.*, CC 8/8/25, fo. 370r
77 *Extracts from the records of the Canongate, passim*
78 Edin. testaments, CC 8/8/1, fo. 73r
79 *Mauchline account books*, 91
80 Edin. testaments, CC 8/8/1, fo. 6v

81 *Ibid.*, CC 8/8/1, fo. 130v
82 *Ibid.*, CC 8/8/1, fo. 60r
83 *Ibid.*, CC 8/8/1, fo. 73r
84 *Ibid.*, CC 8/8/5, fo. 370r
85 *Ibid.*, CC 8/8/1, fo. 60r
86 *Ibid.*, CC 8/8/1, fo. 112v
87 *Ibid.*, CC 8/8/1, fo. 178v
88 *Ibid.*, CC 8/8/10, fo. 47v
89 *Ibid.*, CC 8/8/7, fo. 18r

13

Conclusion

AT the end of the sixteenth century and for long afterwards Scotland's was still a rural society, linked in various ways to the life of the small towns but basically supported by agriculture. Those industries which were expanding, such as coal, salt and linen, drew their raw materials and workforce from the countryside and, inasmuch as they were beginning to be capitalised, were in the hands of the landed classes, especially those of the lairds, whose commercial activities also led to the creation of many burghs of barony. Throughout the age the baronies preserved a localised and conservative way of life.

Within the rural communities, however, changes were taking place which tended towards the entrenchment of the tenant class. Holdings were becoming consolidated and often increasing in size, to which ends there was much mobility and exchange among the tenants and, no doubt, a good deal of subletting. The customary tenures — mainly copyholds of one kind or another — which had emerged in the late-medieval period were characterised by continuity of possession which was due as much to the lord's desire to keep the ground in constant cultivation as to any paternalist concern for the cultivators. This situation appears to have encouraged a practice of customary inheritance which tenants came to regard as a right, known in customary law as *kindly tenure,* the right to succeed to a holding previously possessed by one's nearest of kin. Copyhold tenures, rental and tack, based on the principle of *kindness,* gave almost as much security in practice as the feudal tenures and created an assertive spirit among the kindly tenants.

The feuing of church lands in the sixteenth century was the occasion above all which put the theory of kindly tenancy to the test. The vociferous resentment by kindly tenants of the feuing of their holdings to those 'who had no right or kindness thereto' was a cry of protest as much as a cry for help. The opportunity to gain legal recognition of their customary rights of inheritance once and for all caused many of them to feu their holdings. In this the initiative was partly theirs and partly that of the superiors of church land who were under various pressures to turn their estates over to feu-ferm. Whatever the reasons, at least half of the feu charters of church land went to tenants below the class of laird, very many of them kindly tenants of long-standing, creating a wedge of new, small proprietors in the structure of rural society in certain areas. Because feu-ferm was financially unprofitable to superiors *in the long term,* it was nothing less than the long-drawn-out disendowment of the medieval church in Scotland. It is significant that her property did not in the main return to the class who had endowed her in earlier times, but to many cultivators of the ground.

How the tenants-at-will or, as they should perhaps be called, occupants-at-will fared in this period and how large a proportion of the population they represented, we shall probably never know, for these people are, on the whole, unrecorded. They may, however, be identified with the cottars and labourers and with sub-tenants, many of whom may have had no written rights. It may be that as small feus were eaten up by bigger landlords in the seventeenth century and later and as tenant farms were amalgamated on secular estates, there was left exposed a great mass of tenants-at-will who became specially vulnerable in the agricultural changes of the later seventeenth and eighteenth centuries. Because they appear to be all that were left of the old kindly tenants, it has been assumed that kindly tenants were always these vulnerable folk, occupying their land at the landlord's will but with no written rights. But, as we have seen, these were not the kindly tenants we hear of in the sixteenth century when, so long as the kindly principle was honoured, and many kindly tenants could afford to feu their holdings and become owner-occupiers, there was a sort of boom in proprietorship and a good deal of tenant-continuity. We even saw that, in the sixteenth century, there was the possibility of improvement in the position of cottars, largely because of the stability of the rural classes above them. The decline in the position of the Scottish tenant between the later sixteenth century and the earlier eighteenth is something that requires to be investigated.

We have to remember, however, that the redistribution of the church's wealth, which began *before* the Reformation crisis, took place on two levels: the *property* by feuing, in the way that has been described, and the *superiority* by the practice of granting commendatorships, as a result of which the superiors, that is, those entitled to receive the rents, were often virtual laymen or career-conscious church-men, drawn from noble and baronial families, who used the church's patrimony for their own secular and dynastic ends. Towards the end of the sixteenth century the effects of the commendatory system were 'frozen' as the crown began to turn nominal church estates into genuinely secular lordships, the earlier *erections,* as they were called, going to families who already enjoyed commendatorships and the later ones, at the beginning of the seventeenth century, to a closely associated group of men who held government offices or posts in the royal household, some of whom were King James VI's friends who accompanied him to England in 1603.[1] It can be argued that these men, the Lords of Erection, gained more in pres-tige than they did in actual wealth, for an estate which had been feued brought in less as time went on than one which was still leased; feu-duty was fixed and, therefore, depreciated in an age of rising prices and land value, whereas rents could be increased (although not without protest) and the grain rent could be sold at market prices in a year of scarcity. Besides, a landlord had less control over a feuar than over a tenant. The sons of the Lords of Erection inherited after them and some built mansion houses on the sites of monasteries, after the English pattern. Sir John Scott of Scotstarvet, from his own little tower house, described Newbattle:

And the father and son did so metamorphose the buildings that it cannot be known that ever it did belong to the church, by reason of the fair new fabric and stately edifices built thereon; . . . instead of the old monks has succeeded the deer.[2]

Secularisation was complete.

In the sixteenth century a kind of devolution of political and social initiative accompanied that loss of spiritual leadership by the ecclesiastical establishment and renewal of the bases of religious life which we call the Reformation. According to at least one foreign observer, who happened to write down his impressions, the nobility seemed to be losing ground to the lairds, burgesses and middling sort of men.[3] Professionally trained laymen, some of them of humble origin, were filling positions in law and royal service, a pattern also found in England and Europe. In some senses the 'small man' had the wind of change in his favour; the beginning of the seventeenth century, when King James boasted that he could govern Scotland peacefully with his pen, was the great age of the *portioners* and the *bonnet lairds,* and the *feuars* who, given the chance, began to climb the social ladder. This was the natural thing for all classes to do in an age when society was still hierarchical, reminding us of the end of the *Satire of the Thrie Estatis,* where John the Commonweal appears in the garments of his betters. There were economic returns as well as social advantage for, with the decline of Anglo-Scottish hostilities and increased security of tenure, there was an incentive to better cultivation.

In recent years historical research has revealed elements of continuity, improvement and even optimism in the political, economic and religious life of sixteenth-century Scotland. The present study has tried to illustrate the stability and, at the same time, new opportunities which were to be found in the life of the countryside.

> Greit aboundance and blind prosperitie,
> Oftymes makis ane evill conclusioun;
> The sweitest lyfe, thairfoir, in this cuntrie
> Is sickerness, with small possessioun.
> Henryson, *The Two Mice.*

Notes

1 *A.P.S.,* IV, 321-61
2 Scott of Scotstarvet, Sir John, *The Staggering State of Scottish Statesmen*
3 *Calendar of State Papers relating to Scotland,* IV, 432

Appendix A
Change in Landholding Patterns

THE source material here illustrates the changing social pattern, from tenancy to proprietorship, that is, from tack and rental to feu-ferm, on the lands of Coupar Angus abbey, in the barony of Glasgow and on the lands of Paisley abbey in Renfrewshire in the period covered by this book.

In the left-hand columns are details of how the lands were feued, according to surviving feu charters, and in the right-hand columns is shown the earlier pattern of tenancy. The material demonstrates how customary inheritance worked in these areas and how the coming of feu-ferm either entrenched or replaced tenant families.

References for the feu charters mentioned in the left-hand columns do not appear in the Appendix but the author's Ph.D. thesis, 'The social and economic implications of the feuing of ecclesiastical property in Scotland in the late fifteenth and sixteenth centuries', available for consultation in Edinburgh University Library, contains an alphabetical list of all known feuars of kirklands, with references to their feu charters.

The following are the Sources referred to as *'Rental'* in the right-hand columns of the Appendix:

Coupar Angus *Register of Cupar Abbey,* 2 vols, ed. C. Rogers, Grampian Club, 1879-80
Glasgow *Diocesan Registers of Glasgow,* vol. 1, ed. C. Rogers, Grampian Club, 1875
Paisley *The Abbey of Paisley,* Appendix, pp. cxli-clxxiv, J. C. Lees, 1878

THE LANDS OF COUPAR ANGUS ABBEY

FEUING	TENANCY FROM RENTAL
	a. *Perthshire*

ABERBOTHRIE

Rental 2/90 1542
— Robert Rollok: eighth part of Grange of A.

1558/9
Parts of Grange of A. feued to *Donald Rollok,* s. of Robt R., the abbot's servant: occ. by Donald and his subtenants.
(Rental 2/723 Paid 530 merks, composition for his charter. Nov. 1560)

ARTHURSTANE

Rental 1/317 c. 1532 x 1536
—Robert Turnbull: quarter of A.
2/188 1542
—Robert Turnbull: quarter of A.

1559
Quarter of A. feued to *Robert Turnbull:*
occ. by him

1567
Three-quarters of A. feued to *John, earl of
Atholl:* occ. by John Blair, Thomas Hill,
John Henry and Andrew Duncan.

Later resigned by the earl and feued to
Robert Aysoun, s. of Pat. A. of Tullyman.
(same occupants named)

BAITSCHEILL

Rental 2/184 1542
—John Pilmure: 2 acres of B.

1559
2 acres of B. feued to *John Pilmure:*
occupied by him

1558/9
2 acres of B. feued to John Campbell of
Cimba; not occupied by him.

BALGIRSHE
1558/9
Feued to *William Blair* of Balgillo; not occupied by him.

BLAKLAW
1558/9
Feued to *John Drummond,* s. of David D. of
Culquhailye, and Janet Campbell, his wife;
not occupied by them.

BALBROGY

Rental 2/41 1547
—James Henderson: half of Over-
Balbrogy.

1580
Half of Over-B. feued to *James Bissat:*
resigned by James Henderson, or Petre.

1580/1
Shadow half of Over-B. feued to *John Henderson,* or Petre; occupied by him.

Rental 2/98 1550
—Colin Campbell: eighth of Wester
Balbrogy.

1558
Eighth of Wester Balbrogy feued to *John
Fallow;* resigned by Colin Campbell and
Isabel Richardson.

1558/9
Quarter of Wester-B. feued to *Colin Campbell*, s. of Mr David C. in Denehead; occupied by his father.
1559/60
Eighth of Wester-B. feued to *John Campbell*: nat s. of Mr David C.; occupied by John Thom.

1558
Quarter of Easter-B. feued to *John Fallow:* resigned by Colin Campbell.
1558
Quarter of Easter-B. feued to *Robert Montgomery:* occupied by him and Andrew Allan 'his subtenant'.

BOGHALL
1578
5 acres in B. feued to *John Craigo* in Wolfhill: doubtful if occupant.

BRUNTHILL
1550
Feued to *Margaret Campbell:* doubtful if occupant.
CAILLEIS
1558/9
Feued to *James Hering* of Glasclune; not occupied by him.

CALSAYEND
1582/3
Toft & Croft in toun of C. feued to *David Moreis;* occupied by him.

CAMPSY
1567
Nether-C. feued to *John, earl of Atholl.*

1578
Feued to *John Craigo;* occupied by him.

CHAPPELTOUN

1558/9
Third of C. feued to *John Campbell.* s. of

Rental 2/80 1550
—Colin Campbell: quarter of Wester-B.

Rental 2/317 c. 1532
—John Thom, elder, and yr.: eighth part of Wester-B.

Rental 2/52 1547
—Tack to Robert Montgomery of quarter of Easter-B. (said to have been 'bruikit befoir' by Andrew Allan)

Rental 2/65 1549
—John Craigo: Over-C., or Wolfhill
ental 2/272 1560
—'Componit with John Craigo for Over Campsy, callit Wolfhill, etc. . . .'

Rental 2/29 1544
—William Rettref: Third of C., formerly occupied by John Campbell.

late Robert C., burgess of Ayr; cultivated by William Rottray.
1558/9
Third feued to *Duncan Campbell* of Glenlyon; occupied by James Johnsoun.
1559
Third of C. feued to *Andrew Campbell;* occupied by him.

Rental 2/60 1547
—Andrew Campbell: Third of C. (N.B. Andrew Campbell mentioned as a tenant in C. in 1542 *Rental* 2/191)

COLTWARD

Rental 2/119 1555
—Thomas Campbell: Lands of C.

1559
Feued to *Archibald Campbell;* cultivated by Thomas C., his father.
1558/9
East and West Cotyards (or Cotward) feued to *John Drummond,* heir of David d. of Culquhailye.

CARSEGRANGE

Rental 2/311 c. 1500
—Robert Turnbell in Bogmill of Carsgrange, mentioned.
Rental 2/112 1554
—Thomas Turnbull, s. of Robt. T.: tack to him.
Rental 2/252 1554
—Composition paid by him for this tack is £66 13s 4d.; i.e. £40 now and the rest before 'the next fair'.

1558
Eighth of C. with Bogmill feued to *Thomas Turnbull;* occupied by him.
(Rental 2/270 Paid £126 13s 4d. composition for his feu charter)

Rental 2/19 c. 1542
—Alexander Jackson in Weterybuts: tack to him of 'Water butts'.
Rental 2/51 1547
—Tack to him of 2 acres of Carsegrange.
Rental 2/117 1554
—Tack to him of eighth part of Carsegrange.

1558/9
Eighth part of C. (with 2 acres resigned to him by William Law) feued to *Alexander Jackson,* in Weterybuttis; occupied by him.
(Rental 2/271 1559 Paid 700 merks composition for his feu charter)

Rental 1/289 1513
—Robert Jackson: eighth of C. with third of 'Jok Zester and Rane Henry's' and another acre.
Rental 2/17 c. 1542
—Robert Jackson: eighth part of C.

CARSEGRANGE, continued

1558/9
Quarter of C. feued to *John Campbell* of Murthly; occupied formerly by Robert Jackson and now by Ranald Henry.

1559
4 acres of C. feued to *Andrew Powry:* cultivated by him.

(Rental 2/272 1560 Paid £10 as composition for his feu charter)

1559
2 acres of C. feued to *James Galloway:* occupied by him, next to the abbey orchard.

(Rental 2/272 1560 Paid £10 as composition for his feu charter)

COWBYRE

1558/9
Third of C. feued to *William Burt.* s. of Andrew B.; occupied by his father.

(Rental 2/273 1562 Agnes Fleming, widow of late Andrew Burt, and Wm. B., her son, paid £100 composition for their feu charter)

1560/1
Third of C. feued to *John Pery:* resigned by Alexander Baxter who had had it in feu.

1572
Third feued to *Walter Leslie:* occupied by him.

Rental 2/92 1550
—Rannald Jackson. or Henry: eighth of C.

Rental 2/34 1546
—Andrew Powry: 4 acres of C. 'and to the fabric of the monastery they have paid £12

Rental 2/121 1555
—Partick Galloway and Janet Keir, his wife, and to James G., their son, and Elizabeth Jackson, his wife: 2 acres of C. occupied by them, 'paying £10 to the fabric of the monastery'.

Rental 2/95 1550
Andrew Burt: third of C. (Rental 2/214 note of teinds due by Andrew Burt 'and his cottars')

Rental 1/172 1473
—Andrew Baxter: Twelfth part of C.
Rental 1/310 N. d
—in tack to Wm. Pery.
Rental 2/96 1550
—John Henderson: tack of third of C.; formerly occupied by late Wm. Pery and now by his widow.

COWBYRE OF KETHICK

Rental 2/51 1545/6
—Finlay Alexander: tenement called Cowbyre of Kethick.

1550
Feued to *Margaret Campbell*, later wife of Walter Lindsay; occupied by Findlay Alexander.

COWPERGRANGE

Rental N.B. Cowpergrange comprises a large number of territories set to various people over the years.

1559/60
Feued to *John Campbell* of Skipinche.

DENEHEAD
1558/9
Easter-D. feued to *Colin Campbell*, s. of Mr David C. of Denehead.
1559
Wester-D. feued to *Robert Turnbull:* occupied by him.

Rental 2/126 1556
—Robert Turnbull in D.; tack of Wester-D.

DRYMMEIS

Rental 2/193 1542
—Occupants given as: James Halden, John Lindsay, Silvester Farquhar, Elizabeth Fife, Walter Millar and David Webster.
Rental 2/133 1557
—James Hering: tack of Wester-D.

1567
Wester-D. feued to *John, earl of Atholl:* no occupants mentioned.

Rental 2/129 1557
—George Turnbull: tack of Middle-D.
Rental 2/130 1553
—Dispute between George and Herbert Turnbull over latter's 'wrangous occupatioun' of certain corn land of Easter-D. Abbot, an arbitrer, stated that the lands belonged to George.

1567
Middle and Easter-D. feued to *George Drummond:* no mention of occupants.

DUNFALLINTE

Rental vol. 1 *passim*
—Leased periodically to tenants of the name of McGow in 15th and early 16th centuries, then to one called 'Gleshane'.

1541
Feued to *Archibald Campbell*, bro. of James C. of Lawers.

FORTHIR

Rental 2/195 1542
—James McNichol and John McNichol given as occupants.
Rental 2/229 1546
—'Componit with 'James McNichol for a 5 year tack of Little-F.
Rental 2/244 1551
—'Componit with' same for a new tack of Little-F.
Rental 2/142 1557
—Tack to John McNichol of Little-F.

1559/60
Little and Mekle F. feued to *James, Lord Ogilvy*.

(Also in *Rental* 2/251 1553
'Componit with William McNichol for his father's tacks'; *Rental* 2/252 1554
'Componit with John McNichol for his grandfather's tack's.')

Rental 2/195 1542
—David Allan and 5 other tenants: tack of Mekle-F.
Rental 2/229 1546
—'The Master of Ogilvy: tack of Mekle-F. 'providand at he put nocht out certane of the tenentis, as his letter of tack proportis.'
Rental 2/175-177 155.
—Katherine Campbell, countess of Crawford and Lord Ogilvy, her son; tack of Mekle-F. mentions, but does not name, 'subtenants'.

GALLONWRAY

Rental 1/316c. 1530s
—Alexander Ramsay: third; John Brown a sixth of G
Rental 2/14 1541
—Alexander Ramsay: part of G.
?1558
Third of G. feued to *Robert Alexander*.
Rental 2/78 1550
—Alexander Ramsay

KEMPHILL

Rental 1/281 1511
—Wm Turnbull: tack of all lands of K.
Rental 2/183 1542
—George Narne and Andrew Perys named as occupants.

1550
Feued to *Margaret Campbell:* not occupied by her.

MOIRTULLICHT
1541
Feued to *Archibald Campbell*, bro. of James C. of Lawers.

KETHICK
1558
6 acres in K. feued to *Wm. Rae* in Cupar: occupied by him.

Rental 2/101 1552
—Wm. Rae: tack of 6 acres in K.

1558/9
2 acres in K. feued to *Andrew Brown:* formerly occupied by James Euart (?Edward).

Rental 2/20 1542
—James Edward: tack of 2 acres in K.
Rental 2/103 1552
—Andrew Brown, Wm. Lowson, his son-inlaw, and Agnes Trent, the latter's wife: tack of 2 acres in K. next to those set to James Edward.

1558/9
2 acres in K. feued to *John Campbell* of Cimba.

1559
Eighth of K. feued to *Archibald Campbell:* cultivated byThomas C., his father.

1571
3 acres in K. feued to *Andrew Donaldson* in Templetoun of Balgrugo; occupied by him.

1581
5 acres in K. feued to *Alexander Leslie:* possibly not the occupant.

1582/3
2 acres in K. feued to *David Moreis:* possibly not the occupant.

LEDCASSY

Rental 2/190 1542
—John Pety: tack of L.

1559
L. with the mill, feued to *John Pety:* occupied by him.

(Rental 2/270 1559 Paid £100 as composition for his feu charter)

Rental 2/224 1544
—'Componit with' John P. for 19 year tack of L. (£40) and 'Componit with' him for a liferent to him and an heir (£10 more).

MILNTHORN
1558/9
Feued, with the mill, to *James Sanders:* probably not the occupant.

Rental 2/189 1542
—Occupants named as Alex. Cumming and John Sowter.

MUIRHOUSIS
1561
Feued to *John Jackson:* occupied by his father.

NEWBIGGING

Rental 2/111 1554
—Annabella Berny: tack of half-N.

1558/9
Half of N. feued to *Alexander Jackson:* occupied by Annabella Berny.

(Rental 2/271 1559 Paid 700 merks for his feu charter of Half-N. and other lands)
1558/9
Half-N. feued to *John Campbell* of Murthly occupied by him.

PERSEY
1559
Over-P. feued to *Mr David Campbell* of Denehead; occupied by him.

Rental 2/73 1550
—Mr David Campbell of Denehead: called tacksman of Easter-P.

1559
(?Wester)-P. feued to *Alexander Rattray:* occupied by him.
(Rental 2/270 1559 Paid £100 composition for his feu charter of Wester-P.)

Rental 2/72-3 1550
—Walter Rattray and his son, Alex. R.: tack of Wester-P.

POLCAK
1558/9
Feued to *Donald Rollok,* s. of Robert R. in Polcak; occupied by him and his subtenants.

Rental 2/191 1542
—Mention of Robert Rollok in Polcak.

SOWTERHOUSE

Rental 2/137 1557
—John Campbell of Cimba: tack of S.

1558/9
Feued to *John Campbell* of Cimba; occupied by him and his subtenants.

TULLIFERGUS
1558/9
Feued to *Duncan Campbell* of Glenlyon; not occupied by him.

Rental 2/94 1550
—George Narne: tack of T.

WESTHORN

Rental 2/225 1545
—Henry Brown: 5 year tack of W.
Rental 2/241 1550
—Another tack to him.
Rental 2/254 1555
—Another tack to him.
Rental 2/127 1557
—Tack to him: paid £10 to the church fabric.

1558/9
Feued to *Henry Brown* and his son, *John B.;* occupied by them.

b. *Forfarshire*

AUCHINDORIE

Rental 1/256 1504
—Thomas Black: to tack of A.
Rental 1/302 1524
—Janet McRay, widow of Thomas Black: tack of A.

P

?1539
Feued to *James Ogilvy*, s. of James, Lord
O.; not the occupant.

AUCHINLEITHE

Rental 2/152 1557
—Mr David Campbell of Denehead: tack
of Brewhouse of A.

1558/9
Brewhouse of A. feued to *Colin Campbell,*
s. of Mr David C. of Denehead; occupied
by the latter and his subtenants.
1559/60
A., with Nether-A., feued to the *Earl of
Argyll;* not the occupant.

BALMYLE
1558
Feued to *Colin Campbell* of Crunan; occupied by him.

Rental 2/120 1555
—Colin Campbell of Crunan: tack of B.

BLACKSTOUN
1558/9
Half of B. feued to *William Blair* of
Balgillo; occupied by him.

CAMBOK

Rental 2/198
—Eight occupants named.

1559/60
Feued to *Archibald, earl of Argyll:* not the
occupant.

CRUNAN
1558
Feued to *Colin Campbell;* occupied by
him.

FREUCHY
1558
¼ Feued to *David Ogilvy* in Newton; not the
occupant.
1558
¼ Feued to *John Ogilvy*, son of above; not
occupant.

GLENBOY

Rental 2/83 1550
—John McFerland: tack of G.
Rental 2/244 1550
—John Myll: tack of East side of G.

1558/9
Feued to *Thos. Kennedy,* fiar of Coiff; not
the occupant.

GLENMARKY

Rental 2/106 1552
—David Ogilvy and Margaret Campbell,
wife: tack of quarter of G.

1558
Quarter of G. feued to *John Ogilvy*, s. of David O. of Newton: occupied by latter.
1559/60
Third *(sic)* feued to *Archibald, earl of Argyll;* not the occupant.

Rental 2/156 1557
—Richard Clerk and John Hall: tack of quarter of G. each.

INVERARITY
1558
Quarter of Easter-I. feued to *Colin Campbell* of Crunan; occupied by him and his subtenants.
1559/60
Parts of Easter-I, feued to *Archibald, earl of Argyll;* not the occupant.

Rental 2/147 1557
—Excambion between Richard Clerk and Colin Campbell — lands of Nether Auchlech and Easter-Inverarity.

1558/9
Quarter and eighth part of Wester-I, feued to *Colin Campbell*, s. of Mr David C. of Denehead; occupied by latter and his sub-tenants.

Rental 2/152 1557
—Mr David Campbell: tack of Wester-Inverarity.

KINGREICH
1558/9
Grange lands of K. feued to *Thomas Kennedy*, fiar of Coiff; not the occupant.

KIRKHILLOK

Rental 2/154 1557
—James Brisone and John Baxter: tack of half K. each.

1558/9
Feued to *John Ogilvy* of Inverarity; not the occupant.

KIRKTOUN OF PITLOCHRIE
1558/9
Feued to *Archibald, earl of Argyll;* not the occupant.

NEWTOUN OF BELLITE

Rental 2/104 1552
—David Ogilvy and Margaret Campbell, wife: tack of N.

1558
Feued to *John Ogilvy*, s. of David O. in Newtoun; occupied by the latter.

THE BARONY OF GLASGOW

FEUING

TENANCY FROM RENTAL

AUCHINARNE

Rental p. 107 1535 Dec. 20
—Duncan Wardane rentalled in 10s of A. by consent of Wm. Thomson.
Rental p.87 1525 Apr. 29
—Robt. Aikin rentalled in 10s of A. by consent of Wille Atkyn.

1581
21s. 8d. feued to *Duncan Wardane* occ. by him & James Brown.
1581
10s. 10d. feued to *Wm. Aikin* 'veteri tenens'.

1581
16s 3d. feued to *David Murehead* occ. by
him & Mariot Armour.

Rental—

AUCHINLOCH
1581
11s. 8d. feued to *John Drew* occ. by him.

Rental p. 129 1545 Feb. 26
—Thos. Drew rentalled in 11s 8d. of A. by
consent of his father Patrick Drew who is
to keep the liferent being 'ane agit man
beddrale'. Instrument recording his consent drawn up by John Drew, notary.
Rental p. 191 1570/1 Jan. 29
—John Drew rentalled in 11s 8d. of A. on
death of his father Thos. D., his mother,
Isobel Cwnyburch keeping liferent.

1581
8s. 9d. feued to *Robt. Aikenhead* occ. by
him.

Rental p. 80 1521 Apr. 27
—John Aykenhead rentalled in 5s 10d. of
A. with his mother's consent.
Rental p. 98 1531 Oct. 31
—Malcolm Kennedy rentalled in 5s. 10d.
of A. with consent of John Aykenhead.
Rental p. 103 1534 July 10
—John Aknyhead rentalled in 5s 10d. of A.
on death of John A.
Rental p. 177 1562 Sept. 13
—John Aykenhead rentalled in 2s. 11d. of
A. with consent of Malcolm Kennedy.
Rental p. 162 1556/7 Feb. 17
—James Kennedy rentalled in 11s 8d. of A.
with consent of Malcolm K. his father, his
mother, Janet Aykenhead keeping liferent.

1581
11s. 8d. feued to *John Provand* 'tenant', occ.
by Allan P. his father.

Rental p. 134 1546 Sept. 6
—Allan Provand rentalled in 11s 8d. of A.
vacant by death of Patrick P. his father.
Rental p. 178 1563 Sept. 16
—John Provain rentalled in 11s 8d. of A.
with consent of his father, latter keeping
liferent, and Marion Angus, his wife, third
part for life.

1581
11s. 8c. feued to *Thos. Provand* and Janet
Brandwood his wife, occ. by them.

Rental p. 191 1570 July 2
—Thos Provand rentalled in 10s. 8d of A.
with consent of Janet Brandwood his wife,
rentalled therein; her father, William B.
keeping liferent.

BADLAY
1580
10 merklands of Badlay, Molanys, Provest's
Hauch, Cuninglaw, feued to *Robert, Lord
Boyd,* and Lady Margaret Colquhoun, his
wife.

Rental p. 107 1535 Nov. 14
—Robert Boyd, son and heir of Robert
Boyd in Kilmarnock, rentalled in these
lands with consent of George Colquhoun
last rentaller, in terms of a contract between Robert, elder, and George; George
and his wife, Margaret Boyd, keeping
liferent.

BLACKLANDS
1586
2 acres called B. feued to *Mr Alexander King,* advocate. Not occupant.

Rental—

BLYTHSWOOD
1563
£3 lands of B. feued to *George,* son of George Elphinston, burgess of Glasgow. Not occupant.

BURROWFIELD
1581
40s. of B. to *Wm. Forret* (with Nicholhous q.v.), occ. by him.

Rental p. 78 1520 Sept. 16
—Thos. Forret rentalled in 40s. of B. which pertained to Widow Agnes Suistar whom he has married.

BRACHANNY
1580
£3 6s. 8d. of B. feued to *Matthew Stewart* of Minto, kt., occ. by him and his tenants.

Rental A number of rentallers appear throughout the Rental; probably the subtenants of Stewart of Minto.

BRUMEHILL
1577
2 merklands of B. feued to *David Wemes,* minister of Glasgow, occ. by him and others.

Rental Number of names appear; probably the 'others' referred to.

CARMYLE
1580
2 merklands of Over-C. feued to *Gabriel Corbat* of Hardwray, occ. by him and his subtenants.

Rental Number of rentallers mentioned; probably the subtenants.

COWSTOUN
1579
Half of C. feued to *John Otterburn (?occ. by him).*

1579
Half of C. feued to Robert Otterburn, held by him in rental and occupied by his father, Michael Otterburn.

Rental p. 152 1553 Nov. 10
—John O. rentalled in 21s. 8d. of C. on death of his father, Andrew Otterburn, Isobel Bryce, his mother, keeping liferent.

—

CRAIGS
bef. 1565 May 29
WesterCraigs (in city of Glasgow) feued to*Alexander Stewart,* tutor of Castlemilk.
(after 1561)
Easter Craigs feued to *John Livingston,* brother of Mr. Thos L. treasurer of Cathedral.

Rental—

—

DALDOWIE
1581
8 merklands of Easter D. feued to *Matthew Stewart* of Minto, kt.

Rental p. 190 1536/7 Jan. 21
—John Stewart of Minto rentalled in 8 merklands of D.; son of late Robert S. of Minto; his mother, Janet Murray, keeping liferent.

Rental p. 169 1558 Oct. 21
—Matthew Stewart, son of John, rentalled in D.; father keeping liferent.

DAVIDSTOUN
1581
15s. 10d. of D. feued to *Walter Drew*, tenant

Rental passim. titles of his family too numerous to be detailed; possession can be traced from 1521. Last relevant entry:—
p.170 1558 Nov. 21
—Walter Drew rentalled in 15s. 7d. of D. on death of his father, Walter D.; his mother, Isobel Stark, keeping liferent.

1581
47s. of D. feued to *John Drew., occ. by him.*
1581
12s. 6d. of D. feued to *John Donaldson,* occ. by him.

Rental passim, from c. 1521.

Rental p. 97 1530 May 23
—John Donaldson rentalled in 12s. 6d. of D. by consent of Janet Fowler, who keeps the liferent.
Rental p. 160 1555 July 27
—John Donaldson rentalled in 12s. 6d. of D. with consent of John D., his father, who, with Euphemia Craig, his wife, keeps the liferent.

DENESIDE
1560
6 roods in D. feued to *Mr. Robert Herbertson,* vicar of Aberuthven, occ. by Patrick Miller.
1563
2 acres, 1 rood in croft called D. feued to *John Herbertson,* son of Robert H., parson of Ayr.

Rental—

DOWHILL
1564
1 acre in D. feued to *George Herbertson,* burgess of Glasgow, and Margt. Mure, wife, occ. by them.
1581
5s. of D. feued to *John Reid* 'tenant'

Rental p.164 1556 Oct. 16
—Matthew Reid rentalled in 5s of D. 'by consent and owergewin of James Down, last rentaller'.

GARBREID
1579
43s. of G. feued to *John Hay,* son of Mr Andrew H., parson of Renfrew, occ. by John Hutchesoun and Wm. Duncan.
1581
16s. 8d. feued to *Wm. Duncan,* occ. by him.

Rental p.72 1515 Apr. 20
—*Alan Duncan* rentalled in 16s 8d. of G.
Rental p. 132 1546 Apr. 24
—William Duncan, son of Alan D. rentalled in 16s. 8d. of G; liferent reserved to Alan and his wife, Janet Corsby.
Rental p. 144 1553 Apr. 3
—John Hutchesoun rentalled in 41s. 8d. of G.; son Costene H. who died rentaller.

1581
41s. 8d. of G. feued to *John Hutchesoun,* occ. by him and his mother, Mariot Wilson, or Jardane.

GARDEROCH
1580
4 merklands of G. feued to *James Fowlis of Colinton;* leased by Agnes Heriot his wife and her predecessors.

Rental p. 76 1518 Dec. 31
—Alan Heriot to be rentalled in 2 parts of G. after his mother's death.
Rental p. 77 1518
—Alan H. rentalled in the lands; entailed to his 2 brothers — Agnes possibly daughter of one of them.

GARNEQUENE
1581
8s. 4d. feued to *John Braindwod,* son of Thos. B., occ. by his father.
1581
5s. of G. feued to *John Eistoun,* son of Patrick E., there, occ. by his father.

Rental p. 106 1535 Aug. 12
—Thos. B. rentalled in 8s. of G. with consent of Aleson Mayn, his mother, she keeping the liferent.
Rental p. 192 1568/9 Feb. 20
—Patrick E. rentalled in 5s. of G. by consent of John Clogy, last rentaller.

GARROCHE
1579
21s. 8d. of G. to *John Hay,* son of Mr Andrew Hay, parson of Renfrew, occ. by John Duncan and — Maxwell 'of which John is rentaller'. (this feu comprises half these lands)
1581
43s. 4d. of G. to *Archibald Wilson,* citizen of Glasgow; 'pertaining to him in rental'.

Rental—

GARTFORROWIE
1581
15s. 6d. feued to *John Watson,* there, occ. by him.
1581
15s. 8d. of G. feued to *Wm. Aitken* 'tenant', occ. by him.

Rental Number of rentallers in G. but none of them have these names.

Rental p. 175 1563/4 Jan. 28
—Wm. Aitken rentalled in 15s. 6d. of G. with consent of his father, John. latter keeping the liferent.

GARTINKIRK
1581
20s. 10d. (i.e. third pt.) of G. feued to *John Stirling* 'tenant', occ. by him.

Rental p. 74 1515 Dec. 20
—Wm. Stirling rentalled in 2 merklands of G.
Rental p. 93 1529 May 28
—Thos. Provand rentalled in 9s. 7½d. of G. with consent of Marion Anderson, widow of Wm. Stirling, and her son, because Thos. is to marry Wm.'s sister, Catryn.
Rental p. 99 1531 May 15
—John Stirling rentalled in 28s. of G. with consent of John S., his father; latter keeping the liferent.
Rental p. 103 1534/5 Feb 27
—Wm. Gray rentalled in 19s. 2d. of G. with consent of Wm. Stirling and Janet Boyd, his wife.
Rental p. 127 1545 June 22
—Wm. Provand, son of (above) Thomas P. rentalled in 19s. 7d. of G.; his mother, Katherine Stirling, keeping the liferent.

1581
28s. 11d. of G. feued to *John Murehead,*
occ. by him.

Rental p. 143 1553 Mar. 30
—John Stirling, son of John S., in G. rentalled in 19s. 2d. of G. with consent of
William Gray, last rentaller, 'which rental
and kyndeness was bought by John Stirling,
elder, by a contract dated 4 Oct. 1549.'
Rental p. 193 1566/7 Mar. 10
—John Stirling rentalled in 18s. 10d. of G.,
by consent of John S., his grandfather, latter and Isobel Baird, his wife, keeping the
liferent.
Rental 1. 193 1566/9 Mar. 20
—George Stirling rentalled in 19s. 2d. of G.
with consent of John Stirling his father, last
rentaller.
Rental p. 191 1570 Apr. 10
—John Murehead rentalled in 28s. 10d. of
G., with consent of Robert Murehead, his
father, latter keeping the liferent.

GORBELLIS
1579
£6 lands of G., with Bridgend, feued to
George Elphinston of Blythswood.

Rental p. 82 1521/2 Mar. 22
—Geo. Elphinston, son of late John E. rentalled in £6 of G. and B. in Govan, with
consent of his mother, Beatrice Wardlaw;
she keeping the liferent.
Rental p. 154 1554 May 10
—George E., burgess of Glasgow and
grandson of Beatrice Wardlaw, rentalled in
the 9 merkland of G. & B. on her death.
Rental p. 179 1563 June 6
—Licence to Eliz. Colquhoun to marry
Wm. Cunningham and to Bruik the £6
lands of G. & B. 'nochtwithstanding our
actis to the contrar'.

GOVAN
1580
6s. 3d. of Easter Govan feued to *Thos. Hill,*
occ. by him, and 25s. of Meikle Govan,
also occ. by him.
(N.B. he is called Thos. Hill, son of James
Hill, parson of Erskine whose predecessors
had held the lands in rental. The 25s. of
Meikle Govan, above, is called, in the feu
charter, 'Drumbrek quarter', or 'Ibrokis';
the liferent is reserved to Mariot Leiche,
his mother.)

Rental p. 158 1554/5 Jan. 26
—sir James Hill rentalled in 12s. 6d. of
Meikle Govan, with consent and 'owergev-
ing' of Thomas Anderson, last possessor.
Rental p. 166 1557 May 3
—James Rowane rentalled in 6s. 8d. of
'estend of Gavane' with consent and overgiving of sir James Hill, last rentaller.
Rental p. 182 1564 Oct. 11
—sir James Hill rentalled in 6s. 3d. of
Drumbrek quarter of Meikle Govan with
consent of John Liche, last rentaller, the
latter and Margt. Barnart, his wife, keeping
the liferent (these two now sir James's
parents-in-law?).
Rental p. 183 1564/6 Mar. 12
—sir James Hill rentalled in Drumbrek's
quarter with consent of Alexander Leiche,
last rentaller.

1581
6s. 8d. of Meikle-G. feued to *Mr Henry Gibson.*

1581
28s. 8d. of Meikle-G. feued to *John Rolland* in Grenehead and Mariot Gibson, his wife, occ. by him (i.e. the westquarter).
1581(?)
20s. in Meikle-G. feued to *John Rolland* in Grenehead (i.e. the Tucherhill quarter)
1581 (?)
18s. 9d. of Meikle-G. (in the west quarter) feued to *John Rolland* in Westscheill, occ. by him.
1581
12s. 6d of Meikle-G. fued to *Andrew Paterson* in West scheill, occ. by him and his tenants (i.e. in the Tucherquarter).

1581
7 merklands of Haggs, Govan-Scheills, and Titwood feued to *John Maxwell* of Nether-Pollock, occ. by him.

25s. of Little Govan feued to *Robert Mitchell,* occ. by him and David Anderson.

Rental p. 100 1532 Apr. 3
—Stevin Rolland rentalled in 18s. of Meikle Govan, with consent of his father, John R.; latter, with his wife, Agnes Leiche, keeping the liferent.

Rental p. 110 1537 Nov. 28
—James Rolland rentalled in 12s. 6d. of Meikle Govan, with consent of Agnes Leiche, his mother.
Rental p. 168 1558 Apr. 1
—John Rolland elder – son of 'Stene Rowane', rentalled in 18s. 9d. of Meikle-G. with consent of Steven and Violet Anderson, 'his future wife'; they keeping the liferent, (is this the John Rolland in Westscheill, opposite?).
Rental p. 186 1566 Dec. 12
—John Rolland rentalled in 6s. 8d. of Meikle-G. by vendition of John Cuthbert.
Rental p. 182 1564 Oct. 10
—James Paterson rentalled in 6s. 8d. of Toqhairhill quarter in Meikle-G. with consent of John Leiche; the latter, and his wife, Margt Barnard, keeping the liferent.
Rental p. 88 1527/8 Feb. 26
—George Maxwell of Cowglen rentalled, with his son, John Maxwell, in 70s. lands of Titwood with consent of Margt. Binning, widow of John Fowler.
Rental p. 88 1527/8 Feb. 26
—George Maxwell of Cowglen and his son, John, rentalled in the 4 merklands of Govan Haggs, Govan Scheills, with consent and renunciation of Robert, bishop of Orkney, his brother, George's mother keeping the liferent.

Rental p. 114 1539 June 11
—David Anderson rentalled in 5s. of Little-G. on the death of Wm. Anderson, his father; Marion Neilson, his mother, keeping the liferent.

Rental p. 150 1553 July 17
—Robert Mitchell in Little-G., rentalled in 5s. of Little-G. with consent and overgiving of John Andrew and Thos. Andrew, his father.

Rental p. 175 1563/4 Jan. 26
—Robert Mitchell rentalled in 5s. of Little-G. with consent of John Andrew, last rentaller.

Rental p. 150 1553 July 17
—David Anderson in Little Govan rentalled in 30d. of Little-G. with consent of John Andrew and Thos. A., his father.

JOHNSTOUN
1581
21s. 9d. of J. feued to *John Aiking,* occ by his father, John A.

Rental p. 124 1544 Oct. 31
—John Aiking rentalled in 21s. 9d. of J. on death of his father, Thomas Aiking.

KENMURE
1580
14s. 2d. of K. feued to *Gabriel Corbet* of Hardwray, occ. by him and his subtenants.
1580
43s. 4d. of K. feued to *John Hutchesoun* younger, and Helen Sempill, his wife, occ. by their predecessors in rental.

Rental p. 77 1520 June 14
—Mr Mychell Hutchesoun rentalled in 43s. 4d. of K.
Rental p. 138 1547/8 Mar. 21
—John H., son of late Mr Mychell H., rentalled in 43s. 4d. of K., Margaret Lindsay, his mother keeping the liferent.

KEPPOCK
1581
43s. 4d. of K. feued to *Robt Michell* in Little-G., (occ. by him).

Rental p. 150 1553 July 17
—Robt. Michell in Little-G. rentalled in 40s. in 'Cappocht' by consent and overgiving of Robert Hall and Thomas Pettegrew.

LAMBHILL
1579
2 merklands of L. feued to *Thos. Hutchesoun* in L. and Helen Herbertson, his wife. Held in rental by Thomas and his predecessors.

Rental p. 167 1557/8 Jan. 21
—Thos Hutchesoun rentalled in 13s. 4d. of L. with consent and overgiving of Janet Sprewll, last rentaller and of her husband, David Hutchesoun, (in 1529 it had belonged to a Hutchesoun who 'overgave' it to a Sprewll p. 96)
Rental p. 171 1558 Nov. 21
—Beatrix Hutchesoun rentalled in 13s. 4d. of L. with consent of David H., her father; he and Margaret Bartaine, her mother, keeping the liferent.
(N.B. This part must have gone to Thos. after 1558 in order to make up the 2 merklands feued to him in 1579.)

LENAGE-HAUCH
1581
4 acres in the L. feued to *Margaret Dunlop* 'tenant', and Archibald Lyoun, her husband, occ. by them.

Rental p. 167 1557/8 Jan. 23
—Andrew Dunlop rentalled in 3¼ acres of L. by vendition of Elizabeth Morton, rentaller, and consent of Robert Mitchell, her husband.
Rental p. 181 1564 May 2
—Margaret Dunlop rentalled in 4 acres of L. on death of her father, Andrew D.; her mother, Cristine Cottis, keeping the liferent.

LUGYHILL
1579
1 merkland of L. feued to *Gavin Hamilton* of, Hill, occ. by him and his predecessors.

Rental p. 185 1566 July 16
—James Hamilton rentalled in 13s. 4d. of L. by consent of Archibald Hamilton, his grandfather, last rentaller.

LUMLOCH
1581
13s. 4d. of L. feued to *Thos Aiken* occ. by
him.
1581
13s 4d. of L. feued to *William Horne*, occ.
by him.

Rental p. 142 1553 Mar. 27
—Archibald Horne rentalled in 13s. 4d. of
L. with consent of Thomas Leyis, last ren-
taller.

1581
6s. 8d. of L. feued to *John Murehead*
'tenant', occ. by him.
1581
16s. 8d. of L. feued to *John Newing,* occ. by
him.

Rental p. 165 1557 Apr. 8
—Gavin Newin rentalled in 16s 8d. of L.
with consent and overgiving of Wm. Low-
dien son of Wm. L., last rentaller.

1581
50s. of L. feued to *Wm. Blair* of Blairstoun;
rented by him and his predecessors.

Rental p. 153 1553/4 Mar. 17
—Katherine Blair, daughter of Alan B. of
Barastoun, granddaughter to William
Lowdein in L. rentalled in place of the late
Ezabel Lowdein, daughter of the late Alex-
ander Lowdein, and also in place of
William L., son of Wm. L. burgess of
Glasgow; rentalled in 33s. 4d. of Lumloch.
Rental p. 163 1557 Apr. 8
Walter Blair, son of Alan B. in
Barastoun rentalled in 16s. 8d. of L. with
consent and overgiving of Katherine Blair,
his sister, last rentaller.
Rental p. 174 1562 Oct. 9
—William Blair rentalled in 16s. 8d. of L.
on the death of his brother, Walter.

NEWPARK
1579
Lands called N. feued to *Robt., Lord Boyd.*

Rental—

PARTICK
1581
20s. of Over-Newtoun of P. feued to *Robert
Mitchell,* (occ. by him).

Rental—

MEADOWFLAT & RAMMISHORNE
1580
33s. 4d. of M & R feued to *James Fowlis* of
Colinton, and Agnes Heriot, his wife, of
which her predecessors had been rentallers.

Rental p.76 1518 Dec. 31
—Alan Heriot rentalled in Rammishorne
& Medowflat, with consent of his mother.
1581
Rental p. 128 1545/6 Jan. 28
—Arthur Sinclair rentalled in 33s. 4d. of
Rammishorne and Medowflat with consent
of Mr Robt. Hereot, last rentaller; the latter
keeping the liferent.
Rental p.161 1555 Nov. 9
—Archibald Hereot rentalled in 33s. 4d. of
Rammishorne and Medowflat with consent
of Mr Henry Sinclair, dean of Glasgow,
brother to the late Arthur Sinclair, last ren-
taller; Mr Robt. Hereot & Helen Swinton,
wife, keeping liferent.

Rental p. 161 1555 Nov. 9
—Archibald Hereot rentalled in 33s. 4d. of Rammishorne and Medowflat with consent of Mr Henry Sinclair, dean of Glasgow, brother to the late Arthur Sinclair, last rentaller; Mr Robt. Hereot & Helen Swinton, wife, keeping liferent.

Rental p. 172 1558/9 Feb. 27
—Licence to Elin Swinton, widow of the late Mr Robt Hereot, to marry Mr Edward Hendersoun and keep liferent of Rammishorne and Medowflat.

Rental p. 186 1566/7 Mar. 14
—Agnes Hereot rentalled in Rammishorne and Medowflat as heir to her father, the late Mr Robert Hereot, last rentaller; Helen Swinton, her mother, now wife of Mr Edward Hendersoun, keeping the liferent.

PARSON'S CROFT
1573
13 acres called P. feued to *Mr David Rollok* of Kincladye and Mariot Livingstoune, his wife, occ. by John Johnstoun and John Anderson.

Rental—

PARSON'S HAUCH
1573
Lands of P., or Rankynnishauch, feued to *Mr David Rollok,* as above.

PARSON'S LAND
1570
Lands called P. feued to *Archibald Lyoun,* burgess of Glasgow, occ. by him and his predecessors (in front of Brumelands).

POSSIL
1581
10s. 10d. of P. feued to *Mr Henry Gibson,* occ. by him.

PROVAND
1562
£20 lands of P. (in 19 separate territories) feued to *Thomas Baillie* of Ravenscraig.

Rental The territories making up the £20 lands of Provand are treated separately; Baillie's name does not appear.

PROVANSIDE
1586
1 acre in P. feued to *Mr Alex. King,* advocate. Not occ. by him.

Rental—

PROVOST'S HAUCH
1580
Piece of land called P. feued to *Robert Lord Boyd.* Not occ. by him.

RUCHILL
1579
1 merk in R. feued to *Ninian Anderson*, belonging to him and his predecessors in rental.

Rental—

1581
13s. 4d. in R. feued to *Michael Baird,* belonging to him and his predecessors in rental.

Rental p. 45 1511 Aug. 12
—John Baird rentalled in 13s. 4d. of R. with consent of Edward Mercial the possessor.
Rental 1. 158 1554/5 Feb. 13
—Wm. Baird, son of John B., rentalled in 13s. 4d. on his father's death; Elin Mershell, his mother, keeping the liferent.
Rental p. 193 1569 May 10
—Michael Baird is rentalled in 13s. 4d. of R. on death of his father, William B.

TOWCORS
1580
2 merklands of T. feued to *Gabriel Corbet* of Harwray, occ. by him and his subtenants.

WEST SCHEILL
1581
19s. of W. S. feued to *Andrew Paterson* younger, occ. by him.

Rental p. 74 1515 Dec. 20
—Andrew Scheill, or Paterson, rentalled in 21s. of W. S.

Rental p. 101 1532/3 Jan. 16
— John Paterson, or Scheill, rentalled in 16s of W. S. with consent of John Scheill.
Rental p. 103 1534 July 14
—John Paterson, or Scheill, rentalled in 5s. of W. S. with consent of John Scheill, his father.
Rental 137 1546/7 Jan. 31
—Andrew Paterson, son of late John P., and Marion Hyll, his future wife, rentalled in 16s. and in 2s. 8d. of W. S. on the death of his father, John Paterson. His mother, Marion Knox, to marry Thomas Hyll, but keep liferent.

1581
30s. of W. S. & a quarter of W. S. (occ. by his mother, Eliz. Montgomery, and her husband, John Rolland) feued to *James Scheills*, or *Johnstoun*, burgess of Renfrew, occ. by him and his prececessors.

Rental p. 85 1525 Apr. 30
—Andrew Johnsoun rentalled in 15s. of W. S. with consent of John Allan.
Rental p. 99 1531 Nov. 3
—Ninian Johnsoun, or Scheill, rentalled in 30s. of W. S. with consent of Andrew Johnsoun, his father (& 'John MacNayr mareit his dochter upoun the said Ninian Scheill').
Rental p. 123 1543 Sept. 26
—James Johnsoun, or Scheill, rentalled in 30s. of W. S. with consent of Andrew Johnsoun, or Scheld, his father, Andrew keeping the liferent.

Rental p. 170 1558 Nov. 6
—James Johnsoun rentalled in 30s. of W.
S. on death of James Johnsoun (?his
father), Elizabeth Montgomery, his
mother, keeping liferent.

WHITEINCH MEDOW
1579
W. feued to *Robert, Lord Boyd*. Not occ. by
him.

Rental—

WOODSIDE
1579
5 merklands of W. feued to *George
Elphinstoun* of Blythswood.

1579
5 merklands of W. feued to *Ninian Anderson*, and Janet Elphinston, his wife; held in
rental by him and his predecessors.

Rental p. 162 1556/7 Mar. 7
—George Elphinston, 2nd son of Geo. E.,
rentalled in 33s. 4d. of W. with consent of
his eldest brother, and on his father's
death; Besse Colquhoun, his mother, keeping liferent.
Rental p. 180 1563 July 31
—Beatrix Tait and Ninian Anderson rentalled in 33s. 4d. of W. on the death of
Robert Tait, her father; Margaret Luff, her
mother, keeping the liferent.
(N.B. ?Beatrix Tait first wife of feuar opposite.)

BURROWFIELD
1580/1
20s. to *Mr Robert Wilkie*, minister, Kilmarnock. 'Occupied by his predecessors.'

THE LANDS OF PAISLEY ABBEY IN RENFREWSHIRE

FEUING   *TENANCY FROM RENTAL*

ARKILSTON

Rental p. cxlii-cxliii
(part)
Robert Urry
John Urry, s. of above (1536)
John Urry, bro. of Robert.
(part)
John Thomson
John Thomson, eld. s. of above (1544)
Hugh Hamilton (1546/7)
John Hamilton, bro. of Hugh (1547/8)
Patrick Hamilton, bro. of John (1554)
(part)
Robert Landals
John Landals
(part)
David Crag
William Crag, s. of above.

1581
Whole lands feued to *Michael Elphinston*,
bro. of Lord E.

ARTHURLIE
1579
Feued to *Walter Adinston,* occupied by *John Paterson* and his subtenants.

Rental p. cli
(part)
Thos. Stewart, 'son of Gilbert'
Thos. Stewart, son of above (1541).
(part)
Matthew Stewart
John Stewart, s. of above.
(part)
John Stewart, 'son of James'.
(part)
Archibald Boyd
James Boyd, son of above (1537).
(part)

1559
18s. lands of A. feued to *John Stewart* in Auchingowin; occupied by him and formerly by his father, the late Thos. Stewart.

John Stewart, 'son of Andrew'
Alan Stewart, 'son of John'
(this part divided into three)
viz:
John Stewart, son of James S.
James Stewart, son of Thomas Stewart
John Stewart, son of Matthew Stewart.
(part)
John Stewart, son of Matthew Stewart.
(part)
James Stewart of Lochheid, s. of Thos. S.

AUCHINHAYNE

Rental p. clviii (40s. land)
(part)
Thomas Orr
James Orr. eld. s. of above (1553)
(part)
John Allanson
Robt. Paterson, eld. s. of above (1545)
—Paterson, eld. s. of above (1554).
(part)
William Maldisheid
Edward Ramsay (1526).

1583
10s. of A. feued to *William Orr,* occupied by him.

Rental p. clxv (£5 land)
(part)
Finlay McGregor
William Johnson, yr., with consent of above (1553).
(part)
William Johnson
William Johnson, yr., (1540/1)
Geo. Johnson, s. of above (1544/5).
(part)
John Brison
Patrick Brison, s. of above.

(part)
James Brison (1545).
(part)
John Edmeston
Patrick Johnson (1549).
(part)
John Fleming
John & Robert Fleming, equally (1548).

1580
37s. 6d. of A. feued to *David Erskine,*
commendator of Dryburgh; occupied by
James Bryson, Robert Fleming and John
Fleming.

AUCHINTOSHAN

Rental p. clxii (£5 land)
(part)
William Donald
John Johnson.
(part)
William Paterson
John Paterson, s. of above (1531)
James Paterson, eld. s. of above.

1580
£3 of A. feued to *David Erskine,*
commendator of Dryburgh; occupied by
Wm. Brison, John McRire and Patrick
Finlay.

AUCHYNIS
1568
A. feued to *Alexander Cunningham:*
occupied by John and James Erskine, his
subtenants.

Rental p. clii
Set to Gabriel Cunningham of Craigends
(1539/40).

AULDHOUSE
1567
5 merklands of Auldhouse feued to *John
Maxwell,* occupied by him.

BALWARTHILL
1580
With Craigbanyoch, feued to *David
Erskine,* commendator of Dryburgh; oc-
cupied by John Hamilton and Finlay
Houstoun.

BAR
1544
10 merklands of Bar feued to *James Glen.*

Rental p. clv (10 merklands)
Set to James of Glen.

BARNCROFT
1581
B. feued to *William Stewart* in Gallowhills,
occupied by him.

BARMAYTH
1583
B. feued to *John-Orr* 20s. lands of Over-B.,
occupied by himself, his father and their
predecessors as tenants.

BARNIS

Rental p. cxlvi
(part)
Robert & Thomas Knok, equally
Mariot Hamilton, wid. Thos Knok.
(part bel. to Thos.)—Knok
his son
Robt. Knok, s. of —K. above.

1560/1
£4 lands of B. feued to *Gavin*, son of *Gavin Hamilton*, commendator of Kilwinning; occupied by John Knox 'and other neighbours'.

BARMOYLOCH

Rental p. cxxxiv 1522
Set to John Norwell.

1583
B. feued to *John Norwell*, occupied by him.

BARROGER

Rental p. lvi 1465
Set to John Stewart and Alan S., his nat. son.

1580/1
30s. of B. feued to *Alexander Stewart* in Barroger, occupied by him, by John Stewart 'and others of his name'.
1582
6s. of B. feued to *John Blair* of Blair; occupied by Thomas Stewart of Dykis.

BARSCAWAN

Rental p. cxlvi
(part)
John Adam
Matthew Adam, eld. s. of above (1540)
Gilbert Adam, eld. s. of above.
(part)
William Hoggsyard
John Hoggsyard, on death of above (1540).

1567/8
4 merklands of B. feued to *sir Thomas Dickson*, vicar of Torphichen; occupied by Matthew Adam and James Hoggart.

BLACKHOLE
1503
Tenement of land called B. feued to *Andrew Payntor*, or *Ros*.

BLACKSTOUN

Rental p. clii
(part)
James Erskine & John Symmer
John Aikin.
(part)
Thomas Sympill.

Q

1580
10s. lands of B. feued to *Thomas Crawford*
of Jordanhill; occupied by Thomas and
John Hamilton.

BOURTREIS
1581
6s. of B. feued to Janet Stewart, widow of
Matthew Stewart, yr. in Boutreis, and to
her son, *Matthew Stewart,* in feu, occupied
by them.
1581
12s. of B. feued to *Thomas Stewart,*
occupied by him.

BRADYLAND

1565
20s. lands of B. feued to Arthur Maxwell,
occupied by him and by his father, Gavin
Maxwell.

Rental p. cxlvi
(part)
Gavin Maxwell
Arthur Maxwell.

BRAIDFIELD

Rental 1522
p. cxxvii
Set William Brison; James Douglas;
Martin Cuthbert; Finlay McGregor
p. cxxviii
John Spreull; John McRaryk; John Lang;
Domony Lang.

1565
£4 lands of B. feued to *Gavin Kneland,*
occupied by him and his tenants.

BROMELANDS
(within the 'terris campestris' of the burgh)
1490
2 acres feued to *John McNellis.*
1513
2 acres feued to *John Pyrry.*
1513
2 acres feued to *John Pyrry.*
1545
2 acres feued to *Elizabeth Brown.*

Rental
p. cliv Occupants given as: Mr Wm.
Steward; James Payntor; William Pyrry;
Matthew Wilson; Robert Smith; sir Henry
Bard; Robert Bissat.

BRYDESTOUN
1582
16s. 8d. feued to *John Blair* of Blair; occupied by Robert Boyd.

CAME

Rental p. clx (£4 lands)
(part)
James Brown
John Brown, s. of above (1531).
(part)
David Hamilton
John Aiken

Humphrey Aikin, s. of above (1554)
(part)
John Allanson
Thos. Allanson, s. of above (1545/6).
(part)
John Robison
Patrick Cochrane (1537).
(part)
James Blackburn
(divided)
viz'
John Jameson (1532)
Humphrey Jameson, s. of above (1538/9).

1583
C. feued to *John Cochrane*, eldest son of
Patrick C., occupied by them.

CARRIAGEHILL

Rental p. cxlv (4 merklands)
(part)
John Wilson
John Wilson, s. of above.
(part)
Janet Slater
sir Robert Slater (1528/9).
(part)
John Hector, eld.
sir Robert Slater (1528/9).
(part)
John Hector, yr.
Peter Algeo (1537/8).

1567/8
13s. 4d. of C. feued to *Peter Algeo*, burgess
of Paisley, occupied by him.

CASTLEHEAD

Rental. p. cliv Occupants given as: John Jop
and John Allanson

1543
C. feued to *John Wilson.*

CAUSAYSIDE
1490
3 roods and another tenement of land there
feued to *John Hector.*
1490
Piece of land there, running from the
public way to St Mirin's burn, feued to
Hugh Marshall, burgess of Paisley.
1490
½ acre in C. feued to *William Weir.*
N. d. 1(?c. 1540s) 1¼ roods in C. feued to
John Aikin.

Rental
p. cliii-cliv Occupants given as:
Hugh Marshall; Hugh Forest; sir Robert
Slater; John Alanson; John Hector, eld;
John Hector, yr.; Andrew Steward;

Bartilmo Steward; John Luff; David Slater; John Slater; Patrick Shelis; John Symson; Robert Luff; Malcolm Gardner.

CLAYFAULDS
1581
C. feued to *John Gilchrist;* occupied by James and John White.

CUNYNGAIR
1576/7
C. or Broumeholme, feued to *Robert Algeo.*

COCHNOCH-EASTER

Rental
p. clxiv (£6 13s. 4d. land)
Set to John Houston of Houston (1529)
(in margin) 'in Few' to Andrew Hamilton and his heirs.

1546 x 1571
Easter-C. feued to *John Hamilton,* son of Andrew H., captain of Dumbarton castle, on Andrew's resignation.
1546 x 1571
Easter-C. feued to *William Duchell* in liferent, and to *Andrew D.,* his son in feu.

COCHNOCH-WESTER

Rental
p. clxiii (£6 13s.4d.)
(part)
Gilbert Boill
James Boill, eld. s. of above
Andrew Hamilton, captain of Dumbarton castle and John Hamilton, his son (1550).
(part)
Robert Slater.
(part)
Agnes Buchanan
Patrick Forsyth
Walter Forsyth, s. of above (1554).
(part)
John Lee
James Lee, s. of above (1554).
(part)
William Neven
Andrew Hamilton (1551).
(part)
John Paterson
Robert Paterson, s. of above (1531)
(margin:
half set to Andrew Hamilton and John H., his son 1551).
(part)
James Brison
Gilbert Porterfield, on death of above (1583)
John Porterfield, s. of above (1553).
(part)
James Thomson
Andrew Hamilton (1550).

(part)
William Hog
John Hog

1580
Half of Wester-C. feued to *David Erskine,*
commendator of Dryburgh: occupied by
Walter Forsyth; John Hog; James Hog;
William Brison; James Erskine.

CORSEBAR

Rental p. cxlvi
C. and Thomasbar set to Mr Walter Maxwell for his lifetime and then to Gabriel
Maxwell, son and heir to the late John M.
of Stanely, paying 250 marks for his rental
28 Feb. 1537/8.

1555
5 merklands of C. feued to *Gabriel Maxwell,* laird of Stanlie; occupied by him and
his tenants.

CORSEFLAT

Rental p. cxliv
(part)
Set to George Houstoun.

1560/1
Half of C. feued to *Mr John Houstoun,*
canon of Glasgow, in liferent and to Henry
Houstoun, his brother, in feu; previously
leased to them.

CULBOY EASTER

Rental p. clxv (£5 land)
(part)
Patrick Moreis.
(part)
William Henderson
Archibald Henderson, eld. s. of above
(1543)
(part)
John Henderson
John Henderson, eld., s. of above.
(1551)
Robt. Hamilton in Dunterclunan, with
consent of above (1552).
(part)
John Fynne
John Fynnesoun, eld. s. of above
Archibald Henderson &
Robt. Fynny (1555)
(set to them because of failure of John Fyn-
nesoun to pay his dues).

1560/1
Easter-C. feued to *Gavin Hamilton,* s. of
Gavin H., commendator of Kilwinning;
occupied by Patrick Moreis and 'other
neighbours'.

CULBOY WESTER
1560/1
£6 lands of Wester-C. feued to *Gavin
Hamilton,* son of Gavin H., commendator
of Kilwinning; occupied by Walter
McRerick and 'other neighbours'.

DARSKAITH

1544
20s. lands of D. feued to *John Stewart*, in Woodside; occupied by him.
1580/1
10s. lands and Wood of D. feued to *William Stewart* of Woodside; occupied by him.

Rental p. cxlvii
Set to John Stewart
John Stewart, yr. (1536/7).

DRUMGRANE

Rental p. cl
(part)
James Hamilton.
(part)
John Anderson, yr.
(part)
John Cochrane
Andrew Spreull
Andrew Spreull & Christine Hamilton, his wife, & Patrick Spreull, their eldest son (1549).
Patrick Spreull, as above (1552).
(part)
John Anderson, elder
John Anderson, yr.
John Hamilton.
(part)
Thomas Jop
John Jop, eld. s. of above.
(part)
Alexander Rawf
sir Alexander Rawf, s. of above
John Hamilton of Newbiggins.
(part)
Mr Robert Stewart.
(part)
Andrew Spreull
Patrick Sprewll (1522).
(part)
Nicholas Bar
Margaret Dickson
Margaret McGe & Wm. Stewart, her son.
Nicholas Bar (1541)
Alexander Bar, s. of above (1547).
(part)
John Hamilton
John Stuart & Margaret McGe, his wife.

1560/1
38s. 6d. of D. feued to *William Mure* of Glanderstoun and Eliz. Hamilton, his wife; occupied by Eliz. Edmonston.

DRUMTOCHIR

Rental
p. clxiv (£4 6s 8d. land)
(part)
John Sprewill
Thomas Sprewill, s. of above.
(part)
James Douglas
James Douglas, eld. s. of above (1529/30).
(part)
James Fynnesoun.
(part)
Robert Donaldson
Robt: Hamilton of Dunterclunan.
(part)
William *(blank)*
James Douglas, elder, with consent of above.

1580
Half lands of Mylntoun of D. and Mill lands feued to *David Erskine,* commendator of Dryburgh, with a piece called the Mylland; occupied by Thomas Spreull.

EASTWOOD
1562
Domain and kirklands of E. feued to *John Maxwell* in Auldhouse.

EDINBARNAT

Rental
p. clxv (£4 6s. 8d. lands)
(part)
Janet Houstoun
Stephen Spreull (1527).
(part)
Alexander Houstoun
Finlay Houstoun (1538).
(part)
John Edmonston
Stephen Spreull and Katherine Hall, his wife, with his consent (1549).

1580
¼ of E. and Craigbanyock feued to *David Erskine,* commendator of Dryburgh; occupied by John Hamilton and Finlay Houstoun.

FERGUSLIE

Rental
p. cxliv (£6 land
Set to Ninian Wallace (1531)
John Hamilton, abbey graniter (1538/9)
John Hamilton, s. of above (1541/2).

1543
Feued to *John Hamilton;* occupied by him.

FULTOUNS

Rental p. cli
(part)
Robert Brown
John Brown, eld. s. of above (1543)
(part)
John Buyt
John Hamilton, abbey graniter (1545).
(part)
Archibald Hamilton
John Adam, yr.
(part)
John Symson, 's. of Robert'
John Symson, eld. s. of above.
(part)
John Symson, 's. of William'
John Symson, s. of above
Robert Symson, s. of above (1550).
(part)
John Knok of Wrayes
John Brown, on death of above (1535/6)
Wm. Sempill of Thirdpart, with consent of eldest son of above
John Hamilton of Ferguslie, with consent of above.
(part)
John Brown
John Hall.

1580
Mill and Mill-lands of F. feued to *Thomas Crawford* of Jordanehill

GALLOWHILLS OVER

Rental
p. cxliv
(part)
James Wilson
John Wilson, eld. s. of above (1544).
(pat)
Robert Bully
Elizabeth McGe & Wm. Stewart, her son (1546/7).
(par)
James White
John White, eld. s. of above (1550).

c. 1580
20s. of Over-G. feued to *William Stewart* of Gallowhills, Another 20s. of Over-G.; occupied by John Wilson.

GALLOWHILLS NETHER

Rental
p. cxliv
(part)
William White
James White, eld. s. of above
John White, eld. s. of above (1550).
(part)
Andrew Bully.

(Middle part)
Charles hamilton
Gilchrist Gilmour
Robert Gilmour, s. of above (1544/5)
John Hamilton of Feguslie (1551).

1546 x 1571
Half of Nether-G. feued to *John Gilchrist.*
1554
13s. 4d. of Nether-G. feued to *John White;*
occupied by him.

GALLOWHILLS (not specified which
part).
1490
2 acres in G. feued to *John Quarrior,
burgess of Paisley.*

GLASGOW
1505
Tenement of land belonging to the Abbot
in the street called Stokwell, Glasgow,
feued to *Allan Stewart* of Cardonald.
1558
Garden called Ronald's yard, in Glasgow
and the house built on it feued to *George
Huchesoun,* clerk.

Tenement of land belonging to the Abot in
the street called Stokwell, Glasgow, feued
to *Allan Stewart* of Cardonald.

GLEN
1544c. 30 June
50 merklands of Glen feued to *Robert,
Master of Semphill* 'for money and for his
help against the English and heretics'; the
charter is subscribed by Chatelherault.
Occupants given as:—
William Lord Sempill; Ninian Lord Ross;
Robert Orr; Thomas Shaw; John
Ranaldsoun; John Orr; John Kirkwood,
yr.; John Allasoun; Thomas Kirkwood;
John Kirkwood, eld.; John Norwell; John
Glen; William Orr; James Bryden;
Robert Glen; William Allasoun; John Orr;
Robert Briden; John Aitkin; William
Montgomery; Thomas Orr; John Shaw;
John Kibbill; Patrick Cochrane; James
Allan; John Brown; James Blakburn;
Humphrey Jamesoun; John Orr; Ninian
Atkin; Margaret Marshall; John Cochran;
Janet Orr; John Allason.
(Parts of GLEN feued, and noted
separately are — BAR; MYLBANK;
KERSE; JAFFRAYTAK;
MAVISBANK; LANGYARD;
AUCHINHAME; CAME, q.v.)

(N.B. in the rental the lands making up
those of Glen are dealt with separately —
as they are in this table. Grant of the whole
territory to Lord Sempill in 1544 given opposite because of the politico-religious
significance of the grant.)

GUISHOUSLANDS
1546 x 1571
4 acres called the G. feued to *John
Gilchrist;* occupied by Isabel Auchindour,
the widow of John White.

GUNACHANYS
1504
Tenement in Paisley called the G. feued to
Gilcrest Leyth.

HILLINGTON

Rental
p. cxliii (9 merklands)
(part)
Robert Steyn
John Steyn, bro. of above.
(part of the above)
Set to John Hamilton of Ferguslie
Robert Hamilton, s. of above (1553/4).
(part)
Henry Lochheid
—Lochheid, s. of above (1553/4).
(part)
John Kebill
David Kebill, eld. s. of above
James Wilson (part of above) (1555/6).
(part)
William Bully
Thomas Darroch.

1581
H., with Arkilston, feued to *Michael Elphinston,* bro. of Robert, Lord Elphinston.

INCHE

Rental
p. cxli
(part)
John Langmure (1525)
Robert Hamilton, burgess of Paisley (1531)
John Hamilton, s. of above
John Hamilton of Ferguslie, graniter (1548)
William Sempill of Third-part, with consent of above (1550)
James Snodgers (1554).

1581
15s. of I. feued to *William Snodgers,* son of James S., in Inche; occupied by his father.

(Thirteen other parts of Inche set to other families; no feu charters to any of these have been found.)

JAFFRAYTAK

Rental
p. clvi (23s 4d. land)
Set to John Orr
John Orr, eld. s. of above (1552)

1556
23s. 4d. of J. feued to *John Orr;* occupied by him.

KERSE, WESTER

Rental
p. clvi (43s. 4d. lands)

(part)
Alan Kirkwood
James Allasone, who married daughter of above (1532/3).
(part)
John Kirkwood, yr.
(part)
Robert Kirkwood
Robert Kirkwood, s. of above (1552).
(part)
John Kirkwood, elder
James Kirkwood, eld. s. of above (1553).

1566
10s. 10d. of Wester-K. feued to *Robert Kirkwood,* yr.; occupied by him.

KNAIFSLAND

Rental p. cxlviii (5s. land)
Set to Catherine Watson 'pro vita quia pauperam'.

1554
5s. lands of K. feued to *John White.*
Before 1554
5 acres called K. feued to *John Gilchrist.*

LADYHOUS
1505/6
Tenement called L. feued to *John Steward,* cook, burgess of Paisley.
1517
Tenement called L. feued to *James Wache.*

KILPATRICK-WESTER

Rental p. clx (£6 13s. 4d. land)
(part)
George Brounside
John Brounside, s. of above (1551).
(part)
Humphrey Brounside
(this part divided)
(1/3 pt) Robt Brounside
(1/3 pt) John Brounside.
(part)
John Johnsoun
William Johnsoun, s. of above
(1/3 of this part to Geo Brounside, yr.)
William Brounside (1552).
(part)
Robt. Strabok
Finlay Brok, eld. s. of above (1547/8).
(part)
Conan Brounside
Patrick Brounside, eld. s. of above (1545).
(part)
William Brounside
Robert Brounside (1534).
(part)
William Lang
John Howston
John Howston, s. of above (1545).

1580
10 merklands of Wester-K. feued to *David Erskine*, commendator of Dryburgh.

KILPATRICK-EASTER

Rental p. clxi (10 merklands)
(part)
Alan Lang
Wm. Brounside.
(part)
David Henderson
James Strabok
John Strabok, eld. s. of above (1554).
(part)
Widow of John Brison
(part of above)
David Henderson, with her sonsent
(another part of above)
James Finlay (1533).
(part)
William Finlaw
John Paterson.
(part)
John Alanson
(part)
James Finlay
John Johnson (1533)
John Johnson, eld. s. of above (1555/6).

1580
10 merklands of Easter-K. feued to *David Erskine*, commendator of Dryburgh.

LANGYARD

Rental p. clvii (2 merklands)
(part)
Robert Orr
James Orr.
(part)
William Riche
James Riche, s. of above
John Hamilton (1541)
Robert, Lord Sempill (1553/4).

1542/3
Tenement called the L. feued to *Robert Slater*, with 2 acres.
1580/1
13s. 4d. of L. feued to *Andrew, Master of Sempill*.

LOCHEND
1582
16s. 8d. of L. feued to *John Blair* of Blair; occupied by Thomas Stewart.

LYNWOOD
1580
4s. of L. feued to *Thomas Crawford* of Jordanhill.

MARKISWORTH
1567/8
13s. 4d. of M. feued to *Peter Algeo*, burgess of Paisley; occupied by him.

MAVISBANK

Rental p. clvi (10s. land)
Set to Richard Orr
John Glen, on death of above
James Orr

1583
20 merklands of M. feued to *John Aitkin* and Janet Glen, his wife.

MEKLERIGGS

Rental p. cxlv (£8 land)
(part)
Robert Slater
Arthur Slater, eld. s. of above (1548).
(part)
David Slater
John Slater, nephew of above (1548/9).
(part)
Robert Anderson
Robert Anderson, eld. s. of above
 John Anderson, eld. s. of above (1550).
(part)
John Robison.

1581
40s. in M. feued to *Robert Slater*, eldest son of Arthur Slater, there; occupied by them.
1581
20s. in M. feued to *John Slater*, eld.; occupied by him.
1581
10s. in M. feued to *John Wilson;* occupied by his father.

MIDDLETON
1580
10s. of M. feued to *Thomas Crawford* of Jordanhill.

MONKSHAW WOOD
before 1571
3 acres below the dyke of M. feued to *John Gilchrist.*
1581
Piece of land called M. feued to *John Gilchrist* of Sandiford, custodian of the wood.

MOREISLAND

Rental p. clxii (26s. 8d. land)
(part)
Patrick Lang
James Lang, s. of above (1538/9)
James Lang, son of above (1554/5)
(part)
Finlay Marchand
William Cunningham (1548).

1580
2 merklands of M. feued to *David Erskine*, commendator of Dryburgh.

MEIRBURNE
1580/1
20s. lands of M. feued to *Alex. Stewart* in Barroger; occupied by John Stewart in Barroger and Alexander, 'and others of his name'.
1582
13s. 4d. of Nether-M. feued to *John Blair* of Blair; occupied by Thos Stewart.
1582
6s. 8d. of M. feued to *Janet Stewart*, widow of Matthew S., in Bourtreis, and to *Matthew Stewart*, her son; occupied by them.

MYLBANK

Rental p. clv (24s land)
(part)
Robert Orr
James Orr, s. of above (1545).
(part)
James Orr & John Ranaldson
Thomas Shaw & John Ranaldson, s. of above (1547/8)
James Glen of Bar.

1580/1
Andrew, Master of Sempill
6s. of Easter-M.; occupied by him and his subtenants.

MYLLAND
1580
Piece of land called M. feued to *David Erskine*, commendator of Dryburgh.

NETHERWARD
Before 1571
Lands of N., or Horesward, feued to *John Gilchrist.*

NEWTOUN
1574
2 merklands of N. feued to *Cuthbert Sempill* in Auchinbothie; occupied by him.

OVERWARD
1581
Lands of Overward, feued to *William Stewart* in Gallowhills; occupied by him.

OXSCHAWHEAD

Rental p. cliv (36s. land)
Occupants given as John Whiteford; Meg White; Elen White.

1490
2 acres in O. feued to *John Whiteford*, bailie of Paisley burgh.

QUARRELLHILL
1490
4 acres in Q. feued to *John Whiteford,* bailie
of Paisley burgh.

OXSCHAWSIDE
1490
1 acre in O. feued to *John McKnellis.*

1490
1 acre in O. feued to John Quarrior, burgess
of Paisley.

1490
1 acre in O. feued to *Robt. Smyth,* burgess
of Paisley.

1490
3 roods, 20 falls land in O. feued to *James
Urry,* burgess of Paisley.

1495
1 acre in O. feued to *John Bulle.*

1509
½ acre in O. feued to *Wm. Kerr.*

1518/19
½ acre in O. feued to *Alan Wilson.*

1543
½ acre in O. feued to *Allan Clark.*

PAISLEY Burgh of

1. *BARNYARD*

1511
Tenement of land at foot of B. feued to
William Pyrry.

1511
Tenement of land at foot of B. feued to
John Androsoun.

1511
Tenement of land at foot of B. feued to
John Arthur.

1511
Tenement of land in B. feued to *John Alexander.*

1512/13
Tenement of land in B. feued to *William
Smith.*

1513/14
Tenement of land in B. feued to *Andrew
Wallace.*

Rental p. cliii (£6 13s. 8d. lands)
Occupants given as:—
John Whiteford; John Simson; Andrew
Quarrior; John Wes; John Sunderland;
Stene Henderson; Conne Steyne; John
Bully; Robert Brown; Robert Urry.

1541
Tenement there feued to *Mr James Stewart*,
burgess of Paisley.

2. *BLADOYARD*

1490
3 roods 10 falls land in B. feued to *John
Algeo*, burgess of Paisley.

3 *MOSSGAIT*

1541
Tenement of land and garden in M. feued
to *Mr James Stewart*, burgess of Paisley.

4 *PASLAYTAK*

1500
Tenement called P. feued to *Richard
Brigtoun.*

1541/2
Tenement called P. feued to *John Dowhill*,
burgess of Paisley.

5. *PRIORSCROFT*

1490
Piece of land in P. feued to *Partick Wilson*,
burgess of Paisley.

1499
1 acre in P. feued to *Robert Taner.*

1490
7 'ulnas' of land in P. feued to *Andrew Payntor.*

1490
1 acre in P. feued to *Andrew Payntor*,
burgess of Paisley.

1526
1 acre in P. feued to *Thomas Morton.*

1541
1/3 of acre in P. feued to *Katherine Mor-
sone.*

1541/2
1 rood of land in P. feued to *Egidia Pyrry.*

1542
Tenement of land in Pl feued to *Thomas
Ralsoun.*

1542/3
½ acre, 13 falls, 2 'ulnas' land in P. feued to
Felicite Fork.

Rental p. cliii (£8 4s.)
Occupants given as:—
John Whiteford; Patrick Mossman; James
Payntor; Thom Morton; Robert Bissat;
Elyn White; William Brown; Janet Lech; Mr
William Steward; William Pyrry; John
Alexander; Gilbert Alexander; Thom White;
Arche Gibsoun; Robert Smith.

1544/5
Tenement of land in P. feued to *William Stewart.*

1545
1 rood in P. feued to *Patrick Brown,* burgess of Paisley.

6. *LAND WITHIN THE BURGH AND 'TERRIS CAMPESTRIS', UNSPECIFIED*

1432
Certain 'chapellands' in *toun* of Paisley feued to *John Scheylis.*

1490
Tenement of land and croft of 16 acres feued to *Alan Stewart,* burgess of Paisley.

1490
2 'particates, 3 ulnas' feued to *Wm. Scott.*

1490
2 acres feued to *David Slater,* burgess of Paisley.

1490
Tenement and croft feued to *John Slater,* yr., burgess of Paisley.

1490
2 acrew of land feued to *David Slater.*

1490
4½ acres feued to *John Ray.*

1490
2 acres feued to *Andrew Payntor.*

1490
A piece of land feued to *Andrew Payntor.*

1490
Tenement of land and garden feued to *Roland Muir.*

1490
Tenement of land and garden feued to *Robert Moderwell.*

1490
Tenement of land feued to *John Luff,* burgess of Paisley.

1490
Tenement of land feued to *John Hamilton,* burgess of Paisley.

1490
Tenement of land feued to *John Alansoun.*

R

1490
¼ acre of land feued to *John Fiff* burgess of Paisley.

1490
Tenement of land and garden, with a croft and an acre, feued to *Robert Canezeis,* bailie of Paisley.

1490
Tenement of land and garden feued to *Wm. Brown,* burgess of Paisley.

1490
1¼ acres feued to *David Whiteford,* bailie of Paisley.

1490
2 acres, 1 rood, 20 falls land to *John Hamilton,* burgess of Paisley.

1497
28 falls of land feued to *Andrew Murray.*

1497
Tenement of land feued to *John Slater.*

1497/8
1 rood of land feued to *Andrew Murray.*

1498
Tenement of land feued to *Richard Brigton,* burgess of Paisley.

1501
3 acres feued to *Wm. Johnston.*

1501
2 tenements of land feued to *William Johnsoun.*

1504
Tenement of land feued to *Mr Wm Steward.*

1505/6
3 acres, 1 rood, 5 falls feued to *Malcom Gardner.*

1505/6
Tenement of land feued to *Thomas Inglis.*

1505/6
Tenement of land feued to *John Brown.*

1507
Tenement of land feued to *Thomas White,* burgess of Paisley.

1508
1 rood land feued to *Gilbert Alexandersoun.*

1510
Tenement of land and garden feued to *John Henderson,* burgess of Paisley.

1510
Tenement of land and garden feued to *William Pyrry,* burgess of Paisley.

1510
2 tenements of land feued to *Patrick Scheylis.*

1513
Tenement of land and garden feued to *Robert White,* 'for his special service'.

1513/14
Tenement of land feued to *Stephen Wes.*

1517
Tenement of land feued to *Nicholas Stewart.*

1521/2
Tenement of land feued to *Patrick Mossman.*

1572
1 acre of land feued to *Robert Henderson,* yr., burgess of Paisley.

1533
1/3 acre feued to *Thos Henrison,* burgess of Paisley.

1533
1 acre of land feued to *Robert Simson,* burgess of Paisley.

1536
Tenement of land feued to *Robert Wilson.*

1536
Tenement and garden feued to *James Moderwell.*

c. 1540
Tenement of land feued to *John Steward.*

1540
1/3 of tenement beside the River Cart feued to *John Fork,* yr.

1540
Tenement of land feued to *Stephen Stobo.*

1540
Tenement of land feued to *Alexander Ralsoun.*

1540
Tenement of land feued to *Thomas Wilson.*

1541
1¼ roods feued to *Wm Steward* of Blackhall.

1542
Tenement of land feued to *Martha Hamilton,* dau. Robt. H. of Paisley.

1542
Tenement of land bel. to certain chaplainries feued to *John Stewart,* burgess of Paisley.

1542/3
Tenement of land and garden feued to *John Kilpatrick.*

1542/3
2 acres feued to *Robert Slater.*

1542/3
1¼ acres, 8 falls, feued to *John Crag.* yr., s. of David C.

1543/4
Tenement of land feued to *John Henrison.*

1545
Tenement of land and garden feued to *Partick Loure,* burgess of Paisley.

1545
Tenement of land feued to *Robert Stewart.*

1545
Tenement of land and garden feued to *Richard Finlayson.*

1545
Tenement of land feued to *John Black.*

c. 1580s
Piece of land on which the smithy sood, feued to *Robt Ashindor,* janitor of the abbey; formerly occupied by James Luff, smith.

Rental p. cliii (£5 9s. 8d.)
Only occupants named are:—
dene John Scott; Patrick Mosman; Thomas White; John Bully; Robert Brown; John Brown; Patrick Thom; David Crag; Patrick Mosman, 'for his house'.

RICHARTSBAR

Rental p. cxlv (40s land)
(part)
John Ralston
David Ralston, s. of above.

1580/1
Half lands of R. feued to *John Wilson,*
elder, s. of late Thomas W. in R.; occupied
by him.

1580/1
Half lands of R. feued to *John Ralston,* yr.;
occupied by him.

ROUCHBANK

1561
5 merkland feued to *James Hamilton,* s. of
Gavin H. of Orbiston; of which 3 merks
had been resigned by his brother, Arthur,
he himself having been rentalled in the
other part.

SEEDHILL

1490
All the lands of S. feued to *James Crawford,*
burgess of Paisley.

1557/8
Grain mill of S. feued to *William Stewart* of
Cabirsbank.

SNADOUN (Modern Sneddon)

1507
A toft, houses and garden in S. feued to
Alan Henderson.

1507
Another feu to him of half the lands of S.

1541
Half lands of S. feued to *Alan Luff.*

WALKYNSCHAW

1512
Lands of W. feued to *Adam Morton.*

(part)
James Richartsbar
Matthew Wilson, s. of above (1548)
Thos. Wilson, bro of above (1550).

Rental p. cxlvii (5 merklands)
(part)
John Marshall
Edward Steward
John Hamilton of Cunnok (1547/8).

(note in margin)
feued to James Hamilton.
(part)
Thomas Bard
Thomas Huntar
John Hamilton of Cunnok (1547/8).

Rental p. cliii (with Wellmeadow, worth £6
10s.)
No occupants given.

Rental p. cliii (£6 land)
Occupants given as:—
Peter Neil
James Crag.

WARDMEADOW

> *Rental* p. cliv (26s. 8d. lands)
> Occupants given as:—
> Stephen Henderson.
> Gilbert Alexanderson.

1511
Half of W. feued to *Stephen Henderson.*

1542/3
Half the W. feued to *Robert Henderson.*

WATTERRAW

1545/6
Tenement in the W. feued to *Thomas Bulle.*

WOODSIDE

1545
20s. lands of W. feued to *John Stewart;*
occupied by him.

MEIKLERIGGS

1581/2
10s. to *Robert Wilson.*
Occupied by him.

Appendix B
Some Place Names of Sixteenth-Century Scotland

THE place names that mattered and were familiar to the sixteenth-century Scot were not, as with us, those of towns twenty, fifty or even a hundred miles away, of many of which he would never have heard, but those to be found in his own and many other baronies descriptive of the physical formation, use, ownership and cultivation patterns of the land itself. Tracing these names on a modern map, where a surprising number of them still survive, is often the nearest we can come to the rural world of four hundred years ago, so much of which has been swept away in the agricultural and industrial revolutions and the urbanisation of the last two hundred years.

The following selection of sixteenth-century field and croft names, many of them, of course, of much earlier origin, was compiled from details in feu charters of church lands in many parts of the country. The locations generally indicate the name of a barony or the vicinity of a monastery but in some cases are more precise, depending on the information in the text of the charter. Their appearance here as a tailpiece is only to preserve a flavour of rural life, no attempt being made to give their meanings. In any case, many of the descriptive names speak for themselves. However, further information on Scottish place names can be found in W. F. H. Nicolaisen, *Scottish Place-Names, Their Study and Significance* (London, 1976).

Abbot	
Abbotscroft	Scone
Abbotshall	Ellon: Kirkcaldy
Abbotshill	Crossraguel
Acre	
Brewacres	Haddington
Brewinacres	Duffus
Kilacre	Stevenston: Anstruther
Meadowacre	Arbroath
Milnacre	Dryburgh
Stableacre	Spynie
Whiteacre	Kinloss
Kairtoracre	Scone
Cruikitacre	Scone
Sevenacres	Kilwinning

Vicar's acre	Bolton
Serjeant's acre	Strabrock (Uphall)
Alehouse	
Ailhouscroft	Glenbuckat; Kirkton of Rayne
Alehoustak	Kinloss
Almoner	
Almoner's croft	Arbroath
Almoner's field	Dunfermline
Ammurryland	Scone
Almerycruik	Lindores
Almerieclose	Arbroath
Appletreeleaves, lands of	Melrose
Archdeacon	
Archdeacon's croft	Dumfries (archdeacon of Glasgow)
Beirland	Kirkcudbright burgh, common beirlands of
Beyond-the-mure	Lands of, Carrick
Bishop	
Bishoptoun	Whithorn
Bishopcroft	Dornoch
Bishopmeadow	Dunblane
Blacklands	Kilwinning; Glasgow; Failford
Brewster	
Brewster's pairt	Milton of Craigie, Dundee
Brewsterland	Paisley
But, Butts	
The six butts	Crofts called, Perthshire
Hempbutts	Anstruther
Brumebut	Kilwinning
Watterbutts	Carsegrange, Carse of Gowrie
Byre	
Byirhill	Failford; Kilwinning; Kinloss; St Andrews
Byres	Kilwinning
Newbyre	Newbattle
Byrefield	Culross
Byregrange	Culross
Calsay	
Calsayland	Lincluden
Causeyside	Paisley
Causayend	Coupar Angus
Cellarer	
Cellarer's cruik	Kinloss
Cellarer's meadow	Lindores; Melrose
Chancellor	
Chancellor's croft	Dunkeld
Coittis (Coats)	
Cauldcottis	Inveresk; Pluscarden; Elcho
Saltcottis	St Ninian's, Stirling; Kerse
Coitland	Foulden
Langcott	Kinloss
Butchercoitt	Tweeddale
Damscoittis	Kincardine, Aberdeenshire
Constable	
Constablecroft	Cullen
Cornland	Failford
Costertoun	Musselburgh
Croft	
Abbotscroft	Scone
Trinitycroft	Scone

Lyon croft	Scone
Sacristan's croft	Scone; Coldingham
Smiddycroft	Denmylne; Fearn; Clatt; Darnick; Spynie
Dovecotcroft	Scone
Guiscroft	Scone
Dempstercroft	Scone
Alehouscroft	Glenbuckat: Kirktoun of Rayne
Parson's croft	Kincardine O'Neill; Methlick; Kirkbean; Aberdeen
Fratercroft	Kirkbean
Freircroft (Friarcroft)	Dunbar; Stirling; Irvine
Langcroft	Dunbar; Dunblane
Meiklecroft	Ketnes
Brebiner's croft	Balkny (Ross)
Coopercroft	Cowie
Milncroft	Newbattle
Barncroft	Paisley; Balmerino; Cullen
Langrigcroft	Aberdeen
Croft called 'Fill the cup'	Aberdeen
Cruikitcroft	Fordyce
Almoner's Croft	Arbroath
Graniter's croft	Arbroath
Deracroft	Banquhory-Ternan
Barber's croft	Arbroath
Croftheads	Furnival
Bishopcroft	Dornoch
Southcroft	Coldingham (18 acres called)
Saltoncroft	Culross
Waterston's croft	Dunblane
Dischecroft	Dunfermline
Godbairnscroft	Holyrood
Peirtreecroft	Traquair
Brewerycroft	Fearn
Gudescroft	Kilwinning
Stablecroft	Kilwinning
Gilmuliscroft	Kylesmure
Walkercroft	Melrose
Dewiscroft	Cullen
Mid-Drownaris croft	Cullen
Monkscroft	Pittenweem
Comptescroft	Coldstream
Cruik	
Kilncruik	Cromarty
Friarcruik	Whithorn; Kinloss
Castlecruik	Whithorn
Cellarercruik	Kinloss
Milncruik	Kinloss
Portercruik	Kinloss
Burdiscruik	Coldingham
Cuningair (Rabbit warren)	Paisley; Arbroath
Daill	
Aikirdaillis	Monkton (Kyle)
Crowkyrdaill	Dingwall
Borrowdaillis	Dunbar
Dammisdaill	Inverness
Blackdaillis	Cromarty
Guisdale	Cromarty
Wedukdaill	Linlithgow
Davoch	Elgin; Beauly; Fearn; Nigg

Dovecot

Doucatland	Scone; Coldstream

Fauld

Priestisfauld	Stevenston
Lempotfauld	St Leonard's, Ayr
Fauldincroft	Failford
Langfauld	Strathaven
Richefald	Kilwinning
Muryfauld	Parish of Keith
Bogfauld	Parish of Keith
Cowtfald	Kinloss
Peirfald	Kylesmure
Stotfauld	Spynie
Clayfaulds	Paisley
Auldfaulds	Murthill
Corsfalds	Balmerino
Fermelands	North Berwick; Dryburgh

Field

Stirkfield	Stobo
Westfield	Dundee
Parson's field	Kilwinning
Middlefield	Kylesmure
Sorrolesfield	Melrose
Braidfield	Paisley
Punderlaw field	Arbroath
Outfield of Byres	Balmerino
Treasurer's field	Dornoch
Chanter field	Dornoch
Northfield	Coldingham (c. 30 acres called)
Southfield	Dunfermline (40 acres called)
Middlethird of Clipperfield	Broughton, Edinburgh

Flat

Lochflat	Midlothian
Commonflat	Langton
Wellflat	Kirkintilloch
Barnflat	Failford
Scottonflat	Torphichen
Huntflat	Failford (30 acres called)
Byreflat	Kilwinning
Staneflat	Kilwinning
Kilflat	Kilwinning; Kinloss
Damflat	Kinloss
Meadowflat	Newbattle
Corsflat	Paisley; St Boswells
Guttirflat	Culross
Middleflat	Kerse
The Flat	Smailholm ($\frac{1}{2}$ husbandland called)

Gallows

Gallowhill	Dingwall; Scrabster; Paisley
Gallowgait	Glasgow
Gallowmuir	Forgandenny; Scone
Gallowdenehill	Newbattle

Green

The Green	Dumbarton
Green of Muir	Balhousie
Greenyard	Dunbar
Greenfoot	Kilwinning
Nethergreen and Overgreen	Arbroath
Barngreen	Arbroath
Green	Balmerino

Bogangreen	Coldingham
Greenside	Holyrood
Hauch	
Hauchs	Langton
Langhauch	Dunbar
Pyperhauch	Parish of Keith
Milnhauch	Haddington; Dryburgh
Cherrietreehauch	Kilmaurs
Greishauch	Dunbar
Sandyhauch	Dunbar
Ceidmanhauch	Dunbar
Friarhauch	Dumfries
Whitehauch	Kylesmure
Lymmerhauch	Kylesmure
Cruikithauch	Melrose
Hayning	Kilwinning
Hays	Arbroath
Hirst	
Stirkhirst and Whithirst	Kilwinning
Hole	
Berrihoill	Balmerino
Todhoillis	Kilwinning
Hole of Clien	Scone
Kirk-Door-Keys	Two acres at Leuchars parish kirk; Arable land near Brechin
Land(s)	
Ky lands	Islay
Maryland	Abernethy; Dunbar; Forgandenny
Femaisterisland	Forgandenny
Officer's land	Darnick
Skralingisland	Darnick
Monkland	Haddington; Crossraguel
Freirsland	Melrose
Bordland	Torphichen; Penninghame
Brewland	Kylesmure; Paisley
Cottarisland	Kylesmure
Ladyland	Monkton (Kyle); Little Dunkeld
Subcellarer's land	Melrose
Harperland	Spynie
Soutarland	Strabrock
Baxterland	Spynie
Barbersland	Holyrood
Millersland	Culross
Hangmanisland	Musselburgh
Masounland	Dunfermline
Quarriersland	Kinghorn Wester
Wrightislands	Edinburgh
Cooperlands	Kerse
Knaifsland	Paisley
Grievisland	Paisley
Guishousland	Paisley
Mairland	Arbroath
Smithlands	Stow; Arbroath
Disterland	Arbroath
Caponland	Coldingham
Maltmanisland	Crossraguel
Shipland	Inverness
Sandilands	Dunbar
Flemingislands	Ketnes
Meg White's land	Avondale, Lanarkshire

Brandisland	Cullen
Loan	
Loan of damside	Scone
Loneheid of Ruthven	Aberdeenshire
Lowpenstanehill	near Dunbar
Meadow	
Braidmeadow	Kilwinning; Kylesmure
Butmeadow	Kilwinning
Dene William Wood's meadow	Kilwinning
Swandam meadow	Kilwinning
Dalglen meadow	Kilwinning
Roundmeadow	Kilwinning
Priorsmeadow	Kilwinning
Meiklemeadow	Kilwinning
Saltgirs meadow	Lindores
Langmeadow	Newstead, Melrose
Meadowhead	Cromarty
Meadowend	Dunfermline
Wellmeadow	Paisley
Skinnarismeadow	Pittenweem
Bogmeadow	Failford
Kingsmeadow	Peebles
Monks meadow	Dirleton
Blackfauldsmeadow	Failford
Yardmeadow	Kilwinning
Inch meadow	Paisley
Mylords meadow	St Andrews
Gaistmeadow	Arbroath
Hallmeadow	Arbroath
Meikle half	Barony of Rerick (3 acres called)
Middle third pairt	Tullygreg, Aberdeenshire
Outsteads	Duns
Pettycommons	
Land called	Culross
Acres called	Dunfermline
Ploughlands	
Plewlands	Dundonald
Easter pleuch of Millegan	Strathisla
Plewland	Maxton
Wester pleuch of the	
Midset of Auchinhuiff	Strathisla
Pundler	
Pundlerlands	Dunbar; Kerse
Punderlaw	Arbroath
Quarrell (Quarry)	
Quarrelflat	Failford
Quarrelhill	Paisley
Quarter	
Westquarter	Coldstream
Westwoodquarter	Carrington
Sunnyquarter	Lindores
Rig(s)	
Greatrig	Langton; Dundonald
Hoprig	Oldhamstocks
Gawriggs	Dundonald
Knightisrig	Dalkeith
Murieriggs	Lindores
Monkrig	Haddington
Meikleriggs	Paisley
Rudriggs	Clatt, Aberdeenshire
Burnriggs	Coldingham

Braidrig	Carsegrange
Sett (Seat)	
Clerkseat	Strathisla
Oversett of Kinminitie	Strathisla
Newsett of Wester Crannach	Strathisla
Frosterseat	Pluscarden
Kingseat	Aberdeenshire
Shed	
Clasched	Montrose
Lawschedd	Conveth parish
Saltershed	Dunbar
Friendlished	Kylesmure
'Thrie scheddis'	Canonry of Ross
Sheills (Shields)	
Spittalshields	Montrose
Listonshields	Old Liston
Janetshields	Strathisla
Brintshields	Kylesmure
Clerkinshields	Rescobie
Fishershields	Auchmithie, Arbroath
Baitscheill	Coupar Angus
Slidderiestanes	Dunbar
Tenshillingside	Kylesmure
Terrarer	
Terrarer's meadow	Dunfermline
Ward	
Priorward	St Andrews; Pluscarden
The Ward	Dunbar (10½ acres)
Jamesward	Kilwinning
Oxenward	Kilwinning
Littleward	Kilwinning
Stokward	Kilwinning
Overward	Paisley
Netherward	Paisley
Coltward	Coupar Angus
Acornward	Dunfermline
Greatward	Dunkeld
Northward	Dunfermline
Yard	
Chapelyard	Tongland; Dirleton; Carsegrange
Newyards	Dumfries
Whiteyard	Failford
Kilnyard	Failford
Hemp yard	Pittenweem
Huddisyard	Beith; Kilwinning
Beyneyard	Kilwinning
Lessyard	Kilwinning
Grassyards	Kylesmure
Bladoyard	Paisley
Commonyards	Arbroath

Table of Events

Scotland and England	Europe
1458 Act anent feu-ferm	
1485 Henry VIII becomes king of England	
1487 James III of Scotland receives papal permission to nominate to prelacies	
1488 James IV becomes king of Scots	
1495 King's College, Aberdeen founded	
1503 Marriage of James IV and Margaret Tudor	1503 Julius II becomes pope
1507 Printing introduced into Scotland	1509 John Calvin born
1512 St Leonard's college, St Andrews, founded	
1513 Battle of Flodden; James IV killed; James V becomes king of Scots	1513 Machiavelli's *The Prince* printed
	1514 Peace made between Henry VIII and Louis XII of France
1515 Albany arrives in Scotland to be made regent for James V	1515 Francis I becomes king of France; invades Italy
1516 Sir Thomas More's *Utopia* printed	
	1517 Treaty of Rouen between France and Scotland
	Luther posts his 95 theses on the church door at Wittenberg
	1519 Debate at Leipzig between Luther and Eck
	1519 Beginning of the Zwinglian reforms in Switzerland

1519 Charles V becomes Holy Roman Emperor

1520 'Cleanse the Causeway' fight in Edinburgh between Hamiltons and Douglases

1520 Field of the Cloth of Gold; meeting of Henry VIII and Francis I

1521 John Major's *History of Greater Britain* printed

1521 Diet of Worms; Luther outlawed; war declared between Charles V and Francis I

Luther's *New Testament* printed

1524 Regent Albany leaves Scotland

1524 Peasants' revolt in Germany

1525 Legislation against importation of Lutheran books into Scotland; William Tyndale begins printing *New Testament* in English

1525 Defeat of Francis I at Pavia

1527 The sack of Rome

1528 James V's personal rule begins; Patrick Hamilton burned for heresy at St Andrews

1529 Diet of Speyer; Lutherans called Protestants

1531 Zwingli killed at Zurich in battle against the Catholic League

1532 Endowment of the College of Justice in Scotland

1533 Henry VIII marries Anne Boleyn

1534 English Act of Supremacy

1535 Sir Thomas More beheaded

1536 Suppression of English monasteries begins

1536 Calvin's *Institutes* printed

1537 James V marries Madeleine of France

1538 James V marries Mary of Guise;

St Mary's college, St Andrews founded

1539 Coverdale's translation of Bible printed

1540 *Satyre of the Thrie Estatis* performed at Linlithgow

1540 Jesuit Order recognised by the Pope

1541 Calvin's theocratic state set up in Geneva

1542 Battle of Solway Moss; death of James V; birth of Mary, Queen of Scots

1543 Earl of Arran declared governor; Treaty of Greenwich for Queen Mary to marry Prince Edward

1543 Copernicus' *Revolution of the Celestial Orbs* printed

1544   English invasion of Scotland on cancellation of Treaty of Greenwich

1545   English invasion of Scotland

1545   Council of Trent opens

1546   George Wishart burned for heresy; Cardinal Beaton assassinated

1547   Death of Henry VIII; battle of Pinkie

1548   Treaty of Haddington for Queen Mary to marry French Dauphin

1549   John Knox made preacher at Berwick, after release from French galleys

1552   War declared between Charles V and Henry II of France

1554   Queen Mary Tudor marries Prince Philip of Spain; Foxe's *Book of Martyrs* printed

1554   Knox goes to Frankfurt as pastor

1555   Knox visits Scotland from Geneva

1555   Henry II of France invades Italy

1556   Philip II becomes king of Spain

1557   First Band of the Lords of the Congregation

Knox goes to Geneva as pastor

1558   Elizabeth becomes queen of England

1558   Marriage of Dauphin of France and Mary, Queen of Scots

1559   John Knox returns to Scotland

1559   Treaty of Casteau Cambresis by which France abandons claims in Italy

1560   Treaty of Berwick; English help for Lords of the Congregation

Treaty of Edinburgh; French leave Scotland

Reformation parliament meets and ratifies the Confession of Faith

1561   Queen Mary returns to Scotland after death of Francis II

1562   Legislation on 'Thirds of Benefices'

1563   Attempt to erect public Catholic worship in west of Scotland

1565   Marriage of Queen Mary and Lord Darnley

1566   Murder of David Riccio

Birth of Prince James

1567   Murder of Darnley
        Marriage of Queen Mary and
the earl of Bothwell
        Deposition of Queen Mary
1568   Battle of Langside after
Queen Mary's escape from prison; her
flight to England
1570   Assassination of the Regent
Moray
1571   Death of the Regent Lennox
1572   Death of John Knox
        Death of the Regent Mar
        Earl of Morton becomes
Regent
1573   End of civil war between
Queen Mary's supporters and those
of the young King James VI
1578   Second Book of Discipline;
        Morton demits office of
Regent
1581   Execution of Morton
1582   The 'Ruthven Raid'
1583   Edinburgh university founded
1587   Execution of Mary, queen of
Scots
1592   The 'Golden Acts' recognising
presbyterian church organisation
1593   Marischal college, Aberdeen
founded
1599   First, private, edition of King
James's book, *Basilikon Doron*
1600   The Gowrie Conspiracy
1603   King James VI of Scotland
succeeds to the throne of England on
the death of Queen Elizabeth

1567   Spanish army under Alva
enters Netherlands to suppress revolt

1572   Massacre of St Bartholemew's
Eve in France

1581   Netherlands proclaim their
independence of Spain

1588   Defeat of the Spanish Armada

1598   Edict of Nantes, recognising
the Huguenots in France

Glossary

Note: Since historical word-usage continually changes, the following definitions apply only to the period and context of this book.

Acredales	small allocations of arable land granted in addition to, and sometimes in proportion to, the main tenant holdings in a farm or settlement.
Almoner	official distributor of alms, attached to a religious institution; land or rents might be mortified to his office, e.g. *the almoner's (elimosiner's) field.*
Arles	earnest-money paid to a servant on being hired or contracted.
Arrest	to seize property by legal authority.
Assedation	a setting of land, by tack or feu.
Assise	the jury in the barony or regality court.
Augmentation	increase in rent as the result of feuing; reckoned as a distinct entity in the feu-duty.
Aumbry	cupboard, usually for household utensils.
Bailie	the chief executive officer in a barony; presided over the barony court.
Bairn's pairt	the third of a parent's moveables due to a child on the former's death.
Barnman	thresher.
Barony	basic unit of local government in landward parts of medieval and early-modern Scotland.
Bere	the common name for the four-rowed barley grown in Scotland.
Birlaymen	*ad hoc* judges appointed by the barony court, often in cases of neighbourhood (q.v.).
Bloodwit	liability to penalty for bloodshed; the penalty itself.

248

Boll	dry measure, usually of grain; customary payment to servants originally in grain, e.g. *ploughman's boll.*
Bonage	harvest work due by tenants; commutation therefor, e.g. *boon work, bonservice, bonsilver.*
Bond	written legal obligation to repay money or perform a service.
Bone shearing	service of shearing in harvest.
Bonnet laird	small proprietor.
Bounteth	gratuity or gift added to a servant's fee.
Bowgang	farm set in pasture for cows.
Bowman	man put in charge of a bowgang.
Bowstead	steading erected on a bowgang or grazing farm.
Butt	small piece of land separate from main holding; excluded in ploughing.
Caput	head-place of a barony, originally the dwelling of the baron.
Carriage	customary service demanded from tenants; might be long or short carriages, from outwith or within the barony.
Casualties	incidental items of annual income to a baron, e.g. *herezeld, relief.*
Caution	surety.
Chamberlain	chief financial officer of an estate.
Chandler	candlestick.
Charge	credit side of the chamberlain's accounts.
Clare constat	document recognising an heir and entitling him to infeftment in his property.
Commendation	*see* commendator
Commendator	the holder of the revenues of a monastery, appointed by the pope, with secular recommendation, not an elected head of the monastery; commendatorships were granted to both clerics and laymen.
Commonty	common pasture land.
Commutation	money equivalent of a payment in kind or labour service.
Composition	agreed payment for a tack or charter.
Conjunct fee	joint-holding by a husband and wife in feudal law.
Copyhold	customary tenure of which the evidence was a copy from the landlord's rental.
Cordiner	shoemaker.

Cotland	land held by a cottar (q.v.).
Cottar	the holder of a cotland, usually under a husbandman and owing labour-services to him, but sometimes holding directly from the baron, with fewer rights and responsibilities than a husbandman.
Cottoun	settlement entirely set to cottars.
Croft	small piece of land enclosed for tillage and pasture
Cuppill	a pair of sloping rafters, or a standard length in building, of about 12 feet.
Custom	payments rendered by use and wont.
Daill (law)	an allocated share of land, formally demarcated.
Daill (wood)	a deal or plank of wood for building.
Daker	10 hides.
Defalcation	deduction.
Deforce	to prevent an officer from carrying out his duties.
Delf	a pit, a place dug out.
Delt	allocated.
Dempster	the officer who pronounced the judgement of the court; sometimes *deemster* or *doomster*.
Discharge	a receipt for payment of money or the delivery of goods; the debit side of the chamberlain's accounts.
Doom	the judgement or decision of a court.
Duplicand	double usual payment, e.g. double feu-duty paid at the entry of an heir.
Elimosiner	*see* almoner.
Ell	standard length, usually of cloth, c. 37-38 inches.
Entail	settlement of the succession to heritable property by specifying the line of heirs.
Entry	the point at which a tenant formally took up possession.
Entry silver	money payment on the formal taking up of possession.
Escheat	to confiscate moveables; the moveables themselves, often gifted or sold by the crown.
Eveners	persons appointed by the barony court to demarcate land.
Evidents	written evidence of a right to land.

Farmtoun	settlement, with arable and pasture land and dwellings.
Fauld	an enclosed piece of ground used for cultivation.
Fee	the regular payment to a hired or contracted servant.
Fence	to legally confiscate goods or land; to formally forbid interruption of a court of law; an enclosure.
Ferme	originally, land let at a fixed rent; the rent itself; that part of the barony rents paid in kind, usually grain.
Feu-duty	annual payment to the superior by a feuar.
Feu-ferm	land-tenure in which an annual feu-duty of money and grain are paid for heritable property instead of the old ward-duty.
Free-gear	moveable wealth of a deceased person after debts have been deducted from the total moveables.
Freeholder	proprietor.
Forrow cow	cow not in calf.
Gear	moveable goods.
Goods	stock (animals).
Grange	farm and associated administrative buildings established by a monastery on outlying parts of its estates.
Graniter	officer responsible for collection of the grain rent.
Grassum	down payment for a tack or feu-charter; periodic payment from a feuar in terms of his charter.
Head-dyke	outer, boundary dyke of a farmtoun's territory.
Heirship	the best of all categories of moveables reserved for the heir.
Herezeld	death-duty on a husbandman's moveable estate, usually an animal.
Heritor	proprietor.
Holm	meadow; low-lying land by a river.
Husbandland	holding of a husbandman; originally 26 Scots acres.
Husbandman	one who actually cultivates the land; holder of a husbandland; the most substantial of the rural tenantry.
In commendam	*see* commendator.

Indweller	a resident in a burgh who did not have burgess rights; a resident in a town which was not a burgh, e.g. Leith.
Infeft	legally instated in possession of heritable property.
Infield	part of the farm constantly under crops.
Inlaik	loss or damage.
Kane	customary payments from tenants, usually in kind.
Kindly	*see* kindness.
Kindness	claim to customary inheritance on the basis of kinship with the previous holder.
Kirklands	land of which a churchman or ecclesiastical institution was superior.
Knaifship	perquisites of the miller's assistant.
Labourer	agricultural worker, with no rights in the land.
Labour services	customary agricultural work due by tenants to the landlord.
Land(s)	house(s) in a burgh.
Lead	to transport grain, coal or other commodity.
Loan	common way through a rural township leading to the arable and pasture land.
Mailing	ground for which maill (rent) is paid; a holding.
Maill	rent, commonly money-rent.
Mailler	one who pays rent; tenant.
Mains	part of the barony reserved for the lord's use, cultivated directly and not set to others.
Marriage	feudal casualty payable on the marriage of an heir.
Mart	carcase of an animal slaughtered at Martinmas; animal due to be rendered by a tenant at Martinmas.
Meadow	grassland mowed for hay, often marshy and near a river.
Moss	boggy ground or moorland, yielding peat.
Multure	tax, usually in grain, on crop ground at the barony mill.
Neighbourhood	mutual obligations among members of a community, in particular to observe the boundaries of one another's holdings.
Notary	one licensed to record legal transactions.
Outfield	land which was periodically allowed to lie

	fallow, not constantly cropped like the infield (q.v.).
Outsett	small new croft for cultivation by hand rather than by ploughing.
Oxgang	division of arable land, nominally as much as a plough team could work in a year.
Petty commons	small revenues shared by members of a monastic community.
Ploughgate	division of arable land, eight oxgangs.
Policy	use of the land, essentially towards its improvement.
Portion	monk's pension allocated from the monastic revenues.
Portioner	one who owns part of a property; a small proprietor, often a feuar.
Precept	authorisation by a superior for a proprietor's or heir's infeftment in property; a simple authorisation by one person to another to act on his behalf.
Prelacy	a major ecclesiastical benefice such as a bishopric or abbacy.
Profits	returns from land and stock in a current year.
Protocol book	notary's register.
Regality	unit of local government in which the lord enjoyed certain exemptions from royal authority.
Relief	feudal casualty paid to the lord on entry of an heir.
Relieve	to compensate a cautioner (guarantor) who has paid on behalf of a debtor, the debtor's obligation to relieve his cautioner being known as a bond of relief.
Rental	rental book or rent roll of the superior; working rental or check-list of rents due, compiled for the use of the chamberlain; the written title of a rentaller (q.v.), consisting of a copy from the lord's rental book of his entry as a tenant.
Rentaller	a tenant who held for life, the written evidence of whose right was a rental (q.v.).
Repledge	to recall an accused person to his lord's court from the jurisdiction of another.
Rests	arrears or outstanding payments.
Riding book	account book compiled during the collec-

	tion (riding) of the teinds (q.v.).
Room	a holding or piece of occupied land.
Rundale	pattern of cultivation in which the strips were similar to but larger than in run-rig.
Run-rig	division of cultivation rigs among tenants, those of individual tenants being scattered throughout the cultivated area; rundale was a variant in which the rigs were more consolidated.
Saltfat	saltcellar.
Sasine	infeftment, or the act of formally taking possession; the instrument of sasine is evidence of having been infeft.
Serjeant	an inferior officer of a court, e.g. the barony court.
Shed(land)	a piece of land clearly marked off from its surroundings.
Shielings	summer pastures on high ground.
Siller (silver)	cash part of the rent or commutation money paid instead of rent in kind or labour services. E.g. teiling (tilling) siller, rin-mart siller in place of an animal due at Martinmas; dyke siller in place of the building and maintenance of dykes; dam siller for the upkeep of a dam; fed-oxen siller in place of the customary payment of an ox; boon siller, or bon siller, in place of harvest work.
Slaughter	the killing of a person, where the killer or killers were known. (Note: in a case of murder the killers were unknown at the time and had to be discovered and accused).
Soutar	cobbler.
Sowme	share of grazing.
Steading	the farm buildings; originally the farm or holding itself.
Steelbow	a customary tenure under which the farmer received stock and seed with the farm.
Stirk	a bullock or heifer between the ages of 1-2 years.
Stob	a stake; to stake out land.
Sucken	tenants on land thirled to a mill.
Superior(ity)	someone who makes a grant of property to another in return for annual payment; the right to receive the annual payment.
Sworn men	barony men sworn in for the purpose of

making a considered statement to the barony court on the facts of a case or the background to it.

Tack	lease.
Tack-duty	annual payment for a tack.
Tacksman	holder of a tack, usually a substantial tack of rents or teinds as distinct from the tenant's tack of the piece of land which he cultivated.
Teinds	tenth of the produce of land in a parish divided between parson and vicar but, in practice, often set in tack.
Tenandry	holding of a tenant.
Tenant-at-will	occupant without written rights of possession, allowed to remain 'at the lord's will'.
Tenant-in-chief	vassal holding directly from the crown.
Terrarer	monastic official responsible for setting the ground.
Thirds	tax, equivalent to a third of income, paid on benefices after 1562; the crown and the reformed ministry.
Thirlage	obligation to have grain grown in the barony ground at the barony mill.
Toft	piece of land for cultivation, attached to a house.
Toun	settlement.
Utencils and domicils	household goods (in a testament)
Vassal	in feudal law, one who holds land from a superior.
Violent	by force; without legal right, e.g. violent occupation.
Voucher	written evidence that a payment had been made; often the receipted account, kept by the chamberlain in support of the discharge side of his accounts.
Wadset	to grant away land as security for debt; a wadsetter was a proprietor who held land in security until the debtor paid.
Wage	extraordinary payment to a servant.
Ward	superior's rights in property during minority of the heir; service rendered in return for holding land.
Warning	formal notice to tenants to remove within forty days.
Waulk mill	fulling mill.

T

Wedder	male sheep bred for fleece and mutton.
Wedder silver	commutation for the customary payment of a wedder (q.v.).
Wobstar	weaver.
Wrongful occupation	possession of land without evidence of legal right.

Sources and Bibliography

1. Manuscript
a) *Central government*
Register of abbreviates of feu charters of kirklands (S.R.O.)
Acta dominorum concilii (S.R.O.)
Acta dominorum concilii et sessionis (S.R.O.)
Register of acts and decreets (S.R.O.)
Register of deeds, old series (S.R.O.)
Register of the privy seal (S.R.O.)
The books of assumption (S.R.O.)
Secretary's register of sasines for Banff (S.R.O.)
Secretary's register of sasines for Ayr (S.R.O.)
b) *Local courts* (other than those in private archives)
Alloway barony court book (S.R.O.) B 6/28/1
Keillour barony court book (S.R.O.)RH 11/41/1
Glasgow regality court book (S.R.O.) RH 11/32/3/1
Carrick bailie court book (S.R.O.) RH 11/14/1
Hamilton regality accounts (S.R.O.) RH 11/36/1
Argyll regality accounts (S.R.O.) RH 11/6/1
Wamphray barony court book (S.R.O.) RH 11/69/1
Edinburgh commissariot records, Registers of Testaments (S.R.O.) CC 8/8
Glasgow commissariot records, Registers of Testaments (S.R.O.) CC 9/7
c) *Church records*
Register of feu charters of Paisley abbey (Paisley public library)
Register of tacks of Dunfermline abbey (S.R.O.) CH 6/3/1
Register of tacks of Holyrood abbey (S.R.O.) CH 6/4/1
Register of the archbishopric of St Andrews (N.L.S.) Adv. Mss. 17/1/3
d) *Private archives*
Newbattle muniments (S.R.O.) GD 40
Leven and Melville muniments (S.R.O.) GD 26
Morton muniments (S.R.O.) GD 150
Fraser charters (S.R.O.) GD 86
Eglinton muniments (S.R.O.) GD 3

Breadalbane muniments (S.R.O.) GD 112
Broughton and Cally muniments (S.R.O.) GD 10
Collection of John C. Brodie (S.R.O.) GD 247
Airlie muniments (S.R.O.) GD 16
Yester writs (S.R.O.) GD 28
Collection of the Society of Antiquaries of Scotland (S.R.O.) GD 103
Yule collection (S.R.O.) GD 90
Hamilton muniments (Lennoxlove)
Dalhousie muniments (S.R.O.) GD 45
Curle collection (S.R.O.) GD 111
Monro of Allan muniments (S.R.O.) GD 71
Montrose muniments (S.R.O.) GD 220
Douglas collection (S.R.O.) GD 98
Dunecht writs (S.R.O.) RD 42
Errol charters (formerly S.R.O., GD 175) Microfilm, RH 1/6
Pitreavie papers (S.R.O.) GD 91
Records of King James VI Hospital, Perth (S.R.O.) GD 79
Kinross House papers (S.R.O.) GD 29
Pittenweem writs (S.R.O.) GD 62
Swinton charters (S.R.O.) GD 12
Crawford muniments (S.R.O.) GD 20
Scott of Raeburn muniments (S.R.O.) GD 104
Blair of Blair muniments (S.R.O.) GD 167
Collection of Messrs Shepherd and Wedderburn (S.R.O.) GD 242
Closeburn writs (S.R.O.) GD 19
Northesk muniments (S.R.O.) GD 130
e) *Other manuscript sources*
Rental of Scone abbey (S.R.O.) RH 9/3/163
Account book of Lochleven (S.R.O.) RH 9/1/2
Rental of Lord Menteith's bowgangs (S.R.O.) RH 9/3/84
Rental of the lordship of Hamilton (S.R.O.) RH 11/36/1
Accounts of William Douglas of Lochleven (S.R.O.) RH 9/1/3
Register House charters (S.R.O.) RH6
2. Printed works
a) *Primary, including narrative sources*
The court book of the barony of Carnwath, ed. W. C. Dickinson (S.H.S.) 1937
The register of Cupar abbey, 2 vols, ed. C. Rogers (Grampian Club) 1879
The diocesan registers of Glasgow, 2 vols, ed. J. Bain (Grampian Club) 1875
The register of the great seal, vol. III, ed. J. B. Paul and Thomas Thomson, 1883;
vol IV, ed. Thomas Thomson, 1885; vol. V, ed. Thomas Thomson, 1886
The court book of the barony of Urie, ed. D. G. Barron (S.H.S.) 1892
Extracts from the regality court of Spynie, in Miscellany 11 of the Spalding Club,
1842
Regality court book of Dunfermline, ed. J. Webster and A. A. M. Duncan, 1953
Register of the privy seal, vol 111, ed. D. H. Fleming and J. Beveridge, 1936; vol

IV, ed. J. Beveridge, 1952; vol. V, ed. J. Beveridge and G. Donaldson, 1957; vol. VI, ed. G. Donaldson, 1963; vol. VII, ed. G. Donaldson, 1966

Registrum epsicopatus Glasguensis, vol. 1, ed. Cosmo Innes (Bannatyne Club) 1843

Liber de S. Marie de Mailros, 2 vols, ed. Cosmo Innes (Bannatyne Club) 1837

Rentale Dunkeldense, ed. R. K. Hannay (S.H.S.) 1915

Liber S. Marie de Calchou, 2 vols, ed. Cosmo Innes (Bannatyne Club) 1846

Rentale Sancti Andree, ed. R. K. Hannay (S.H.S.) 1913

History of Greater Britain, John Major, ed. A. Constable and A. J. G. MacKay (S.H.S.) 1892

Liber S. Thome de Aberbrothoc, vol. 11, ed. Cosmo Innes (Bannatyne Club) 1855

Registrum episcopatus Aberdonensis, 2 vols, ed. Cosmo Innes (Maitland Club) 1845

Acts of the lords of council in public affairs, 1501-54, ed. R. K. Hannay, 1932

Melrose regality records, vol. 111, ed. C. Romanes (S.H.S.) 1917

The acts of the parliaments of Scotland, vols. I, II and III, ed. Thomas Thomson, 1814

Registrum de Dunfermelyn, ed. Cosmo Innes (Bannatyne Club) 1842

Registrum episcopatus Moraviensis, ed. Cosmo Innes (Bannatyne Club) 1837

Collections of Ayrshire and Galloway Archaeological Association, vol. I; Charters of Kilwinning abbey, 1878

History of the Reformation in Scotland, John Knox, ed. W. C. Dickinson, 1949

Liber ecclesie de Scon (Bannatyne Club) 1843

History of the affairs of the church and state, Robert Keith, vol. I (Spottiswood Society) 1844

Reports of the Historical Manuscripts Commission, Nos 4 and 158

Charters of Crossraguel abbey, 2 vols, ed. F. C. Hunter Blair (Ayrshire and Galloway Archaeological Association) 1886

Register of the Privy Council of Scotland, vol. I, ed. J. H. Burton, 1877; vol. II, ed. J. H. Burton, 1878; vol. III, ed. D. Masson, 1880

The Old Statistical Account of Scotland, vol. IX, 1793

The New Statistical Account of Scotland, vol. XIII, 1842

Calendar of Laing charters, ed. J. Anderson, 1899

The Practiks of Sir James Balfour of Pittendreich, 2 vols, ed. P. G. B. McNeill (Stair Society) 1962

Accounts of the Collectors of Thirds of Benefices, ed. G. Donaldson (S.H.S.) 1949

Extracts from the records of the Canongate, 1561-88 (Maitland Miscellany, II, pt. 2) 1840

Extracts from the protocols of the Town Clerks of Glasgow, vol. 11, ed. R. Renwick, 1896

Autobiography and Diary, James Melville (Wodrow Society) 1842

Accounts of the Treasurer of Scotland, vol. XI, ed. J. B. Paul, 1916; vol. XII, ed. C. T. McInnes, 1970

Statutes of the Scottish Church, ed. D. Patrick (S.H.S.) 1907

b) *Secondary*

Anson, Peter F.	*A monastery in Moray*, 1959
Campbell, J.	*Balmerino and its abbey*, 1899
Chalmers, George	*Caledonia*, vol. VI, 1890
Donaldson, Gordon	*Scotland: James V to James VII*, 1965
Donaldson, Gordon	*The Scottish Reformation*, 1960
Fleming, David Hay	*The Scottish Reformation*, 1910
Franklin, T. B.	*A History of Scottish Farming*, 1952
Goody, J. and others, ed.	*Family and Inheritance, Rural Society in Western Europe, 1200-1800*, 1976
Gordon, J. F. S.	*Book of the Chronicles of Keith*, 1880
Grant, I. F.	*Social and Economic Development of Scotland before 1603*, 1930
Grant, J. and Leslie, W.	*Survey of the province of Moray*, 1798
Hannay, R. K.	'Church lands at the Reformation', in *S.H.R.*, vol. XVI, 1919
Hay, George	*History of Arbroath*, 1876
Innes, Cosmo	*Early sketches of Scottish History and Social progress*, 1861
Kerridge, Eric	*Agrarian Problems in the Sixteenth Century and After*, 1969
Lees, J. Cameron	*The Abbey of Paisley*, 1878; contains primary material
Lythe, S. G. E.	*The Economy of Scotland, 1550-1625, in its European setting*, 1960
Mackie, R. L. and Cruden, S.	*The Abbey of Arbroath; official guide* (H.M.S.O.) 1954
McDowall, W.	*Chronicles of Lincluden*, 1886; contains primary material
McGibbon, D. and Ross, T.	*Castellated and Domestic Architecture of Scotland*, 5 vols, 1887-92
McRoberts, D., ed.	*Essays on the Scottish Reformation*, 1962
Murray, J. G.	*The Book of Burgie*, 1930
Robertson, George	*Particular Description of Ayrshire*, 1820
Sanderson, M. H. B.	*The Mauchline Account Books of Melrose Abbey, (A.A.N.H.S.), 1975; contains primary material*
Smout, T. C.	*A History of the Scottish People, 1560-1830*, 1969
Stuart, J.	*Records of the abbey of Kinloss*, 1872; contains primary material
—	*Royal Commission on Ancient and Historical Monuments (Scotland), Report on Fife, Kinross and Clackmannan*, 1933

Index

Note: place-names in Appendix A, modernised where possible, have been included in the Index